/12

Maurice Prendergast

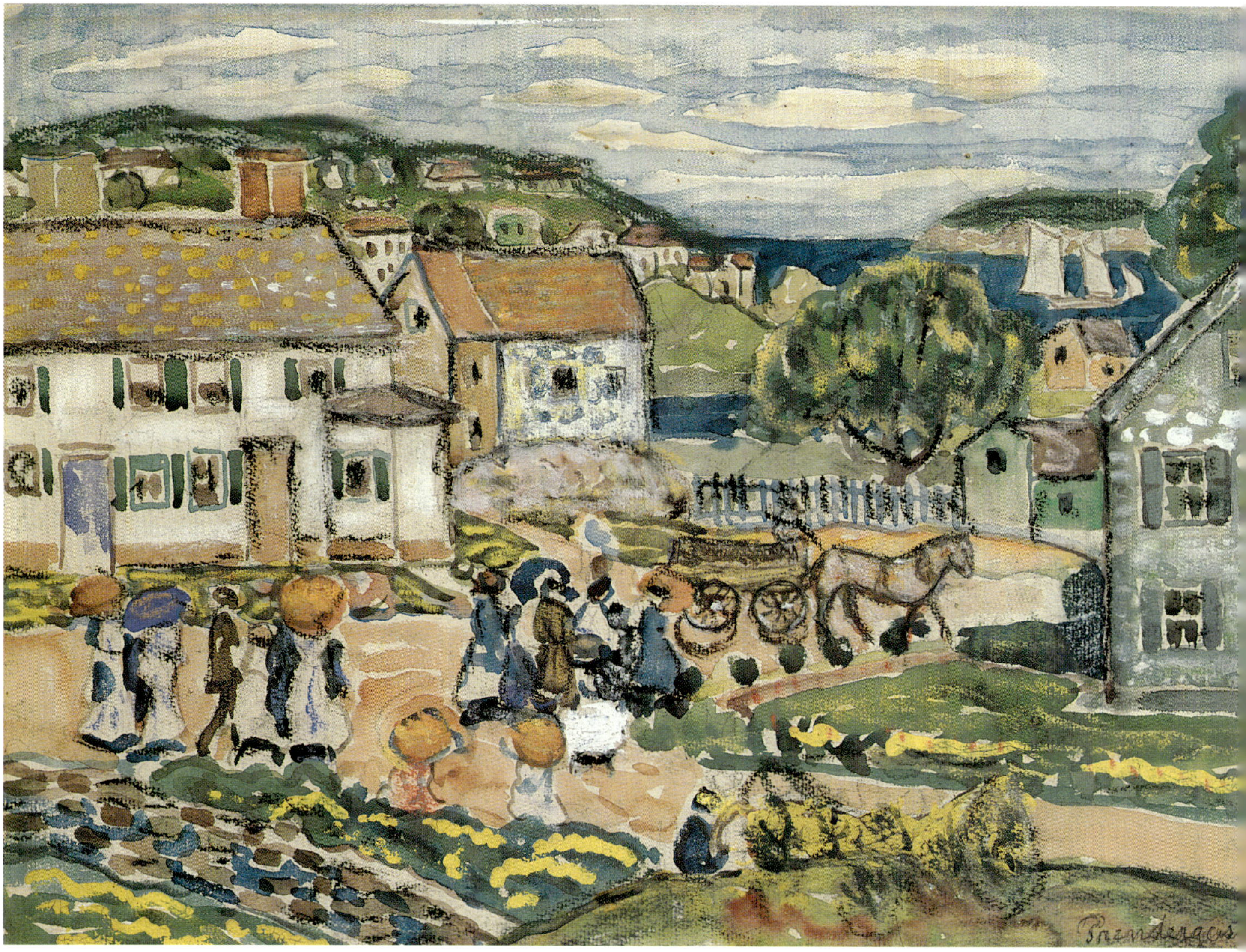

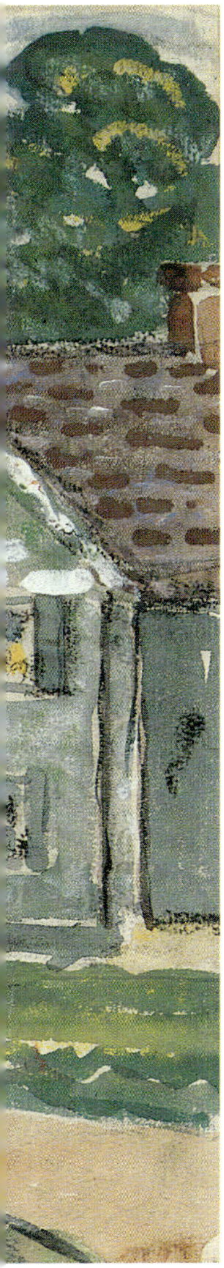

The Art of Leisure

Maurice Prendergast in the Williams College Museum *of* Art

Nancy Mowll Mathews

Eugénie Prendergast Curator

PRODUCED BY STOREY COMMUNICATIONS, INC.

President: *M. John Storey*
Executive Vice President: *Martha M. Storey*
Vice President and Publisher: *Pamela B. Art*
Acquisitions Editor: *Deirdre Lynch*
Designer: *Betty Kodela*
Editor: *Dan Callahan*
Production Assistance: *Robert Pini, Jen Rork*

Printed in the United States by Excelsior Printing Company
10 9 8 7 6 5 4 3 2 1

Library of Congress Cataloging-in-Publication Data

Williams College Museum of Art
The art of leisure : Maurice Prendergast in the Williams College Museum of Art / Nancy Mowll Mathews, Eugénie Prendergast Curator.
p. cm.
Includes bibliographical references and indexes.
ISBN 0-913697-24-9
1. Prendergast, Maurice Brazil, 1858–1924—Catalogs. 2. Williams College. Museum of Art—Catalogs. 3. Art—Massachusetts—Williamstown—Catalogs. 4. Leisure in art. I. Prendergast, Maurice Brazil, 1858–1924. II. Mathews, Nancy Mowll. III. Prendergast, Eugénie. IV. Title. V. Title: Art of leisure
N6537.P68 A4 1999
759.13—dc21

99-10129
CIP
Rev.

ISBN 0-913697-24-9

COVER: Detail of CR 640 *Low Tide, Nantasket,* ca. 1896-97

FRONTISPIECE: CR 1201 *Marblehead*, ca. 1914-15

Williams College Museum of Art
Main Street
Williamstown, Massachusetts 01267

ABBREVIATIONS:

CR	CATALOGUE RAISONNÉ
AAA	ARCHIVES OF AMERICAN ART
WCMA	WILLIAMS COLLEGE MUSEUM OF ART

MARGINALIA:

CR 1773 *My Lady Nicotine,* ca. 1895, pp. 5, 16, 53

CR 1481 *Sketchbook,* ca. 1900–05, p. 49

All works illustrated are in the Williams College Museum of Art unless otherwise noted.

Contents

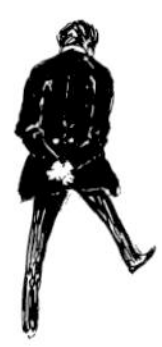

Foreword

Linda Shearer
Director

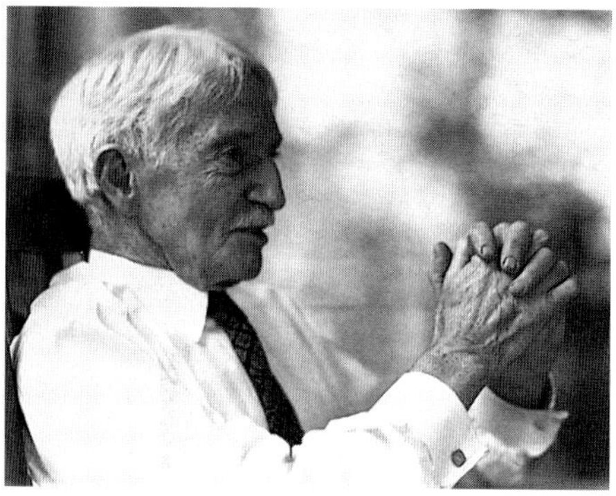

Charles Prendergast (1863–1948), ca. 1946

The art of Maurice Prendergast has been intimately connected with the Williams College Museum of Art for so many years that it comes as something of a surprise that a catalogue of the museum's collection has not previously been published. This volume completes the series of Prendergast catalogues that the museum embarked upon in 1983. The series now includes the *Catalogue Raisonné* of Maurice and Charles Prendergast (1990); the catalogue of the traveling loan exhibition, *Maurice Prendergast* (1990); the catalogue of our collection of Charles Prendergast, *"Beauties of a Quiet Kind": The Art of Charles Prendergast* (1993); and this volume, *The Art of Leisure: Maurice Prendergast in the Williams College Museum of Art.* In addition to providing scholars and the general public with thorough and reliable information about these two American artists, the series is also a tribute to the museum's great benefactor, Eugénie Prendergast (1894–1994).

Eugénie Vankemmel could not have anticipated the role she would play in American art history when she married the gentle Charles Prendergast in 1927. The couple had met in Paris two years earlier when Charles, still mourning the death of his brother Maurice (d. 1924), had been persuaded to travel abroad to lift his spirits. Having left her birthplace near Lille in northern France during the First World War, Eugénie was in her early thirties and working in a hotel in Paris. She would care tenderly and devotedly for her husband until his death in 1948 and then, in the almost five decades until her own death in 1994, for the art that Charles and Maurice left behind.

Mrs. Prendergast soon learned the ways of the American art world. She became well known as a canny negotiator by dealers, collectors, and museum directors who specialized in the art of that period. But her ongoing passion was the promotion of art as an educational tool. Many smaller community and academic museums benefited from her generous gifts of works of art and financial support for educational outreach. In addition, her dream was to see the Prendergasts' art thoroughly researched and published—a dream that was finally realized through her association with the Williams College Museum of Art, which began in 1982. In the last years of her life, she was able to hold in her hands all but this, the final volume in the series of scholarly catalogues on Maurice and Charles Prendergast.

Many people have contributed to this extraordinary research and publication effort. My predecessor, Tom Krens, must be recognized for the part he played in establishing the close association between the museum and Mrs. Prendergast, and, along with him, Williams College presidents emeriti John W. Chandler and Francis C. Oakley. The scholars who conducted the initial research for the *Catalogue Raisonné,* Carol Clark, Gwendolyn Owens, and our own Nancy Mowll Mathews, deserve continuing recognition for giving future Prendergast research such a solid foundation. Over the years, many other staff members, interns, and outside scholars have made substantial contributions to this body of knowledge, and to each of them I extend our heartfelt thanks for their role in helping us to complete this important work.

For the present volume, the list of acknowledgments is more manageable. The Prendergast Committee, consisting of John Boyd, Joseph Butler, and Catherine Genvert, very kindly assisted us in sorting out Mrs. Prendergast's wishes for the future of the program at the Williams College Museum of Art, including such projects as this one. Nancy Mowll Mathews, the museum's Eugénie Prendergast Curator, has brought this volume to fruition with her characteristic intelligence, creativity, and dedication. Assisting her have been Ann Greenwood, Edith Schwartz, and Rachel Tassone from the Williams College Museum of Art staff. Graduate student interns Sarah Powers M.A. '97, Alexis Goodin M.A. '98, Tiffany Reed M.A. '98, Dorothy Moss M.A. '99, as well as undergraduates Margaret Adler '99, Kaiva Klimanis '98, and Anna Mulliken '99, have been invaluable to the overall project. Finally, we would like to give special thanks to Deirdre Lynch, Robert Pini, Dan Callahan, Jen Rork, Betty Kodela, and the rest of the staff of Storey Communications for adjusting to the specific needs and idiosyncrasies of museum publications.

It is an honor to dedicate this volume to Eugénie Prendergast, whose generosity, foresight, and perseverance have made so much possible at the Williams College Museum of Art.

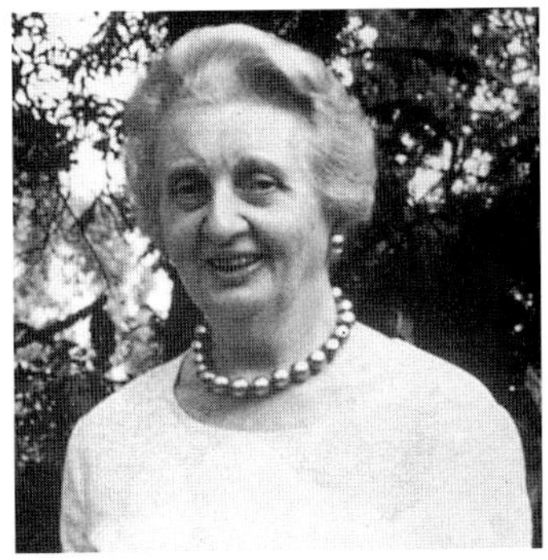

Eugénie Vankemmel Prendergast (1894–1994), ca. 1960

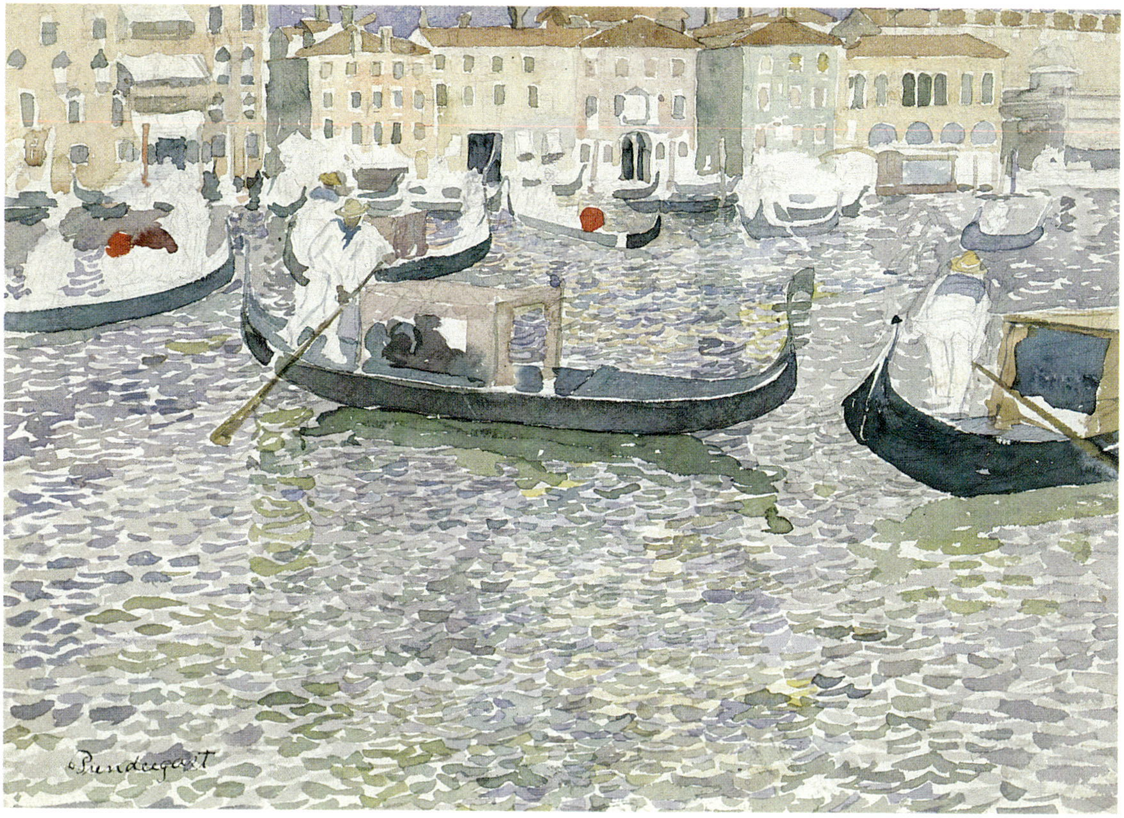

CR 712 *Grand Canal, Venice,* ca. 1898–99

Chronology

1857 On February 23 in St. John's, Newfoundland, Mary Malvina Germaine, the fourth daughter of H.M. Germaine, M.D., of Boston, marries Maurice Prendergast [Sr.] (family bible, Prendergast Archive, Williams College Museum of Art [WCMA]).

1858 Maurice Brazil Prendergast and his twin sister, Lucy Catherine, are born and baptized on October 10 in St. John's, Newfoundland (family bible; St. John's Basilica baptism records). Lucy Catherine dies "at the age of 18 or 20" (draft of a letter from Eugénie Prendergast to Peter Wick, July 8, 1960, Prendergast Archive, WCMA).

1860 A brother, Richard Thomas Prendergast (with a stillborn twin sister), is born on November 19, but dies in 1864 (family bible).

1863 Charles James Prendergast is born on May 27 and baptized on June 24 in St. John's, Newfoundland (family bible; St. John's Basilica baptism records).

1864–1865 Maurice Prendergast [Sr.] is listed as a grocer at 138 Water Street, St. John's, in the *Newfoundland Directory*.

1868 In November the Prendergast family moves to Boston (U.S. naturalization papers of Maurice Prendergast [Sr.], 1881).

1868–1872 Maurice and Charles attend Rice Grammar School for Boys on Dartmouth Street in Boston. Maurice finishes eight years of schooling (ca. 1872) and goes to work wrapping packages at the dry goods store of Loring and Waterhouse (Brooks, 1938; Basso, 1946b).

1872–1877 Maurice Prendergast [Sr.?] is listed as "laborer" in the 1872, 1873, and 1874 *Boston City Directory* and as "confectioner" in 1875, 1876, and 1877 with a home address at 86 West Dedham Street, Boston.

1878 Maurice Brazil Prendergast is listed for the first time in the *Boston City Directory* (as "clerk") with a home address at 86 West Dedham Street.

1879 Maurice's home address remains the same, but he is listed in the *Boston City Directory* as "designer" with a business address at 266 Washington Street, Boston.

1881 Maurice Prendergast [Sr.] is naturalized as a U.S. citizen on June 24 (U.S. naturalization papers).

1882–1893 During these years, the *Boston City Directory* lists the family as living at 119 Center Street, Roxbury. No occupation is noted for the father. From 1886 until 1890, Maurice registers his business address as 1 Province Street in downtown Boston, which would place him at the firm of Peter Gill, designer of show cards (Glavin, 1982).

1883 Maurice's mother, Mary Malvina Germaine Prendergast, dies on November 27 (family bible).

1884 Maurice shows his work to a Mrs. Waterbury, who suggests that he study abroad (Milliken, 1926).

1886–1887 Charles travels twice to England on a cattle boat, the second time with Maurice (Basso, 1946b). Two watercolors by Maurice that depict scenes in Wales are dated 1886 (CR 509 and CR 510), and a sketchbook (CR 1475), which contains addresses in North Wales, also has a sketch inscribed "May 1, 87, Everett [Massachusetts]." After their return, Maurice continues to letter show cards and Charles becomes a traveling salesman for a fine-arts shop (Basso, 1946b).

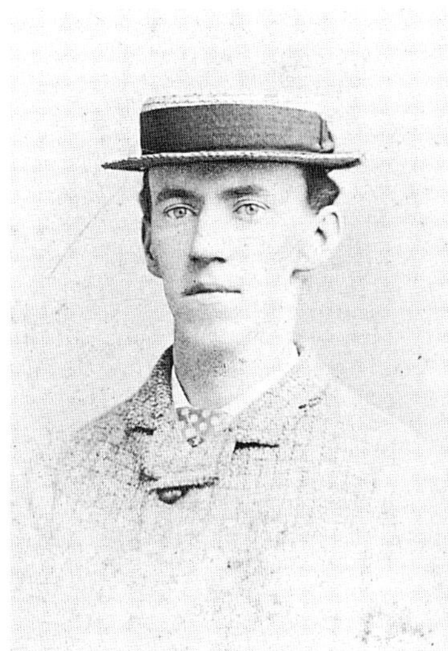

Maurice Prendergast, ca. 1875

1889 During the summer, Maurice paints in Westport, Maine (Rhys 1960).

1891–1894 Maurice and Charles arrive in Paris by January 1891 (CR 517). Maurice studies at the Académie Julian (bill for classes, Prendergast Archive, WCMA) and also at Colarossi's studio, as does Charles (Charles's biographical data form for associate membership, National Academy of Design, ca. 1939). The brothers meet James W. Morrice (letter from Maurice to Charles, ca. June 13, 1907, Prendergast Archive, WCMA), with whom Maurice spends the summers painting at Tréport, Dieppe, and Dinard. Charles returns to Boston by 1892. Although living in Paris, Maurice is listed as "decorator" in the *Boston City Directory* (1891–1892).

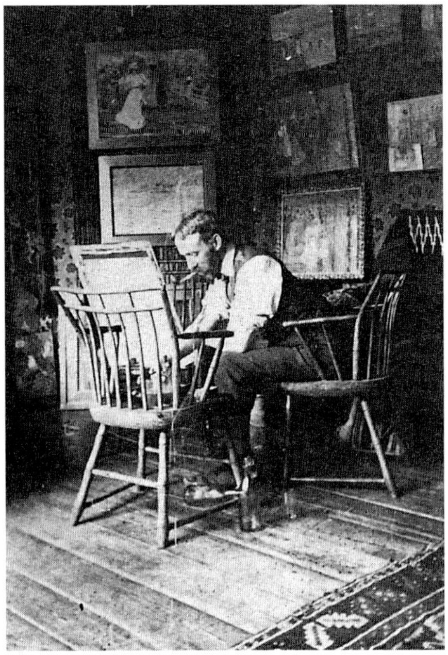

Maurice Prendergast, ca. 1900

1893 Still abroad, Maurice is listed as "artist" for the first time in the *Boston City Directory*. Maurice's sketches are stolen by Michael Dignam and then published under Dignam's name in London by The Studio (Brooks, 1938).

1894 Maurice returns to Boston on September 1 on the SS *Cephalonia* from Liverpool (passenger arrival list). Maurice and Charles board at the Brookline Avenue corner of Francis Street, Boston *(Boston City Directory).*

1895 First known inclusion of works by Maurice in an exhibition (Boston Art Club).

1895–1896 Maurice, Charles, and their father move to 83 Hillside Avenue, Roxbury, where they continue to reside until 1896 *(Boston City Directory).*

1896 Maurice lists his address in a late 1896 exhibition at the Pennsylvania Academy of the Fine Arts as Trinity Court, Boston, a residence of apartments and studios (Hitchings, 1989).

1897 Maurice begins to exhibit in New York at the Water Color Club. Charles lists himself as "artist" for the first time and is living with his father and brother at the Ormonde, 641 Huntington Avenue, Boston, where they will remain until the spring of 1898 (*Boston City Directory* and Hitchings, 1989).

1898 Maurice applies for a U.S. passport on June 29.

1898–1899 Financed by Sarah Choate Sears (Milliken, 1926), Maurice travels to Italy and stays for about 18 months. His itinerary probably included Venice, Padua, Florence, Siena, Orvieto, Rome, Naples, and Capri (Pepper, 1910). Maurice, Charles, and their father are listed as living at 27 Winthrop Street, Winchester (1899 *Woburn and Winchester City Directory*), where they have been since at least April 1898.

1899 While he is still in Italy, 16 of Maurice's Italian watercolors are shown at the Eastman Chase Gallery in Boston, possibly constituting his first one-person exhibition. William Macbeth invites Maurice to exhibit in his New York gallery. In Maurice's absence, Charles responds positively on September 29 (Macbeth Galleries Papers, Archives of American Art [AAA]). Maurice plans to leave Italy on November 16 (sketchbook, CR 1479).

1900 Maurice shows watercolors and monotypes with Hermann Dudley Murphy at the Art Institute of Chicago, January 3–28. The 1900 Census lists Maurice, Charles, and their father at 81 Walnut Street in Winchester. Maurice has his first major one-person exhibition of watercolors and monotypes at the gallery of William Macbeth, March 9–24. Maurice mentions a sketching trip planned from July 18 until mid-September (letter from Maurice to William Macbeth, July 17, 1900, AAA). By November Maurice has moved to 83 Walnut Street, Winchester, where he and his brother will continue to live at least until 1903 and their father until his death in 1901.

1901 Maurice Prendergast [Sr.] dies and is buried on September 23 (family bible). Maurice wins a Bronze Medal at the Pan-American Exposition in Buffalo, New York. Maurice's second major one-person show (watercolors and monotypes) is seen in Detroit and Cincinnati.

1902 During the summer, Maurice and Charles visit the Oliver Williams family in Annisquam, Massachusetts, and Maurice paints a picture of Esther Williams and her newborn son, Thomas (CR 49).

1903 Charles and Hermann Dudley Murphy establish a frame-making business (Carrig-Rohane Papers, AAA), and Maurice works with Charles on Thomas Lawson's commission of two large frames (Derby, 1989). Although Maurice, Charles, and their father are not listed in the *Boston City Directory* from 1899 through 1904, Maurice maintained a studio at 56 Mount Vernon Street, Boston, for he gives that address in exhibition catalogues beginning in April 1903.

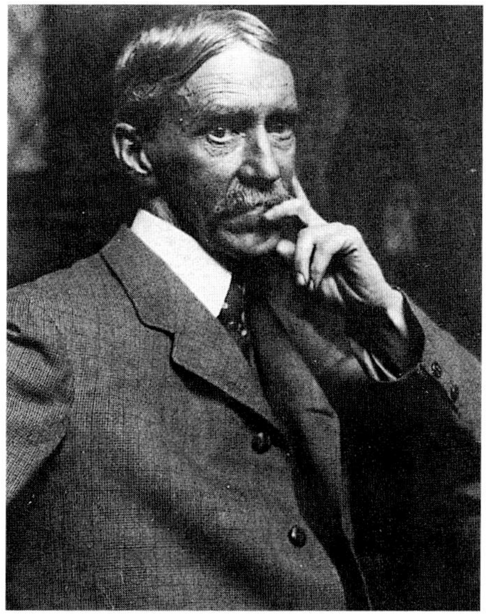
Maurice Prendergast, ca. 1907

1904 Maurice exhibits at the National Arts Club and is first affiliated with Robert Henri, William Glackens, George Luks, John Sloan, and Arthur B. Davies, future members of The Eight. Maurice stays at 115 West 56th Street in New York during the spring and summer (letter from Maurice to Esther Williams, April 27, 1904, Williams Papers, AAA).

1905–1906 Maurice and Charles are living at 56 Mount Vernon Street, Boston, where they will remain until they move to New York in 1914 *(Boston City Directory).* Maurice, however, moves to new lodgings at 65 Pinckney Street on October 19, 1905 (sketchbook, CR 1483) and lists this address in the 1906 *Boston City Directory.* In the 1913 and 1914 *Boston City Directory,* Maurice is listed as boarding at 60½ West Cedar Street, indicating that during these years he uses 56 Mount Vernon Street, where Charles continues to reside, only as a studio. Maurice's work is interrupted in order to find a cure for his loss of hearing. Joining the L Street Brownies in Boston, he begins a regimen of swimming and sunning to protect his health (sketchbook, CR 1483, and letters from Maurice to Esther Williams, May 14 and November 10, 1905, Williams Papers, AAA).

1907 Maurice sails to France on May 19 and arrives in Le Havre on May 28. Itinerary, according to letters from Maurice to Charles (Prendergast Archive, WCMA) and to Esther Williams (AAA), May–June 1907:

Paris, by May 31

Versailles, June 15

St.-Malo, June 31 to end of August

Back to Paris in September

Maurice plans to sail back to Boston on October 26 (letter from Maurice to Esther Williams, October 10, 1907, Williams Papers, AAA).

1908 Maurice participates in the exhibition of The Eight at Macbeth Galleries, February 3–15. Maurice plans to spend the summer in

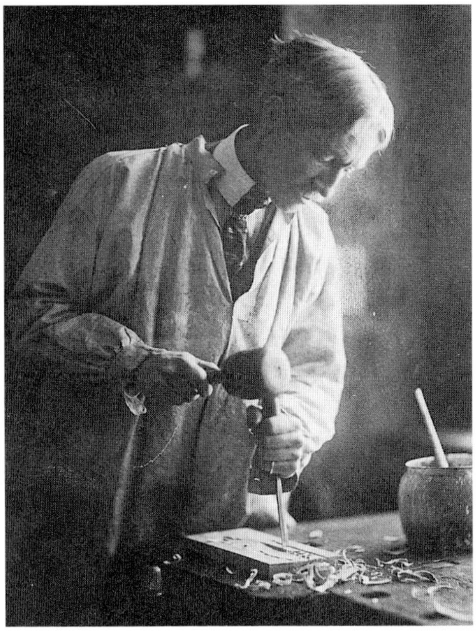

Charles Prendergast, ca. 1912

Annisquam (letter from Maurice to Esther Williams, May 31, 1908, Williams Papers, AAA).

1910 Maurice takes part in the Exhibition of Independent Artists, April 1–27, in New York. Charles Hovey Pepper publishes the first article on Maurice in *The World To-Day.* Maurice travels to New Hampshire in the fall and exhibits watercolors of the trip at the Boston Water Color Club in February 1911.

1911 Charles travels to Italy from about June 15 through October. Maurice follows him in August and during the autumn becomes ill. Maurice undergoes prostate surgery at the Cosmopolitan Hospital in Venice (letters from Maurice to Esther Williams, Williams Papers, AAA, and to Charles, Prendergast Archive, WCMA; September–December 1911).

1912 On January 31 Maurice sails home on the White Star Line's SS *Canopic,* which stops in Palermo (Glavin, 1976). Maurice joins the Association of American Painters and Sculptors to organize the Armory Show and is appointed to the foreign and American selection committees (Brown, 1963). In April Maurice has a one-person exhibition at the Women's Cosmopolitan Club, New York. Maurice spends the summer with the Glackens family in Bellport, Long Island (Glackens, 1957). Maurice paints in New Hampshire (Milliken, 1926). Sometime during this year, Charles produces his first carved and painted panel (Basso, 1946a and 1946b).

1913 The Armory Show, in which Maurice exhibits seven works, runs in New York from February 17 to March 15. Maurice is listed in the 1913 and 1914 *Boston City Directory* as boarding at 60½ West Cedar Street, while Charles continues to reside at 56 Mount Vernon Street. In June Maurice undergoes a second prostate surgery, at City Hospital, Boston (letter from Maurice to Walter Pach, June 25, 1913, Pach Papers, AAA). Maurice and Charles spend part of the summer in Brooksville, Maine (letters from Maurice to Walter Pach, July 11, 1913, Pach Papers, AAA, and to John Quinn, August 14, 1913, Quinn Papers, New York Public Library [NYPL]). Maurice and Charles visit New York in early December and stay at the St. Denis Hotel (letter from Maurice to John Quinn, December 10, 1913, Quinn Papers, NYPL).

1914 Maurice travels to Paris and St.-Malo in the spring and plans to return from France in mid-October (letter from Maurice to Esther Williams, May 2, 1914, AAA, and from Charles to John Quinn, June 24, 1914, Quinn Papers, NYPL). Charles receives payment of $1,800 for 18 frames from an insurance company in Philadelphia, which enables the brothers to move from Boston to New York (Basso, 1946b). Maurice and Charles move to 50 Washington Square South in New York on November 1 (letter from Maurice to Edward Root, January 8, 1915, Root Papers, AAA). Maurice is elected president of the Association of American Painters and Sculptors (Brown, 1963).

1915 Maurice has a one-person show at the Carroll Galleries, New York, from February 15 to March 6. Maurice and Charles exhibit together for the first time, March 23–April 24, at the Montross Gallery, New York. In early July, Charles visits the Williams family in Annisquam, and Maurice plans a trip there later in the month (letter from Maurice to Esther Williams, July 14, 1915, Williams Papers, AAA). Maurice and Charles are in Ogunquit, Maine, in early August and Maurice visits Walt Kuhn and his family in York Village, Maine. Maurice plans an autumn trip to the Catskills (letter from Maurice to John Quinn, September 7, 1915, Quinn Papers, NYPL). Maurice is included in *Vanity Fair*'s "Hall of Fame" (vol. 5 [November 1915], p. 56).

1916 Maurice and Charles visit Boston in May (letter from Charles to John Quinn, May 10, 1916, Quinn Papers, NYPL). Maurice visits Boston in November with William Glackens (Glackens, 1957).

1917 Maurice and Charles exhibit with the Society of Independent Artists, April 10–May 6. Charles is elected vice president of this organization. Maurice spends the summer in Annisquam and Gloucester, Massachusetts (Glackens, 1957).

1921 A joint exhibition of the brothers' work is held at Brummer Galleries, New York, April 4–23.

1922 Walter Pach publishes "Maurice Prendergast" in *Shadowland* (vol. 66 [April 1922], pp. 10–11).

1923 In December Maurice is awarded a third-place medal and $1,000 in the Corcoran Gallery ninth biennial. He is in New York Hospital and unable to receive the award in person (letter from Maurice to C. Powell Minnigerode, [December] 7, 1923, Corcoran Gallery Archives).

1924 Maurice dies on February 1 in New York City.

1925 C.W. Kraushaar Art Galleries arrange a memorial show for Maurice, February 16–March 4.

1926 The Cleveland Museum of Art mounts a memorial retrospective of Maurice's work, January 15–February 15.

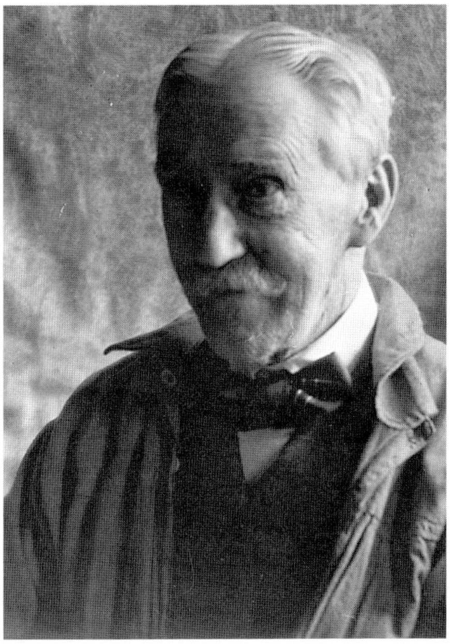

Maurice Prendergast, ca. 1917

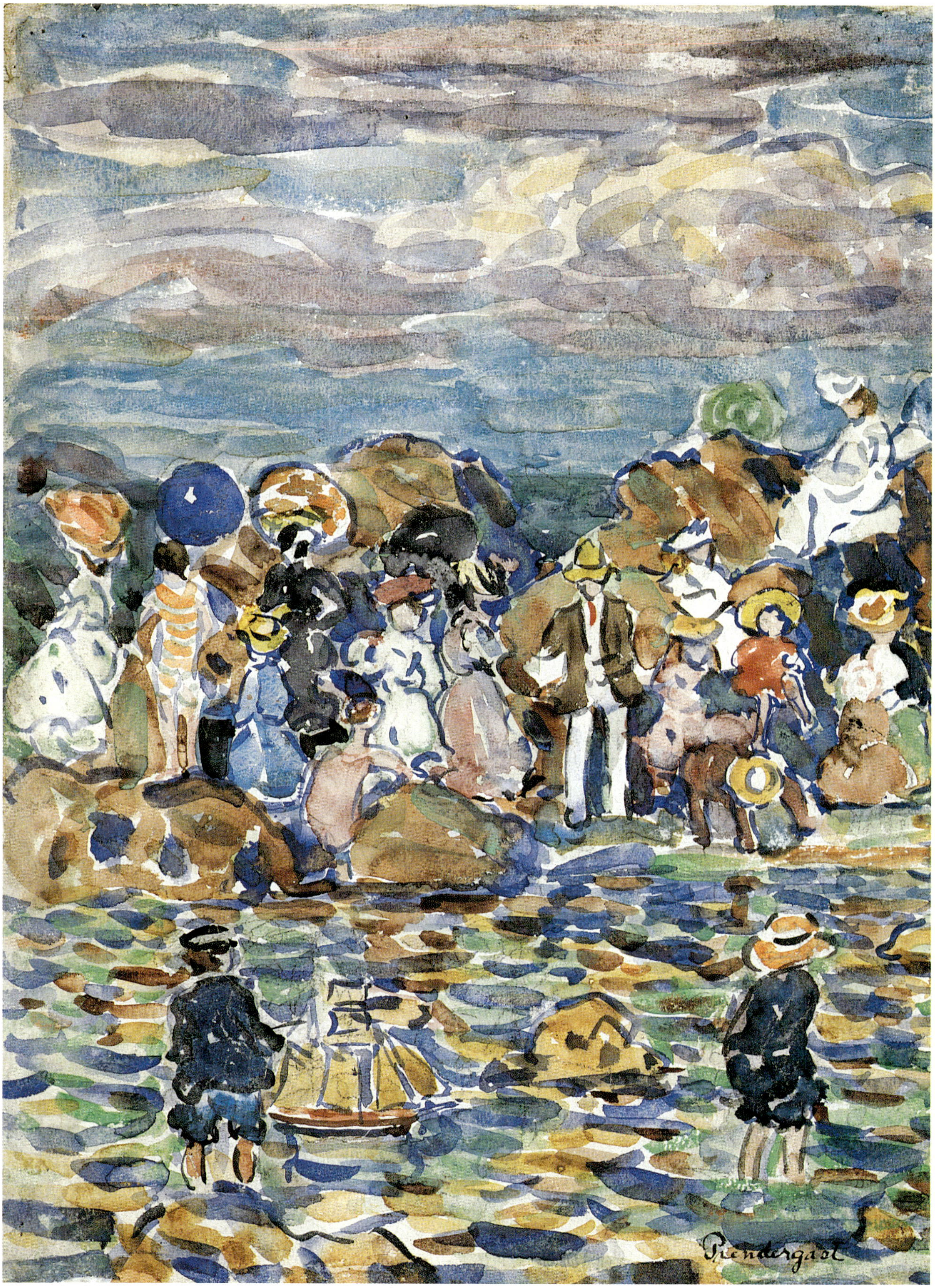

CR 896 *St. Malo*, ca. 1907

Prendergast & Leisure

Nancy Mowll Mathews, *Eugénie Prendergast Curator*

Introduction

By the 1890s, when the young Maurice Prendergast (1858–1924) was searching for an artistic direction, "leisure" had become the grand theme of modern art. Impressionism, with its views of beaches and cafés, spread quickly beyond Paris and emerged as an international phenomenon among avant-garde artists. At the same time, leisure was promoted as the hallmark of a progressive society. Social reformers and the labor movement fought for the universal acceptance of the eight-hour workday and guaranteed paid holidays.[1] They argued that increased leisure time for the individual would bring improvements in health, education, and productivity, which, in turn, would fuel the growth of an enlightened, modern society. With the impetus of political currency, American artists and writers capitalized on the modernity of the subject and, from travelogues to seaside romances, from popular fiction to high art, tourism and other forms of popular relaxation became a central motif.

But few artists were so well suited to capture this moment in the history of American culture as Maurice Prendergast. His talent and personality drew him to the kind of experiences turn-of-the-century leisure offered: the colorful jostling of holiday crowds, the experience of nature mediated by parasol and windswept banner, and the lowering of class and gender barriers to foster a sense of inclusiveness—however fleeting. Unlike contemporaries such as Winslow Homer and Paul Gauguin, who

1. "Between 1884 and 1891, a wave of agitation for the eight-hour day swept western European and American labor." The most publicized mass rallies were held on May Day (May 1) in Chicago in 1886 and across the country in 1890. See Gary Cross, *A Social History of Leisure since 1600* (State College, PA: Venture Publishing, Inc., 1990), pp. 82–84, and chapter 11.

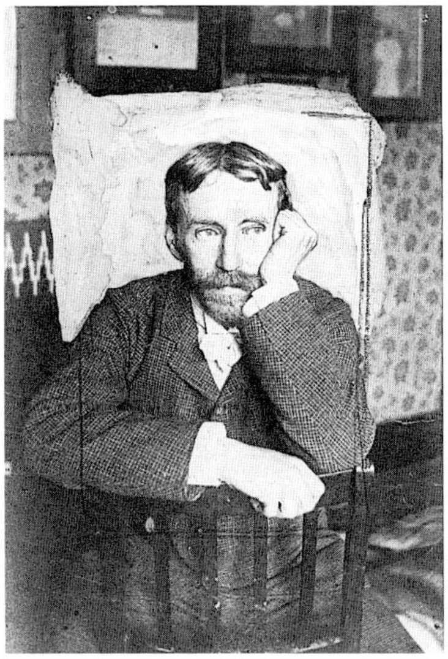

FIG. 1. Maurice Prendergast, ca. 1900

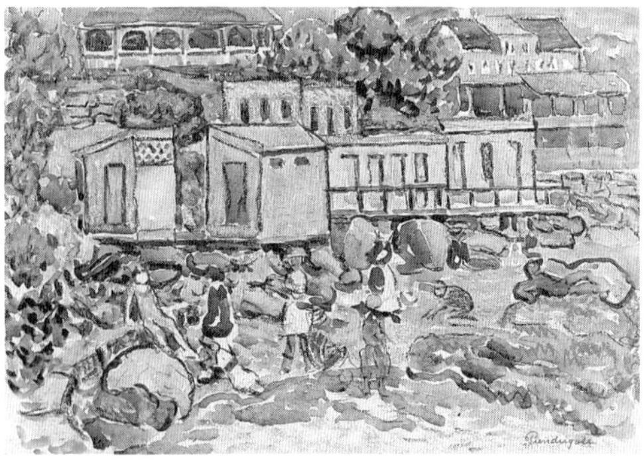

CR 1319 *Beach Resort*, ca. 1919

used travel to produce spectacles divorced from modern life, Prendergast traveled so that he might capture the excitement and significance of the modern tourist. He believed in leisure as an American right, with all the educational, therapeutic, and romantic benefits that were preached by social reformers. He loved the spectacles that were invented to entertain the masses in their newly free hours—beach resorts, amusement parks, festivals of all kinds, and, of course, the movies. From his earliest days as a painter, his deft brush could capture the ephemeral quality of such leisure activities.

But Prendergast's generation also witnessed the decline of leisure as it had been promoted in the first heady days of labor reform in the 1890s. By 1910, the rickety resort hotels and amusement parks that had sprung up overnight had begun to collapse, burn, or be closed down by stricter building codes. The automobile had a devastating effect on the group experience of leisure-time travel that had been fostered by the railroad in the nineteenth century. The First World War brought quick disillusionment about the "civilized" advances of modern society. As early-twentieth-century modernism erupted in art and literature, it swept aside the themes of modern life that had been promoted by naturalism and caused a reevaluation of the comfortable park and beach scenes of a few years before.

Prendergast was one of the first American artists to embrace modernist theories that reexamined the relationship of art to nature, and he quickly began to experiment with new versions of the subjects that had become his hallmark in the 1890s. During a trip to Paris in 1907, he discovered the radical color and brushwork of Paul Cézanne and the Fauves and immediately applied them to his studies of the French resort of St.-Malo. In the teens he monumentalized leisure, combining modern abstraction with echoes of a golden age. Borrowing simplified forms from ancient and "primitive" art, he turned the park-bench conversation and the seaside picnic into timeless idylls.

True to his age, leisure became the great theme of Prendergast's art. Over time, attitudes and values changed, but he never lost his reverence for a subject that he felt made people more civilized and more human. Nor did he forget that art itself was a leisure-time spectacle. Like a movie producer or an amusement park carney, he was a showman in the best sense of the word. He produced art to seduce and charm his audience—all the while asking them to sharpen their senses and broaden their horizons.

The following eight essays examine the different facets of leisure that Maurice Prendergast explored in the thirty years of his career as a painter. Taking one or two works as a touchstone, each essay weaves the art into its social and personal context. The result is not so much a complete overview of the life and art of Maurice Prendergast as it is a sampling of the circumstances and assumptions that lay behind the innocently playful images so familiar to us today.

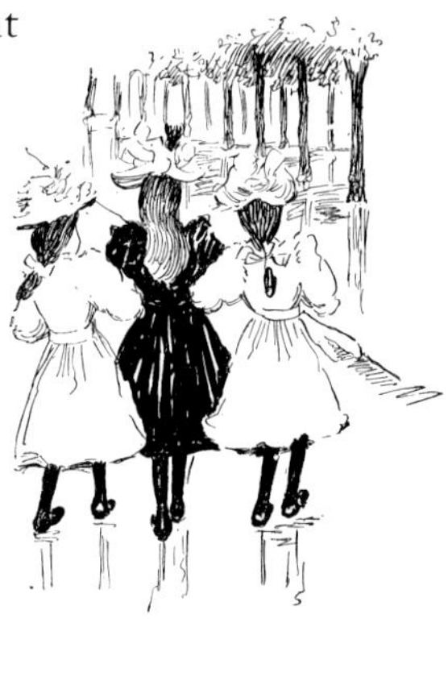

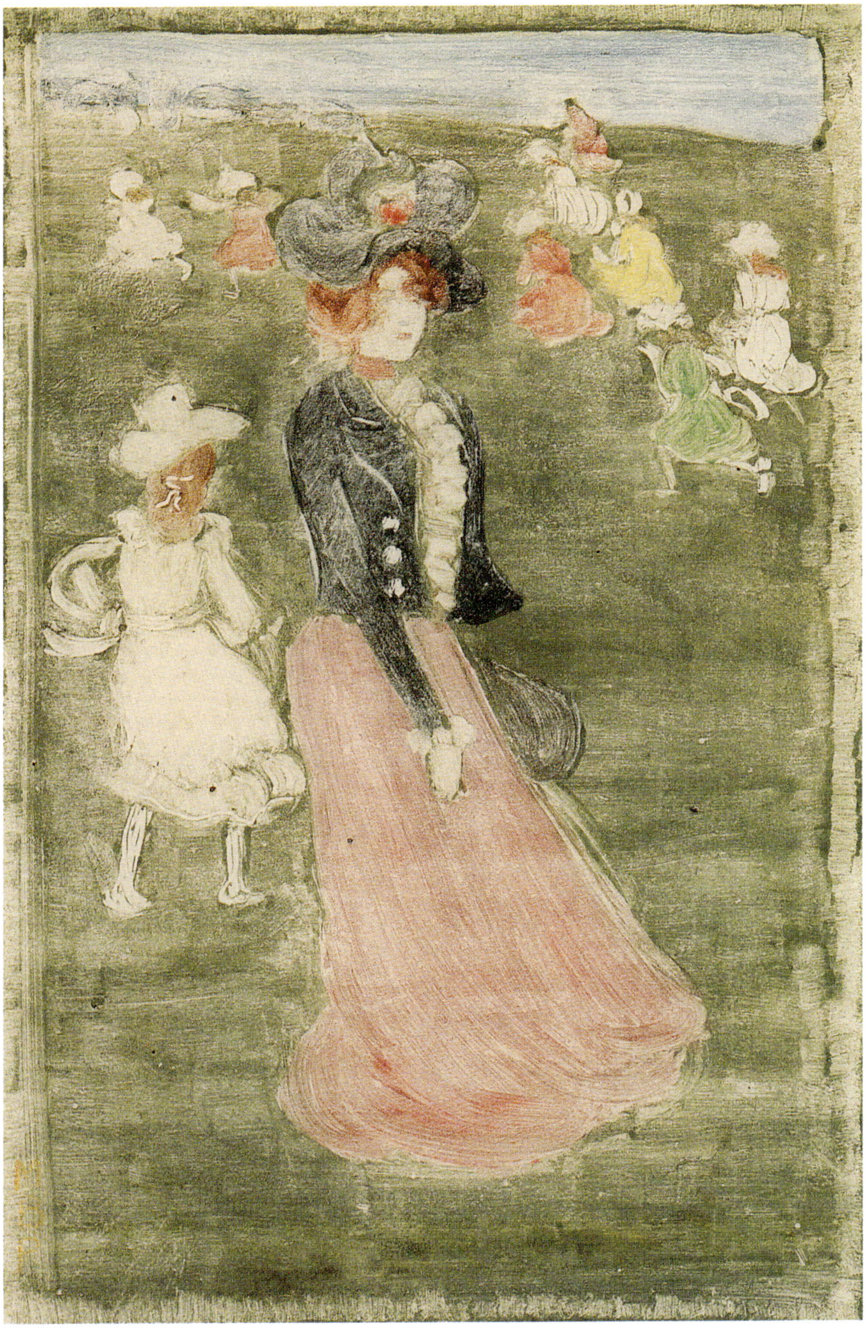

CR 1660 *Lady in Pink Skirt*, ca. 1895–97

Franklin Park, Boston

Maurice Prendergast was a Bostonian. Although he was already ten years old when his family moved there from St. John's, Newfoundland, it was in Boston that he received his principal education and began his career as an artist. His parents were solidly middle class (his father ran the family's general merchandise store in St. John's, and his mother was the daughter of a Boston physician), but apparently financial reverses prevented them from providing Maurice and his younger brother Charles with education beyond the age of fourteen. At that time the brothers went out to work—both gravitating toward the visual arts. By 1879, at twenty-one, Maurice had become a "designer," or commercial artist.

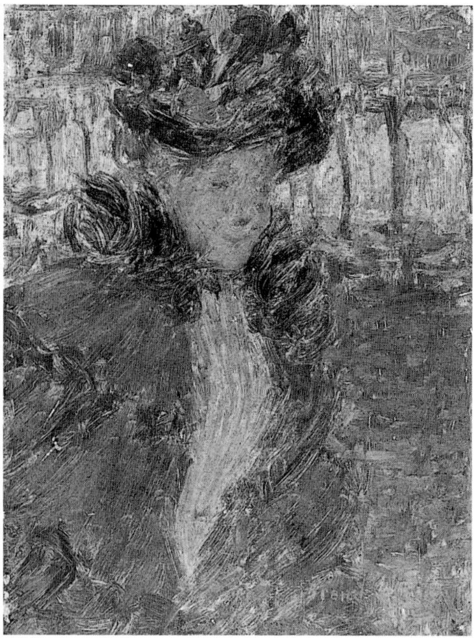

CR 16 *Woman in Paris*, ca. 1892–94

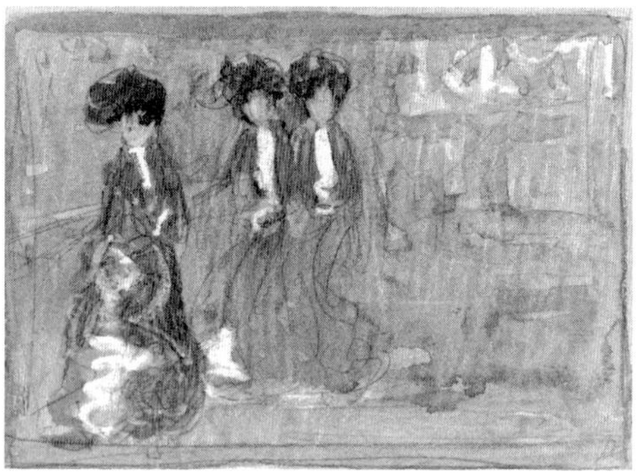

CR 554 *Paris*, ca. 1893–94

By 1891, Maurice and Charles were financially able to travel together to Paris to join the throngs of American art students hoping to advance their careers with foreign credentials. Although Charles soon returned to Boston, Maurice stayed on in Paris for four years, learning the latest styles and making art world connections that would allow him to switch from commercial art to fine-art painting. Life in Paris was stimulating, and he managed to sell some small Parisian sketches while there; but he knew he could not afford to stay. He would have to test his new career back in Boston.

Prendergast's natural tendency was to make his sites identifiable. In the earliest known sketchbook (1887, Museum of Fine Arts, Boston, CR 1475), the sketches are frequently inscribed with place-names such as "Hawarden," "N. Wales," and "Everett." Even early figure drawings evoked a specific location, such as a Parisian café, or were clearly identified with a site such as "St. Servan," "Dinard," or "Paris." This was standard practice for an artist hoping to appeal to the tourist trade, but it also reveals Prendergast's fundamental respect for place and his desire to communicate the experience of being in an actual location rather than just recording a charming scene.

When he returned to Boston, he had to adapt what he had learned abroad to the circumstances at home. In France he had carefully painted peasants and fishermen, but back home he ignored the New England farmers and fishing industry that occupied other American artists like Winslow Homer. Instead he tried to maintain his worldly viewpoint as a tourist; consistent with his French work, he chose scenes that would serve as souvenirs of a pleasant holiday rather than symbols of American hard work.

He was fortunate to come back to Boston at a time when it was becoming more like Paris in its integration of areas for work and leisure. Since it was a coastal city, nearby beaches were being turned into amusement centers for day-trippers. Furthermore, the ambitious ring of large urban parks, termed the "emerald necklace," was coming to completion under the direction of the great American landscape architect Frederick Law Olmsted. The system traversed the city, linking the original downtown park—the Boston Common—to new recreation areas in the suburbs, such as Franklin Park, and then snaking back to the sea at South Boston Pier. As each section was opened to the public in the 1890s, self-congratulatory publicity in Boston newspapers drew crowds of novelty seekers, including the Prendergast brothers and their circle of young artists. Prendergast's first American subjects, therefore, were the bustling thoroughfares of Boston's fashionable haunts—the heart of the city, the temporary, curving structure of the South Boston Pier, and the expanses of Franklin Park.

Lady in Pink Skirt (CR 1660) is one of a series of monotypes and watercolors associated with Franklin Park that Prendergast started in 1895 and began to exhibit in 1897.[2] The monotype technique used by Prendergast and such friends as Hermann Dudley Murphy (1867–1945) involved painting in colored printer's ink onto a metal plate and passing it through a printing press so that the ink came off onto a sheet of fine paper. Occasionally another faint print or two could be pulled from the plate before all the ink was completely removed. But because the plate was not permanently altered (as in an etching, engraving, or other traditional print media), the "edition" ended at that point. The result was a delicately muted image that combined the flexibility of the brushstroke in oil with the translucence of watercolor. The monotype was popular among experimental painters of the 1890s because it had the flat, abstract qualities of a Japanese print.

The ephemeral nature of this print technique also suited Prendergast's desire to represent a fleeting moment. Writers on Prendergast in the 1890s responded effusively. "The *Franklin Park*," said one critic, "is a charming sketch of children in the open air, flecked with bright color and full of animation and festivity."[3] The children chasing balloons in Franklin Park scenes are shown with skirts and ribbons flying while a more sedate but windblown woman looks on.

What the critics do not mention is what is more unusual to us today—the fact that the playground is full of girls and only girls. This is not true of Prendergast's depictions of other locations. While Prendergast tends to favor little girls, he seldom paints a beach or street scene without the occasional little boy. In segregating his park scenes by sex, he records one of the social theories behind the public park movement: that both boys and girls need exercise, but exercise of different kinds. At Franklin Park, the Playstead, a vast level playing field, was created for organized sports (primarily baseball) to be played by boys. Girls were expected to ramble over the hilly sections of the park in less organized games of running and chasing. To Prendergast's credit, he shows the girls in vigorous movement, which gives an edge to what would otherwise be an overly decorative representation and may account for his popularity among female viewers.

The woman in the foreground in her ruffled blouse and elegant suit became a favorite motif of Prendergast in these years. She appears in at least three other monotypes of Franklin Park and a watercolor, *Figures Under the Flag* (CR 825), which is related to yet another monotype. The repetition of this figure reveals Prendergast's interest in reusing successful designs and his belief that certain "types" were especially meaningful. To this day, *Lady in Pink Skirt* conveys the cutting-edge fashion of the new leisure activities of the 1890s—whether new parks or new seaside promenades. Young and attractive, she is the "available" woman in the romantic fantasies that spring up in the relaxed atmosphere of holiday destinations.

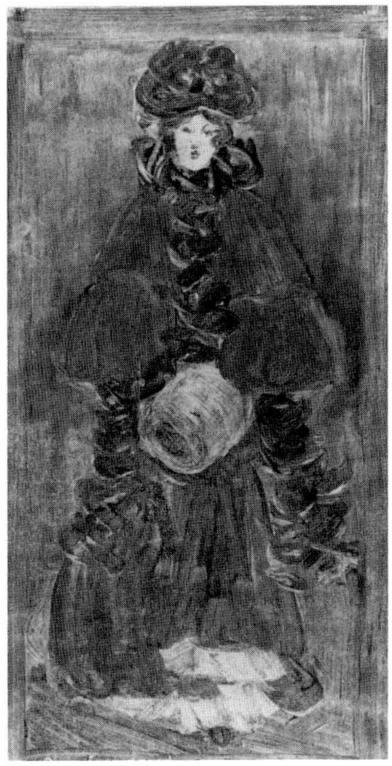

CR 1744 *Lady with Red Cape and Muff,* ca. 1900–02

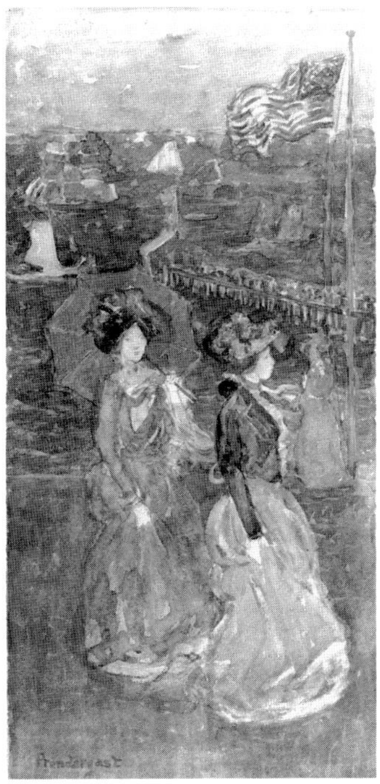

CR 825 *Figures Under the Flag,* ca. 1900–05

2. None in the series is inscribed with the location of the scene; in fact two are titled *The Breezy Common*, prompting the mistaken idea that they represent the Boston Common. But works of similar description were exhibited under the title *Franklin Park* (see "The Water Color Club," *The Sun*, Nov. 14, 1897, p. 7), and many, such as CR 611, 612, 614, 615, and 1639, have traditionally borne the same title.

3. "Eleventh Annual Exhibit of the Water Color Club," *Boston Evening Transcript*, Feb. 25, 1898, p. 5.

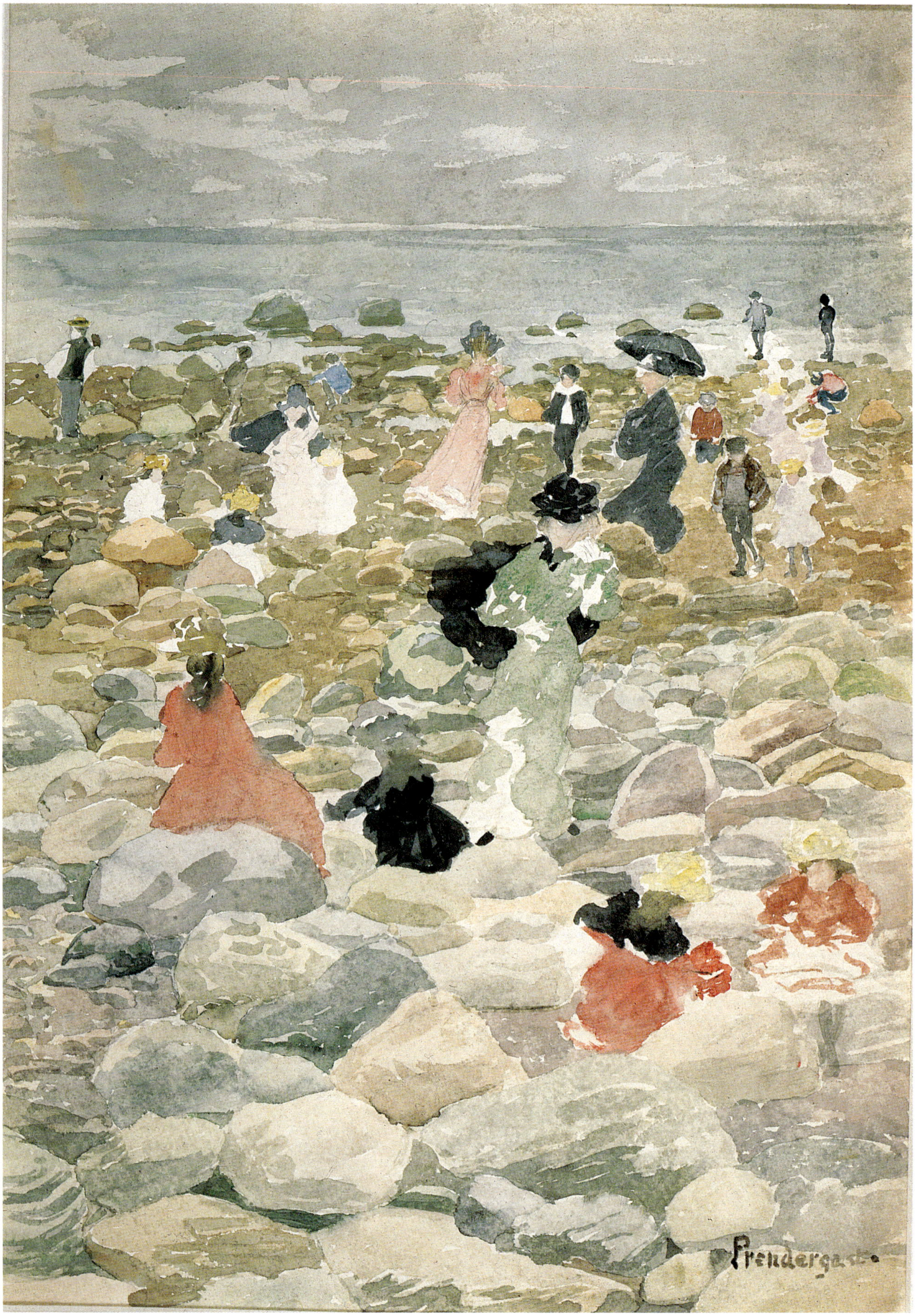

CR 640 *Low Tide, Nantasket*, ca. 1896–97

The South Shore

Leisure activities in the late nineteenth century were primarily carried out in large groups. The railroad and its sister modes of transportation, the streetcar and the steamer, made travel to holiday destinations easier and faster. Even the lower classes could make use of their new time off by taking the local electric railways to nearby ocean parks. But the price society paid for this new mobility was a loss of privacy. Trains carrying hundreds of people replaced the old horse-drawn coaches; huge vacation hotels, often built by the railroad companies, offered cramped bedrooms but spacious public verandas and dining rooms. Families with their servants traveled together and expected to spend the major part of their vacation time socializing with other families like theirs. Classes were involuntarily thrown together in the public spaces such as railroad stations and boardwalks, but as a rule hotels and even resort towns catered to a particular segment of society.

Segregation by class during holidays served an important function for nineteenth-century society. Holidays were not just for personal relaxation; they also offered a setting for making or strengthening ties with other families and provided young people with a safe arena for supervised courtship. These social aspects of leisure time in the 1890s account for Prendergast's attention to the poses of people in conversation and observation (of nature and of each other) in such works as *Low Tide, Nantasket* (CR 640) and *Surf, Nantasket* (CR 834). Women were central to the process of family and social bonding that took place at seaside resorts. Very often the mother and children would settle in for the summer while the father commuted from the city only on weekends. The women, too, "worked" during the holidays, supervising their transplanted households and maintaining a demanding social schedule. The dressy clothes that they wear on the beach attest to their consciousness of being observed and judged by the social circles at their chosen resort.

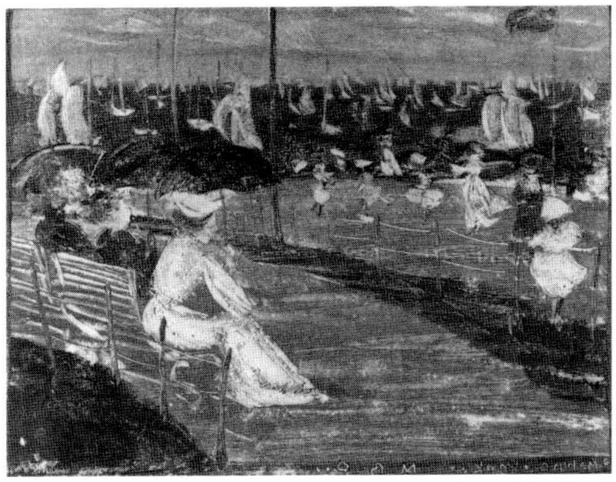

CR 1679 *Marine Park, South Boston,* ca. 1895–97

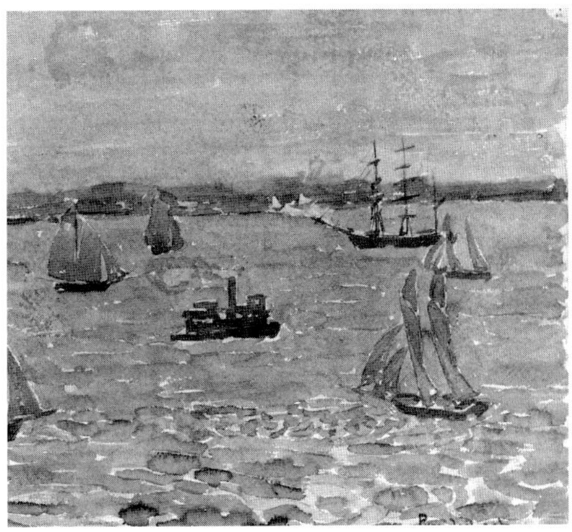

CR 820 *Boston Harbor,* ca. 1900–05

Prendergast's first beach scenes date from the summer of 1896, when he concentrated on the new public leisure destinations in and around Boston. In his titles, he identified the new Marine Park, which included Castle Island and the curved South Boston Pier. It was a bathing beach and promenade, but it was planned by Frederick Law Olmsted to be the final link in the "emerald necklace." It easily served the residents of downtown and suburban Boston for a Sunday picnic or an early-evening stroll. He also identified Crescent Beach, the hooked, southern end of Revere Beach, which became the most visited Boston-area beach at the turn of the century. He did not use the title "Nantasket" in exhibition catalogues or inscriptions; nevertheless, many of the beach scenes have acquired that site identification, and it seems to be a logical one. Nantasket is a sandy peninsula that juts out from Cohasset through the ocean toward Boston. Although by land it was too far for a day trip, by sea there were special steamers that connected Boston Harbor to Nantasket in less than an hour.

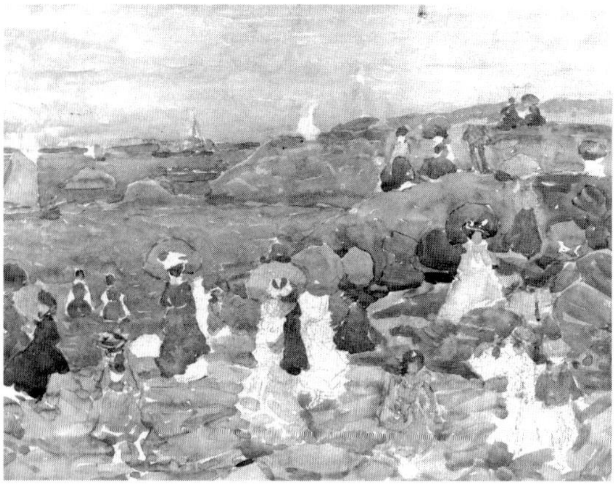

CR 667 *Rocky Coast*, ca. 1896–97

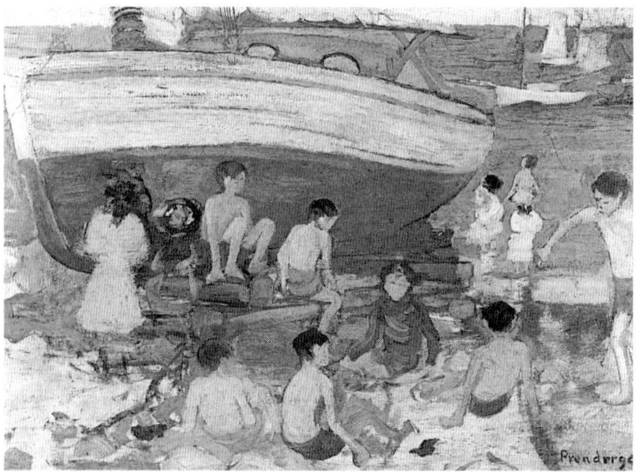

CR 28 *Low Tide*, ca. 1895–97

Nantasket was the leading seaside resort of the South Shore throughout the nineteenth century. Although not as elite as Nahant on the North Shore, it served a respectable summer crowd as well as the day-trippers from Boston.

In the 1890s, Nantasket underwent renovation to clean up the less savory parts of the peninsula, which had grown up around the "only liquor oasis between Boston and Provincetown."[4] It even figured in the most ambitious plan (never carried out) of the Olmsted team to bring healthful leisure to Bostonians, which was to extend the ring of parks south to Hingham, out to World's End, and then by bridge to Nantasket.

Prendergast's representations of the new, cleaned-up "urban" beaches such as Marine Park, Revere Beach, and Nantasket, along with his Franklin Park scenes, were exhibited to great acclaim in Boston, and also were sent to exhibitions in New York, Philadelphia, and Chicago in the late 1890s. They were considered to be as "modern" as some of the popular European seascapes, yet they were identifiably American. As one critic wrote, "Modern art . . . has found one of its distinctive expressions in pure and bright and positive color. This example is extraordinary. It is a splendid bouquet of flowers, or a cluster of radiant jewels. It glows, it flashes. We have seen Italian seashores with figures by Fortuny[5] that were not better."[6] The Boston critic could not be blamed for implying that they were not just American but perhaps even "Boston." Prendergast's paintings celebrated the strides taken by his home city to bring clean, healthful parks and beaches to all its citizens. These paintings would serve civic pride when exhibited at home and establish Boston's progressiveness when exhibited in rival cities.

As an advocate for the leisure spots of the Massachusetts coast, Prendergast helped to transform the national image of New England from maritime power and industrial giant to picturesque vacation destination. When the old fisheries and mills became outdated and industry moved farther west, New England drew on its sites of American history and bucolic landscape to promote tourism. As Dona Brown points out, the new vision of the region was "expressed in an extensive literature—from history and journalism to novels and short stories—and in architectural and landscape reforms that began to transform the appearance of many towns and villages."[7] We might also add that the new vision was expressed in countless paintings, illustrations, and other images of New England in the second half of the nineteenth century—but in Prendergast the vision found its "modern" note.

4. Joseph E. Garland, *Boston's Gold Coast: The North Shore,* 1890–1929 (Boston: Little, Brown and Co., 1981), p. 18.

5. The author may have been talking about either Mariano Fortuny y Marsal (1838–1874) or his son, Mariano Fortuny y Madrazo (1871–1949), both of whom painted in Italy.

6. "The Fine Arts," *Boston Evening Transcript,* April 3, 1897, p. 7.

7. Dona Brown, *Inventing New England: Regional Tourism in the Nineteenth Century* (Washington DC: Smithsonian Institution Press, 1995), p. 9.

In the late 1890s and the first half of the 1900s, Prendergast branched out to all the resorts on the north and south shores of Boston—Cohasset, Nahant, Marblehead, Salem, and Cape Ann. While they differed in character and class level, he painted them with a mixture of elegance and uninhibited "play" (at least on the part of the children) that erased obvious class identification. Some of his favorite resorts were those built for the masses, such as Salem Willows and Bass Rocks, which had huge turn-of-the-century amusement parks with thrilling rides and spectacular sideshows. Prendergast also enjoyed the populist spirit of the large public beaches and genuinely loved swimming. He described a visit to Boston's L Street Beach, not far from Marine Park, in glowing terms:

> *To take off one's cloths* [sic] *and lay full stretched on the sand exposed to the wind and the sun is the finest sensation I know...all ages and classes come here—professional men, I have already met three artists—sports—prize fighters, business men, etc. It is free to all and it is a fine sight to see those naked figures strolling around and taking a dip in the icy water.*[8]

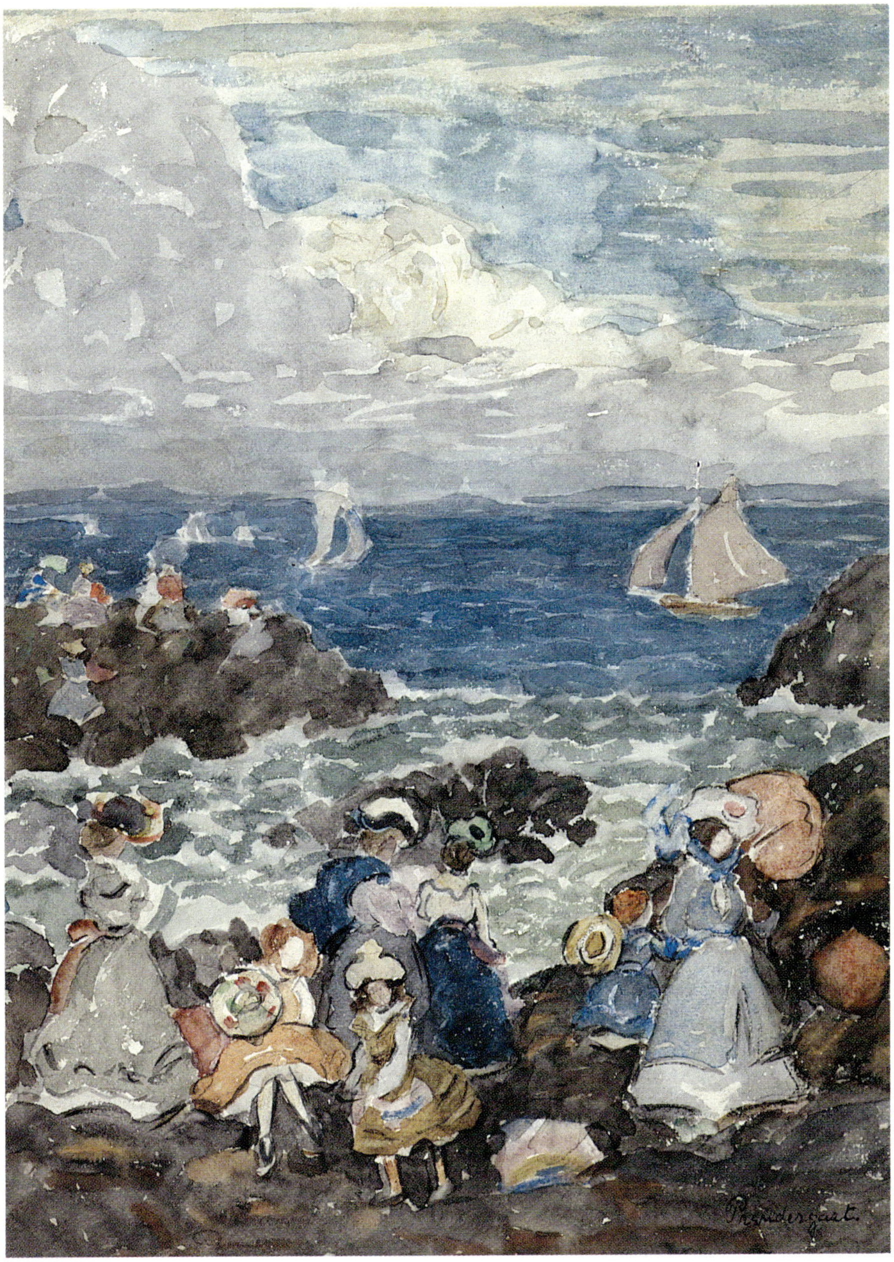

CR 834 *Surf, Nantasket,* ca. 1900–05

On the other hand, he often stayed with his brother at the homes of wealthy friends and patrons, and depicted the more refined society with equal relish. Although the Prendergast brothers were not among the elite of Boston society, as many Boston artists tended to be, they should not be considered too far below that social rung. Their tendency to enjoy spectacles of all kinds shows a great democracy of taste, but they always returned home to the apartment and studio in fashionable Beacon Hill that they moved into in 1902.

8. Maurice B. Prendergast [MBP] to Esther Williams, May 14, 1905, Archives of American Art. Prendergast also went swimming for health reasons. Apparently, in this case, bathing in the cold seawater in May was advised by his doctor to improve his strength.

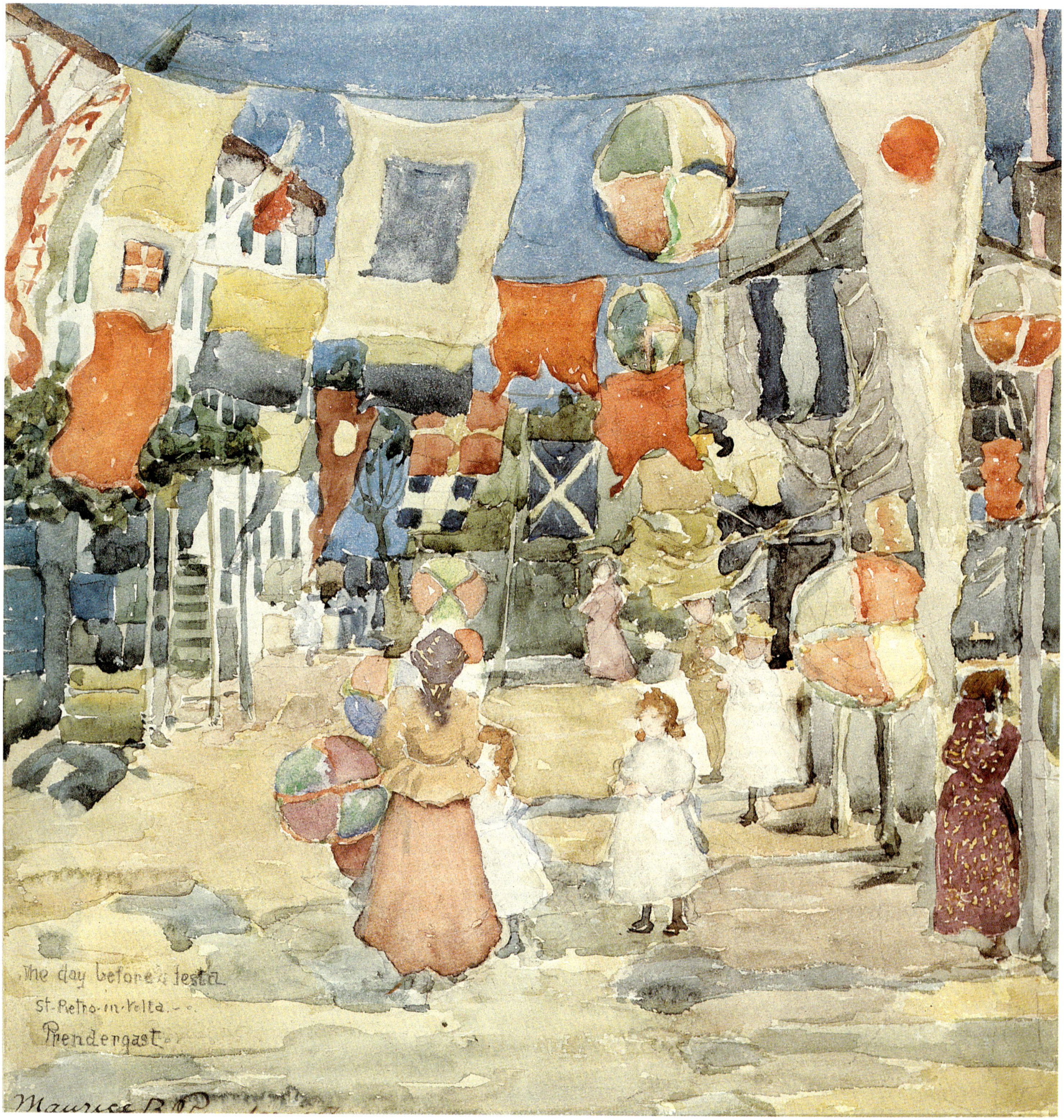

CR 729 *Fiesta-Venice-S. Pietro in Volta*, ca. 1898–99

Foreign Travel

The anonymous critic who compared Prendergast's Boston beach scenes to the Venetian paintings of Fortuny may have put an idea into his head. A year later he was applying for a passport to go to Italy and, thanks to a wealthy friend, he was able to stay for about a year and a half. In the spring of 1899, midway through his trip, he began sending home finished watercolors to be shown in the annual Boston Water Color Club exhibition and then in a one-person show at the Eastman Chase Gallery. His patron, the Boston artist and collector Sarah Choate Sears (1858–1935), was amply repaid for her generosity by the Italian watercolors she received in return. Prendergast's watercolors from this trip were immediately sought by collectors and dealers alike and continue to this day to be the most treasured of all his works. The success they enjoyed in Boston was quickly communicated to New York. The ambitious young dealer William Macbeth, who would be a major force behind radical art during the next decade in America, contacted Prendergast in September and arranged to be his dealer for the next decade, bringing the artist to national prominence.

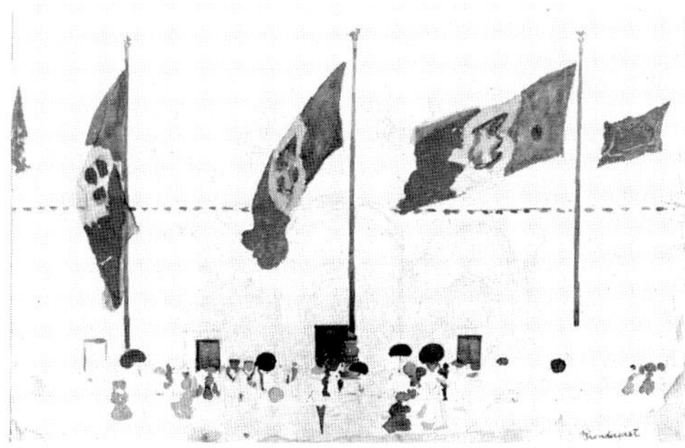

CR 678 *Venice*, ca. 1898–99

Prendergast's Italian watercolors of 1898–99 deserve a place alongside the writings of Mark Twain and Henry James for their masterful characterization of the American experience in Europe. Like Twain's *Innocents Abroad* (1869) and James's many novels and short stories, but especially *The American* (1876–77) and *Daisy Miller* (1883), Prendergast's distinctive vision of Italy was half Baedeker and half joyous consumerism. He visited only the most popular destinations in Italy, gravitating toward the sites that drew the biggest crowds. Not only did he include tourists in his views of famous monuments, but he also created a series that captured unerringly the American tourist experience.

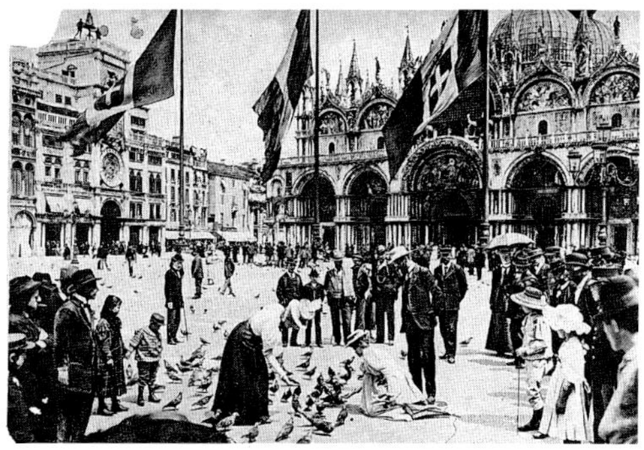

FIG. 2. Piazza San Marco con piccioni, 1897

He wandered around Italy for eighteen months painting Rome, Florence, Siena, Assisi, and Capri. But he concentrated most of his energy on Venice, "the Queen of the Adriatic" and the center for international socializing in Italy. Ever since Napoleon conquered the Italian states and established an Austrian ruling family in Venice, the foreign occupiers had welcomed foreign tourists.[9] By the end of the nineteenth century, organized tours, such as those by Thomas Cook's company, brought hordes of visitors from all over the world. Furthermore, Venice was the preferred destination for foreign artists because of its famous architecture and canals, but also because they enjoyed the opportunity to paint and socialize together. Like Paris, it was a place for artists to vacation among their own kind.

Prendergast's Venetian watercolors reflect his own experience as a tourist. He did not wander off the beaten track. He faithfully painted the most familiar sights of Venice, such as the monuments in and around the piazza San Marco (which coincidentally also included the popular cafés of Venice), the Rialto, and the canals (fig. 2). He carried his Baedeker's guide to Italy[10] with

9. "Venezia, Cara Venezia," *Apollo* (January 1987), p. 47.

10. Now in the Prendergast Archive and Study Center, Williams College Museum of Art.

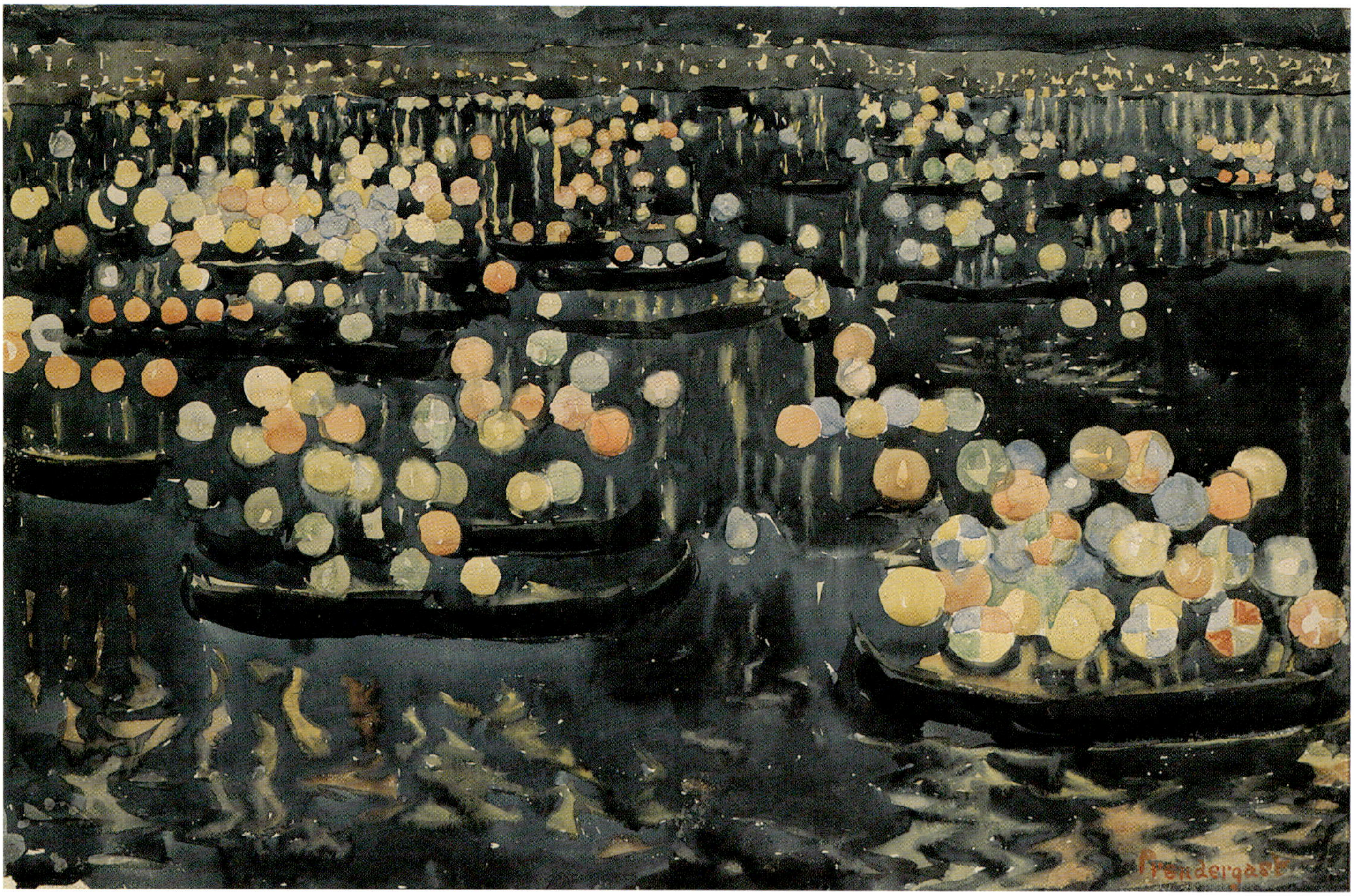

CR 724 *Festa del Redentore*, ca. 1899

him, like any tourist, and seems to have mentally ticked all these sites off the list. Like steamships and railroads, guidebooks made travel simpler and enabled the classes below the most privileged to navigate the complexities of foreign lands. They not only gave information about booking hotels and tipping waiters, but they also listed and annotated the important cultural experiences to be had in each locale. These lists were used by tourists as they would a shopping list, checking off each site as it was "seen"—and giving meaning to the term "acquisition of culture."[11] The clear structure that guidebooks gave to the traveler's experience of foreign "sights" is perhaps echoed in Prendergast's watercolors, which were drawn almost completely in pencil first and then filled in with careful areas of color.

In keeping with its role as a social center, the architectural monuments were not the only spectacles to draw tourists to Venice. The city also organized a number of parades and festivals throughout the summer and fall, which gave the city its lively reputation. These seemingly "ancient" rituals were actually revived or even created in the nineteenth century, spurred by advances in travel and leisure time. Throughout Europe, local festivals were publicized in hopes of bolstering the economy of the region. Folk costumes, banners, games, food, and drink were all part of a spectacle in which tourists could participate.

In Venice, even funeral processions were made picturesque by the costumes and by the banners carried through the streets. Prendergast's *St. Pietro in Volta* [*sic*] (CR 729) depicts preparations for an unidentified festival, possibly the Festa del Redentore (July 19), which was by far the most popular. The woman in the foreground carries round, multicolored lanterns like those seen in his watercolor *Festa del Redentore* (CR 724). The festival itself (still) takes place at night. Those who can afford the expense hire boats decorated with such colored lanterns to take them out onto the Grand Canal. There they spend the night eating, drinking, and watching fireworks. Music wafts over the magical scene. As dawn breaks, the boating parties go to the mouth of the canal to watch the sun come up.

Prendergast's watercolors transport the intended viewer not only to the foreign location but also to the "activity" of tourism. For Americans, Europe was the ultimate leisure destination. It was commonly seen as a reward for a lifetime of hard work, and, like the evening of relaxation after an eight-hour day, it was a time for entertainment and self-improvement. As one of Henry James's American travelers puts it, "[W]e are brought up to think that when we have earned leisure and rest—at some bright hour, when fortune smiles—we may go forth and cross oceans and mountains and see on Italian soil the primal substance . . . of our consoling dreams and our richest fancies."[12]

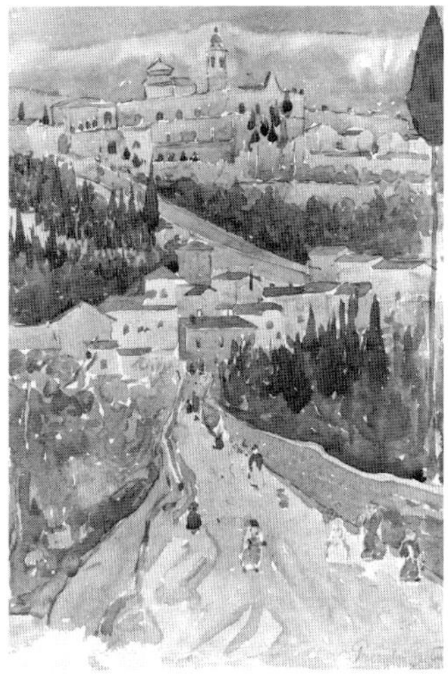

CR 743 *Assisi*, ca. 1898–99

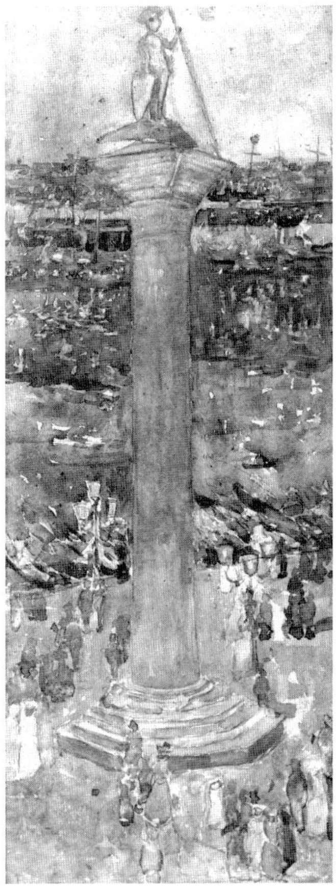

CR 693 *Column of St. Theodore*, ca. 1898–99

11. For more on the function of the guidebook and the "list" of cultural sites, see James Buzard, *The Beaten Track: European Tourism, Literature, and the Ways to Culture*, 1800–1918 (Oxford: Clarendon Press, 1993) pp. 222–23.

12. "At Isella" (1871), as quoted in Buzard, p. 235.

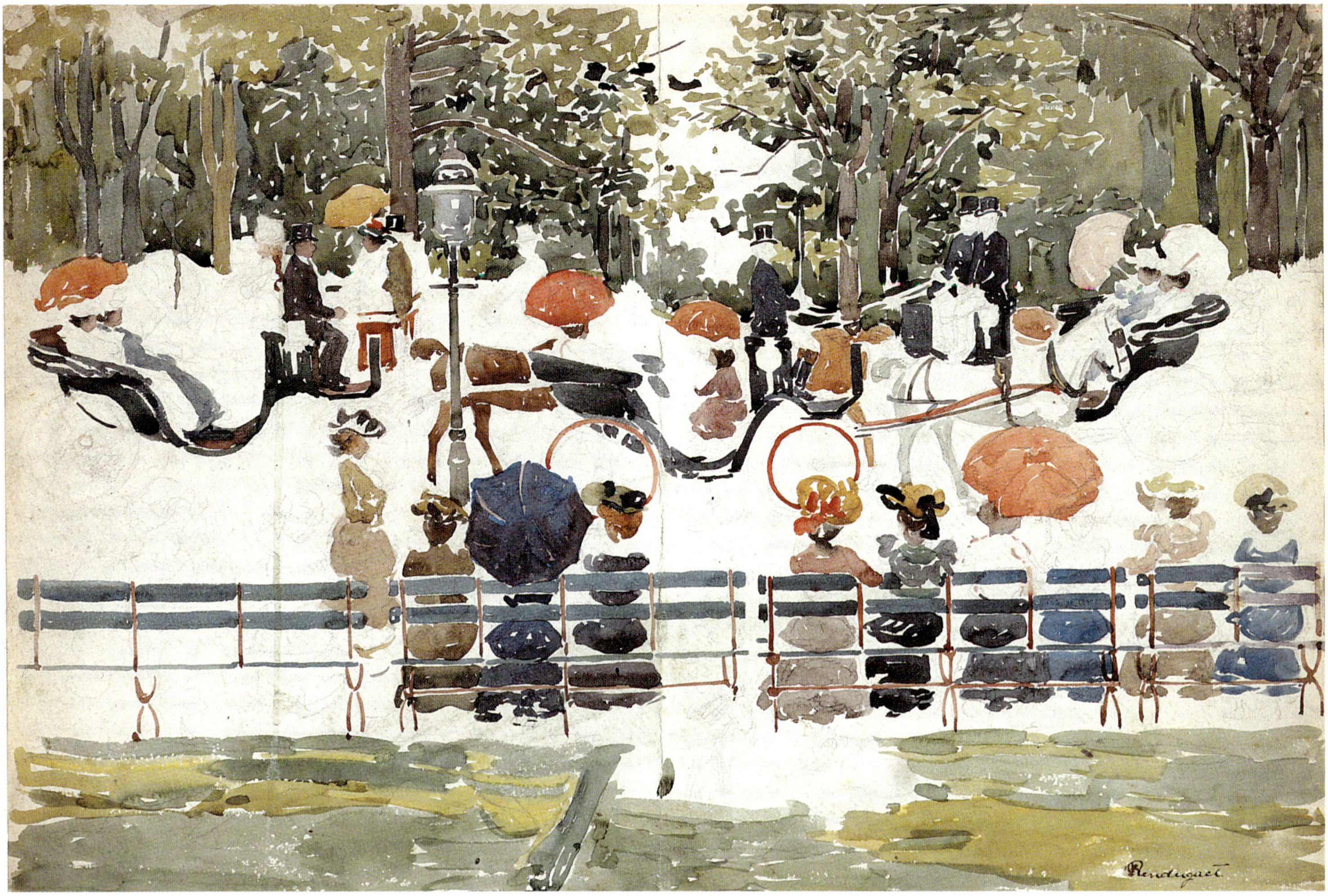

CR 774 *Central Park*, ca. 1901

New York

It was evident by 1900 that New York was the center of the American art world. Both Philadelphia and Boston had long vied with New York for that honor, but New York's extraordinary growth and social dynamism at the turn of the century made all other American cities pale in comparison. To be sure, there were lively art communities in all the major urban areas, including the Mid- and Far West, but it was New York that captured the attention of artists, critics, and collectors nationwide.

Prendergast had begun to send works to New York exhibitions starting in 1897, and in 1899 was invited to hold a solo exhibition in the gallery of the young, aggressive dealer William Macbeth (fig. 3). When this exhibition of watercolors and monotypes was held in March 1900, Prendergast was immediately ranked among the important new artists of the city. He began to spend part of every year in New York, painting alongside urban realists Robert Henri, William Glackens, George Luks, and John Sloan—who would later be referred to as the Ash Can School. He also became a close friend of Arthur B. Davies, who frequented all the modernist art circles that formed in the first two decades of the twentieth century.

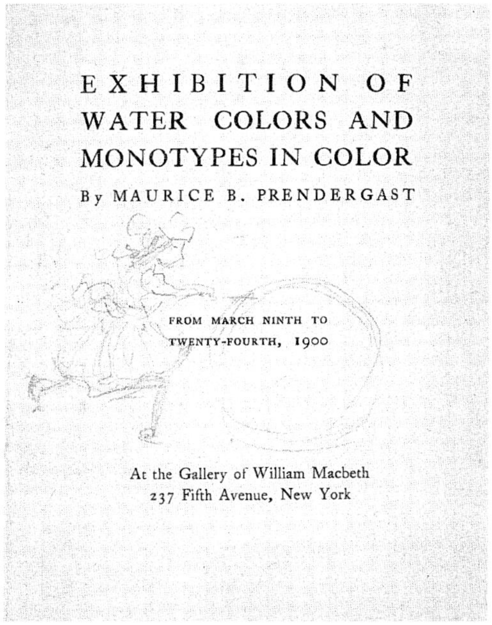

FIG. 3. *Sketch of Girl with Hoop,* pencil on exhibition catalogue, ca. 1900

Fresh from painting the tourist sites of Italy, Prendergast sought American equivalents of those populated urban palaces, churches, and parks. In Boston he painted several views of West Church, which was being used temporarily as a library, and in New York he began to study such sites as Madison Square, Columbus Circle, and the boat docks. But by far his most frequent destination was Central Park, where he produced dozens of watercolors of adults promenading and children playing.

Central Park was the model for Frederick Law Olmsted's designs for Boston's "emerald necklace" and specifically Franklin Park. Central Park had been the architect's first major park design (opened in 1858) and remained his most triumphant. When Prendergast came to it in 1900, after his innovative celebration of Olmsted's work in Boston (Franklin Park, Marine Park, and the South Boston Pier) as well as the parks and squares of Venice and Rome, he looked upon Central Park's distinctive features with a practiced eye.

In the Williams College Museum of Art's unfinished watercolor of Central Park (CR 774), the scene has been flattened into four horizontal bands of activity—from the foreground grass, to the bench-sitters, to the carriages, to the foliage of the trees above. This radical simplification of the composition, along with the bright touches of color in the umbrellas and costumes of the people, gives the watercolor a very modern appearance. Part of its appeal is its unfinished state (see a finished version of this scene, CR 775). The outline of the composition is dramatically silhouetted against the white of the bare paper. It is hard to say why he abandoned the work at this point, and he would be shocked to learn that we find it so pleasing, as he did not exhibit or sell such unfinished works.

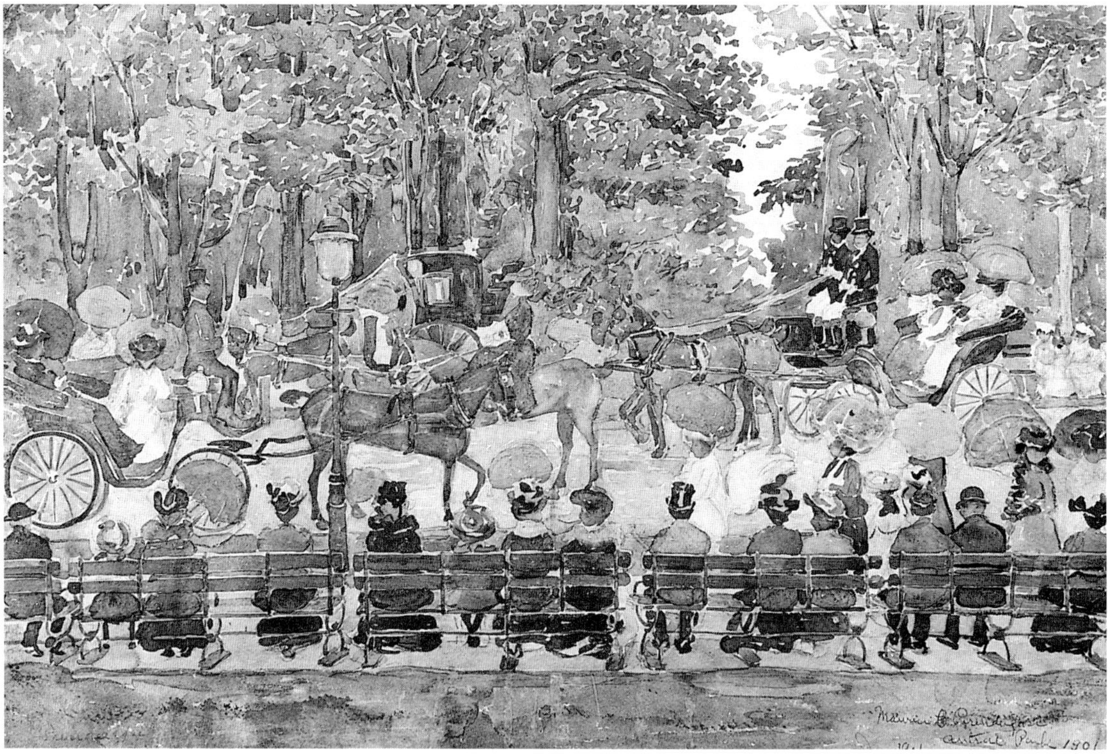

CR 775 *Central Park*, ca. 1901; Whitney Museum of American Art

Yet despite the modernity of this fragmented view of *Central Park* (CR 774), the carriages and the benches evoke the park as it was when it first opened forty years before. This mixture of old and new was crucial to Central Park as Prendergast knew it. He discovered it at the moment when the decades-long "society" domination of the park gave way to increasing pressure from the lower classes and represents in subtle ways the transition that affected the entire city.

The parade of elegant horse-drawn carriages, which Prendergast has sketched fully in pencil but has just begun to fill in with watercolor, is the spectacle the park offers to the "audience" of bench-sitters. It is a reminder that Central Park was first and foremost an equestrian park. The huge size (almost 900 acres) and the miles of paved roads were designed more for horse-power than for the casual stroll. When the carriage drives were completed in 1863, almost two-thirds of the visitors to the park were drawn there by horses.[13] In fact, the presence of such a superior facility for carriages stimulated the private ownership of horses and rigs in New York, an expense that was far beyond the reach of the average citizen.[14] Such excessive spending on carriages made Central Park the site of the most conspicuous display of wealth to be found in the city.

As Prendergast has indicated in his sketch, the occupants of the carriages tended to be female. Taking a drive in the park was considered one of the few

13. Roy Rosenzweig and Elizabeth Blackmar, *The Park and the People: A History of Central Park* (Ithaca: Cornell University Press, 1992), p. 213.

14. Ibid. "It would be hard to come up with a more precise marker of mid-nineteenth-century class status than a carriage. Money and lots of it was the only prerequisite." The typical carriage cost $1,200 or four times the annual salary of the average worker. Then an equal amount would be needed to maintain horses, stables, harness, and coachmen.

"safe" outings in an increasingly crowded and chaotic city, and the women fulfilled their social obligations by congregating this way on a regular basis. Husband or father usually controlled the wealth behind such an expensive activity, but the woman herself was responsible for the most effective presentation of the financial and social clout of the family.

The observers sitting on park benches in the foreground of the composition must be understood as less fortunate than their sisters in the carriages, although it is difficult to see class distinctions in the clothing or demeanor of the two groups. Fashionable gowns and colorful umbrellas are shown equally throughout. But in 1901, benches had an extra significance that has been forgotten in the intervening century. That June, a new practice of renting individual chairs to visitors in the city's parks had brought a storm of protest. Borrowing the idea from Europe, the New York parks commissioner permitted vendors to provide seats for a nickel apiece. Many New Yorkers liked the idea because it freed them from the traditional continuous bench (as seen in *Central Park*), which could be socially uncomfortable. As one writer pointed out, the rental chair would spare you "the ordeal of sitting next to unclean, often drunken, and generally foul-mouthed loafers."[15] But the protesters won out through various forms of civil disobedience, including an organized boycott that turned raucous and became known by the police as "Chair Sunday."[16] In Prendergast's portrayal, our attention is drawn to the "democratic" park bench by the insistent horizontality and the bright blue coloring of the slats. All the bench-sitters are well behaved and unquestionably respectable, a point of some significance to the viewers of 1901, with Chair Sunday fresh in their minds.

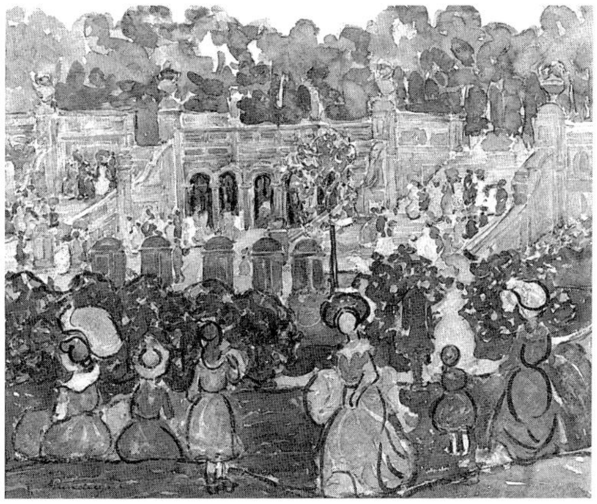

CR 783 *Central Park, New York,* ca. 1900–03

Other seemingly decorative Central Park watercolors, such as the May Day scenes (CR 1182, verso), also refer to the increased use of the park by the city's underclasses. The traditional May Day picnics for children became politicized after 1900 when religious, ethnic, and civic groups, which had been discouraged from using the park for their activities in past decades, began to organize large gatherings attracting as many as 200,000 children.[17] In this unfinished sketch, similar to several finished watercolors,[18] little girls gather around an umbrella-like Maypole—one of many that would have been erected throughout the open areas of the park on May 1.

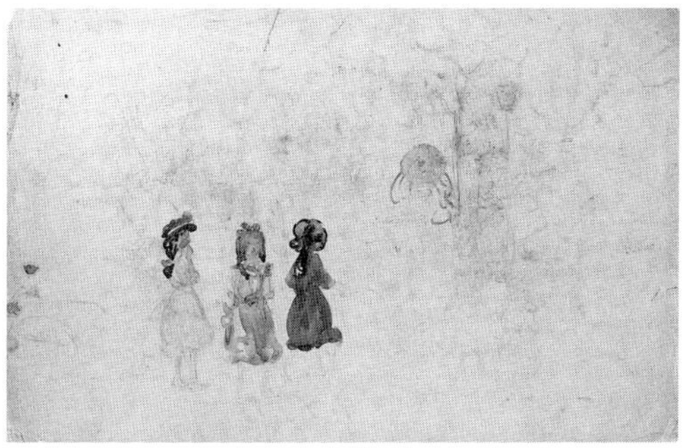

CR 1182 verso *Sketch of Girls and Street Scene,* ca. 1900–03

Today, there seems to be no hint of controversy in the charming pastel colors and innocent enjoyment of the children in Prendergast's watercolors; but for the viewers at the time who associated Prendergast with the socially critical artists of the Ash Can School, these decorative watercolors would have touched on the larger issues of the day.

15. Ibid., p. 384.

16. Ibid., p. 383.

17. Ibid., p. 389.

18. Such as *May Day, Central Park,* 1901 (Cleveland Museum of Art, CR 795) and *Maypole,* 1900–03 (Allen Memorial Art Museum, Oberlin College, Ohio, CR 797).

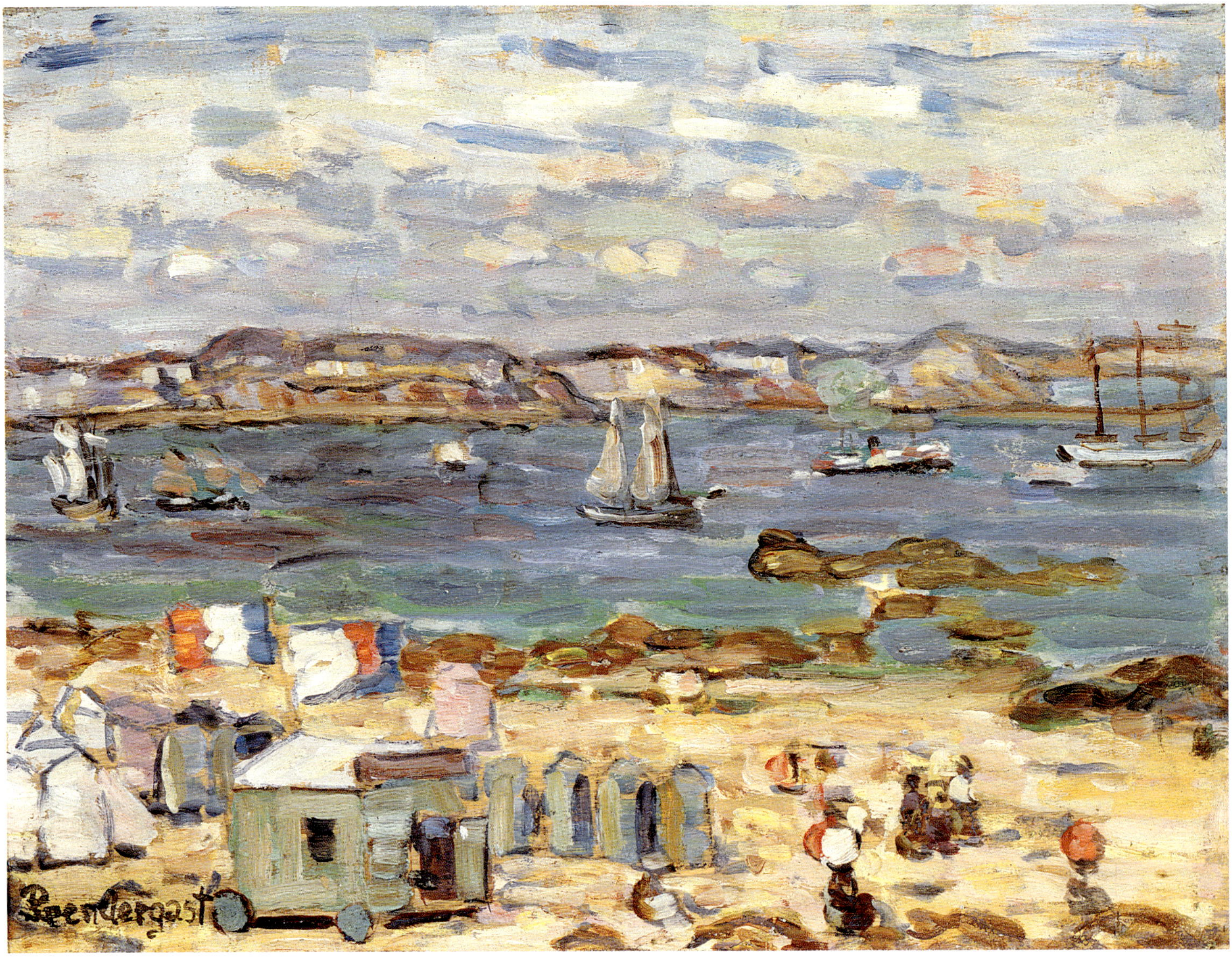

CR 71 *Study St. Malo, No. 12*, ca. 1907

Modern Art

Prendergast exhibited with Robert Henri and the other New York urban artists in 1904[19] and participated regularly in the activities of the group thereafter. In 1907 they decided to hold a second exhibition that would open in February 1908 in the Macbeth Galleries. This show became more of an event than a simple exhibition, traveling around the country and earning the group a lasting label: The Eight. Henri's philosophy of modern art, which he taught in his classes and frequently wrote about, was tied to the modernity of American life, specifically in multicultural New York. Prendergast shared this belief in the early years of their friendship, but as he began to prepare for the exhibition that would showcase the group's common American spirit, he slipped off to France for a summer of painting on the Normandy coast.

He had recently gotten away from the site-specific approach that had driven his earlier park and travel scenes, concentrating less on the associations of the actual location and more on generic effects. Because of this, his trip to France did not seem to contradict the nationalistic goals of the upcoming exhibition. But when bad weather on the coast drove him inland to wait out the rainy spell in Paris, he encountered art and ideas that would change his style forever. The paintings he produced upon his return to the seaside resort of St.-Malo redefined modern art for him and in turn introduced these ideas to art audiences in the ten American cities that hosted the exhibition of The Eight.

During his brief stay in Paris in June 1907, Prendergast absorbed the radical styles of Cézanne, the Neo-Impressionists, and Matisse's group of Fauves. The antinaturalist color and space in these paintings appealed to the artist who had dared to highlight the park bench in *Central Park* (CR 774) with insistent horizontal lines and blue color. In his letters home, he described the most daring of these paintings with awe:

> *Can you imagine a picture which is called Maternity, the mother surrounded by her children, an interior. The mother has a brick red face and arms with a prussian blue dress, the baby has a vermillion face with a green dress . . . . The furniture is indian red, the whole backed with a cadmium yellow wall. The faces are outlined in black black eye brows, black shadows, etc. The effect is startling, but there is something I like about them. I wish we had some of it in Boston or New York. Our exhibitions are so monotonous.*[20]

Prendergast responded to the new art with a professional eye and immediately tried out his own version of these styles. But he also responded to the art as might a tourist. He had experienced firsthand the power of antinaturalistic styles to transport the viewer to a new reality. For

19. "Exhibition of Henri, Sloan, Glackens, Davies, Luks, Prendergast," National Arts Club, January 1904.

20. MBP to Esther Williams, Oct. 10, 1907, Williams Papers, Archives of American Art.

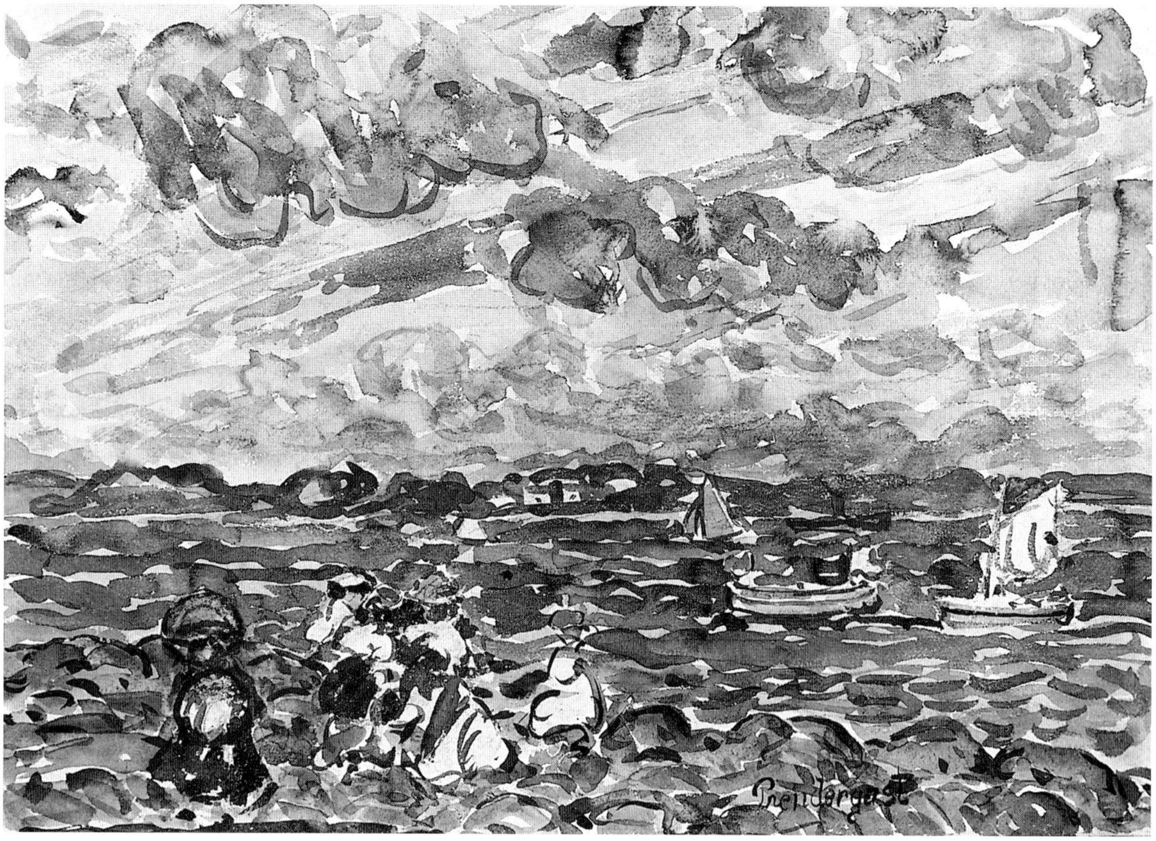

CR 883 *St. Malo*, ca. 1907

Prendergast, the sensation was physical: "I had to run up and down the Boulevards to work off steam," he wrote to an artist friend at home.[21] He quickly grasped how the expressive distortions of modern French art could accomplish what he had always sought in his painting—to transport the viewer to an alternate reality.

When Prendergast returned to the French coast and settled in for a long stay in the fashionable town of St.-Malo, he tried out various techniques to make his typical beach scenes more daring. In the many oil sketches he made on small 11 x 14-inch panels, such as *Study St. Malo, No. 12* (CR 71), one finds the heightened colors that were the direct result of the art he saw in Paris. The pure blues, reds, and greens are more brilliant than any he had used in the past. The boldness of the color is intensified by the crude, visible brushstrokes that are used from foreground to background, minimizing the illusion of three-dimensional space and unifying the paint surface into a sea of choppy colors. The costumes and activities of the people on the beach are less important to the mood of the holiday scene than in previous seaside paintings, but the French flags and the characteristic rolling cabanas used on the tidal beach of St.-Malo inform the American viewer that this is a foreign land.

Even when such obvious signs of location are absent, as in the watercolor *St. Malo* (CR 883), the American viewer in 1908 still reacted to the foreignness of the technique. Impressionist brushwork was no longer a

21. Ibid.

curiosity among the art public, but such a hodgepodge of shapes and colors—to the extent that the figures on the rocks in the background cannot be deciphered—had the shock value that Prendergast sought. One amused critic went along with his intention to use technique to create a new, exotic reality:

> *Prendergast sends [to the exhibition] nearly a score of modest sized canvases, full of spots of color, with many people mainly on the beach at the French St.-Malo, obviously a place where the people are careless about their drawing and construction, and where everything is a jumble of riotous pigment, such as one does not see elsewhere.*[22]

When he saw the reaction of the critics and public to the St.-Malo studies in 1908, Prendergast must have suddenly felt a little like a foreigner himself. Since the 1890s, he had had the sympathy of important critics and collectors, who appreciated the modernity of his approach but mostly admired his naturalism. When he abandoned naturalism, he also lost his old comfortable niche in the American art world, and gradually had to locate other artists, collectors, and critics who shared his interest in modernist experimentation. He made many converts by the charm of his art and the eloquence of his defense of such avant-garde favorites as Cézanne, but it was an uphill battle for a man who had just turned fifty. More often than not, he had to tolerate the jokes that even his friends were tempted to make about his art, such as Arthur Hoeber's memorable jest: "Hung in a group, these canvases of Maurice Prendergast look for all the world like an explosion in a color factory."[23]

22. Arthur Hoeber, "Art and Artists," *Globe and Commercial Advertiser,* Feb. 5, 1908, p. 9.

23. Ibid.

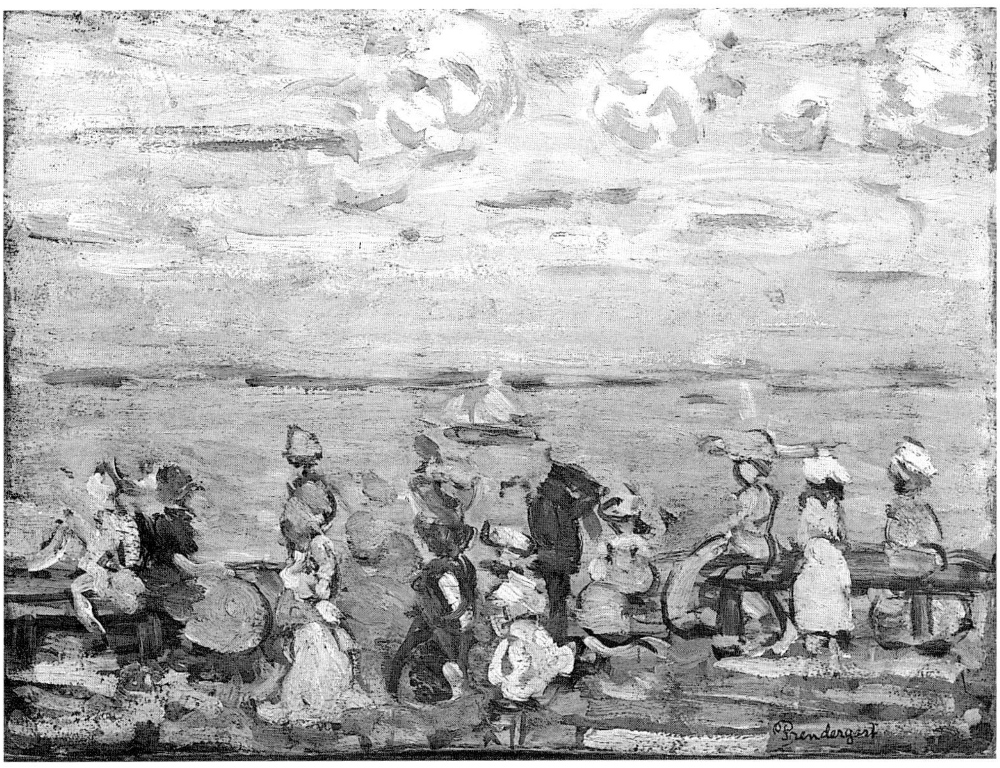

CR 59 *Beach Scene #4,* ca. 1903–06

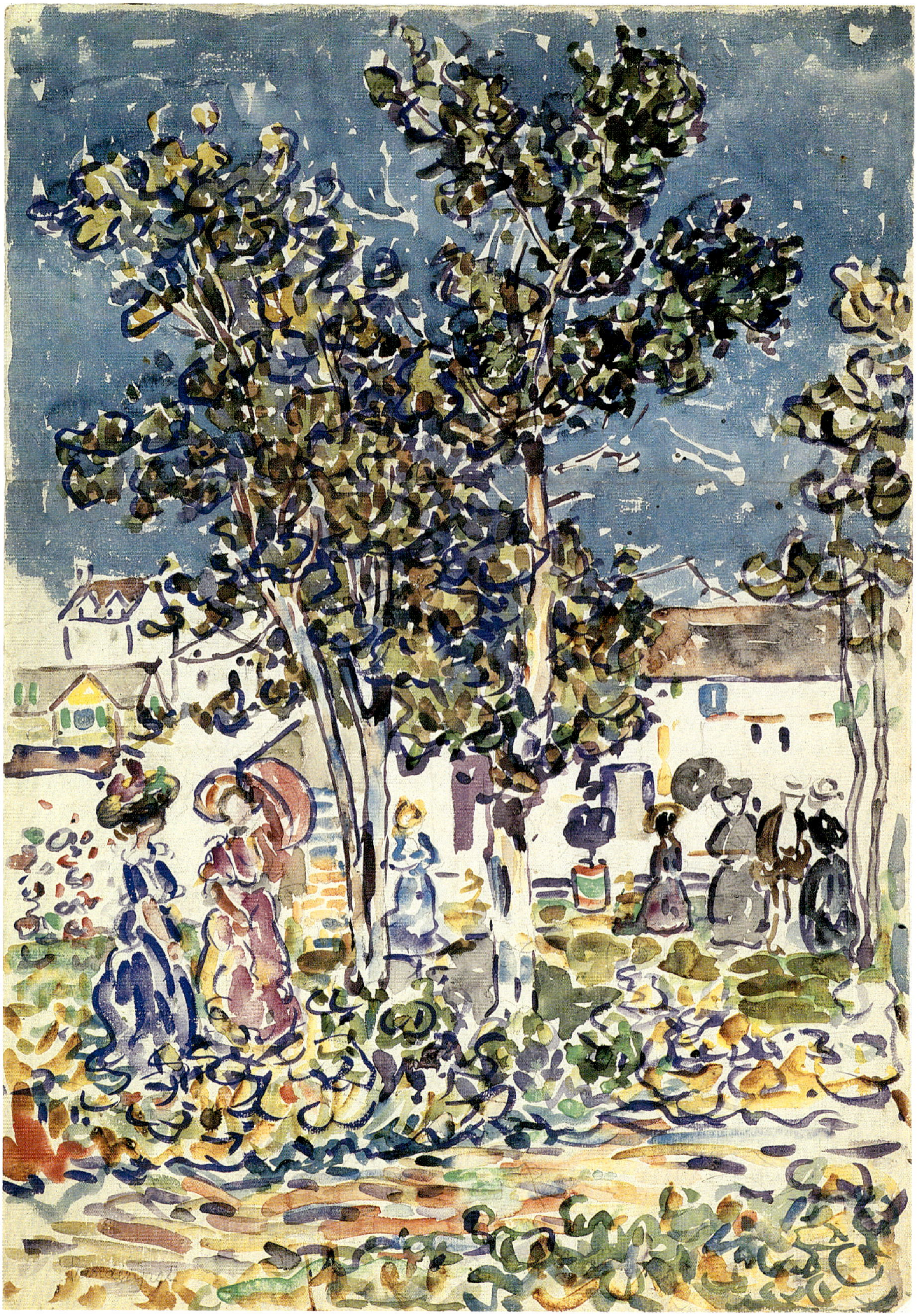

CR 976 *Spring Promenade,* ca. 1910–11

Fantasy

Once Prendergast was convinced that art could be independent of visual reality, he took another look at leisure in "modern" New England. After 1907, many of Prendergast's paintings, such as *Spring Promenade* (CR 976) and *Bathers by the Sea* (CR 281), show actual locations in Massachusetts, Maine, and New Hampshire, but they are now unexpectedly populated by fanciful inhabitants. The humble regional landmarks—houses, birch trees—are so accurately depicted that they seem locatable. But the people are not. They are either nude wood nymphs or so lavishly costumed that they suggest the New England of another, more interesting age.

Such a playfully inconsistent approach to reality is made possible by Prendergast's new style. He unifies the imaginative figures and the accurately observed setting by using loose brushstrokes and freer colors throughout the composition. And he overcomes the potential sentimentality of the historical references with the overt modernity of his technique. His earlier celebration of a specific place and time (modern Boston, New York, Venice) has given way to a "modern" celebration of a timeless and generalized region.

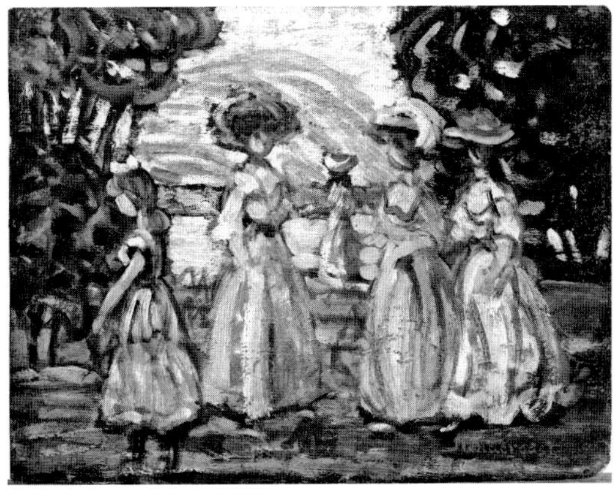

CR 222 *Five Figures in a Park,* ca. 1907–10

The fantasy world of the past had special currency in the most up-to-date art forms around 1910. Modernist groups in Paris led by Matisse and Picasso had revived the traditional female nude in her guise as mythological or primitive creature. Because of the artists' experimental approach to form and color, this exotic woman was ancient and modern at the same time. Prendergast's version of the modern goddess, as in *Bathers by the Sea,* was his first attempt to use the female nude in his paintings and ushered in several other new subjects—still life, dance, the "horse and rider"—that he had picked up from avant-garde European painting.

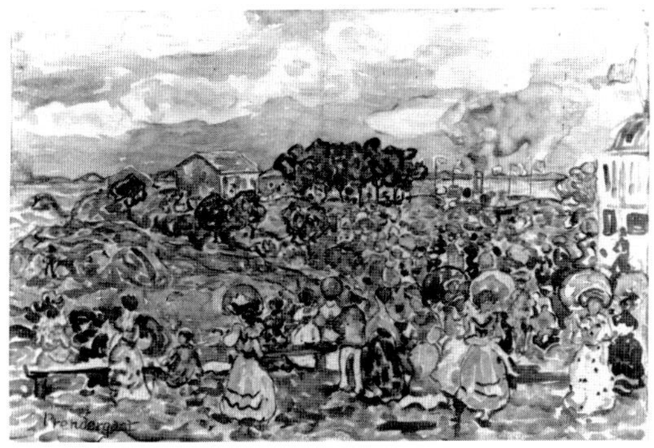

CR 971 *New England Holiday,* ca. 1910–11

The fact that he placed his modern goddess in a New England setting has interesting parallels in two unlikely cultural trends of the early twentieth century: the marketing of New England's history to lure tourists and the shift toward fantasy in the nascent film industry. In both cases, history is reenacted in real settings to spark the imagination of the audience and transport them into the past for the sake of entertainment.

As usual, Prendergast was his own best barometer of current ideas. He traveled frequently during the summers, retracing the familiar paths of eastern Massachusetts, coastal Maine, and the picturesque mountains of New Hampshire. Although he was not an avid visitor of battle sites and historical monuments, he developed a new appreciation of the small New England town and its local forests, lakes, and coastlines. This was a change from his earlier preoccupation with the latest resorts and public parks that sprang up around Boston at the turn of the century. It was a deliberate celebration of the quaint and timeless character of a region that was fast losing its progressive edge.

In 1905, a local historian of Maine's Mount Desert Island wrote that the region welcomed tourists enamored of the past. It had suffered great eco-

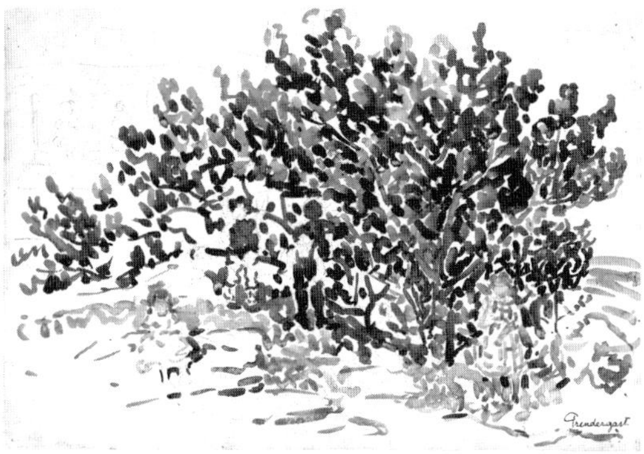

CR 1000 *Children in the Tree*, ca. 1910–11

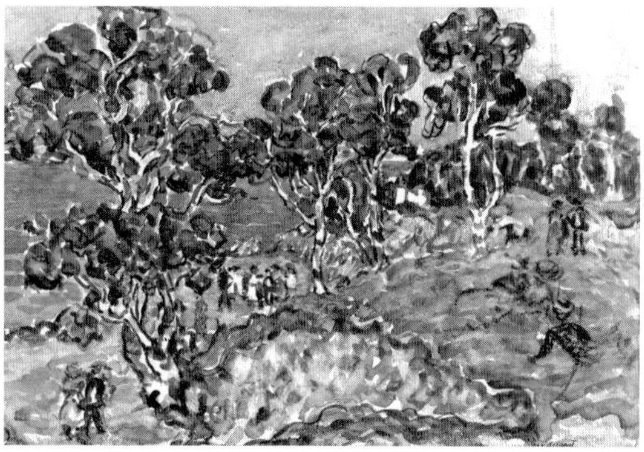

CR 1100 *Birches*, ca. 1910–13

nomic reverses by 1900: "The herring fisheries were becoming less and less profitable, the coasting trade was slack, the hills had been stripped of the last trees suitable for sawing, the thin soil of the farms was practically exhausted."[24] Tourists brought a much needed infusion of cash to local bank accounts.

Furthermore, since the region represented early American life to outsiders, the small town could forgo expensive modernization projects. New England towns abandoned their previous technological competitiveness, so characteristic during the earlier industrialization of the nineteenth century, and began to preserve old buildings, picturesque local shops, and outmoded social and business practices. The untidy, diverse population that had been drawn to New England from all over the world to work in the factories was forgotten in the rush to create a "mythic region called Old New England—rural, preindustrial, and ethnically 'pure'—a reverse image of all that was most unsettling in late nineteenth-century urban life."[25]

Prendergast's paintings after 1907 fit this desire to "invent" a New England impervious to the vagaries of modern industry and fashion. In addition to the unexpected placement of nymphs on the New England coastline, his depictions of colorful small towns (as in *Spring Promenade*) and women in quasi-rococo costume entice the viewer to visit a region where the past lives on.

The unsettling combination of reality and fantasy in Prendergast's work around 1910 parallels another change in American leisure habits—the growing popularity of the motion picture among all classes. Since 1895, when the first successful film projectors were put in use, the movies had provided Americans with a new form of group entertainment. The earliest films capitalized on the ability of the camera to record "real life" with the almost miraculous addition of movement—and were advertised "to those who know something of the artistic side of photography."[26] The very short (less than five minutes) footage of waves rolling in to the beach and of Maypole dances in Central Park were standard offerings on motion picture programs at the turn of the century. Travelogues (Venice, New York, Egypt, and so on) and current events (such as coronations, battle scenes, and disastrous fires) were a logical development and gave films an educational appeal.

Maurice Prendergast, an enthusiastic consumer of spectacles of all kinds, not only was reported to love the movies, but even owned stock in a film company.[27] His paintings of foreign travel, city life, and park and beach scenes clearly owe much to still photography in that period, but they also show an interest in capturing movement that parallels the motion picture phenomenon.

24. George E. Street, *Mount Desert: A History* (Boston: Houghton, Mifflin & Co., 1905), p. 326, as cited in Brown, p. 8.

25. Brown, p. 9.

26. Charles Musser, *The Emergence of Cinema: The American Screen to 1907* (New York: Charles Scribner's Sons, 1990), p. 139.

27. Reminiscences of Daphne Dunbar, who knew the Prendergasts in Boston before 1912, as told to Fred Brady in "Anonymous Friend Reveals Prendergast's Love of Life," *Boston Herald*, Nov. 27, 1960, n.p.

After 1905, however, the audience's demand for narrative spurred the growth of the feature film and linked the motion picture more closely to theater. Films based on modern life and manners were soon joined by historical dramas, biblical epics, and other forms of costume fantasies. Boston's Beacon Theater, built in 1910 strictly for movies, "opened its brass doors with *The Fall of Troy* to a full house of eight hundred persons."[28] The use of actors and real-world sets, such as Vitagraph's *Romeo and Juliet* (1908), which was filmed in Central Park, to portray the world of the imagination produced the same kind of disjunction found in Prendergast's paintings from this period. The "modern" medium of the film, just like Prendergast's "modern" style, helped to reconcile the disparate elements of past and present.

28. Tino Balio, *The American Film Industry* (Madison: The University of Wisconsin Press, 1985), p. 99.

CR 281 *Bathers by the Sea,* ca. 1910–13

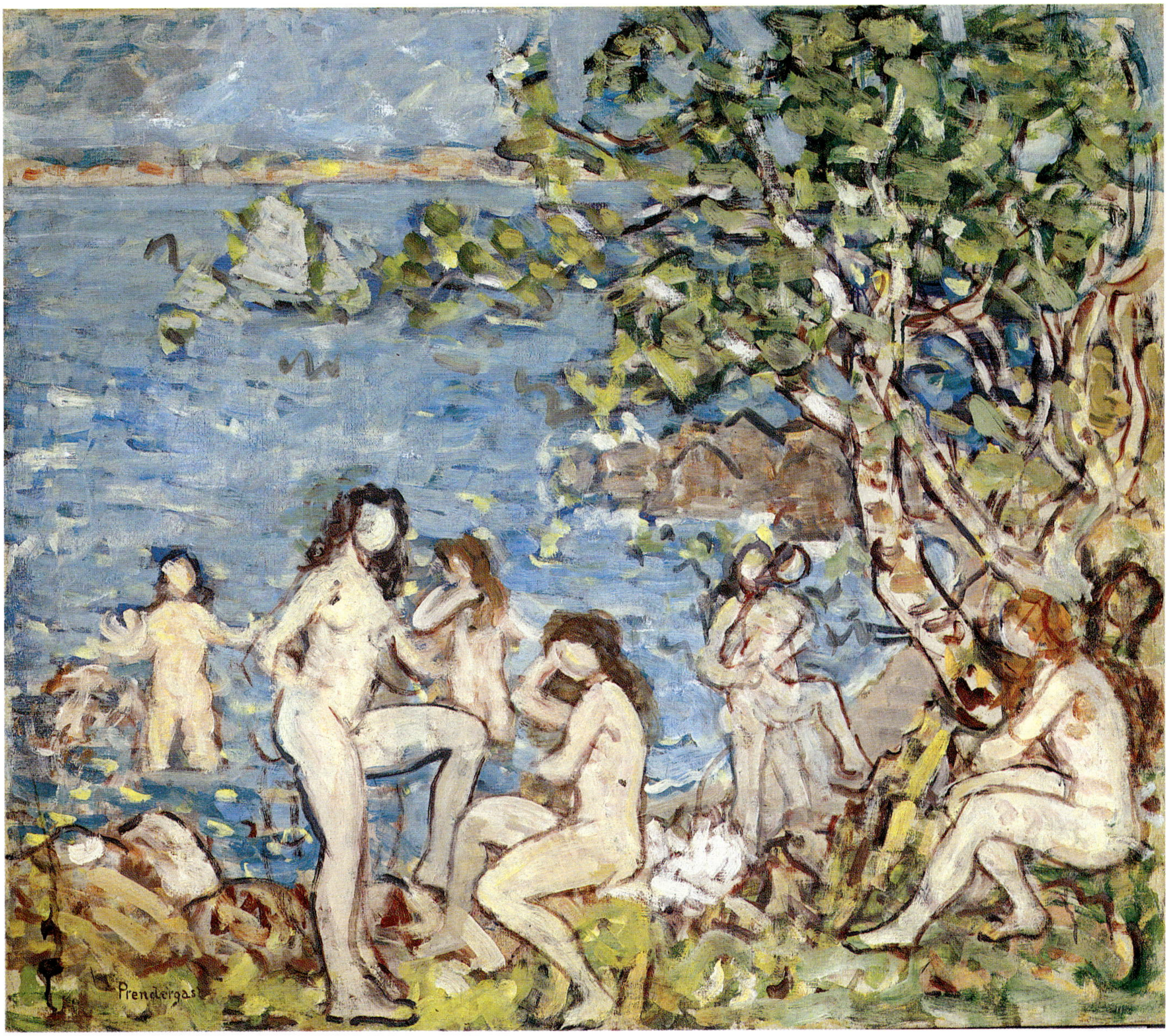

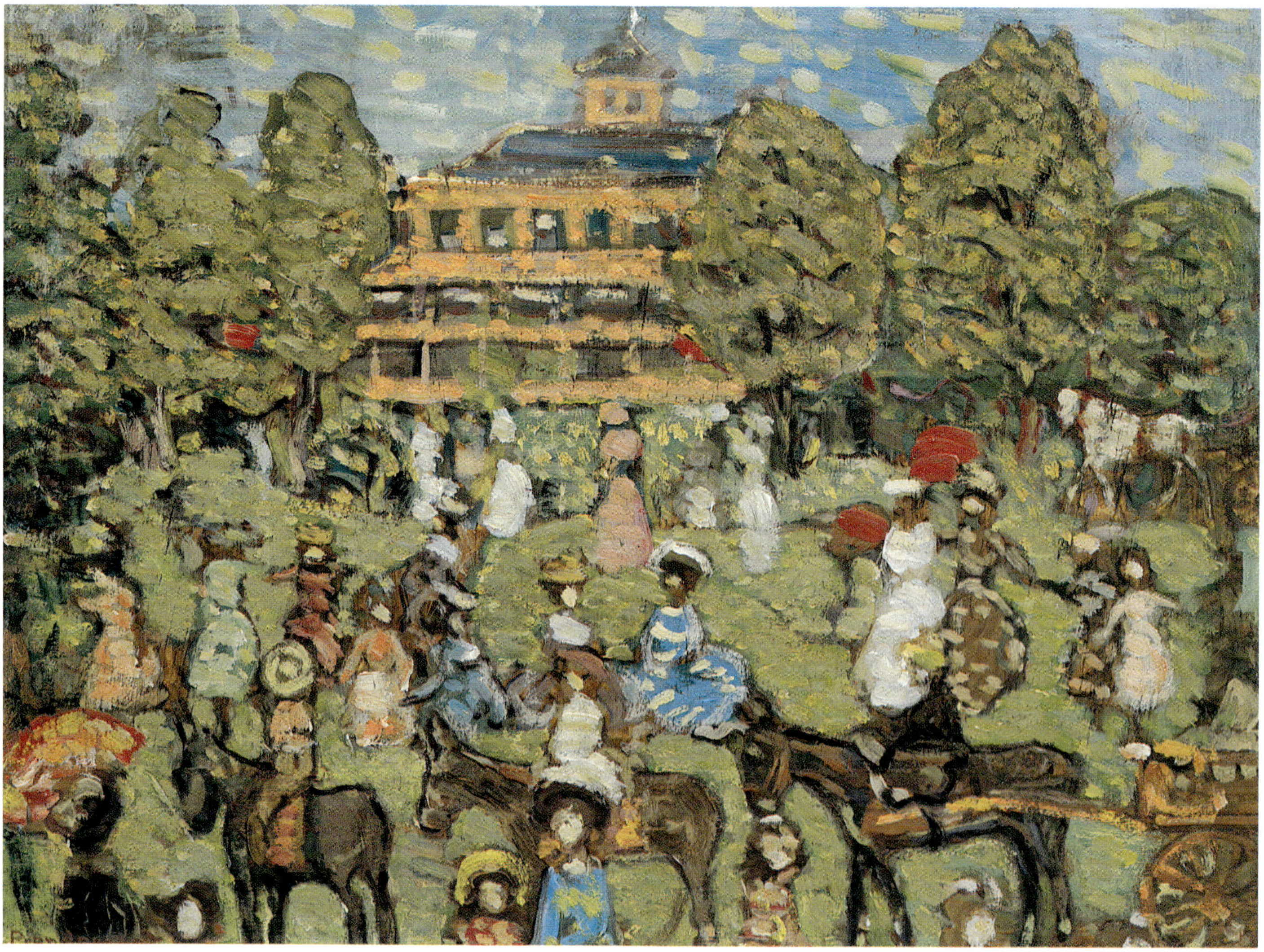

CR 395 *Summer Hotel, Maine*, ca. 1914–15

"O my God!" Art: The American Avant-Garde

Prendergast's interest in what Americans do in their leisure time evolved in the early 1900s to include another new activity: the "blockbuster" art exhibition. Specifically, Prendergast witnessed and responded to the growth of popular involvement in avant-garde art. The infamous Armory Show of 1913, which drew a huge American audience in its three venues (New York, Chicago, and Boston) and evoked reactions from such surprising non-art figures as Theodore Roosevelt, marks the beginning of the large, avant-garde art exhibition as mass entertainment in the United States.

The phenomenon of the exhibition as entertainment has its roots in nineteenth-century Paris, where government support of the arts led to the annual large-scale exhibition known as the Salon and periodic special art exhibitions incorporated into the Paris world's fairs of 1855, 1867, 1878, 1889, and 1900. These huge displays of recent painting and sculpture were geared not only to the French public but also to tourists drawn to Paris from all over the world. As experimental modern artists such as the Impressionists split off to start their own small, group exhibitions, they capitalized on the well-developed art press (both serious and satirical) to publicize their new ideas and relied on an art-hungry audience already in Paris for the Salons.

As Jeffrey Weiss points out in *The Popular Culture of Modern Art,* the most daring avant-garde circles encouraged an atmosphere of mystification and spectacle at their exhibitions that was akin to the popular "revues" or satirical vaudeville shows that proliferated at the turn of the century.[29] The emphasis was on novelty and rejection of past standards. A 1909 article summed up the art climate of prewar Paris: "One hears talk only of 'making a tabula rasa' and of 'starting over.' The work of one's predecessors is now perceived as an intolerable weight. . . . Each counts on being 'original' . . . *Faire nouveau* is the entire program."[30] This modernist mandate fostered a discourse of "excess, impatience and self-promotionalism."[31]

The attention paid to modern art exhibitions in Paris inspired foreign artists and promoters to duplicate the phenomenon in other countries. Huge displays of contemporary painting and sculpture, imported largely from Paris, were consequently staged in London (1910 and 1912), Cologne (1912), and, finally, New York (1913). In addition to promoting the events as transforming cultural experiences, organizers of modern art exhibitions also played to the curiosity of local audiences about exotic cultures.[32] The art on display transported the viewer to a foreign "place" just as actual travel to an unfamiliar land might have.

Although he was ambivalent about the restless search for novelty in the modern art world of the teens, Prendergast's art was strongly affected by his own increased participation in avant-garde exhibitions. His arch comment on the Armory Show, which he had helped organize, was "Too much—O my

29. Jeffrey Weiss, *The Popular Culture of Modern Art: Picasso, Duchamp, and Avant-Gardism* (New Haven: Yale University Press, 1994), see Chapter 1, "Le Journal Joué: Picasso, Collage, and Music-Hall Modernism," pp. 1–49.

30. Camille Mauclair, "The Prejudice of Novelty in Modern Art" (April 1909), in Weiss, p. 53.

31. Weiss, p. 54.

32. Martha Ward, "What's Important about the History of Modern Art Exhibitions?" *Thinking about Exhibitions*, eds. Reesa Greenberg, Bruce W. Ferguson, and Sandy Nairne (London: Routledge, 1996), p. 458.

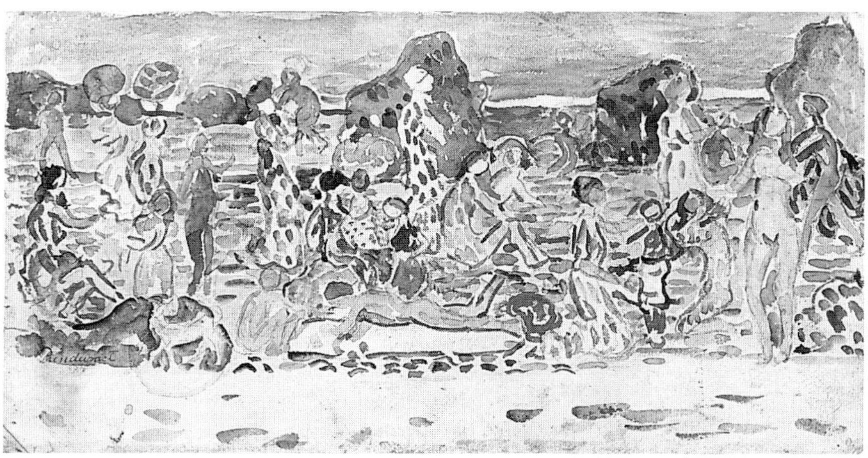

CR 1211 *Summer Day,* ca. 1913–15

God!–art here."[33] But in spite of this naysaying, Prendergast eagerly participated in the bohemian culture of the New York art world that followed in the wake of the Armory Show. In the fall of 1914, he and his brother Charles carried out the move they had long discussed—from Boston to New York. Properly ensconced in an apartment and studio on Washington Square South, they became members of the progressive art scene. It was natural that their closest friends were their age, in their fifties, like Edith and William Glackens and Arthur B. Davies, but the Prendergasts also found themselves exhibiting alongside such young artists associated with the irreverent Dada movement as Marcel Duchamp and Man Ray (fig. 4).

The lifestyle of New York avant-garde artists in the teens was a mixture of street-smart bohemianism and hobnobbing with the wealthy. Collectors like Lizzie Bliss and Gertrude Whitney were famous for their friendship and support of modern artists, including the Prendergast brothers. While the Prendergasts did not have a documented presence in the most outrageous salons in New York, such as those established by the Arensbergs or the Stettheimer sisters, they nevertheless could be found at most dinners and parties—at times even in costume (see fig. 4)—that marked the social side of modern art in the teens.

33. Ira Glackens, *William Glackens and the Eight* (New York: Horizon Press, 1957), p. 183.

CR 1218 *Boat Landing, Dinard,* ca. 1914

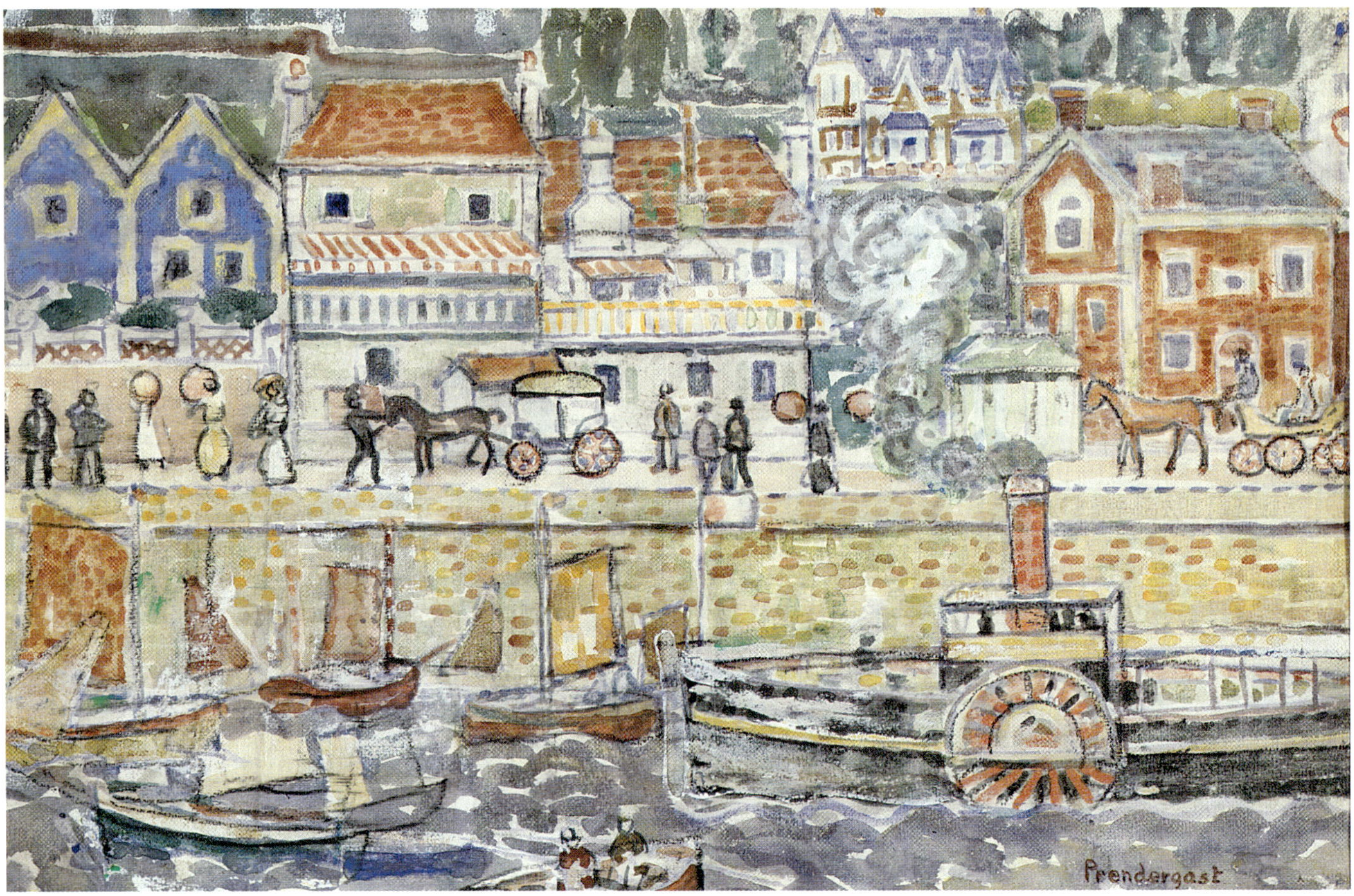

Prendergast's social acceptance into the New York art scene when he was well into middle age was largely due to the respect that the younger artists accorded him for his role in promoting modern art in the United States. By 1915, he had spent twenty years experimenting with the representation of modern life and leisure; and his enthusiasm for spectacle, no matter how novel or commercial, made him acceptable in the like-minded circles of young artists, writers, and collectors. In 1914 he was elected president of the Association of American Painters and Sculptors, the organization that had sponsored the Armory Show. In 1917 both he and Charles were represented in the famous exhibition of The Society of Independent Artists, where Marcel Duchamp showed a urinal as his ready-made "sculpture" *Fountain.*

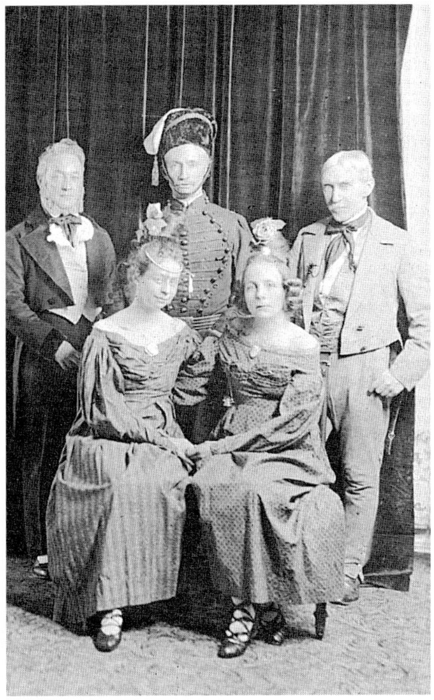

FIG. 4. Maurice B. Prendergast, Charles Prendergast, William J. Glackens, Mrs. L. E. Travis, Edith Dimock (Glackens)—in 1917, at the Illustrators' Ball, Hotel Brevoort, New York

Prendergast's art also played on the restless search for novelty in this period. Although he was unwilling to follow the path set by Duchamp and others, he established his own set of daring characteristics that provoked viewers and critics. A second trip to the Normandy coast of France in the spring of 1914 allowed him to reprise the 1907 beach scenes that had started him on the path to experimental color and form. This time he was more conscious of abstract geometric shapes (as in *Boat Landing, Dinard,* CR 1218) undoubtedly thanks to the ascendance of cubism on the modernist horizon. In addition, he lined up his old dots of color into a regularized pattern that enforced the strong horizontal and vertical lines of the architecture. The resulting blocky, mosaic effects recalled the latest styles from Paris but were obstinately personal. When Prendergast applied this style to New England scenes, as in *Marblehead* (CR 1201) or *Summer Hotel, Maine* (CR 395), the quaintness of the local architecture and the picturesqueness of the hilly coastline were cast into relief by the decorative patterning.

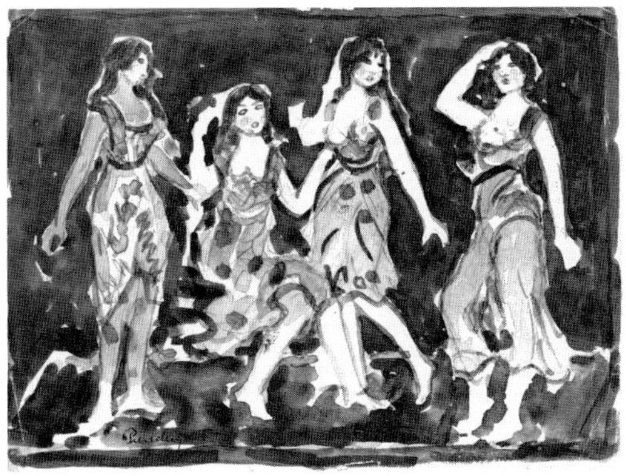

CR 1155 *Four Dancers,* ca. 1912–15

Sympathetic American critics often praised Prendergast's ability to be "modern" without being derivative of French styles, and progressive American amateurs and collectors appreciated his use of identifiable regional subject matter within an avant-garde context. But the general public went to his exhibitions expecting to be amazed and outraged by the much discussed excesses of modern art—and were not disappointed. A critic who spoke for these audiences articulated the typical response: "Mr. Prendergast's . . . compositions are executed in his most incoherent style. Some of the figures are nude and some are draped but all are equally ill drawn."[34] Perhaps Prendergast received his most dramatic compliment of notoriety when the phrase used in 1908 to ridicule his St.-Malo beach scenes, "An explosion in a color factory,"[35] was recalled in 1913 when another critic called Duchamp's *Nude Descending a Staircase* "an explosion in a shingle factory"[36]—one of the most frequently quoted phrases from the early days of the American avant-garde.

34. "Four Boston Painters," *Boston Evening Transcript,* Jan. 8, 1913, p. 25.

35. See "Modern Art," footnote 23.

36. This phrase is usually given to Julian Street in the tongue-in-cheek "Why I Became a Cubist," (*Everybody's Magazine,* June 1913), p. 316.

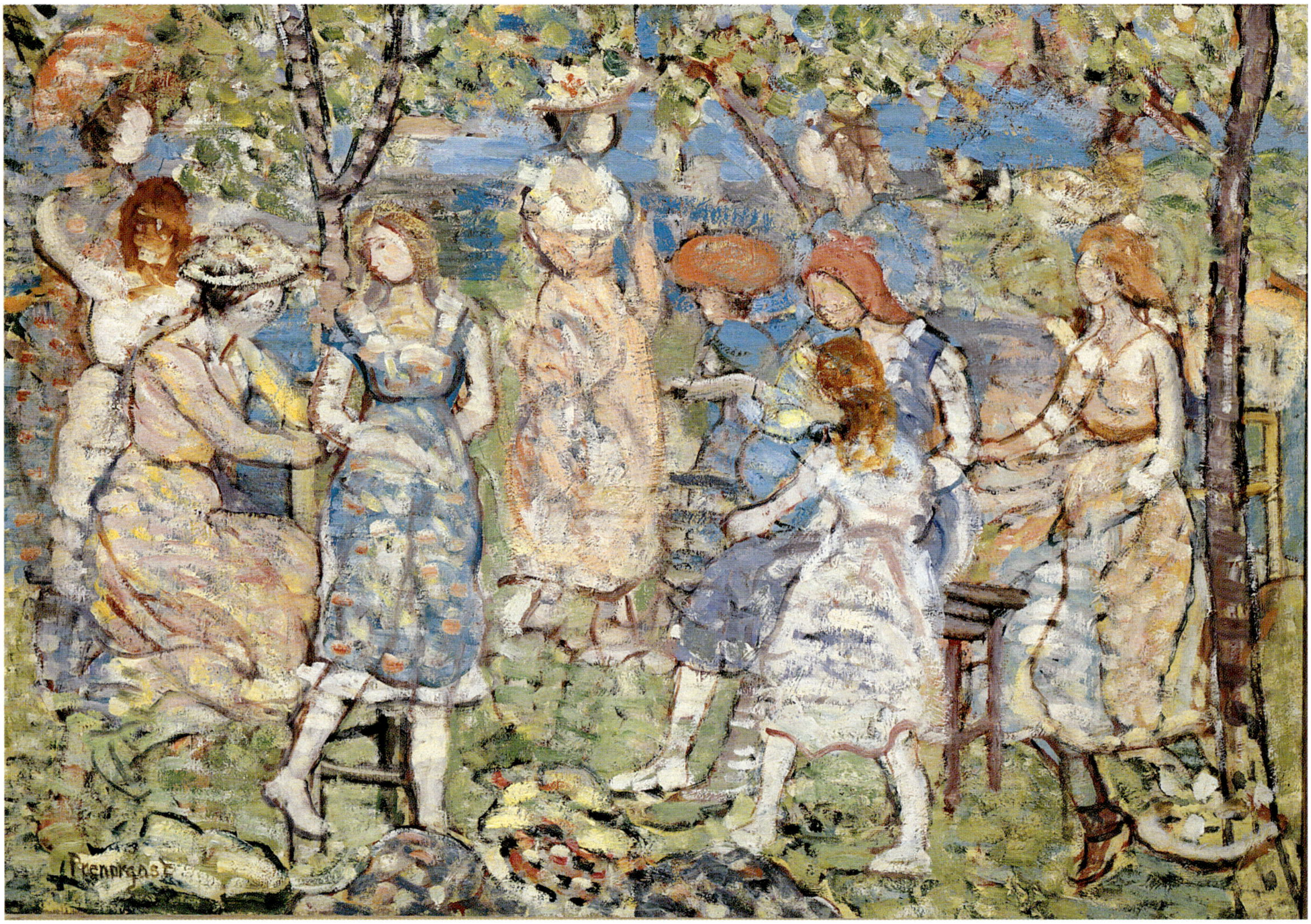

CR 398 *Girls in the Park*, ca. 1914–15

Elegy to Leisure

The large oils of Prendergast's late career almost exclusively depict idyllic park and beach scenes. They are muted, abstracted compositions made up of large female figures turning and gesturing to each other in slow, indecipherable poses. One can see echoes of late Renoir bathers, Puvis de Chavannes's atmospheric historicism, and ancient (Egyptian, Assyrian, and classical) friezes. They were the most critically acclaimed of Prendergast's works and entered major collections, both private and public, during his lifetime.

The idylls coincide with the start of the First World War in 1914 and, in their absolute rejection of such devastating events in the modern world, they are perhaps the most touching of Prendergast's responses to American leisure. As the artist approached sixty, he witnessed the sudden end to the optimism and prosperity that had colored his youthful depiction of the themes of modern life. Many of the grand resort hotels and amusement parks he recorded at the turn of the century had already been abandoned to fire and vandals. Furthermore, the vicious destruction caused by modern warfare abroad had put a temporary stop to American travel to Europe and even affected the economically necessary tourism in New England. Prendergast's instinct was to retreat into a world of his own and eulogize the innocent pleasures that now seemed as distant as the ancient processions in the friezes he emulated.

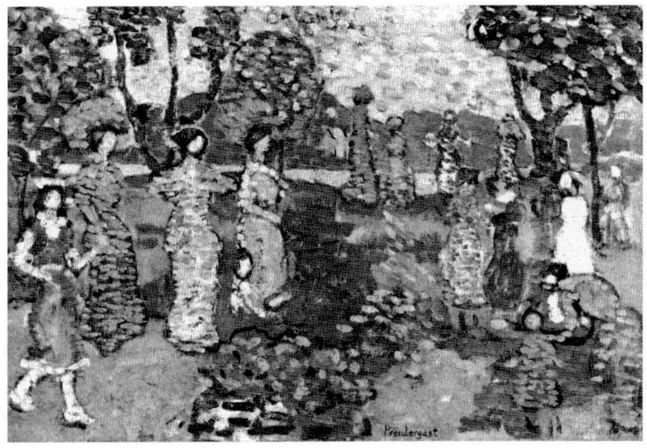

CR 419 *A Day in the Country*, ca. 1914–15

The war also brought many refugee European intellectuals to New York, including the notorious pair Duchamp and Francis Picabia. The competition for leadership of the new art was intense, and Prendergast no longer was interested in confronting the popular styles, such as Dada, head-on. His best patrons like Lizzie Bliss and Albert Barnes encouraged the more lyrical direction of his art, as did many critics who noted his withdrawal from modern strife: "The joy of the sun is within him, and nature serves merely as a dictionary from which to borrow the occasional necessary word. Of all our optimists, Mr. Prendergast is perhaps the blithest."[37]

The optimism in such compositions as *Summer Day, Salem* (CR 436) and *Girls in the Park* (CR 398) may have been palpable to those who were living through the war, but in fact, as history has shown, it was less a belief in the future than it was nostalgia for the past. The values it represented were no longer dominant in American life and never would be again. The two factors with more lasting impact than the war were the rise of the automobile in modern life and the changes in American social structure created by the wave of immigration in the early twentieth century. The quest for pleasures that allowed social groups to bond was giving way to the individualism symbolized by automobile travel and the immigrant work ethic that sacrificed leisure to attainment of the American Dream.

Ironically, the labor policies that had been fought for during Prendergast's youth—the eight-hour day and paid holidays—were instituted almost effortlessly before the end of the war. But in the United States, the concept of the

37. "Art," *New York Tribune*, April 24, 1917, p. 7.

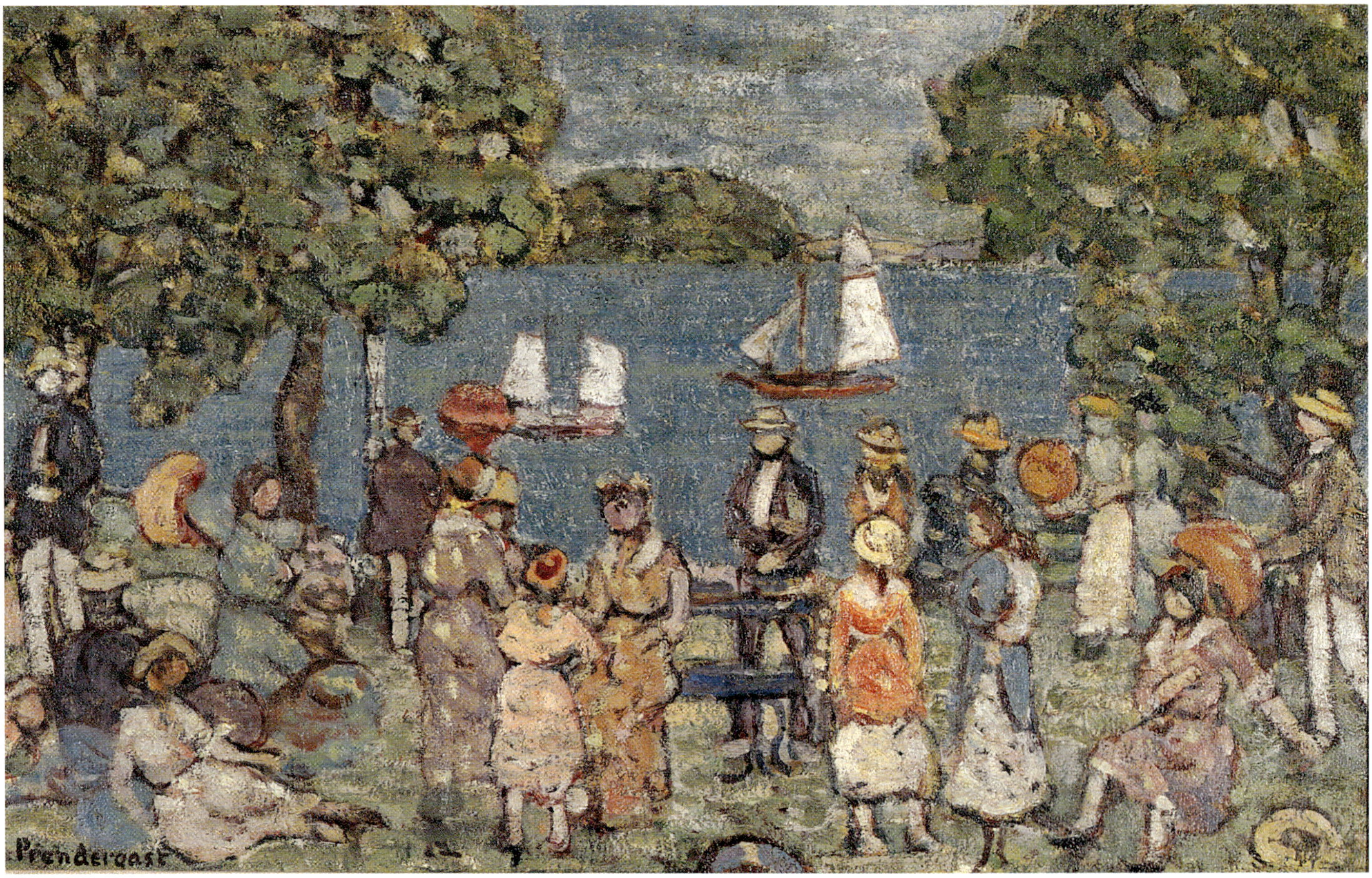

CR 436 *Summer Day, Salem,* ca. 1915–18

monthlong holiday, so dear to Europeans and to the resort structure of the turn of the century, was never guaranteed to the workforce. The length of vacation time remains in this country the shortest of all the developed nations. This restriction shows the power of American business over its workers, but it also reflects a moral code typical of a newcomer society of immigrants who feared the loss of wages and the lethargy produced by prolonged relaxation.[38] The upper classes, whose habit had been to retreat to a mountain or seaside resort for an extended period of time, were gradually forced to curtail their own practices because of the ceaseless pressure of American business.

The automobile, which became a mass form of transportation by 1920, also eroded the leisurely pace and group pleasures that had once been the ideal. As Dona Brown points out, a sense of adventure replaced the once predictable travel by train or streetcar. Tourists in automobiles "liked to 'explore' back roads and towns off the beaten track, staying for only a night or two at each stopping-place."[39] The partnership of hotels and railroads, which had promoted socializing over individual whims, could not compete with the new vision of leisure as "freedom" that the automobile brought with it.

Prendergast's idyllic scenes of a timeless female society—half modern, half classical in dress—monumentalizes a leisurely group experience that he no longer observed around him. The crowds in Salem Willows or Central

38. See Gary Cross, *A Social History of Leisure since 1600,* Chapter 11, "Dilemmas of Leisure and Public Policy: 1900–1920," especially pp. 167–71.

39. Brown, p. 206.

Park on a Sunday afternoon occupied the beaches and lawns for a short, frenetic time. Prendergast's sketchbooks show his attempts to capture the changing poses of swimmers and strollers, parents and children. But in his finished compositions, the sharpness of observation is muted by the tapestry-like paint surface and by the generalized faces and gestures of the women.

An unusual effect found in such works as *Girls in the Park* is the partial overpainting of certain areas, giving them the sense of works in progress. This effect was purposeful, since he exhibited and sold many large-scale canvases in this same state of metamorphosis. While we can only guess at his intention (no mention is made of this device in letters or reviews), it has a strange power to combine the past and the present in a way different from mere historicism. The most obvious symbol of this instability of time is the depiction of the women in modern fashions, painted over with partial outlines of classically nude bodies. In reading the painting as simultaneously ancient and modern—the "essence" of pleasure rather than a specific observation of it—we sense the yearning of a man for whom the passing of time has become a subject in and of itself.

Prendergast's repetition of these motifs in the last decade of his life indicates not only his own interests but also those of his audience. The men and women of his aging generation were now successful collectors, museum directors, and artists, and as a group they sought the optimism in timeless idylls that they had once derived from the spectacles of modern life. Walter Pach, a friend of Prendergast's and a chronicler of modernism in France and America, published a tribute to the artist in 1922, when Prendergast's health was failing and he was given numerous awards and retrospective exhibitions:

> *When he comes nearest to creating a new world is in his joyous fancy of a summer all of light—clear and radiant. His picture is real for us and consonant with our experience: a thing in harmony with the law and adding to the law that we are conscious of in all art, even though we are never able to formulate it.*[40]

For Pach, and for others who participated in the momentous events of the early twentieth century, modern leisure increasingly meant attaining a world beyond the cruelties of change.

Prendergast continued to paint until his death in early 1924. Parks and beach scenes sprang from his brush with their usual regularity—watercolors and sketches in summer, large oils in winter. But as his suffering from prostate cancer increased, his command of the vocabulary of art lessened, until the "unfinished" quality of the work became necessary rather than planned. Prendergast did not live to see an American society in which leisure became the hallmark of modern life as he had once imagined it would; instead he lived as the more typical American of the twentieth century—working until ill health or death brought a much needed respite.

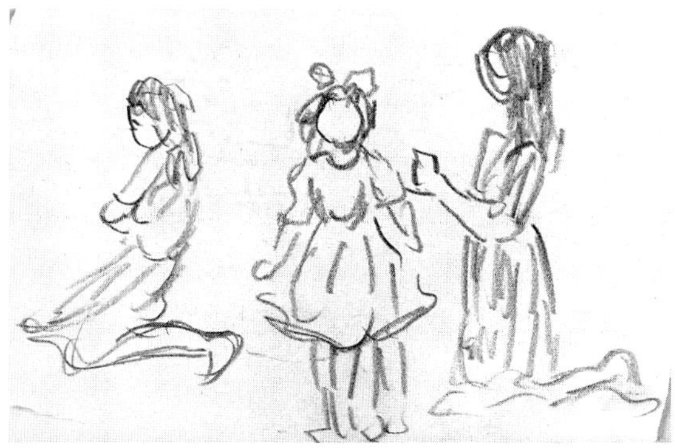

CR 1444 *Sketch of Figures on Beach*, ca. 1912–15

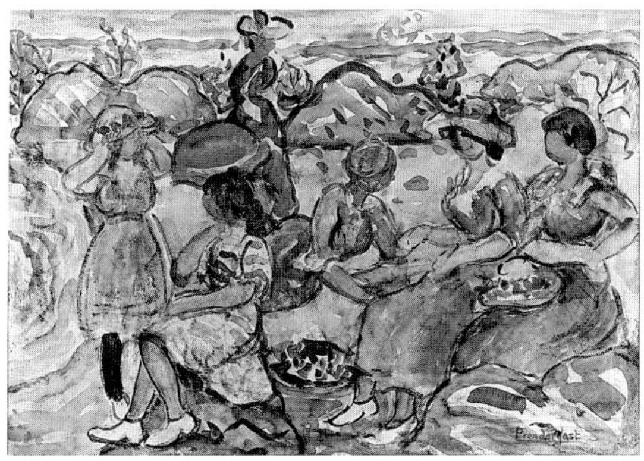

CR 1290 *Six Girls*, ca. 1916–19

40. Walter Pach, "Maurice Prendergast," *Shadowland* (April 1922), p. 75.

Sketchbooks and Other Tools of the Traveling Artist

Alexis Goodin
Williams College Graduate Program in the History of Art, M.A. '98

Maurice Prendergast, an artist who chose the spectacle of modern life for his subject, usually carried with him a small sketchbook. He took to heart the advice given in the art journals he read avidly: "Of all the most fruitful places for study to an artist with any eye for character or natural grace in men and women," queried the author of "The Sketchbook in the Street," "what can surpass the freest of all resorts, the public thoroughfare?"[1]

Of the eighty-eight Prendergast sketchbooks that exist today, five are in the collection of the Williams College Museum of Art. An intermediary between observation and the finished product, sketchbooks were used as a storehouse of new ideas and also as a forum for working the composition and color schemes of these subjects. Three sketchbooks (CRs 1559, 1561, and 1562), which date from the very end of Prendergast's career, ca. 1920–23, demonstrate the artist's preference for immediate, almost stumbled-upon subjects. In these small notebooks (each measures 7¾" x 5¼"), Prendergast produced serene landscapes such as the cluster of houses near the ocean in Rockport (CR 1559), as well as kaleidoscopic beach scenes (CR 1561).[2]

Two earlier sketchbooks in this collection reveal other uses for this medium. In a book dating from 1898 to 1903 (CR 1481), Prendergast sketched elaborate moldings for frame designs that he undoubtedly shared with his artist-brother Charles, a renowned frame maker. A last example, a notebook dated 1912–15, named "The Paris Sketchbook" (CR 1507) for its use during Prendergast's 1914 excursion to France's capital, discloses the artist's careful academic consideration of the human figure: here male and female models are drawn in various poses (pages 8–9). while he mostly used pencil to record scenes from life and in making formal studies, many of the images in the sketchbooks from about 1920 to 1923 are imbued with sumptuous watercolor.[3]

Although it is obvious that Prendergast sketched on-site in pencil, it is more difficult to determine the extent to which he actually painted outdoors. Watercolor is more difficult to manage than is oil in sunny or windy conditions, but many artists routinely painted that way. A close look at the sketchbooks sheds some light on Prendergast's working methods.

1. "The Sketchbook in the Street," *The Studio 1* (1893), p. 187.

2. These sketches were worked into finished watercolors. Pp. 102–03, for example, were used for *Rockport* (ca. 1920–23), Coe Kerr Gallery.

3. According to Charles Parkhurst's calculations, sixteen of the eighty-eight sketchbooks contain watercolors; two hundred watercolor sketches are found within those books. "Color and Coloring in Maurice Prendergast's Sketchbooks," in *Catalogue Raisonné,* p. 71. While watercolor was his primary colorant, on rare occasions the artist introduced colored crayon (CR 1561) and, more frequently, ink washes (CR 1507) into his preliminary work.

While notebooks and graphite pencils had always been portable, advancements in artist materials during the last quarter of the nineteenth century simplified the process of plein-air watercolor sketching. The London-based company Winsor & Newton manufactured several implements, such as the sketchbox and japanned tin boxes for moist watercolors, which increased the mobility of the painter. The japanned tin box, advertised as early as 1875 in the company's *Priced and Illustrated Catalogue of Artists' Materials,* held between six and twenty-four cakes of watercolor paint. The "dead white" colored flaps of the box, which secured the paint tray when the box was closed, doubled as a palette. Winslow Homer (1836–1910) used this kit on his sketching excursions; a fabric "folding Morocco pouch case" allowed him to easily transport the japanned tin box as well as brushes and additional tubes of paint.

It is unknown whether Maurice Prendergast owned travel-ready artist equipment of this type, which would facilitate plein-air watercolor sketching. No artist materials—paints, palettes, brushes—that can definitely be identified as Maurice's have survived since his death in 1924.[4] But in a sketchbook Prendergast used during his trip to Venice in 1912, he wrote "sketchbox" next to a checklist of pigments and brushes, suggesting that he was preparing to paint on location.[5]

His technique also suggests that he was painting quickly as if under difficult conditions. In the later sketchbooks, Prendergast freely applied pigment to selected images, disregarding the boundaries of his pencil underdrawings. Bold, distinct washes of color, like those found on pages 8 and 9 of CR 1561, seem to be haphazardly rendered, implying rapid execution. Whether Prendergast's technique in this case was due to the awkward conditions of plein-air sketching is uncertain. Prendergast's finished style at this time was similarly urgent and indifferent to detail and precision: *The Cove, Gloucester, Mass.* (ca. 1920–23; CR 1383) comprises uniformly thick bands of color and accidental blank or negative space; absent is the precision once used to capture the architectural views of Venice. Finding this spontaneous brushstroke in the later sketchbooks, then, may intimate a preference in style, not necessarily a condition of on-site execution.

Clues within the sketchbooks and an examination of Prendergast's usual working method imply, however, that the artist added watercolor to his sketchbooks only once he returned to the convenience of his studio. Most suggestive of this are the color notations written in the margins of many of his sketches. On the inside cover of sketchbook CR 1559, for example, Prendergast surrounded four small figures with verbal color clues: "Kid white dress/Hat with blue ribbon" is written along the left side

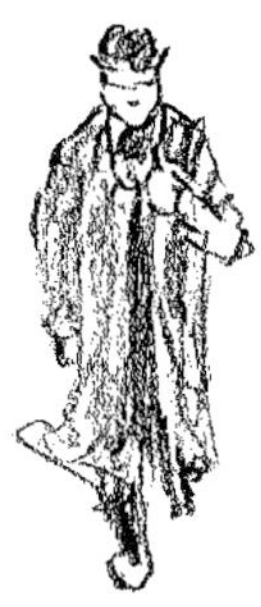

4. His brother Charles, also an artist, inherited the contents of his studio and undoubtedly used any remaining materials.

5. Parkhurst, p.72.

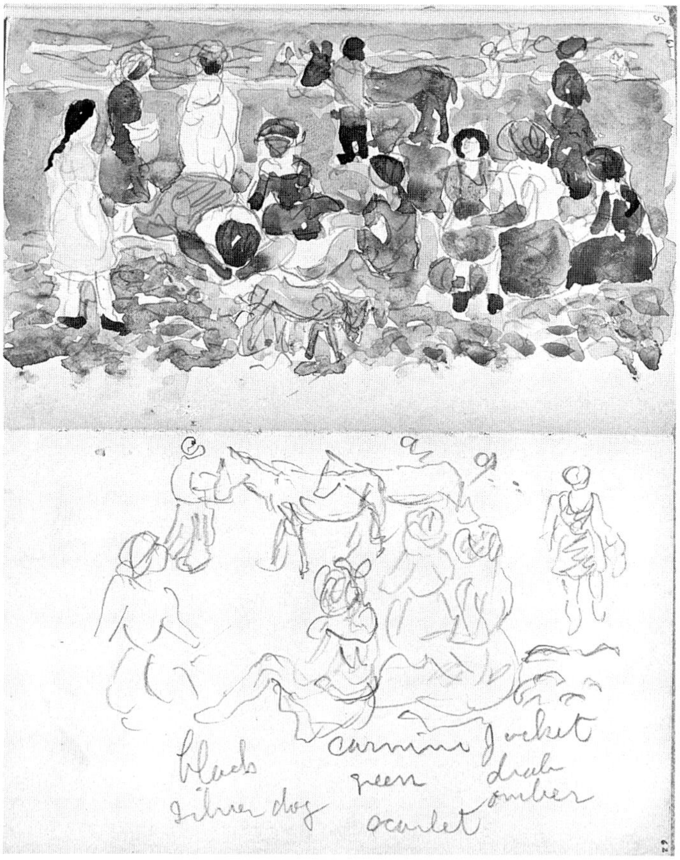

CR 1562 sketchbook, ca. 1920–23

of the page; the instructions "red/white/kid/ blue shirt/black bottom" are in the center.[6]

Although this example was left uncolored, other sketches were completed according to the directions, such as the houses of Rockport on pages 100–101 of sketchbook CR 1559: Here, "ocean blue" corresponds to the color applied to the body of water; "pinks/greens," a more general directive written at the top of the page, is evidenced in the mauve houses and the forest green bushes and trees. Unequipped to paint the colors he witnessed on-site, Prendergast jotted down his observations for future implementation. With the aid of notes, the artist could easily recall the hues that impressed him in nature and construct an image infused with vitality within the confines of his studio. Had Prendergast carried watercolors with him, he could have recorded his impressions of color immediately; in that case, these notes would have been redundant.

Prendergast's working method also suggests that he executed the watercolors indoors. Unlike John Singer Sargent, who hired a servant to carry easels and supplies to predetermined sketching locations so that he could record the details before him accurately, Prendergast, while inspired by firsthand observation, actually created images that were loose interpretations of what he saw. Unfinished works like *Central Park* (CR 774) detail Prendergast's systematic approach to painting. Here, color is plotted deliberately to create a balanced composition: An orangy red pigment, for example, has been evenly applied throughout the page in the form of four elegant parasols. In the studio, Prendergast could experiment with composition and color; he had no need of painting directly from nature, because nature could never offer Prendergast the balance he desired in his works.

An interesting pair of sketches (pages 61–62) in CR 1562 illustrate Prendergast's twofold process of first observing and sketching from nature and then fine-tuning the vision. In the graphite sketch on page 62, six figures—women and children, judging from the dress and size of the figures—and two dogs are situated in a loose circle in the center of the page. In the foreground, three figures recline on rocky ground; a child stands next to one of these figures. In the distance another person gently pets an animal, while one individual, clad in a bathing suit, stands alone to the right. In the margin

6. Like other annotated graphite drawings, this sketch was not washed in color. In this case, the small scale of the figures and the heavy use of graphite would have made it difficult to delineate the colors within their separate spheres. It is possible he had no intention of creating a finished work with such figures, so a preliminary color study would have been superfluous; the verbal instructions were perhaps enough.

below the scene of beachgoers, Prendergast recorded his observations of color. From left to right the following directions appear: “blacks,” “carmine jacket,” “silver dog,” “green,” “drab amber,” and “scarlet.” Although not implemented in this sketch, these colors make a bold appearance on the preceding page, where an almost identical scene of leisure has been reworked to include five additional figures.[7]

Again, Prendergast uses nature as a basis for his work but has enhanced his firsthand experience through manipulation of color, compositional organization, the addition (or subtraction) of figures. In a studio, rather than a plein-air setting, Prendergast would have had the opportunity to reorganize the scene to his taste and to infuse it with the desired color. As further evidence of studio execution, smudge marks and puddling colors are absent, suggesting that a clean, flat surface was at his disposal and the necessary time was taken to produce this image.

That Prendergast applied watercolor to his sketches from life in the studio in no way detracts from the spontaneous feel of these images. The free application of paint and the sensuous colors employed create visually arresting, vibrant pictures. A unique hybrid of observation and imagination, the sketchbooks provide insight into Prendergast's artistic process and are inspiring works of art in themselves.

Prendergast's Travel Books

Tiffany Reed
Williams College Graduate Program in the History of Art, M.A. '98

Pyramids rising out of the arid Egyptian desert, breathtaking peaks of the French Alps breaking through the clouds, gondolas gliding through the waterways of Venice. Vivid images of foreign lands have inspired people to go beyond their backyards for centuries—even if only in their imagination. The increased ease of steamship and railroad transportation in the post–Civil War era made foreign places more accessible to people from all walks of life, including artists such as Maurice Prendergast. Artists at the turn of the century were not so different from us today in our hunger for images of and information about the exotic and the unfamiliar. Literature and photographs allowed both armchair and actual travelers of the nineteenth century to peer over the distant horizon.

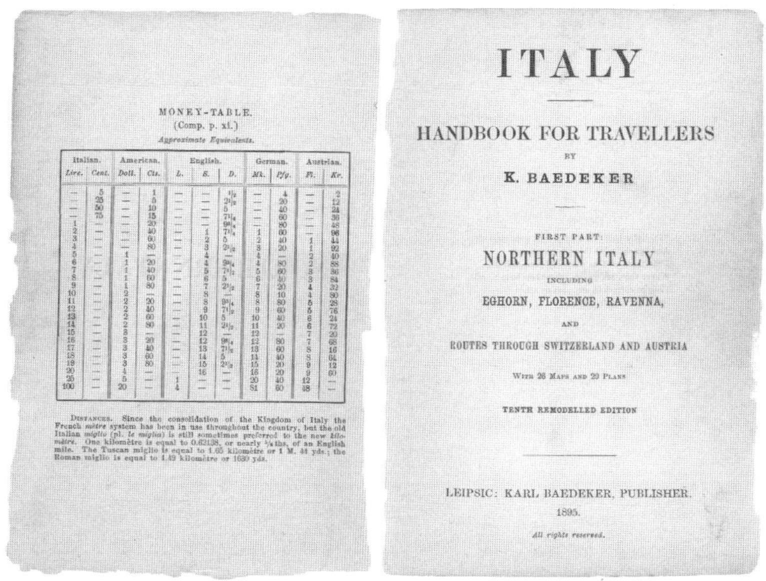

MONEY-TABLE.
(Comp. p. xi.)
Approximate Equivalents.

Italian.		American.		English.			German.		Austrian.	
Lire.	*Cent.*	*Doll.*	*Cts.*	*L.*	*S.*	*D.*	*Mk.*	*Pfg.*	*Fl.*	*Kr.*
—	5	—	1	—	—	1/2	—	4	—	2
—	25	—	5	—	—	2 1/2	—	20	—	12
—	50	—	10	—	—	5	—	40	—	24
—	75	—	15	—	—	7 1/4	—	60	—	36
1	—	—	20	—	—	9 3/4	—	80	—	48
2	—	—	40	—	1	7 1/4	1	60	—	96
3	—	—	60	—	2	5	2	40	1	44
4	—	—	80	—	3	2 1/2	3	20	1	92
5	—	1	—	—	4	—	4	—	2	40
6	—	1	20	—	4	9 3/4	4	80	2	88
7	—	1	40	—	5	7 1/2	5	60	3	36
8	—	1	60	—	6	5	6	40	3	84
9	—	1	80	—	7	2 1/2	7	20	4	32
10	—	2	—	—	8	—	8	10	4	80
11	—	2	20	—	8	9 3/4	8	80	5	28
12	—	2	40	—	9	7 1/2	9	60	5	76
13	—	2	60	—	10	5	10	40	6	24
14	—	2	80	—	11	2 1/2	11	20	6	72
15	—	3	—	—	12	—	12	—	7	20
16	—	3	20	—	12	9 3/4	12	80	7	68
17	—	3	40	—	13	7 1/2	13	60	8	16
18	—	3	60	—	14	5	14	40	8	64
19	—	3	80	—	15	2 1/2	15	20	9	12
20	—	4	—	—	16	—	16	20	9	60
25	—	5	—	1	—	—	20	40	12	—
100	—	20	—	4	—	—	81	60	48	—

DISTANCES. Since the consolidation of the Kingdom of Italy the French *mètre* system has been in use throughout the country, but the old Italian *miglio* (pl. *le miglia*) is still sometimes preferred to the new *kilomètre*. One kilomètre is equal to 0.62138, or nearly 5/8ths, of an English mile. The Tuscan miglio is equal to 1.65 kilomètre or 1 M. 44 yds.; the Roman miglio is equal to 1.49 kilomètre or 1630 yds.

ITALY

HANDBOOK FOR TRAVELLERS

BY

K. BAEDEKER

FIRST PART:

NORTHERN ITALY

INCLUDING

LEGHORN, FLORENCE, RAVENNA,

AND

ROUTES THROUGH SWITZERLAND AND AUSTRIA

With 26 Maps and 29 Plans

TENTH REMODELLED EDITION

LEIPSIC: KARL BAEDEKER, PUBLISHER.

1895.

All rights reserved.

FIG. 5

7. For the watercolor sketch on page 61, Prendergast transposed several figures from the graphite sketch, reduced the amount of pencil shading he employed to delineate garments, and subtly varied the clothing and position of the figures. For example, the child standing near the seated woman now wears an orange dress, and the artist has chosen to delineate her legs and shoes.

FIG. 6

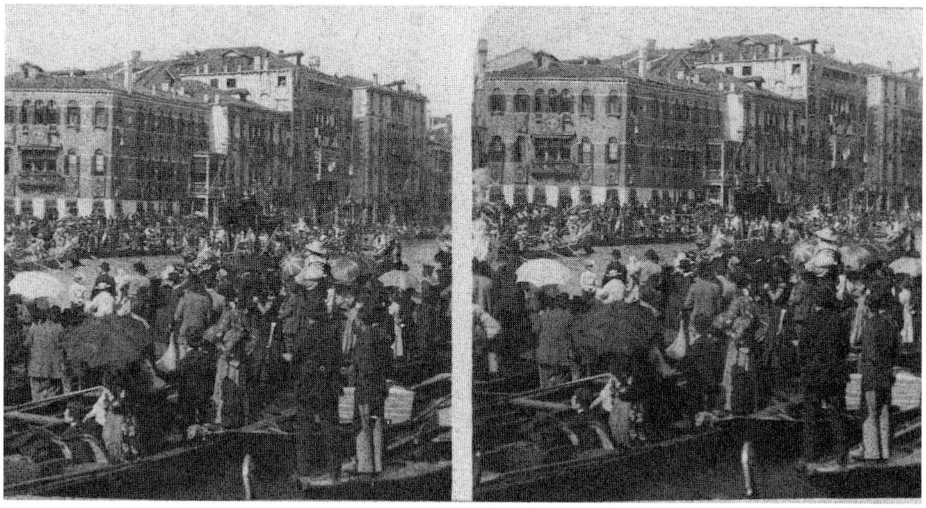

These words and images were used in preparation for a journey, as well as to relive their adventures after their return. Examining the library[8] of Prendergast gives us an idea of how he and other artists at the turn of the century relied upon visual information to bridge the distance between themselves and the great unknown.

There are several types of literature useful to the traveler preparing for a journey. Guidebooks list in detail not only how to get there and what to see, but also where to eat and where to stay. Prendergast surely would have relied upon this type of information, found in *The Maritime Traveller: A Handbook for Travellers* (1875)[9] for his trips throughout New England. A popular series with a rating system much like that used in modern examples, the Baedeker guidebooks included such information as where to buy photographs. For a trip to Italy in 1898–99 including Venice, Padua, Florence, Siena, Orvieto, Rome, Naples, and Capri, Prendergast purchased Baedeker's *Italy: Handbook for Travelers* (1895, fig. 5). He consulted Baedeker's *Italy: From the Alps to Naples* (1909) for his return to Italy in 1911. Prendergast also used Baedeker's *Southern France* (1914) for a trip in 1914 to Paris and St.-Malo. Evident in the well-worn spine and thumbed pages, it is certain that these guidebooks provided an important service to Prendergast in his travels at home and abroad.

Prendergast did his homework before venturing into these foreign lands, reading books on the art, language, and literature of the locale in order to be a more informed visitor. His own personal collection of art-related information includes catalogues of museum collections such as Gisela Richter's *Metropolitan Museum of Art: The Classical Collection* (1917) and Frederick Mayer's *The Louvre* (n.d.). Books such as *Rousseau's Pensées*, *The Art Teaching of John Ruskin* (Collingwood, 1891), *French*

8. Books belonging to Maurice and Charles Prendergast survived in the collection of Eugénie Prendergast and are now in the Prendergast Archive and Study Center, WCMA. It is only a fragmentary sampling of the complete library as it must have once existed in the artists' home.

9. Full bibliographical citations as well as a list of all the books can be found in Mathews, *The Art of Charles Prendergast*, Williams College Museum of Art. 1993, pp. 111–113.

Maxims of Art (Pène du Bois, 1894), and *Cézanne Mappe* (1912) surely would have provided an artistic framework for his three trips to France. He was particularly interested in Italian painting, and returned to Venice in 1911. In anticipation, Prendergast read books including *Giotto* (Thode, 1910), *Florentine Painters of the Renaissance* (1907), *Venetian Painters of the Renaissance* (Berenson, 1906), *Venice Seen by the Painter* (Motta, n.d.), and *Art in Northern Italy* (1911). Prendergast also sought a literary context for art, especially that of France and Italy. For a trip to Paris, Tréport, Dieppe, and Dinard in 1891–94, Prendergast probably perused *Thackeray's Paris Sketchbook* (Titmarsh, 1886) and James McNeill Whistler's *The Gentle Art of Making Enemies*. *Virgil's Aeneid* (1896) and *Select Orations of Marcus Tullius Cicero* (1896) were supplemented by Murray's *Manual of Mythology* (1895). Communication is of key importance during travel; *The English-Italian Conversational Dictionary* and the *The English-French Conversational Dictionary* can be counted among the titles in Prendergast's library. Other sources that he may have consulted include the travel books of Thomas Cook, an organizer of international guided tours, and personal accounts of travel abroad.

In one of his guidebooks, Prendergast marked places to buy photographs at the Palazzo Vecchio, indicating an interest in this type of image (Baedeker, 1909). He also owned photographs of the architectural landmarks of Rome, *Ricordo di Roma: Parte 1 and Parte 2,* purchased while in Italy. Generally the products of professional firms, travel photographs were clear, detailed, lasting records of the exotic places that existed beyond the horizon (fig. 6). Viewed before a trip, they anticipated what would be seen. During a trip, they were collected as souvenirs of the journey and proof of the visit. These souvenirs could be shared and also served as a visual reminder of the events of the trip for years to come. Photography's accuracy was especially important for artists like Prendergast who were interested in the specifics of the foreign location.[10]

Travel books and photographs were used not only by those who traveled to the actual places, but also by those who saw these materials as substitutes for travel or needed to broaden their intellectual horizons. Prendergast owned many books on places he never visited, such as Egypt (*Art in Egypt,* 1912), Russia (*Peasant Art in Russia,* 1912), and Japan (*Picture Book with Flowers and Birds,* 1884). In this regard, Prendergast's travel library is the best reminder that travel is, after all, a flight of the imagination—fueled and sustained by the lasting power of words and images.

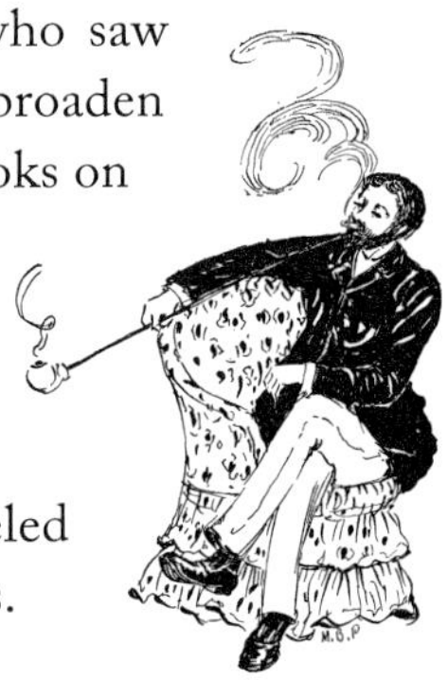

10. The Prendergasts' collection of photographs is currently in the Prendergast Archive and Study Center, WCMA. The full collection is also available on microfilm through the Archives of American Art.

Guide to the Use of the Catalogue

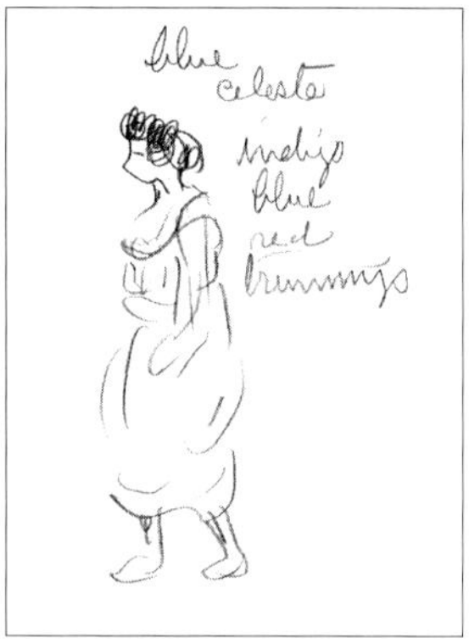

CR 1561 sketchbook, ca. 1920–23

The 318 works by Maurice Prendergast in the following catalogue have been arranged first by medium (oil, watercolor and pastel, drawing, and prints) and then by approximate date. The numbers used to establish the sequence of the objects have been drawn from the Prendergast *Catalogue Raisonné* (CR) published by the Williams College Museum of Art in 1990. Gaps between the numbers in this catalogue indicate works belonging to other collections. The CR number and the museum's accession number are the two most useful identifiers of each object, and we have refrained from adding a new numbering system for the sake of this publication.

Each catalogue entry includes title, alternate titles if any, approximate date, medium, dimensions, credit line, accession number, inscriptions, bibliographical citations, and exhibition history. The provenance is assumed to be the following unless otherwise noted:

The artist; to Charles Prendergast, 1924;
to Mrs. Charles Prendergast, 1948; to present collection.

The date of the gift to the Williams College Museum of Art is found in the first two digits of the accession number assigned to the piece by the museum (e.g. 85.10.1 = 1985).

Citations for bibliography and exhibitions are included in the catalogue entries in a shortened form. The full citation can be found in the complete list of Literature and Exhibitions Cited (pages 149–154). A question mark (?) before a citation indicates that we believe that this is the work referred to in the publication or exhibition, but there is not enough documentation to be certain.

If a verso of a work is reproduced, that reproduction always accompanies its recto and may thus be out of chronological sequence.

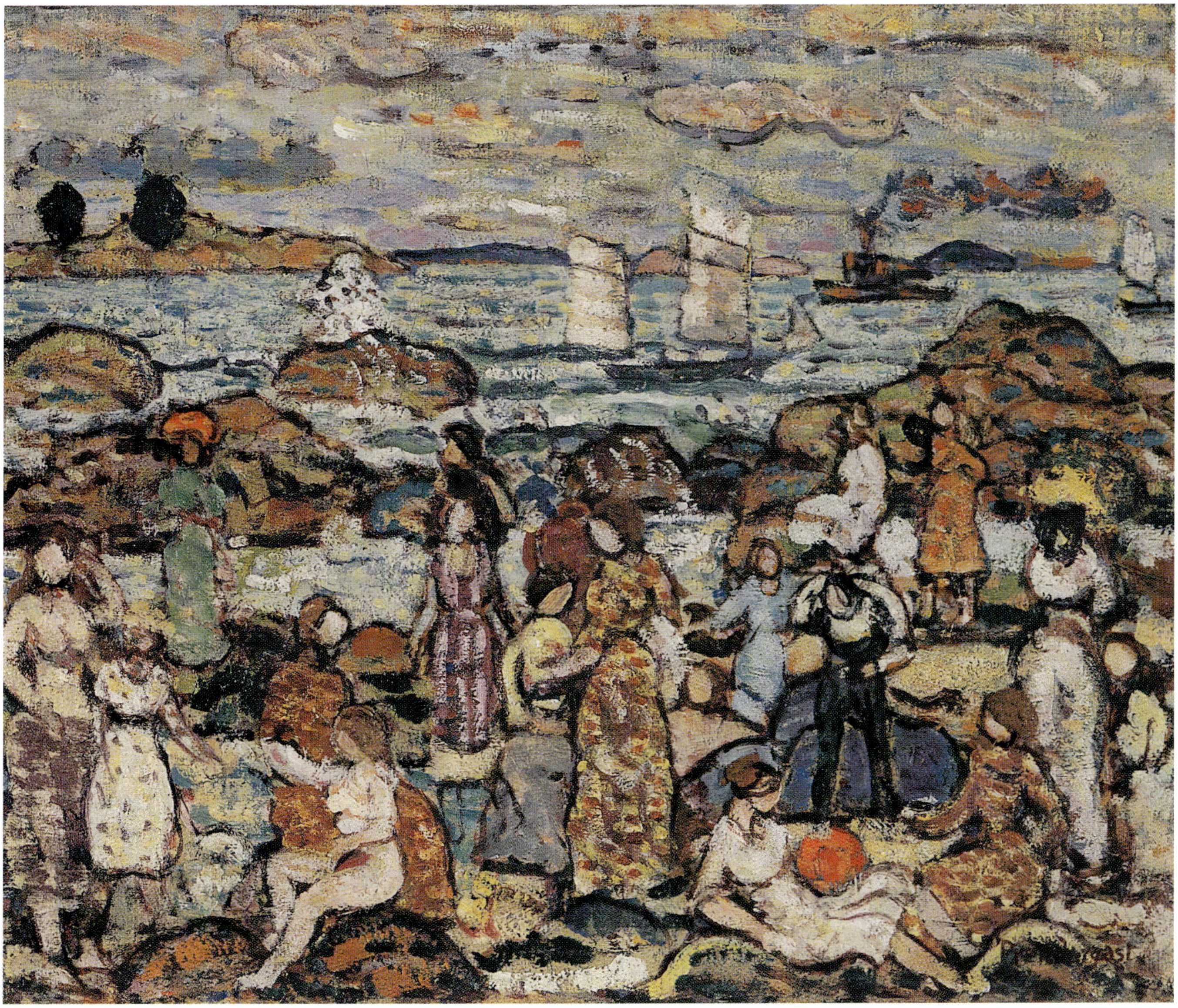

Catalogue of Works

Oils

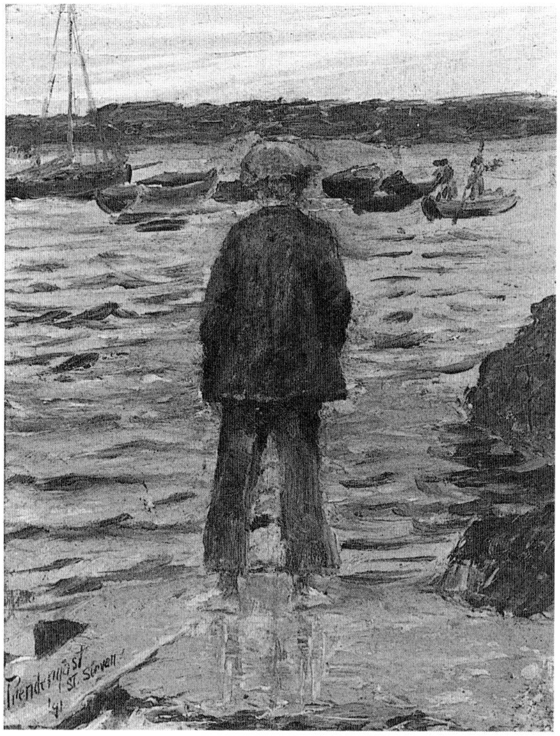

CR 3

CR 3

ST. SERVAN FISHERMAN 1891
St. Servan
Frame by Charles Prendergast
Oil on panel
(10 x 7½ in.; 25.4 x 19.0 cm)
Williams College Museum of Art, bequest of Mrs. Charles Prendergast (95.4.74)

INSCRIPTIONS
l.l. in black: Prendergast/St. Servan/'91

NOTE
This work appears in a photograph (ca. 1900–03) of Charles Prendergast in the studio at 83 Walnut Street, Winchester, MA (Prendergast Archive, Williams College Museum of Art).

CR 15

PROFILE OF A LITTLE GIRL ca. 1892–94
Oil on canvas
(13 x 10½ in.; 34.3 x 26.7 cm)
Williams College Museum of Art, gift of Mrs. Charles Prendergast (86.18.29)

INSCRIPTIONS
l.r. in brown: Prendergast

BIBLIOGRAPHY
Sawyer 1966 (n.p.)

EXHIBITIONS
1966a Knoedler (#6, ill.); 1984b Williams College (no #); 1989c Williams College (no #); 1990f Williams College (no #); 1991a Williams College (no #); 1995b Williams College (no #)

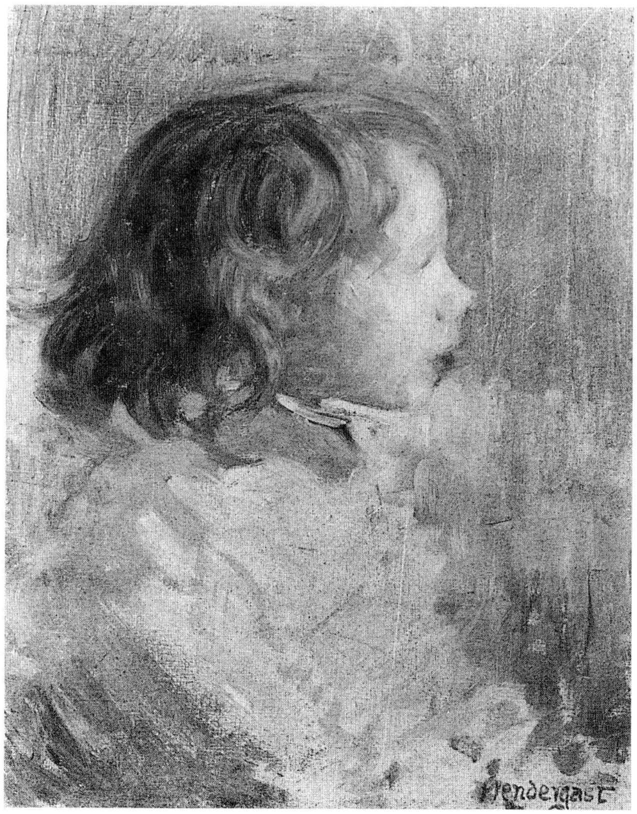

CR 15

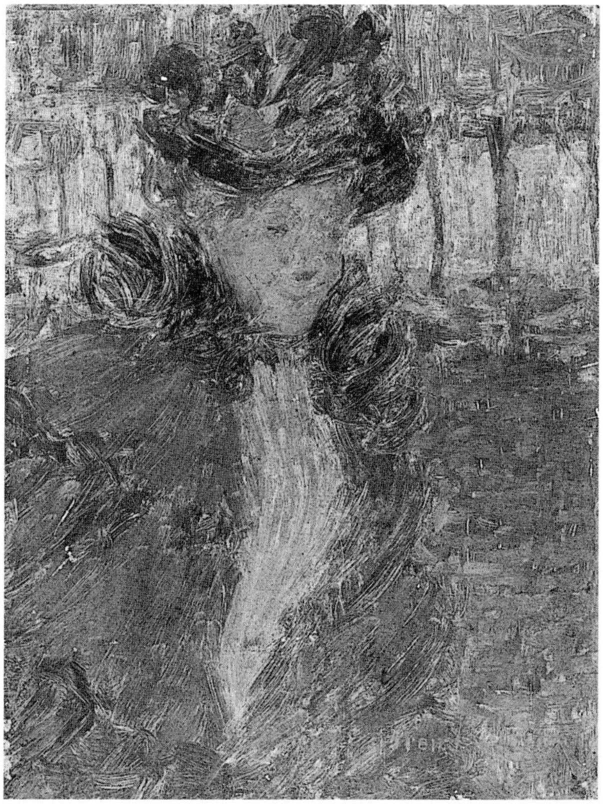

CR 16

CR 16

WOMAN IN PARIS ca. 1892–94
Oil on panel
(8½ x 6¼ in.; 21.6 x 15.9 cm)
Williams College Museum of Art, gift of Mrs. Charles Prendergast (90.11.6)

INSCRIPTIONS
l.r. in red: Prendergast

EXHIBITIONS
1984b Williams College (#5); 1991a Williams College (no #); 1994a Williams College (no #)

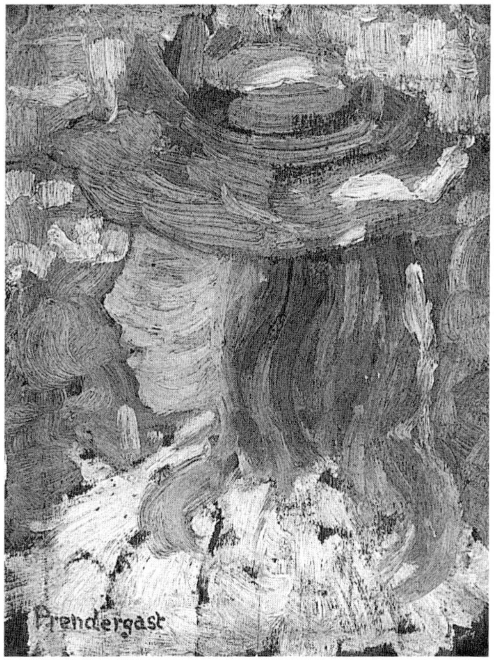

CR 25

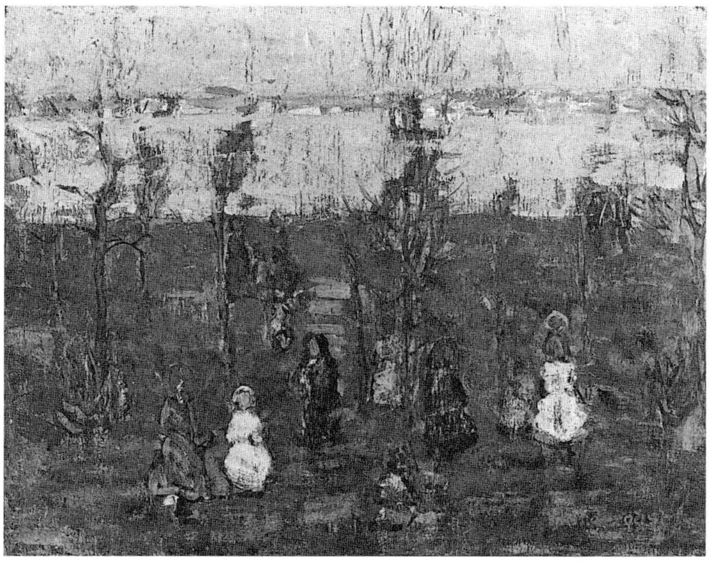

CR 22

CR 22

BOSTON ca. 1895–97
Oil on panel
(10⅝ x 13¾ in.; 27.0 x 34.9 cm)
Williams College Museum of Art, gift of Mrs. Charles Prendergast (84.16.24)

INSCRIPTIONS
l.r. in orange: Prendergast

EXHIBITIONS
1990f Williams College (no #)

CR 25

HEAD OF A GIRL ca. 1895–97
Oil on panel
(6½ x 4½ in.; 16.5 x 11.4 cm)
Williams College Museum of Art, gift of Mrs. Charles Prendergast (90.11.5)

INSCRIPTIONS
l.l. in brown: Prendergast

EXHIBITIONS
1984b Williams College (#3); 1991a Williams College (no #)

CR 28

LOW TIDE ca. 1895–97
Oil on panel
(13½ x 18 in.; 34.3 x 45.7 cm)
Williams College Museum of Art, gift of Mrs. Charles Prendergast (86.18.40)

INSCRIPTIONS
l.r. in brown over yellow: Prendergast

BIBLIOGRAPHY
Rhys 1952 (pp. 63, 149–50); Sawyer 1966 (n.p.); Lauzon 1989 (pp. E: 4, ill.); Mathews 1990 (p. 64; ill.); Mathews 1990a (ill.)

EXHIBITIONS
1938 Addison Gallery (#64); 1966a Knoedler (#5, ill.); 1986 Williams College (no #); 1989d Williams College (no #); 1990c Williams College (#19, ABCD); 1995b Williams College (no #)

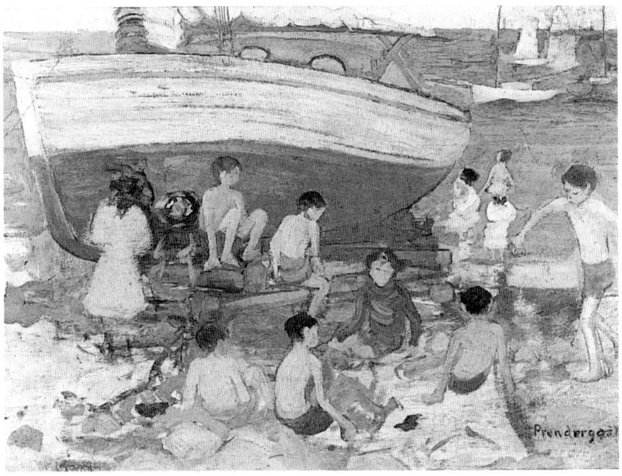

CR 28

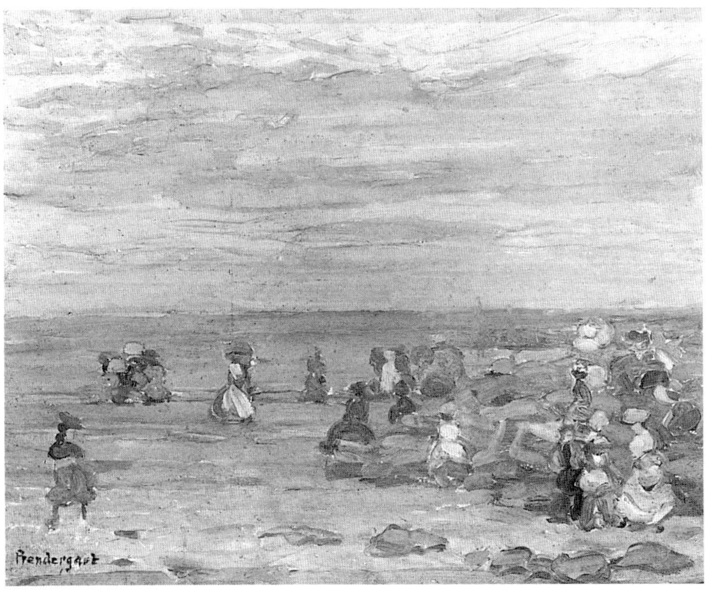

CR 34

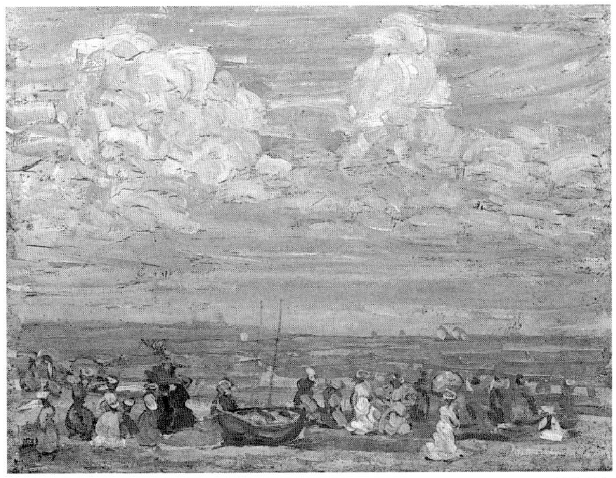
CR 31

CR 31

BEACH SCENE WITH BOAT ca. 1902–04
Oil on panel
(10⅜ x 13½ in.; 26.4 x 34.6 cm)
Williams College Museum of Art, gift of Mrs. Charles Prendergast (84.16.23)

INSCRIPTIONS
Unsigned

EXHIBITIONS
1989d Williams College (no #); 1990b Williams College (no #); 1990f Williams College (no #); 1991a Williams College (no #); 1994a Williams College (no #)

CR 34

SEASCAPE ca. 1902–06
Oil on panel
(10⅝ x 13⅝ in.; 27.0 x 34.6 cm)
Williams College Museum of Art, gift of Mrs. Charles Prendergast (84.16.5)

INSCRIPTIONS
l.l. in brown: Prendergast

EXHIBITIONS
1989d Williams College (no #); 1990b Williams College (no #) verso; 1993 Williams College (no #)

CR 34 verso

WOODLAND ca. 1907–10
Oil

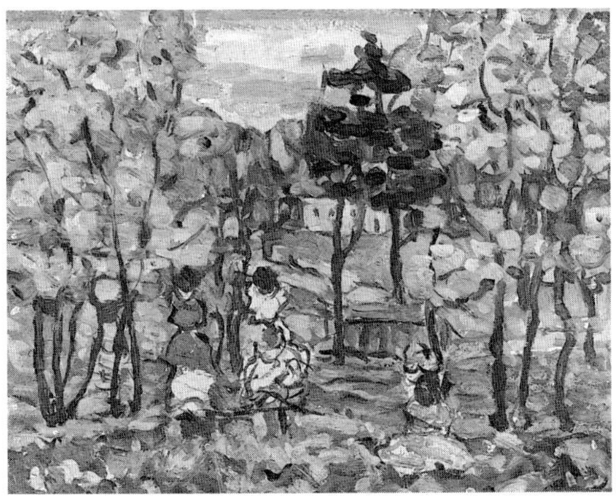
CR 34 verso

CR 35
APPROACHING STORM ca. 1902–04
Frame by Charles Prendergast
Oil on panel
(10½ x 13⅞ in.; 26.7 x 35.2 cm)
Williams College Museum of Art, bequest of Mrs. Charles Prendergast (95.4.76)

INSCRIPTIONS
l.r. in red: Prendergast

BIBLIOGRAPHY
Eglington 1934 (p. 3)

EXHIBITIONS
1934a Whitney (#38); 1938 Addison Gallery (#71); 1988b Williams College

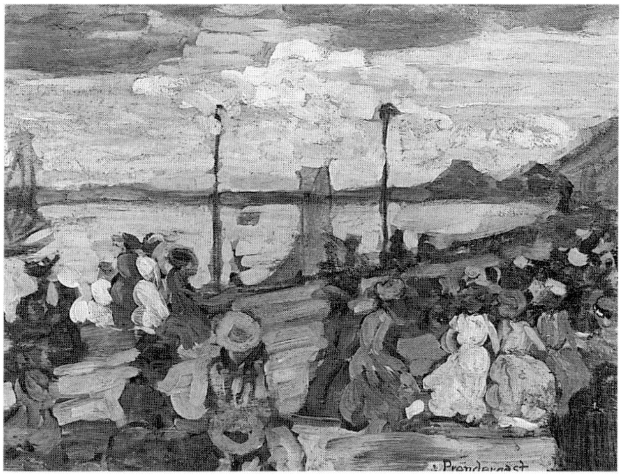

CR 35

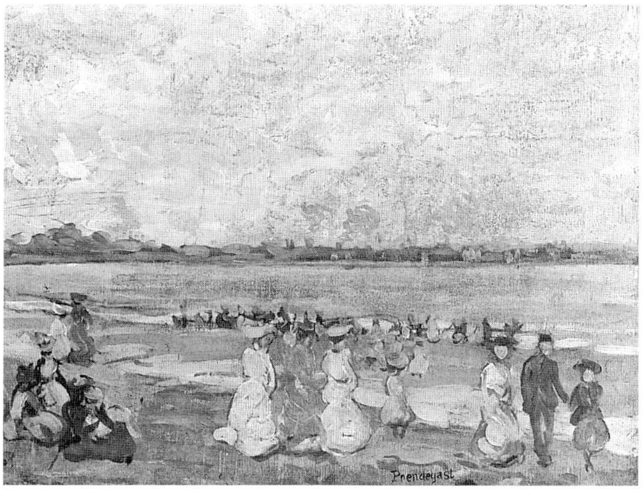

CR 37

CR 37
PROMENADE ON THE BEACH ca. 1902–04
Oil on panel
(10⅜ x 13¾ in.; 26.4 x 34.9 cm)
Williams College Museum of Art, bequest of Mrs. Charles Prendergast (95.4.20)

INSCRIPTIONS
l.r. in black ink: Prendergast

EXHIBITIONS
1938 Addison Gallery (#66)

CR 42
SALEM ca. 1902–04
Oil on panel
(11 x 11 in.; 27.9 x 27.9 cm)
Williams College Museum of Art, bequest of Mrs. Charles Prendergast (95.4.77)

INSCRIPTIONS
l.r. in red: Prendergast

CR 43
LIGHTHOUSE AT THE COVE ca. 1902–04
Oil on panel
(10½ x 13¾ in.; 26.7 x 34.9 cm)
Williams College Museum of Art, bequest of Mrs. Charles Prendergast (95.4.21)

INSCRIPTIONS
l.l. in black ink: Prendergast

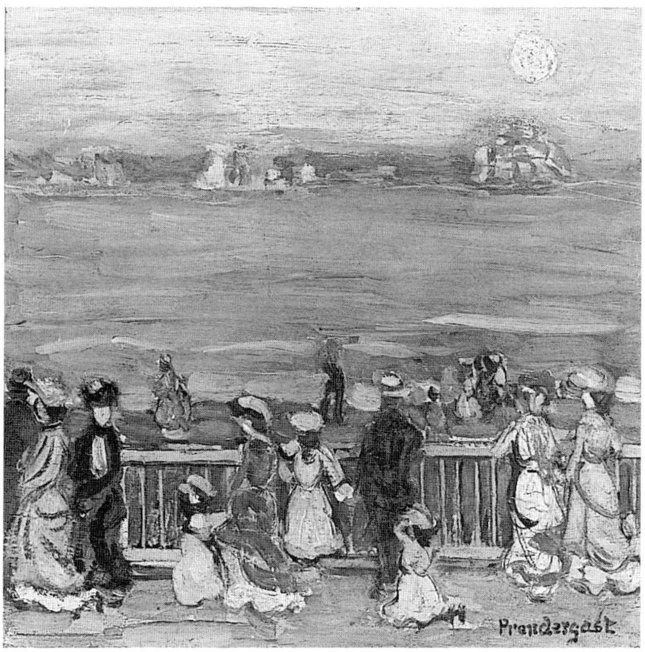

CR 42

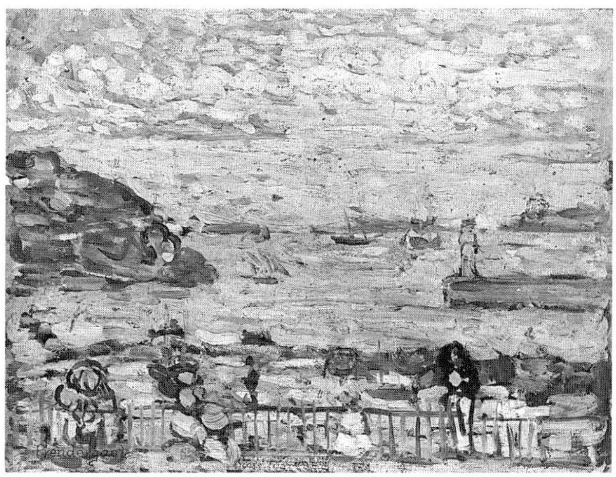

CR 43

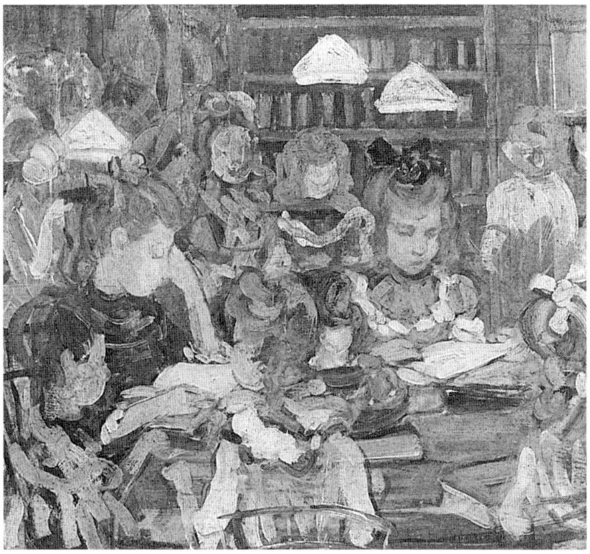

CR 50

CR 50
IN THE LIBRARY ca. 1902–06
Oil on panel
(12⅜ x 13⅜ in.; 31.4 x 34.0 cm)
Williams College Museum of Art, gift of Mrs. Charles Prendergast (86.18.33)

INSCRIPTIONS
Unsigned

EXHIBITIONS
1960 MFA Boston (#7, ill.); 1984b Williams College (#4); 1985b Williams College (no #); 1986 Williams College (no #); 1989c Williams College (no #)

CR 52
FOUR FIGURES BY THE SEA ca. 1903–06
Oil on panel
(10⅜ x 13½ in.; 26.4 x 34.9 cm)
Williams College Museum of Art, gift of Mrs. Charles Prendergast (84.16.3)

INSCRIPTIONS
l.l. in brown: Prendergast

EXHIBITIONS
1989d Williams College (no #); 1990b Williams College (no #) verso; 1990f Williams College (no #) verso

CR 52 verso
BLUE HOUSE WITH RED FLAG ca. 1914–15
Oil

CR 57
ST. MALO ca. 1903–06
Frame by Charles Prendergast
Oil on panel
(5⅜ x 8⅝ in.; 13.7 x 21.9 cm)
Williams College Museum of Art, bequest of Mrs. Charles Prendergast (95.4.73)

INSCRIPTIONS
l.r. in red: MBP [monogram]

EXHIBITIONS
1988b Williams College (frame for *St. Malo* by Charles Prendergast, #59)

NOTE
Although later titled *St. Malo,* this work likely dates from the period just prior to Prendergast's trip to France.

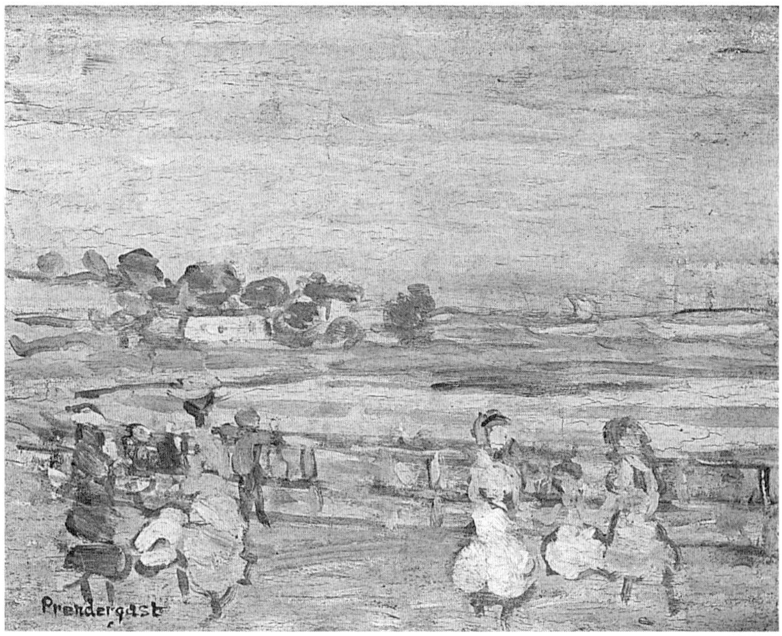

CR 52

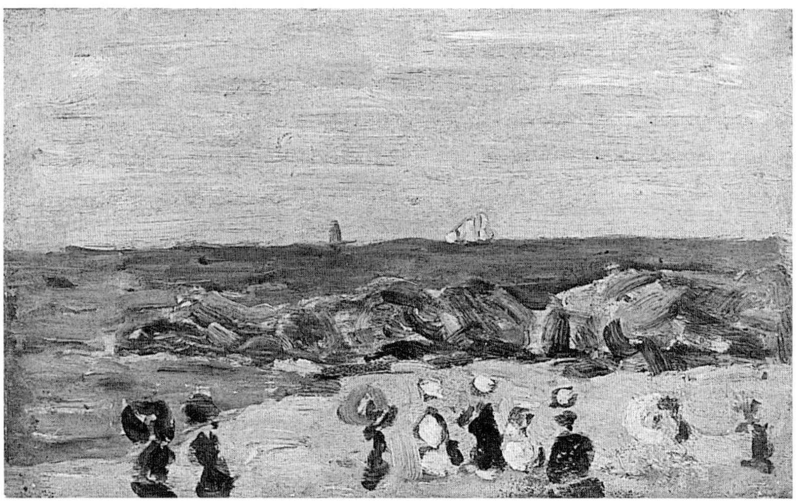

CR 57

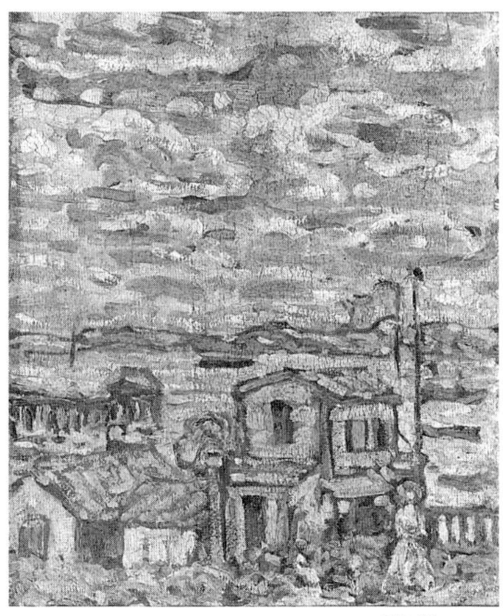

CR 52 verso

CR 59

BEACH SCENE #4 ca. 1903–06
Oil on panel
(10⅜ x 13⅝ in.; 26.2 x 34.6 cm)
Williams College Museum of Art, gift of
Mrs. Charles Prendergast (84.16.21)

INSCRIPTIONS
l.r. in black: Prendergast

BIBLIOGRAPHY
Wattenmaker 1994 (p. 79; ill.)

EXHIBITIONS
1925 Kraushaar (#34); 1925a Chicago AIC (#23); 1926a Cleveland (no #); 1934a Whitney (#64); 1989d Williams College (no #); 1990b Williams College (no #); 1990f Williams College (no #); 1991a Williams College

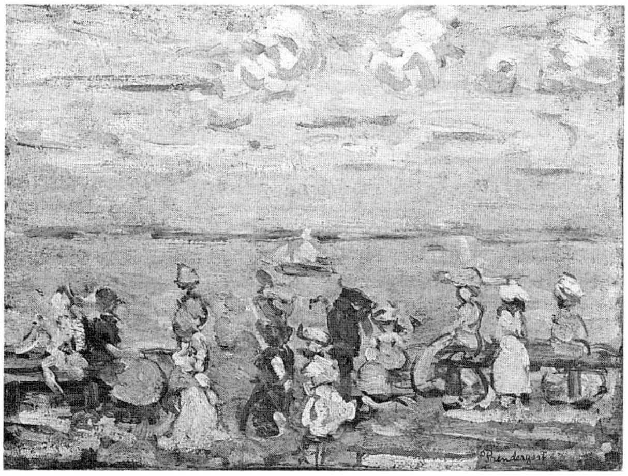

CR 59

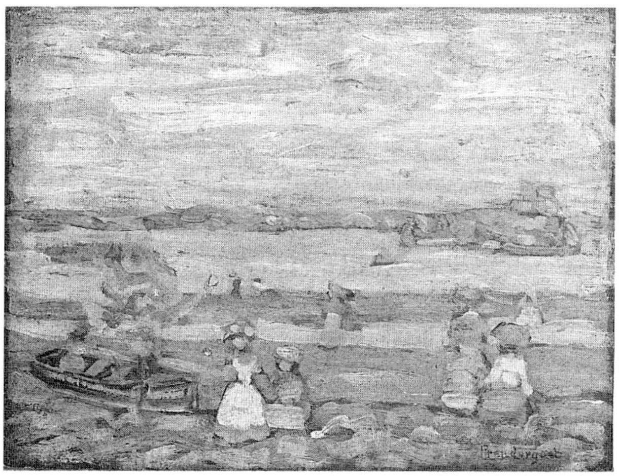

CR 61

CR 61

A GRAY DAY ca. 1903–06
Oil on panel
(10½ x 13⅞ in.; 26.7 x 35.2 cm)
Williams College Museum of Art, gift of
Mrs. Charles Prendergast (84.16.19)

INSCRIPTIONS
l.r. in brown: Prendergast

EXHIBITIONS
1989d Williams College (no #); 1990b Williams College (no #); 1990f Williams College (no #)

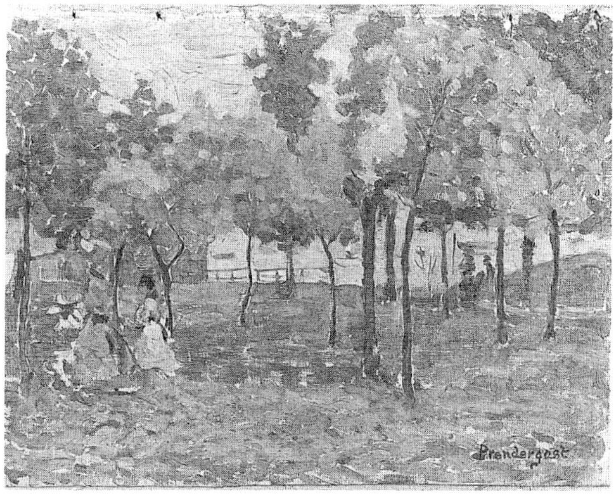

CR 67

CR 67

WATERFRONT PARK ca. 1902–06
Oil on canvas
(10⅞ x 15½ in.; 27.6 x 39.4 cm)
Williams College Museum of Art, bequest of
Mrs. Charles Prendergast (95.4.8)

INSCRIPTIONS
l.r. in red: Prendergast
Cf. a related later work, *Merry-Go-Round* (CR 247).

CR 71

STUDY ST. MALO, NO. 12 ca. 1907
Studies, St. Malo
Oil on panel
(10½ x 13¾ in.; 26.7 x 34.9 cm)
Williams College Museum of Art, gift of
Mrs. Charles Prendergast (91.18.8)

INSCRIPTIONS
l.l. in black: Prendergast

BIBLIOGRAPHY
Newark Evening News 1909a (p. 3, as *Studies, St. Malo*); Rhys 1952 (pp. 34–35, as *Studies, St. Malo*); Wattenmaker 1982 (p. 36)

EXHIBITIONS
1908 Macbeth (#26, #28, #29, or #30); 1990c Williams College (#65. ABCD); 1992 Williams College (no #); 1993 Williams College (no #); 1994a Williams College (no #); 1995b Williams College (no #)
Color plate, p. 32

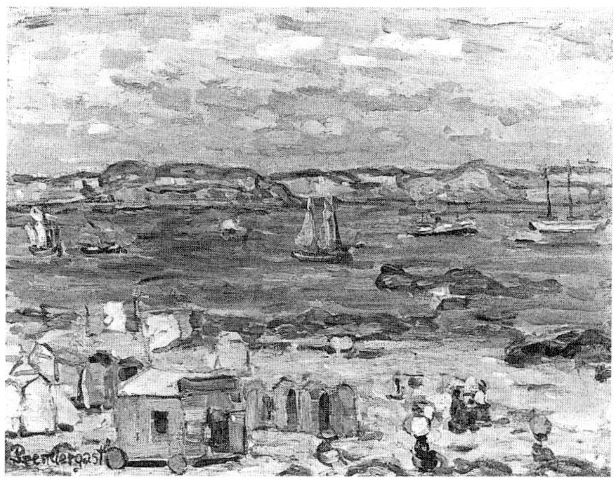

CR 71

CR 91

STUDY ST. MALO, NO. 33 ca. 1907
Studies, St. Malo
Oil on panel
(10½ x 13⅞ in.; 26.7 x 35.2 cm)
Williams College Museum of Art, gift of Mrs. Charles Prendergast (91.18.27)

INSCRIPTIONS
l.l. in black: Prendergast

BIBLIOGRAPHY
Newark Evening News 1909a (p. 3, as *Studies, St. Malo*); Rhys 1952 (pp. 34–35, as *Studies, St. Malo*); Wattenmaker 1982 (p. 36)

EXHIBITIONS
1908 Macbeth (#33)

NOTE
A label on the back of this panel from the 1908 Macbeth exhibition identifies this work as number 33.

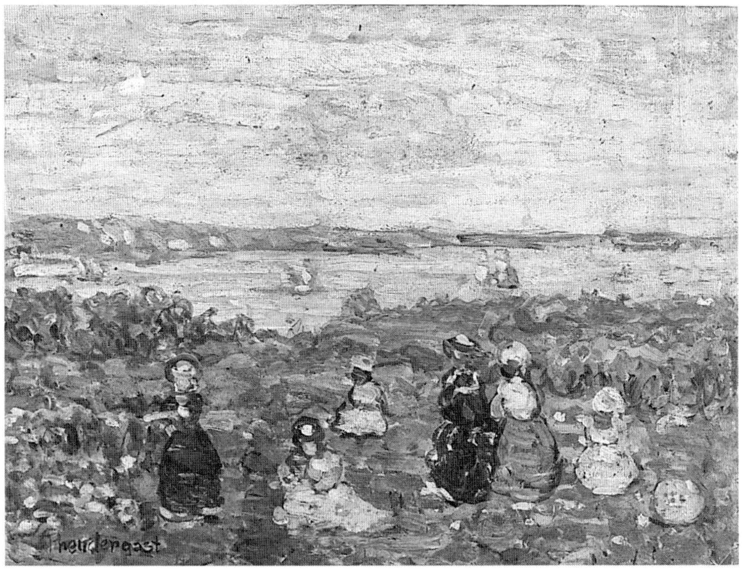

CR 91

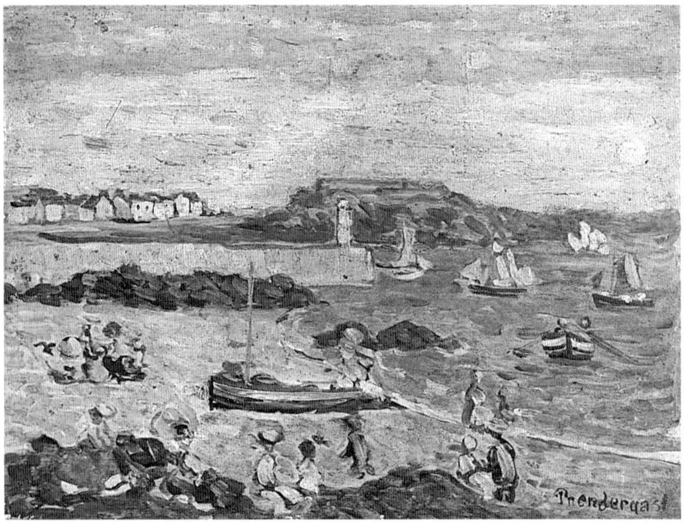

CR 92

CR 92

STUDY ST. MALO, NO. 32 ca. 1907
Studies, St. Malo
Oil on panel
(10½ x 13¾ in.; 26.7 x 34.9 cm)
Williams College Museum of Art, gift of Mrs. Charles Prendergast (91.18.26)

INSCRIPTIONS
l.r. in black: Prendergast

BIBLIOGRAPHY
Newark Evening News 1909a (p. 3, as *Studies, St. Malo*); Rhys 1952 (pp.34–35, as *Studies, St. Malo*); Wattenmaker 1982 (p. 36)

EXHIBITIONS
1908 Macbeth (#32); 1990c Williams College (no #); 1992 Williams College (no #); 1993 Williams College (no #); 1994a Williams College (no #); 1995b Williams College (no #)

NOTE
A label on the back of this panel from the 1908 Macbeth exhibition identifies this work as number 32 in the exhibition.

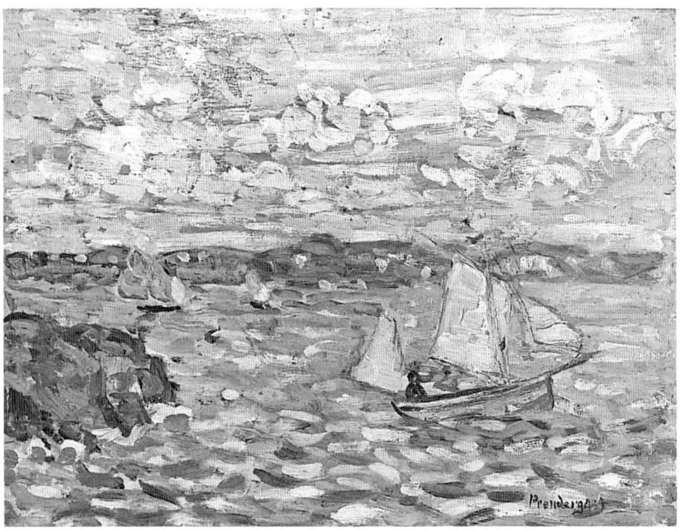

CR 101

CR 101

STUDY ST. MALO NO. 9 ca. 1907
Studies, St. Malo
Oil on panel
(10½ x 13¾ in.; 26.7 x 34.9 cm)
Williams College Museum of Art, gift of Mrs. Charles Prendergast (91.18.25)

INSCRIPTIONS
l.r. in red: Prendergast

BIBLIOGRAPHY
Newark Evening News 1909a (p. 3, as *Studies, St. Malo*); Rhys 1952 (pp. 34–35, as *Studies, St. Malo*); Wattenmaker 1982 (p. 36)

EXHIBITIONS
1908 Macbeth (#26, #28, #29, or #30)

CR 113
TUILERIES GARDENS ca. 1907
Oil on panel
(10½ x 14½ in.; 26.7 x 36.8 cm)
Williams College Museum of Art, bequest of Mrs. Charles Prendergast (95.4.80)

INSCRIPTIONS
l.l. in red: Prendergast

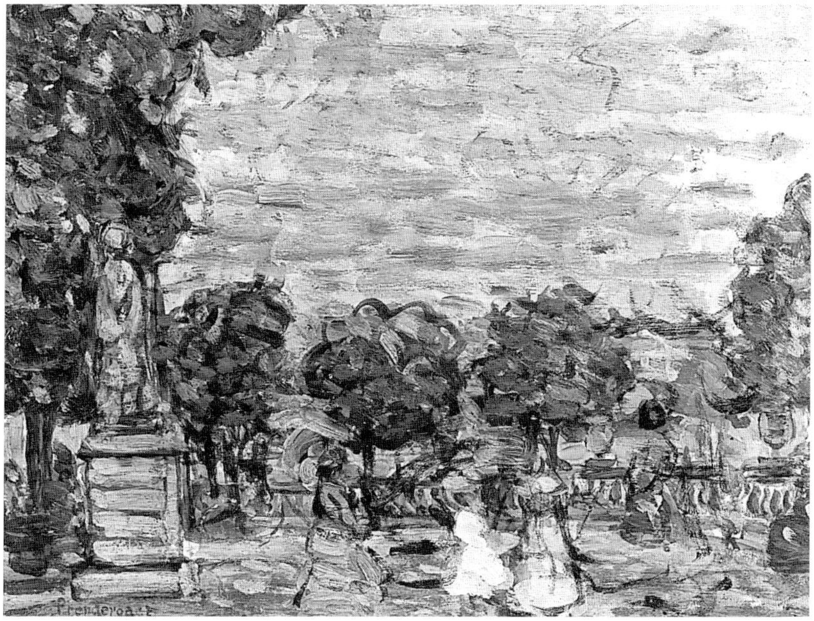

CR 113

CR 113 verso
NEW ENGLAND SCENE ca. 1910–13
Oil

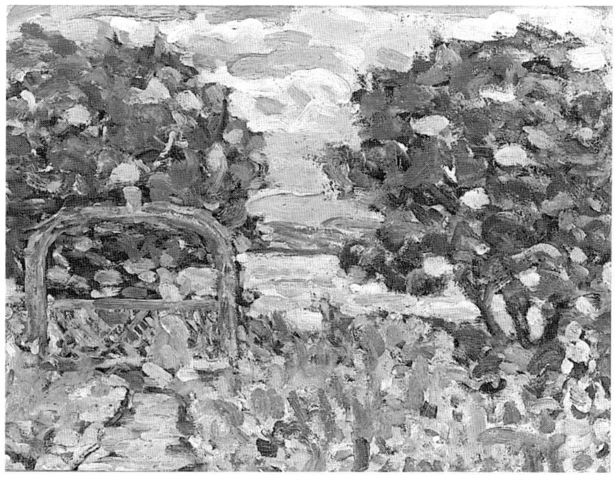

CR 113 verso

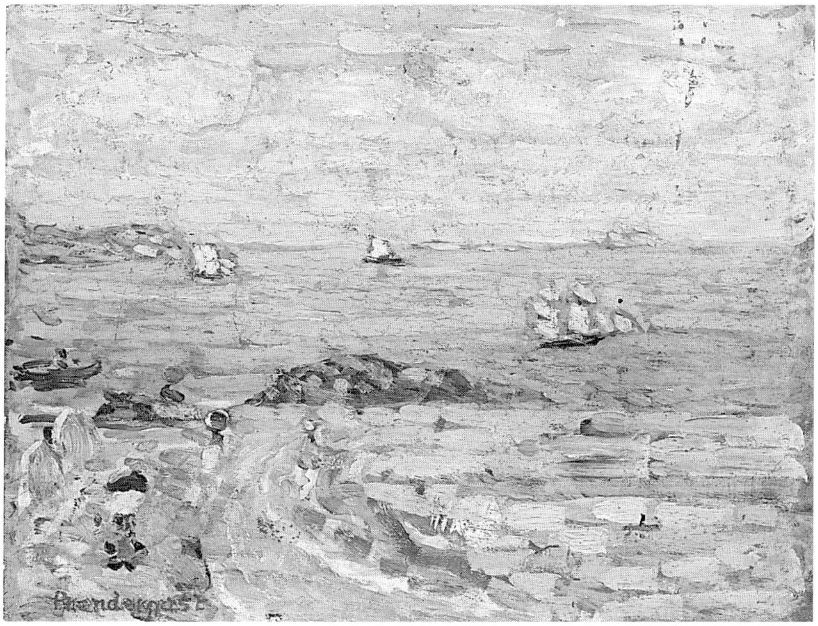

CR 119

CR 119
A SILVER MORNING ca. 1907–10
Oil on panel
(10½ x 13¾ in.; 26.7 x 34.9 cm)
Williams College Museum of Art, gift of Mrs. Charles Prendergast (84.16.22)

INSCRIPTIONS
l.l. in brown: Prendergast

BIBLIOGRAPHY
Lauzon 1989 (p. E: 1, 4)

EXHIBITIONS
1989d Williams College (no #); 1990b Williams College (no #); 1990f Williams College (no #); 1993 Williams College (no #); 1994a Williams College (no #); 1995b Williams College (no #)

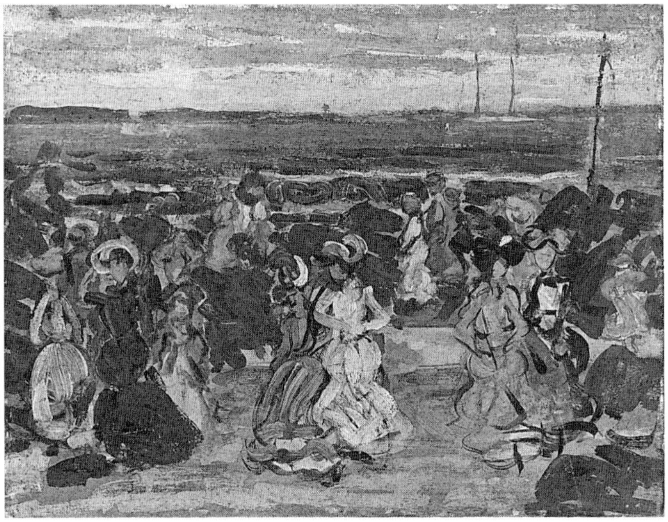

CR 123

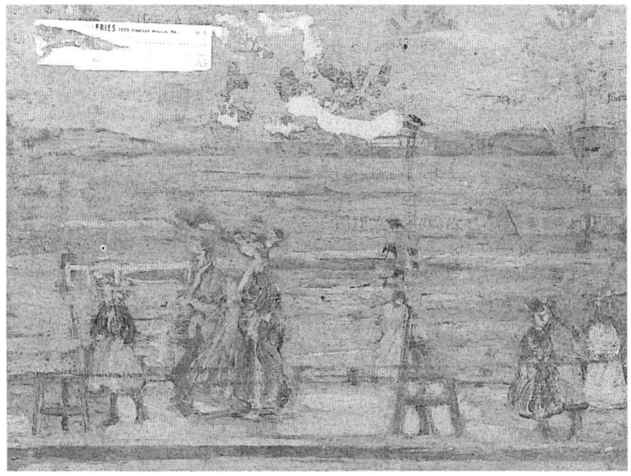

CR 123 verso

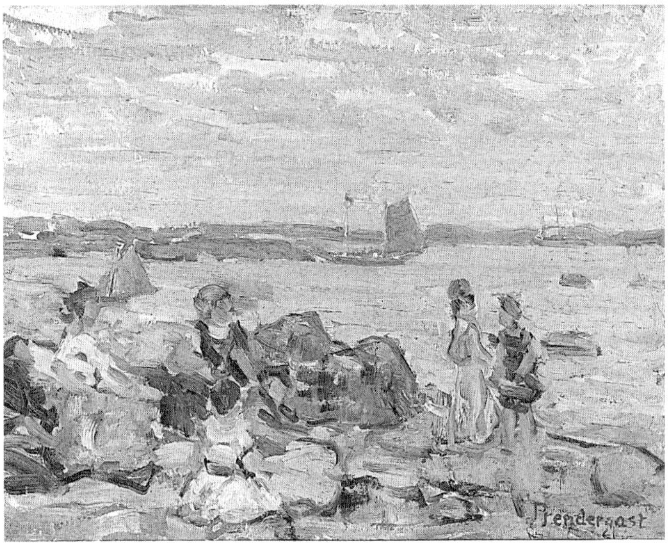

CR 127

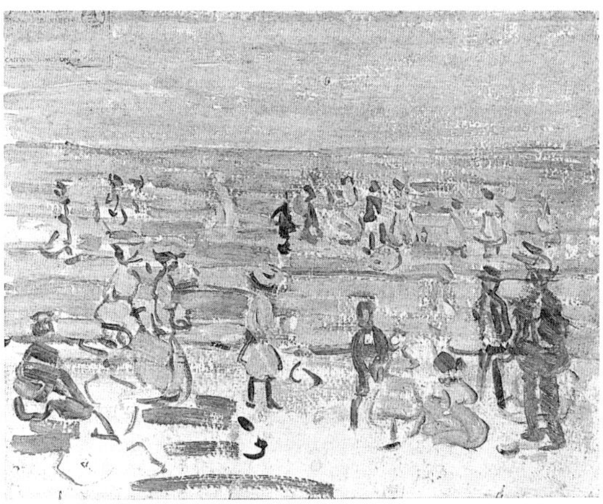

CR 127 verso

CR 123

NORTH SHORE ca. 1907–10
Frame by Charles Prendergast
Oil on panel
(16⅛ x 19⅛ in.; 41.0 x 48.6 cm)
Williams College Museum of Art, gift of Mrs. Charles Prendergast (86.18.37)

INSCRIPTIONS
l.l. (faint): Prendergast

BIBLIOGRAPHY
Lauzon 1989 (p. E: 1, 4)

EXHIBITIONS
1989d Williams College (no #); 1990b Williams College (no #); 1990f Williams College (no #); 1991a Williams College (no #)

CR 123 verso

SEASIDE SCENE
Oil, upper half obscured by remnants of stickers

CR 127

BOATS AND FIGURES BY THE SEA
ca. 1907–10
Oil on board
(10½ x 13⅝ in.; 26.7 x 34.6 cm)
Williams College Museum of Art, gift of Mrs. Charles Prendergast (84.16.4)

INSCRIPTIONS
l.r. in brown: Prendergast

EXHIBITIONS
1989c Williams College (no #); 1989d Williams College (no #); 1990b Williams College (no #); 1990f Williams College (no #) verso

CR 127 verso

SEASIDE
Oil

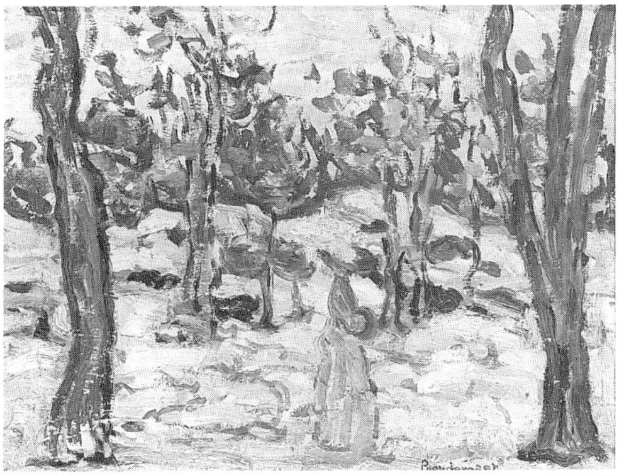

CR 150

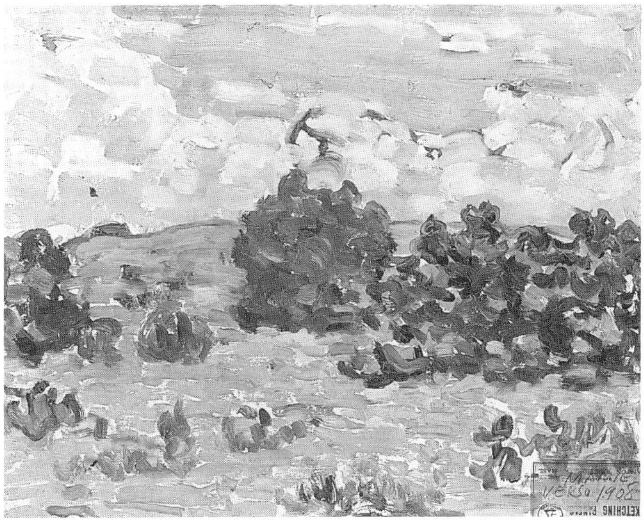

CR 150 verso

CR 150
WINTER LANDSCAPE WITH WOMEN
ca. 1907–10
Oil on board
(10½ x 13½ in.; 26.7 x 34.3 cm)
Williams College Museum of Art, gift of Mrs. Charles Prendergast (84.16.6)

INSCRIPTIONS
l.r. in brown: Prendergast

EXHIBITIONS
1988a Williams College (no #); 1990b Williams College (no #) verso; 1991b Williams College (no #); 1994a Williams College (no #)

CR 150 verso
MAINE
Oil

CR 154
MAYTIME ca. 1907–10
Frame by Charles Prendergast
Oil on panel
(10½ x 15¼ in.; 26.7 x 38.7 cm)
Williams College Museum of Art, bequest of Mrs. Charles Prendergast (95.4.105)

INSCRIPTIONS
l.r. in black: Prendergast

CR 156
SNOWSCAPE ca. 1907–10
Oil on canvas
(20¼ x 24⅜ in.; 51.4 x 61.9 cm)
Williams College Museum of Art, gift of Mrs. Charles Prendergast (91.18.22)

INSCRIPTIONS
l.l. in red: Prendergast

EXHIBITIONS
1990f Williams College (no #); 1994a Williams College (no #)

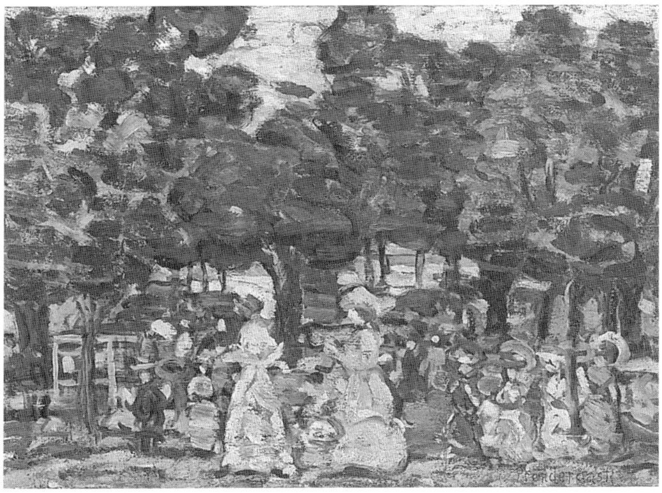

CR 154

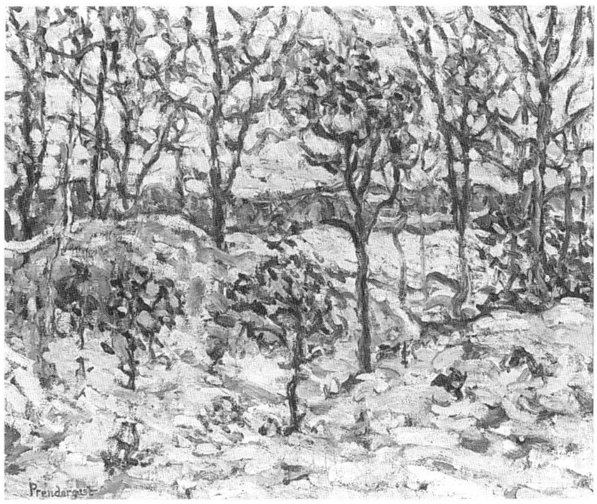

CR 156

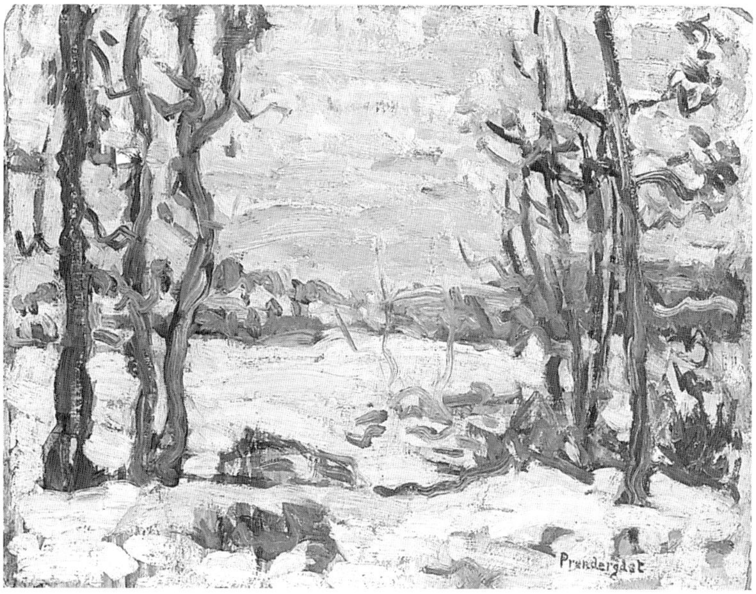

CR 162

CR 162
WINTER SCENE ca. 1907–10
Oil on panel
(10⅝ x 13¾ in.; 27.0 x 34.9 cm)
Williams College Museum of Art, gift of
Mrs. Charles Prendergast (84.16.8)

INSCRIPTIONS
in brown: Prendergast

EXHIBITIONS
1990b Williams College (no #); 1990f Williams College (no #)

CR 165
MAINE ca. 1907–10
Oil on panel
(10⅜ x 13⅜ in.; 26.4 x 34.0 cm)
Williams College Museum of Art, gift of
Mrs. Charles Prendergast (84.16.14)

INSCRIPTIONS
l.r. in brown: Prendergast

EXHIBITIONS
1990b Williams College (no #); 1991b Williams College (no #); 1994a Williams College (no #)

CR 166
LANDSCAPE BY THE SEA ca. 1907–10
Oil on panel
(10½ x 13¾ in.; 26.7 x 34.9 cm)
Williams College Museum of Art, gift of Mrs.
Charles Prendergast (84.16.13)

INSCRIPTIONS
Unsigned

EXHIBITIONS
1990b Williams College (no #)

CR 168
SEASIDE PARK ca. 1907–10
Oil on board
(10⅝ x 13¾ in.; 27.0 x 34.9 cm)
Williams College Museum of Art, gift of
Mrs. Charles Prendergast (84.16.25)

INSCRIPTIONS
l.l. in brown: Prendergast

EXHIBITIONS
1989d Williams College (no #); 1989c Williams College (no #); 1990b Williams College (no #)

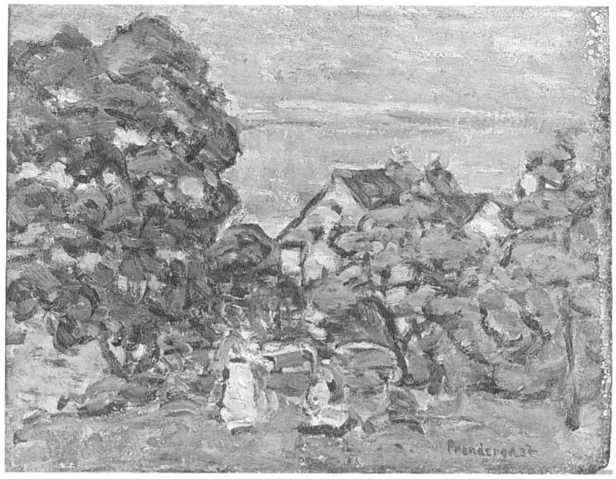

CR 165

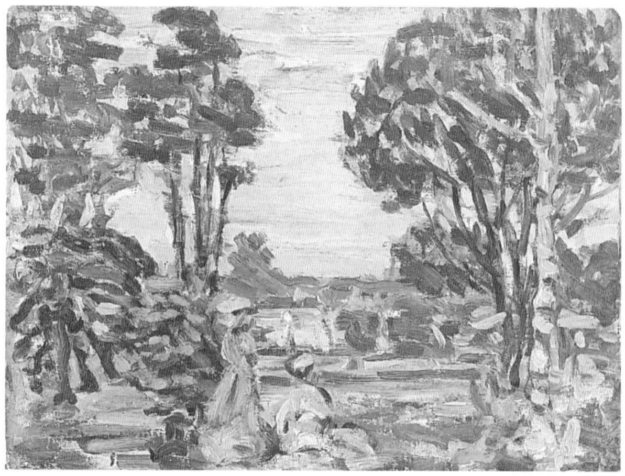

CR 166

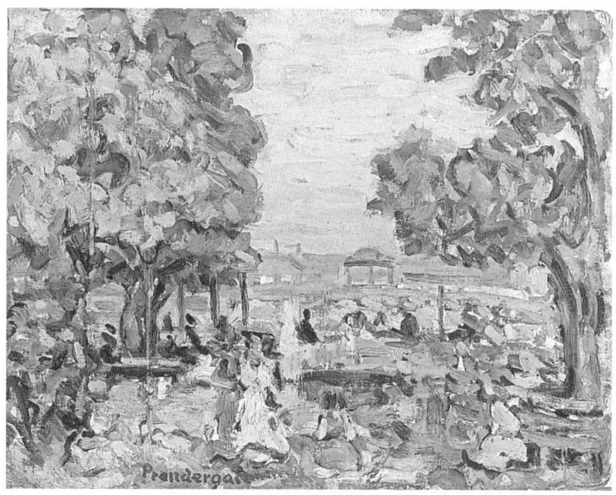

CR 168

CR 169

THREE SAILBOATS ca. 1907–10
Oil on canvas
(15 x 18 in.; 38.1 x 45.7 cm)
Williams College Museum of Art, bequest of Mrs. Charles Prendergast (95.4.12)

INSCRIPTIONS
l.l. in brown: Prendergast

CR 172

MAINE, BLUE HILLS ca. 1907–10
Oil on panel
(10⅜ x 13¾ in.; 26.4 x 34.9 cm)
Williams College Museum of Art, gift of Mrs. Charles Prendergast (84.16.18)

INSCRIPTIONS
l.r. in brown: Prendergast

EXHIBITIONS
1990b Williams College (no #); 1991b Williams College (no #)

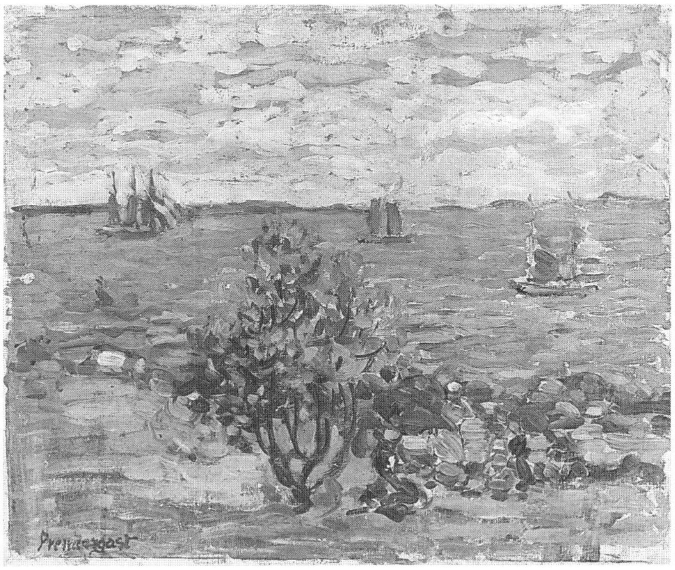

CR 169

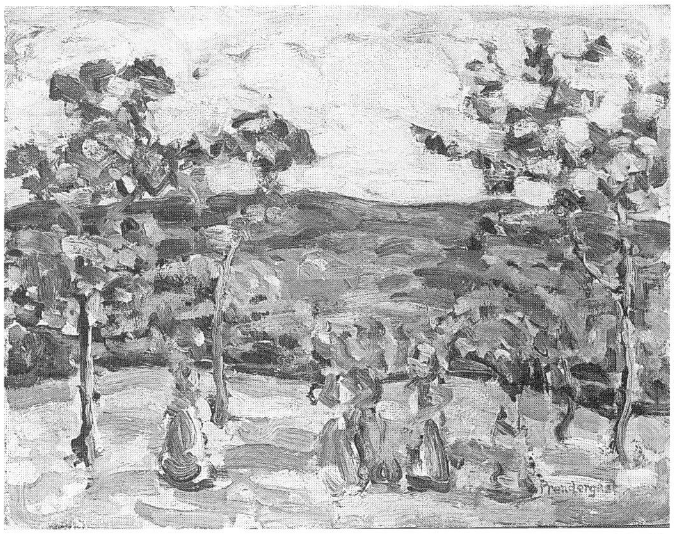

CR 172

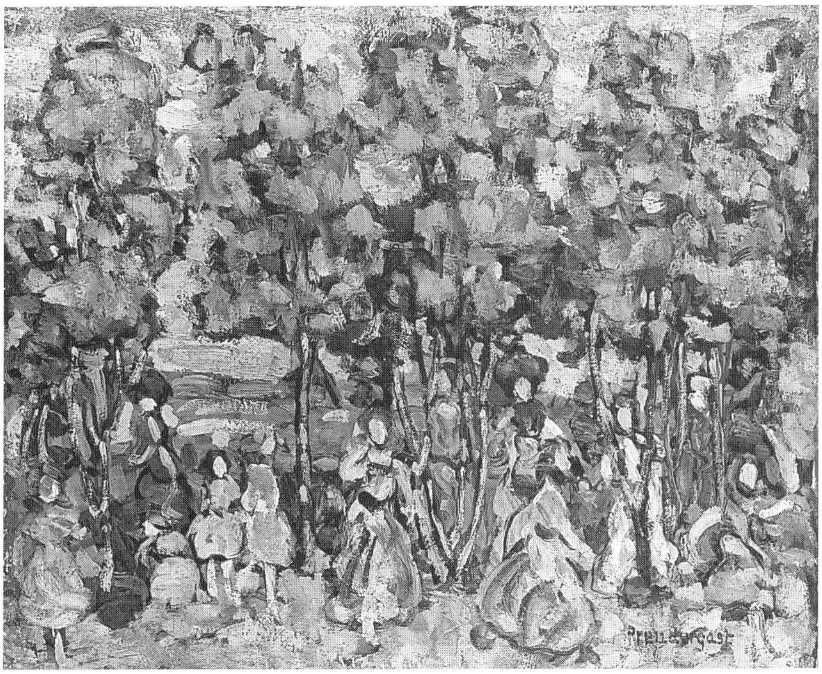

CR 173

CR 173

THE GROVE ca. 1907–10
Oil on panel
(11⅞ x 14⅝ in.; 30.2 x 37.1 cm)
Williams College Museum of Art, gift of Mrs. Charles Prendergast (84.16.7)

INSCRIPTIONS
l.r. in brown: Prendergast

EXHIBITIONS
1988a Williams College (no #); 1990b Williams College (no #); 1990f Williams College (no #); 1991b Williams College (no #)

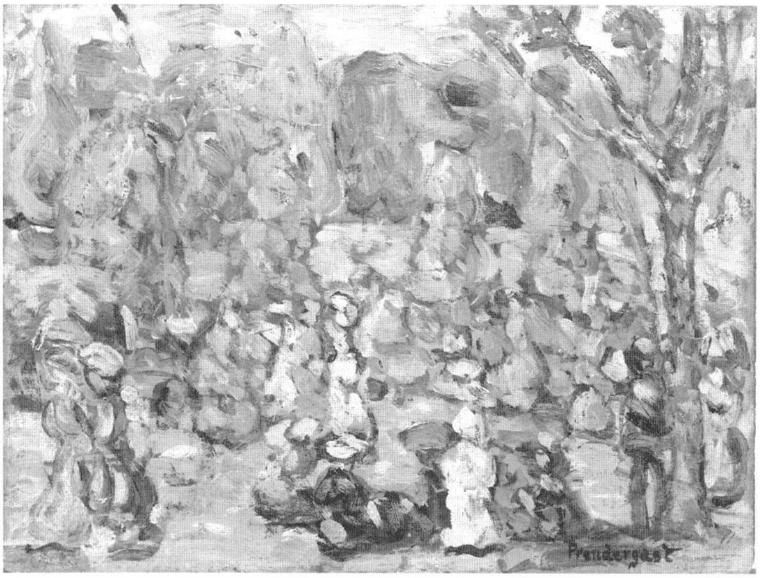

CR 174

CR 174
HOLIDAY ca. 1907–10
Oil on panel
(10⅜ x 13¾ in.; 26.4 x 34.9 cm)
Williams College Museum of Art, gift of Mrs. Charles Prendergast (84.16.20)

INSCRIPTIONS
l.r. in brown: Prendergast

EXHIBITIONS
1988a Williams College (no #); 1990b Williams College (no #); 1991b Williams College (no #)

CR 192
LATE SUMMER ca. 1907–10
Oil on canvas
(19¾ x 31¾ in.; 50.2 x 80.6 cm)
Williams College Museum of Art, gift of Mrs. Charles Prendergast (86.18.43)

INSCRIPTIONS
l.r. in red: Prendergast

EXHIBITIONS
1966a Knoedler (#57); 1969 Knoedler (#84); 1990f Williams College (no #); 1993 Williams College (no #); 1995b Williams College (no #)

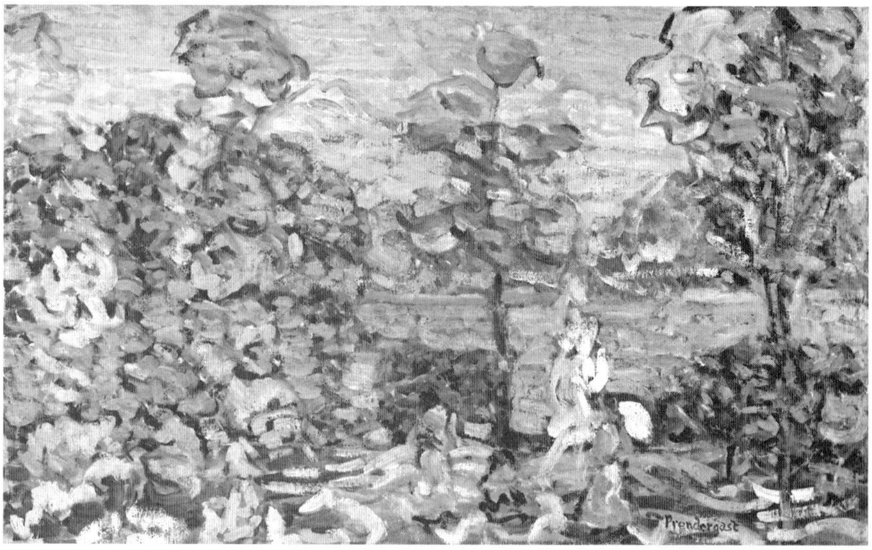

CR 192

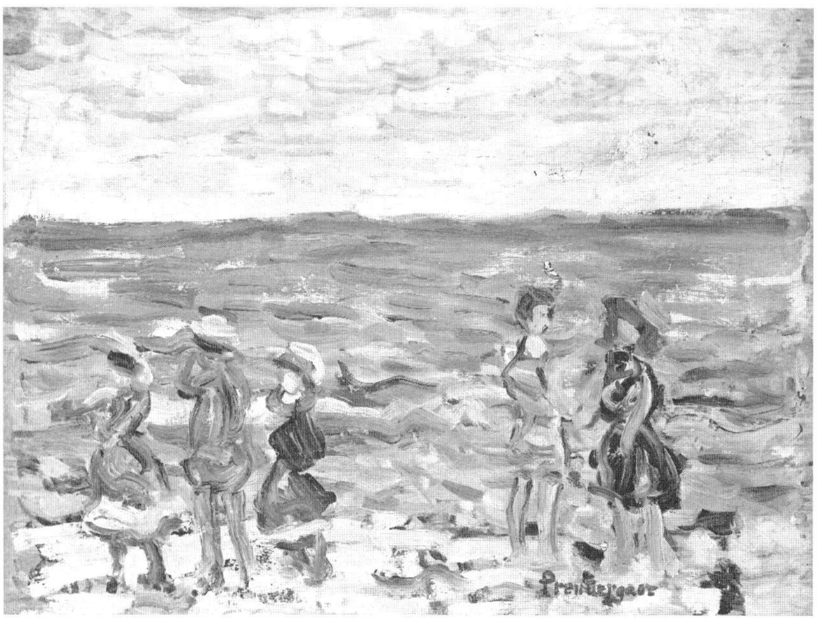

CR 204

CR 204
ON THE BEACH ca. 1907–10
Oil on panel
(10¼ x 13¾ in.; 26.0 x 34.9 cm)
Williams College Museum of Art, gift of Mrs. Charles Prendergast (84.16.17)

INSCRIPTIONS
l.r. in brown: Prendergast

EXHIBITIONS
1989c Williams College (no #); 1989d Williams College (no #); 1990b Williams College (no #)

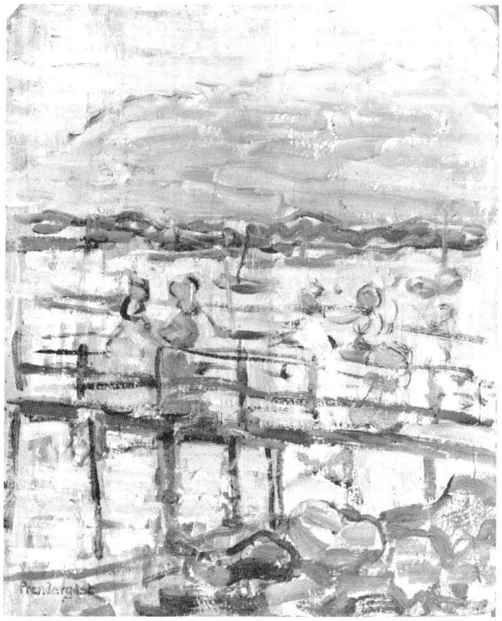

CR 205

CR 205
WINTER SCENE ca. 1907–10
Oil on board
(13⅝ x 10⅝ in.; 34.6 x 27.0 cm)
Williams College Museum of Art, gift of
Mrs. Charles Prendergast (84.16.12)

Inscriptions
l.l. in brown: Prendergast

Exhibitions
1990b Williams College (no #); 1991b
Williams College (no #)

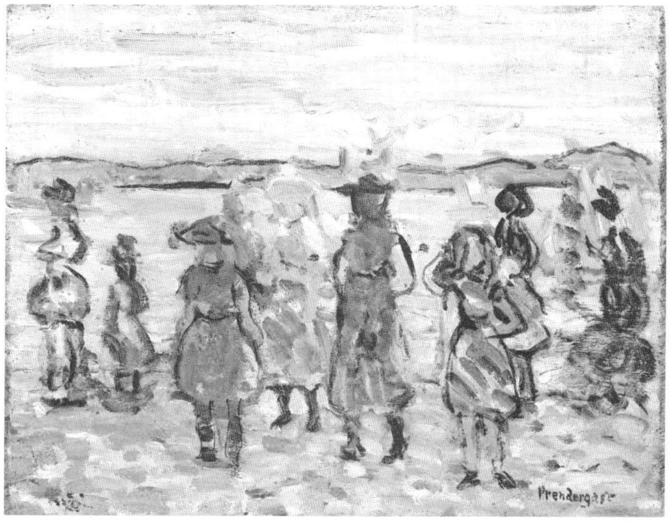

CR 215

CR 215
MEETING ON THE BEACH ca. 1907–10
Oil on panel
(10⅝ x 13¾ in.; 27.0 x 34.9 cm)
Williams College Museum of Art, gift of
Mrs. Charles Prendergast (84.16.15)

Inscriptions
l.r. in brown: Prendergast

Exhibitions
1989d Williams College (no #); 1990b
Williams College (no #)

CR 222
FIVE FIGURES IN A PARK ca. 1907–10
Oil on panel
(10⅝ x 13½ in.; 27.0 x 34.3 cm)
Williams College Museum of Art, gift of
Mrs. Charles Prendergast (84.16.10)

Inscriptions
l.r. in red: Prendergast

Exhibitions
1989c Williams College (no #); 1990b Williams
College (no #); 1990f Williams College (no #);
1992 Williams College (no #)

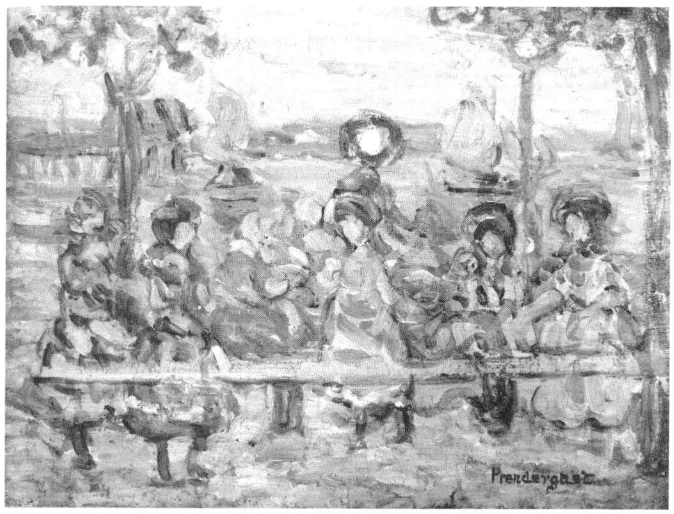

CR 232

CR 232
PARK SCENE ca. 1907–10
Oil on panel
(9⅝ x 12¾ in.; 24.4 x 32.4 cm)
Williams College Museum of Art, gift of
Mrs. Charles Prendergast (84.16.16)

Inscriptions
l.r. in brown: Prendergast

Exhibitions
1989c Williams College (no #); 1990b Williams
College (no #)

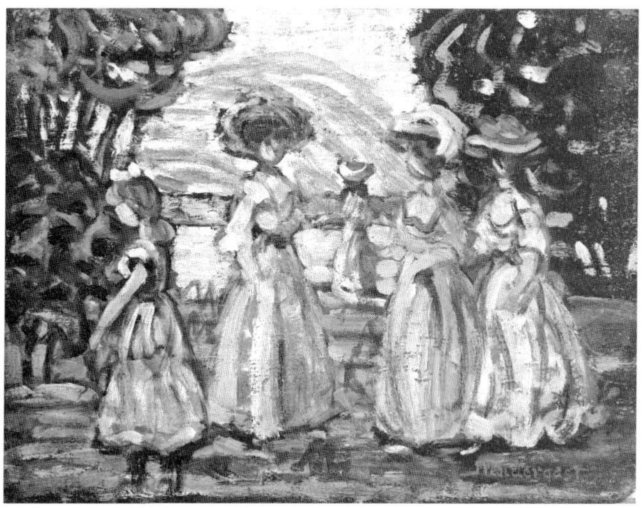

CR 222

CR 238
LAKE IN MAINE ca. 1910–13
Oil on canvas
(18¾ x 22½ in.; 47.6 x 57.1 cm)
Williams College Museum of Art,
bequest of Mrs. Charles Prendergast
(95.4.14)

Inscriptions
l.l. in brown: Prendergast

Exhibitions
1995b Williams College (no #)

CR 241
ALONG THE SHORE ROAD ca. 1910–13
Oil on canvas
(15¾ x 19¾ in.; 40.0 x 50.2 cm)
Williams College Museum of Art,
bequest of Mrs. Charles Prendergast
(95.4.9)

Inscriptions
l.l. in brown: Prendergast

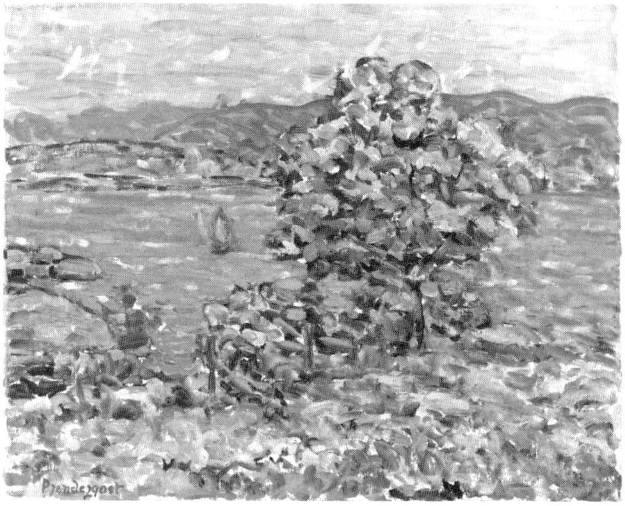
CR 238

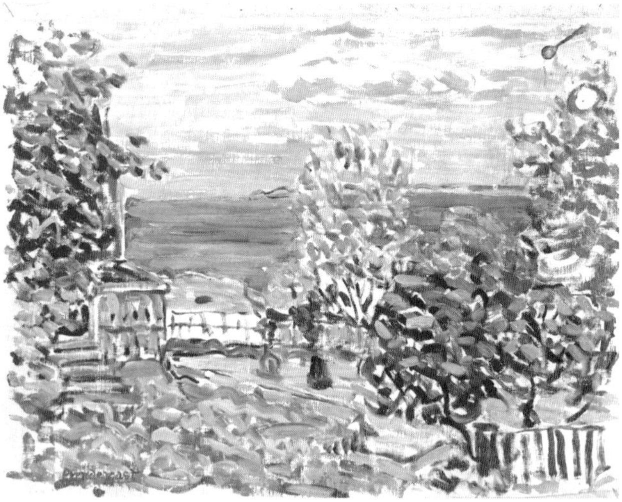
CR 241

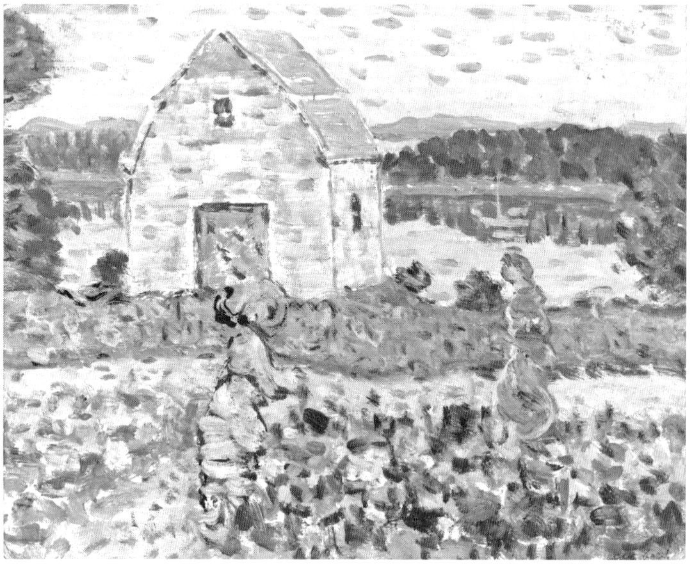
CR 243

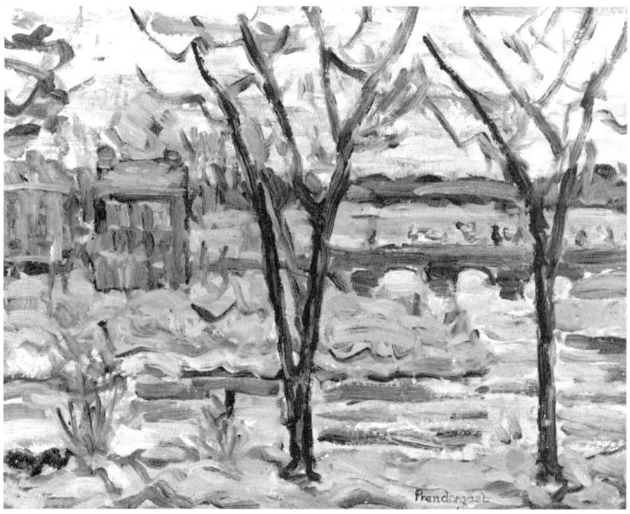
CR 243 verso

CR 243
MAINE BARN ca. 1910–13
Oil on panel
(11 x 14 in.; 28.0 x 35.6 cm)
Williams College Museum of Art, gift of
Mrs. Charles Prendergast (84.16.2)

Inscriptions
Unsigned

Exhibitions
1990b Williams College (no #) verso; 1990f
Williams College (no #); 1991b Williams
College (no #)

CR 243 verso
AUTUMN SCENE BY STREAM
Oil

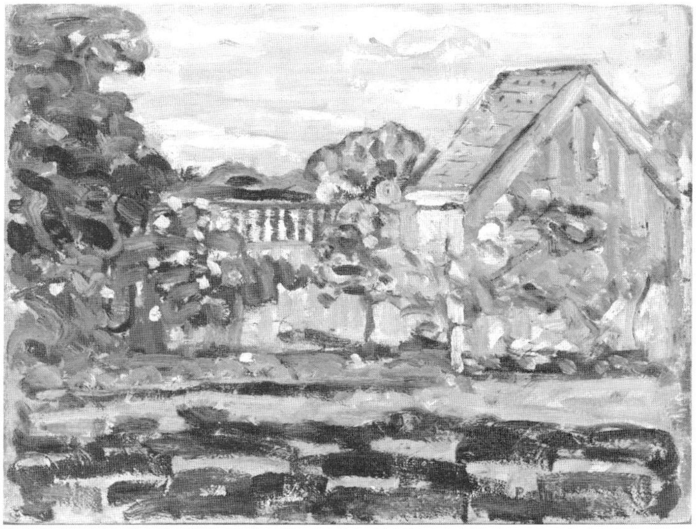

CR 249

CR 249
MAINE ca. 1910–13
Oil on panel
(10⅜ x 13⅞ in.; 26.4 x 35.2 cm)
Williams College Museum of Art, gift of Mrs. Charles Prendergast (84.16.1)

INSCRIPTIONS
l.r. in red: Prendergast

EXHIBITIONS
1990b Williams College (no #); 1990f Williams College (no #); 1991b Williams College (no #)

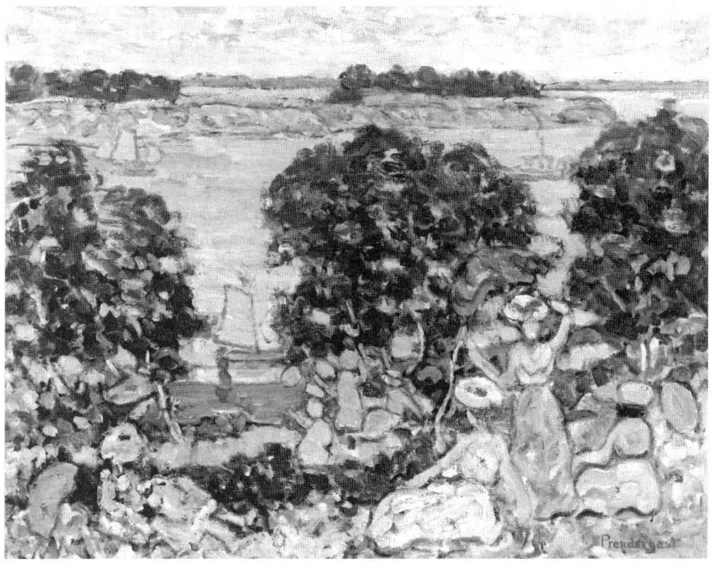

CR 262

CR 262
NEPONSET BAY ca. 1910–13
Oil on canvas
(21¼ x 27¼ in.; 54.0 x 69.2 cm)
Williams College Museum of Art, bequest of Mrs. Charles Prendergast (95.4.83)

INSCRIPTIONS
l.r. in mauve: Prendergast

EXHIBITIONS
1950 Des Moines (no #)

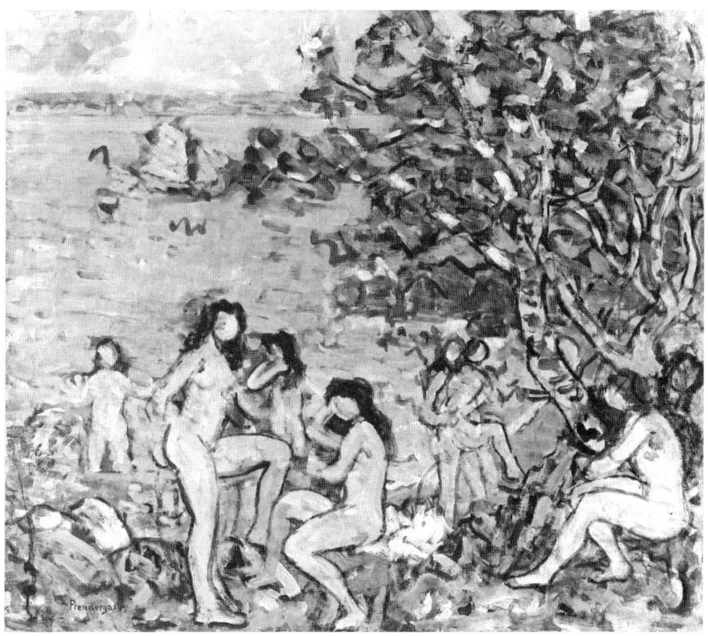

CR 281

CR 281
BATHERS BY THE SEA ca. 1910–13
Oil on canvas
(31 x 35⅛ in.; 78.7 x 89.2 cm)
Williams College Museum of Art, gift of Mrs. Charles Prendergast (83.20.1)

INSCRIPTIONS
l.l. in brown: Prendergast

BIBLIOGRAPHY
Spencer 1985 (p. 30); Lauzon 1989 (pp. E: 1, 4)

EXHIBITIONS
1983a Williams College (no #); 1985b Williams College (no #); 1986 High Museum (no #, p. 147, ill.); 1989b Williams College (#11); 1989c Williams College (no #); 1990a Williams College (no #); 1990f Williams College (no #); 1991a Williams College (no #); 1991b Williams College (no #); 1992 Williams College (no #); 1993 Williams College (no #)
Color plate, p. 39

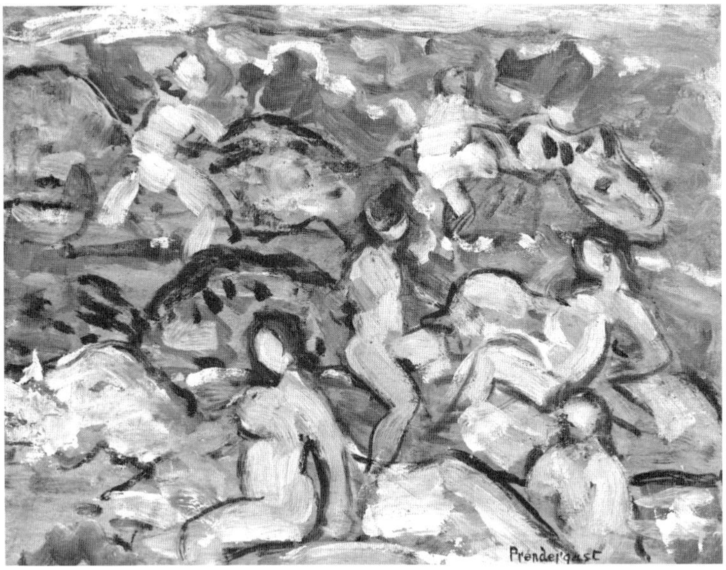

CR 282

CR 282

BATHERS AND ROCKS ca. 1910–13
Oil on panel
(10½ x 13¾ in.; 26.7 x 34.9 cm)
Williams College Museum of Art, bequest of Mrs. Charles Prendergast (95.4.87)

INSCRIPTIONS
l.r. in black: Prendergast

CR 284

FOUR NUDES AT THE SEASHORE
ca. 1910–13
Oil on panel
(10½ x 13¾ in.; 26.7 x 34.9 cm)
Williams College Museum of Art, gift of Mrs. Charles Prendergast (84.16.9)

INSCRIPTIONS
Unsigned

BIBLIOGRAPHY
Mathews 1990 (p. 32; ill.); Wattenmaker 1994 (p. 123; ill.)

EXHIBITIONS
1989c Williams College (no #); 1989d Williams College (no #); 1990c Williams College (Fig. 26.); 1990f Williams College (no #); 1991b Williams College (no #); 1992 Williams College (no #); 1993 Williams College (no #)

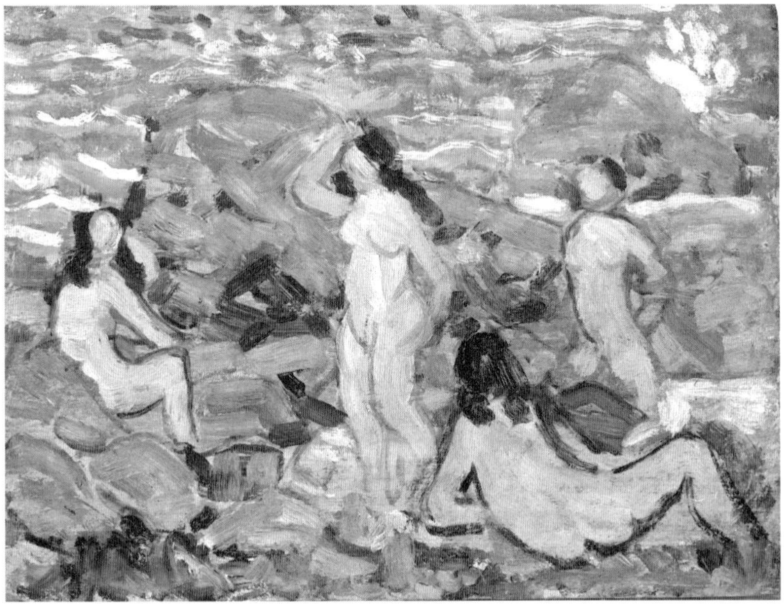

CR 284

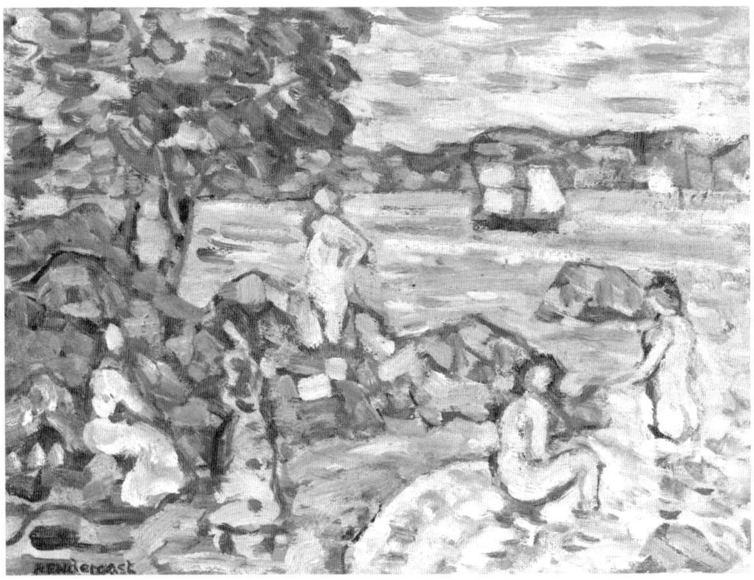

CR 285

CR 285

BATHING ca. 1910–13
Oil on panel
(10 x 13⅜ in.; 25.4 x 34.4 cm)
Williams College Museum of Art, bequest of Mrs. Charles Prendergast (95.4.113)

INSCRIPTIONS
l.l.: Prendergast

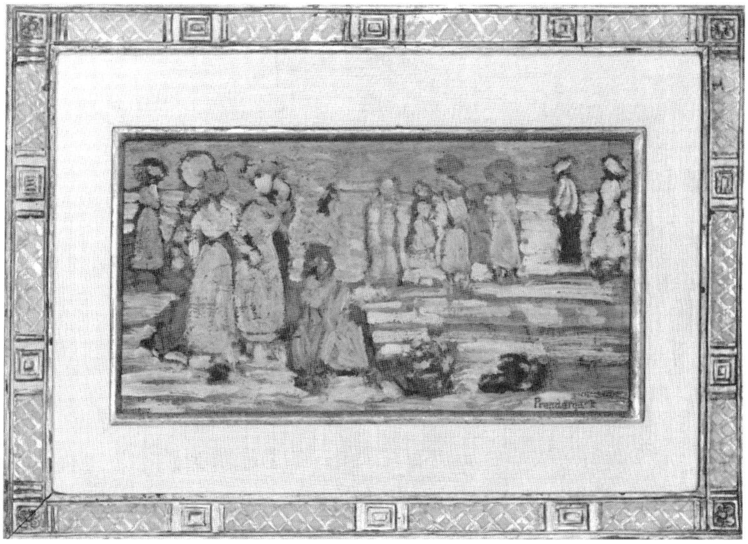

CR 293

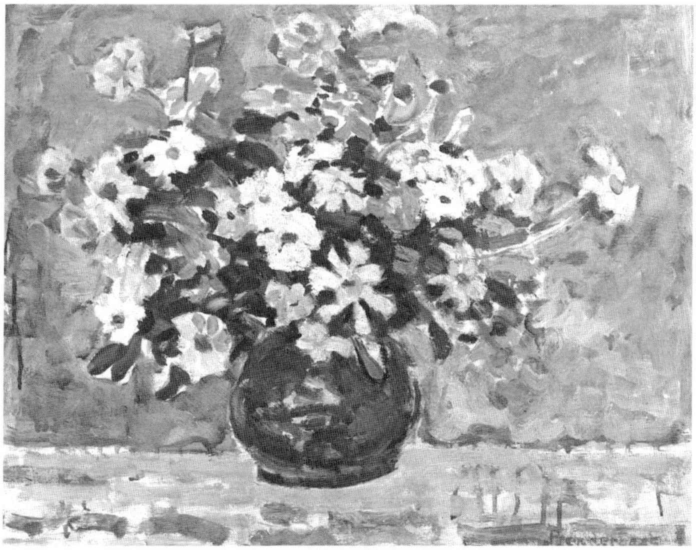

CR 319

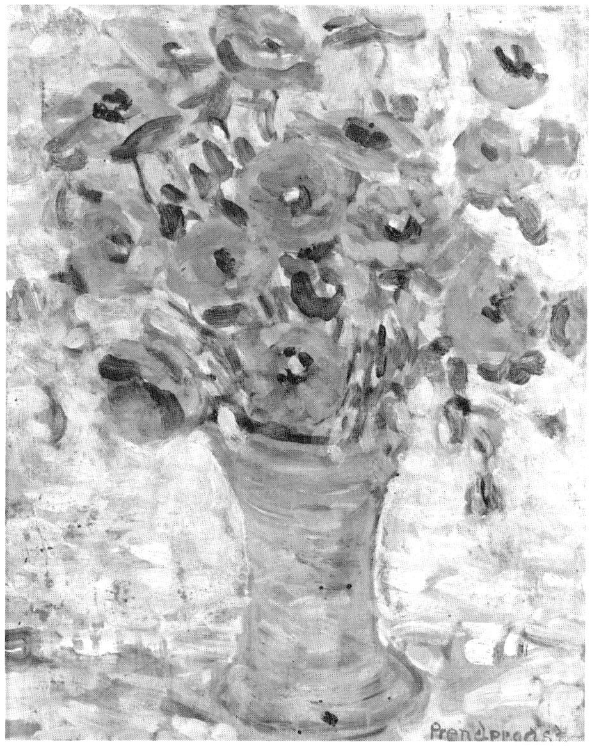

CR 321

CR 293

GREEN SHORE ca. 1910–13
Frame by Charles Prendergast
Oil on panel
(9 x 16½ in.; 22.9 x 41.9 cm)
Williams College Museum of Art, gift of
Mrs. Charles Prendergast (86.18.82)

INSCRIPTIONS
l.r. in brown: Prendergast

BIBLIOGRAPHY
Lauzon 1989 (pp. E: 1, 4; as *Green Shores*)

EXHIBITIONS
1960 Boston MFA (#18, ill.); 1986 Williams College (no #); 1988a Williams College (no #); 1988b Williams College (frame for *Green Shore* by Charles Prendergast, #79); 1989b Williams College (no #); 1989d Williams College (no #); 1990b Williams College (no #); 1991a Williams College (#2); 1991b Williams College (no #)

CR 319

FLOWERS ca. 1910–13
Oil on panel
(14 x 18 in.; 35.6 x 45.7 cm)
Williams College Museum of Art, gift of
Mrs. Charles Prendergast (91.18.14)

INSCRIPTIONS
l.r. in brown: Prendergast

EXHIBITIONS
1990f Williams College (no #); 1991a Williams College (no #); 1991b Williams College (no #); 1993 Williams College (no #)

CR 321

POPPIES IN A BLUE VASE ca. 1910–13
Oil on panel
(13⅝ x 10¼ in.; 34.6 x 26.0 cm)
Williams College Museum of Art, gift of
Mrs. Charles Prendergast (86.18.64)

INSCRIPTIONS
l.r. in red: Prendergast

EXHIBITIONS
1960 Boston MFA (#32, ill.); 1986 Williams College (no #); 1989b Williams College (#13); 1990f Williams College (no #); 1991a Williams College (no #); 1991b Williams College (no #)

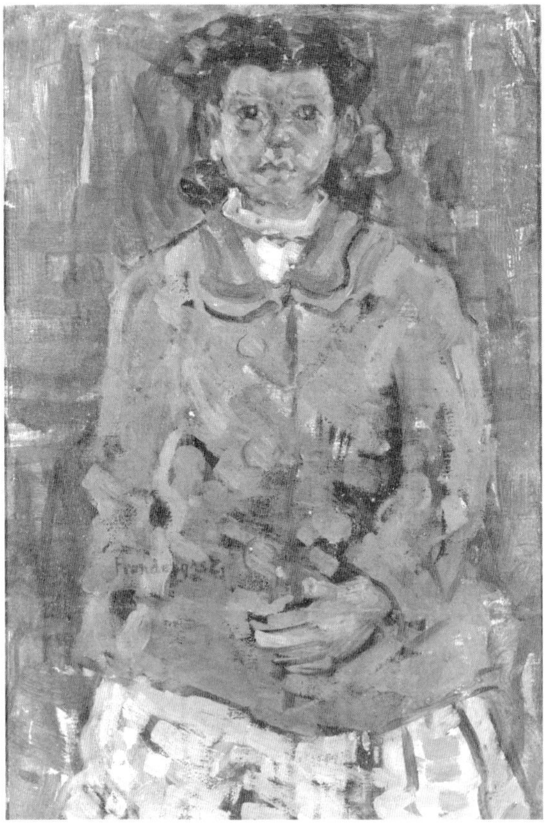

CR 330

CR 330

ITALIAN GIRL ca. 1910–13
Oil on canvas
(19½ x 13¼ in.; 49.5 x 33.7 cm)
Williams College Museum of Art, gift of Mrs. Charles Prendergast (86.18.31)

Inscriptions
left below center in red: Prendergast

Bibliography
Rhys 1960 (p. 48); Genauer 1961b (p. 19; ill.)

Exhibitions
1960 Boston MFA (#23, ill.); 1984b Williams College (#14); 1989c Williams College (no #); 1990f Williams College (no #); 1991a Williams College (no #); 1991b Williams College (no #); 1992 Williams College (no #); 1995b Williams College (no #)

CR 331

TWO GIRLS IN RED—VENICE ca. 1910–13
Oil on canvas
(20¼ x 16½ in.; 51.4 x 41.9 cm)
Williams College Museum of Art, gift of Mrs. Charles Prendergast (86.18.32)

Inscriptions
l.r. in brown: Prendergast

Exhibitions
1984b Williams College (#15); 1990f Williams College (no #); 1991a Williams College (no #); 1991b Williams College (no #)

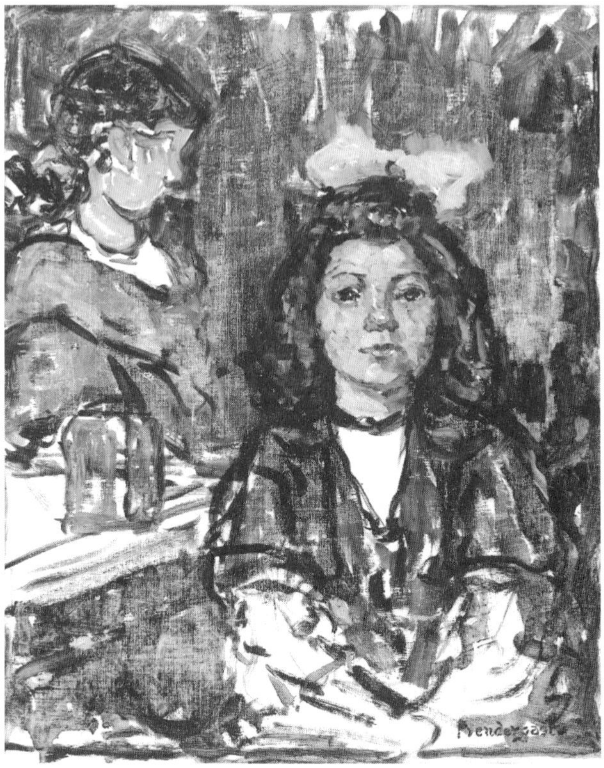

CR 331

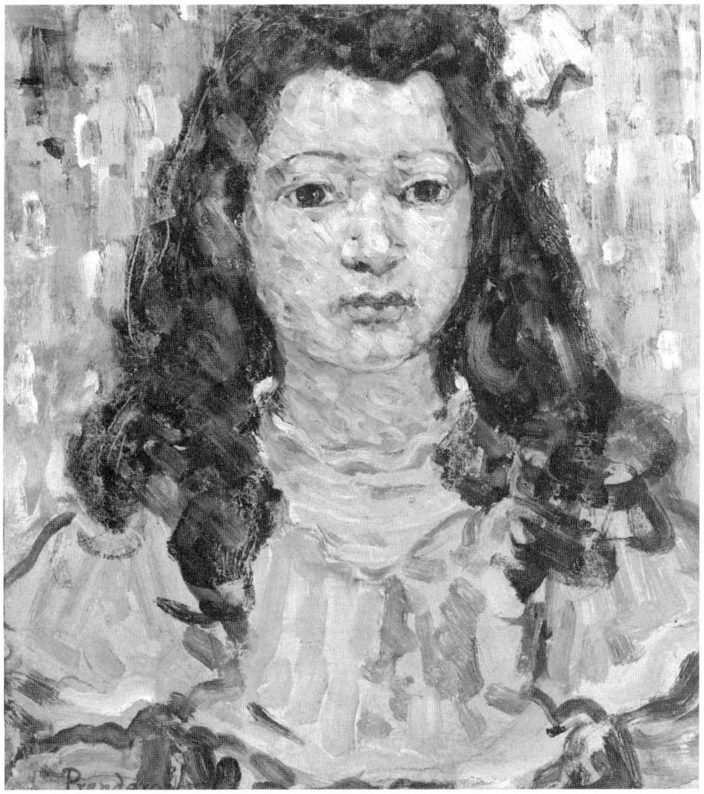

CR 332

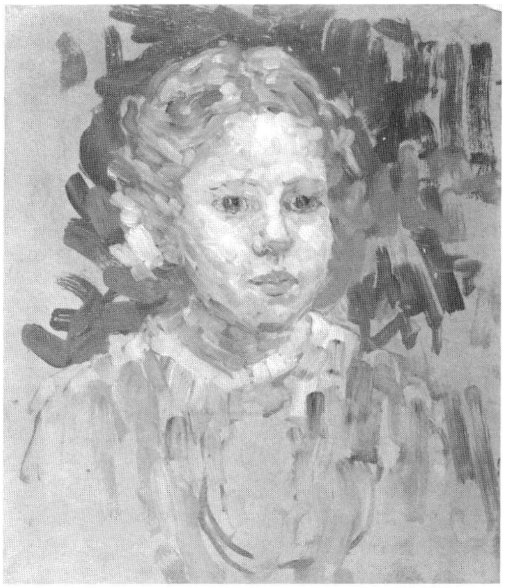

CR 332 verso

CR 332
PORTRAIT OF A YOUNG GIRL ca. 1910–13
Oil on panel
(13½ x 11½ in.; 34.3 x 29.2 cm)
Williams College Museum of Art, gift of Mrs. Charles Prendergast (86.18.30)

INSCRIPTIONS
l.l. in brown: Prendergast

BIBLIOGRAPHY
Sawyer 1966 (n.p.)

EXHIBITIONS
1966a Knoedler (#33, ill.); 1984b Williams College (no #); 1989c Williams College (no #); 1990f Williams College (no #); 1991a Williams College (no #); 1991b Williams College (no #); 1992 Williams College (no #)

CR 332 verso
PORTRAIT OF A BLONDE GIRL
Oil
Cf. related study in sketchbook CR 1507.

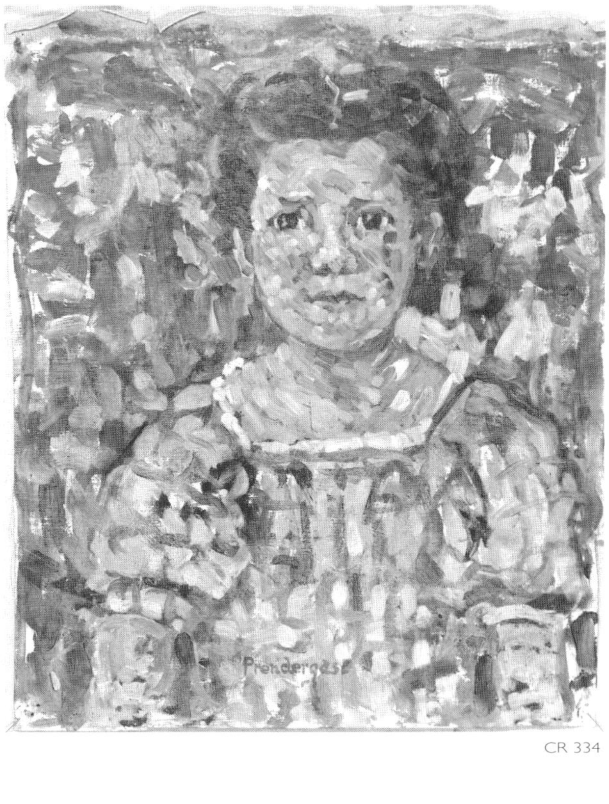

CR 334

CR 334
PORTRAIT OF AN ITALIAN GIRL ca. 1910–13
Oil on canvas
(16 x 12⅞ in.; 40.6 x 32.7 cm)
Williams College Museum of Art, bequest of Mrs. Charles Prendergast (95.4.11)

INSCRIPTIONS
l.c. in red: Prendergast

BIBLIOGRAPHY
Soria 1982 (p. 255)

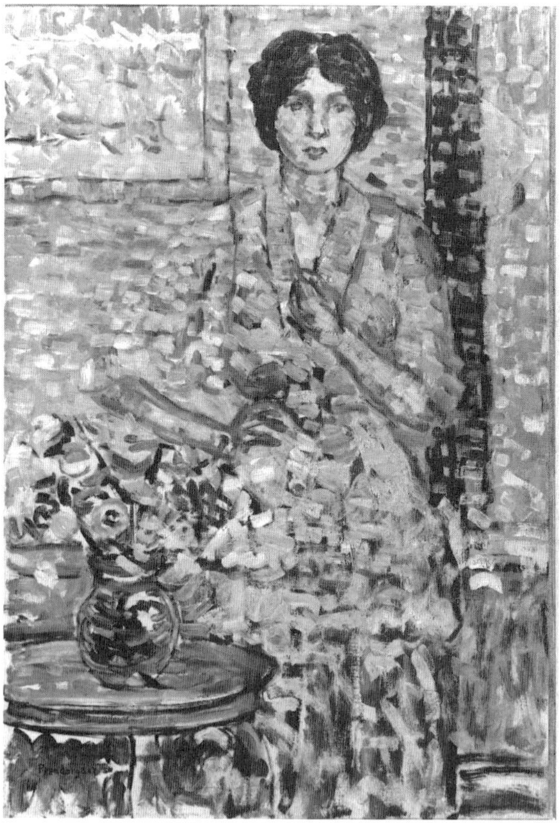

CR 343

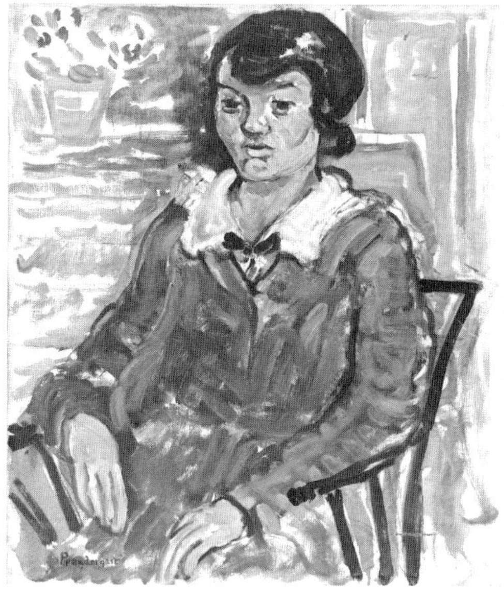

CR 346

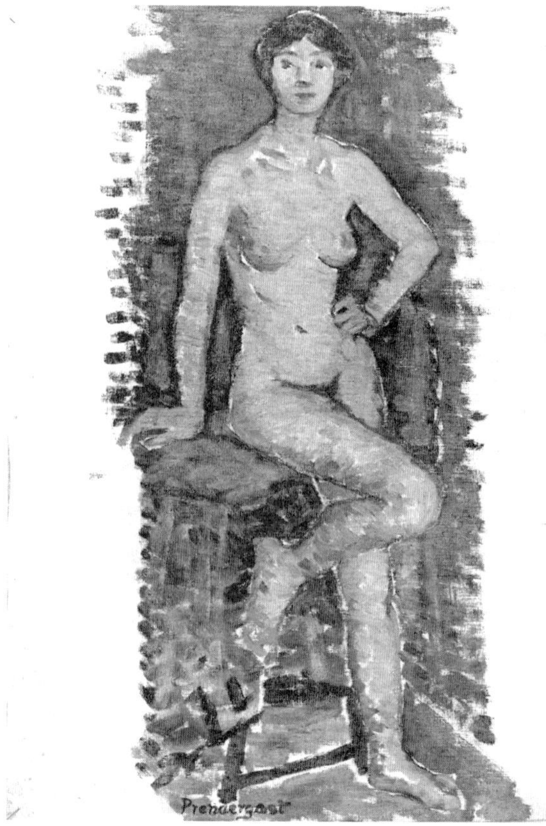

CR 348

CR 343
WOMAN IN GREEN DRESS ca. 1910–13
Portrait of a Girl in Green
Oil on canvas
(35½ x 24 in.; 90.2 x 61.0 cm)
Williams College Museum of Art, gift of Mrs. Charles Prendergast (86.18.4)

INSCRIPTIONS
l.l. in brown: Prendergast

BIBLIOGRAPHY
Porter 1966 (p. 38; ill.); Sawyer 1966 (n.p.); Green 1977 (p. 95; ill.); Sims 1979 (p. 25)

EXHIBITIONS
1966a Knoedler (#25, ill.); 1976 U Maryland (#47, ill.); 1977a Davis & Long (#47); 1983a Williams College (#14, ill.); 1984b Williams College (#16); 1986 Williams College (no #); 1989c Williams College (no #); 1990f Williams College (no #); 1991a Williams College (no #); 1991b Williams College (no #); 1993 Williams College (no #); 1994a Williams College (no #); 1995b Williams College (no #)

CR 346
PORTRAIT OF A WOMAN IN A GREEN JACKET ca. 1910–13
Oil on canvas
(25⅝ x 21¼ in.; 65.1 x 54.0 cm)
Williams College Museum of Art, bequest of Mrs. Charles Prendergast (95.4.15)

INSCRIPTIONS
l.l. in brown: Prendergast

EXHIBITIONS
1995b Williams College (no #)

CR 348
STANDING NUDE MODEL WITH BLUE CLOTH ca. 1910–13
Oil on canvas
(31¼ x 16 in.; 79.4 x 40.6 cm)
Williams College Museum of Art, bequest of Mrs. Charles Prendergast (95.4.10)

INSCRIPTIONS
l.l. in brown: Prendergast

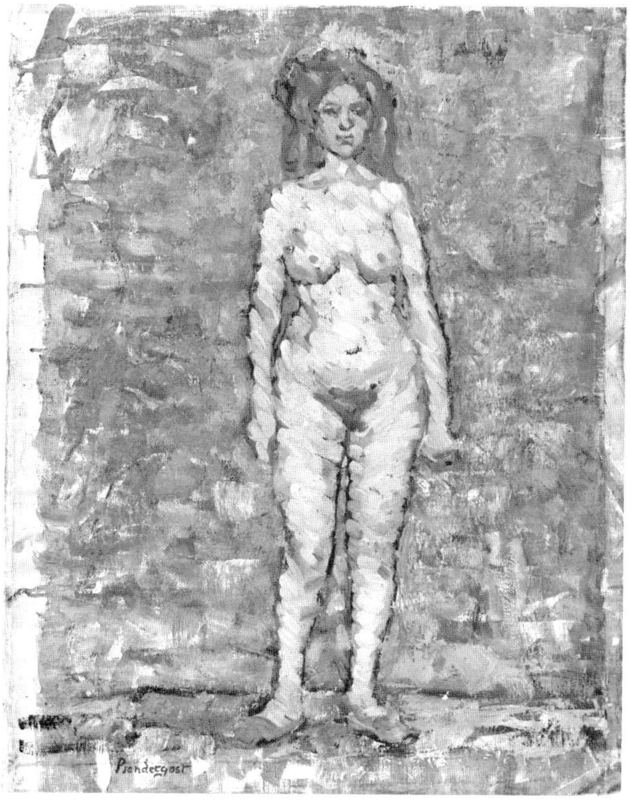

CR 349

CR 349
STANDING NUDE ca. 1910–13
Oil on canvas
(26⅜ x 20⅜ in.; 67.0 x 51.8 cm)
Williams College Museum of Art, bequest of Mrs. Charles Prendergast (95.4.16)

INSCRIPTIONS
l.l. in brown: Prendergast

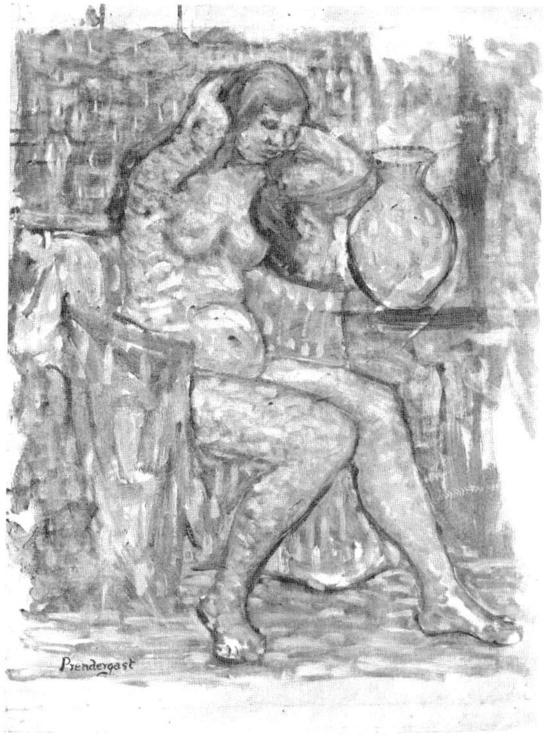

CR 351

CR 351
SEATED NUDE ARRANGING HER HAIR
ca. 1910–13
Oil on canvas
(26½ x 18¾ in.; 67.3 x 47.6 cm)
Williams College Museum of Art, gift of Mrs. Charles Prendergast (86.18.83)

INSCRIPTIONS
l.l. in black: Prendergast

EXHIBITIONS
1989c Williams College (no #); 1991b Williams College (no #); 1992 Williams College (no #)

CR 366
BATHERS IN A COVE ca. 1910–13
Oil on canvas
(15¼ x 22½ in.; 38.7 x 57.1 cm)
Williams College Museum of Art, gift of Mrs. Charles Prendergast (86.18.8)

INSCRIPTIONS
l.r. in black: Prendergast

BIBLIOGRAPHY
Lauzon 1989 (pp. E: 1, 4); Tampa Museum 1989 (pp. 10, 124; ill. p. 91)

EXHIBITIONS
1983a Williams College (#21, ill.); 1985b Williams College (no #); 1986 Williams College (no #); 1989 Tampa Museum (no #; ill. p. 91); 1989c Williams College (no #); 1989d Williams College (no #); 1990f Williams College (no #); 1991a Williams College (no #); 1991b Williams College (no #)

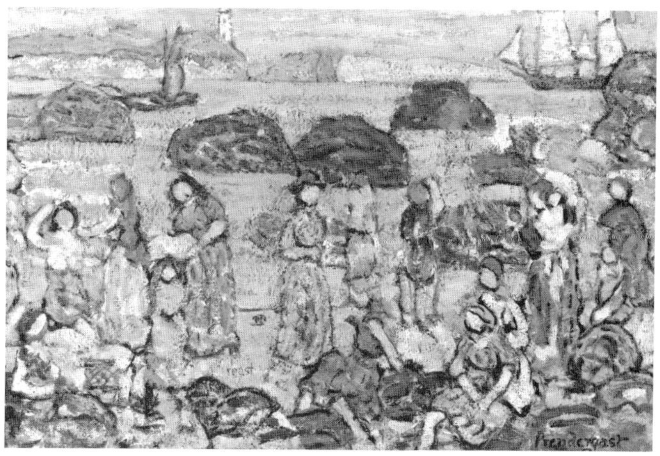

CR 366

CR 366a
BEACH SCENE, MAINE ca. 1910–13
Oil on canvas
(30½ x 34 in.; 77.5 x 87.6 cm)
Williams College Museum of Art, gift of
Mrs. Charles Prendergast (86.18.51)

INSCRIPTIONS
l.r. in red: Prendergast

EXHIBITIONS
1986 Williams College (no #); 1988a Williams College (no #); 1989c Williams College (no #); 1989d Williams College (no #); 1990f Williams College (no #); 1991a Williams College (no #); 1991b Williams College (no #); 1993 Williams College (no #); 1995b Williams College (no #)
Color plate, p. 55

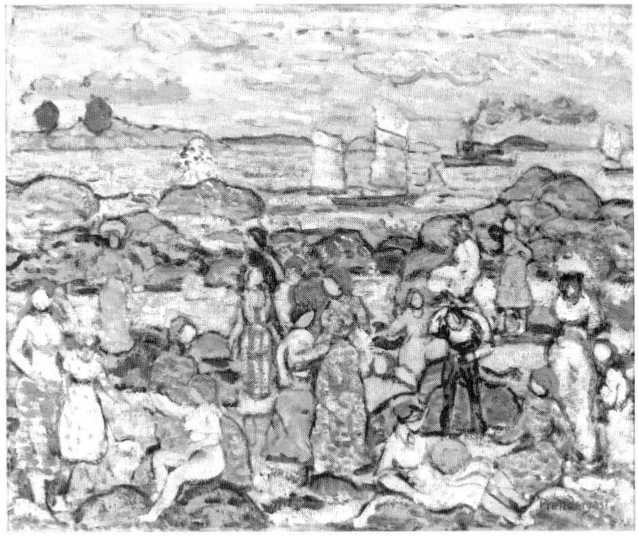
CR 366a

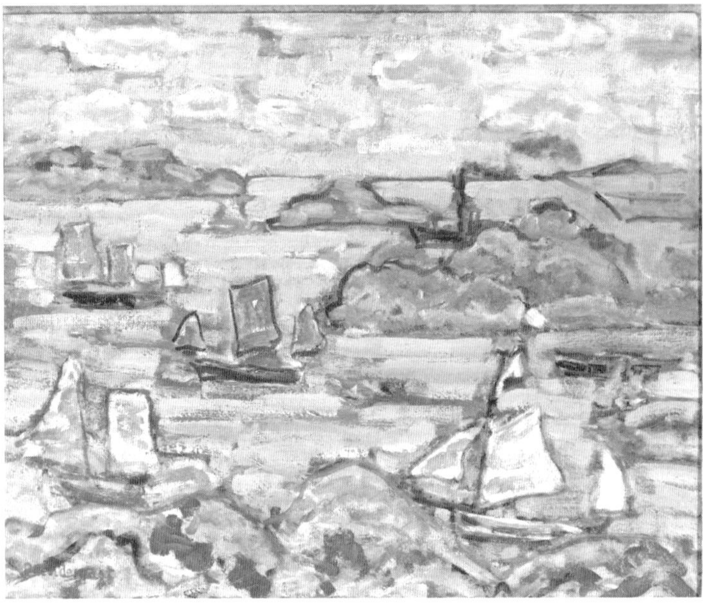
CR 369

CR 369
SAILBOATS, ST. MALO ca. 1910–13
Harbor Scene; St. Malo Rocks and Boats
Oil on canvas
(18½ x 21½ in.; 47.0 x 54.6 cm)
Williams College Museum of Art, gift of
Mrs. Charles Prendergast (86.18.62)

INSCRIPTIONS
l.l. in brown: Prendergast

BIBLIOGRAPHY
Lauzon 1989 (pp. E: 1, 4)

EXHIBITIONS
1986 Williams College (no #); 1989b Williams College (#15); 1990b Williams College (no #); 1990d Williams College (no #); 1990f Williams College (no #); 1991a Williams College (no #); 1991b Williams College (no #)

NOTE
Although "St. Malo" appears in the title of this work, it is unlikely that it was painted there, or that it depicts that site.

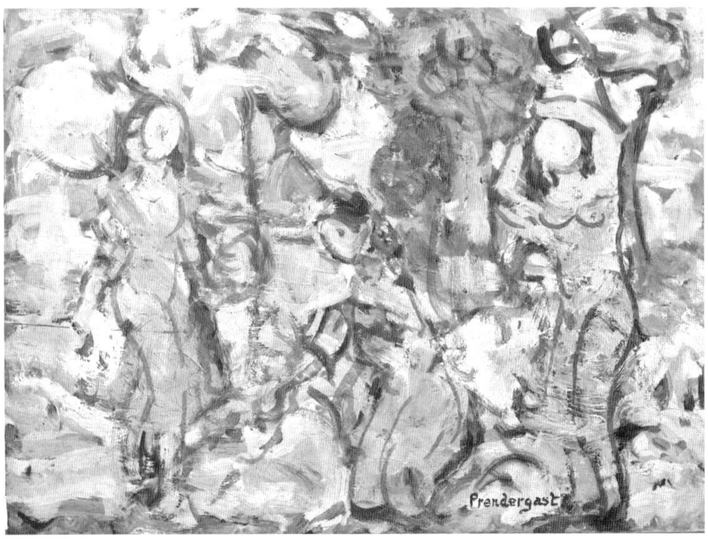

CR 370

CR 370
THREE FIGURES ca. 1914–15
Oil on panel
(10¼ x 13¾ in.; 26.0 x 34.9 cm)
Williams College Museum of Art, gift of
Mrs. Charles Prendergast (84.16.11)

INSCRIPTIONS
l.r. in brown: Prendergast

EXHIBITIONS
1989c Williams College (no #); 1991b Williams College (no #)

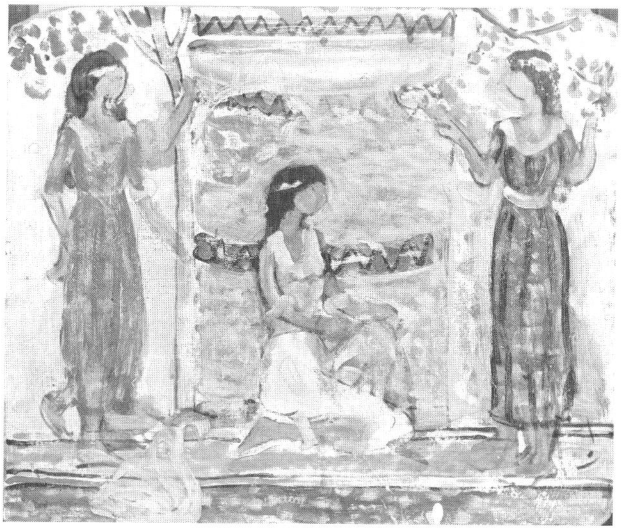

CR 371

CR 371
EXOTIC SCENE ca. 1914–15
Oil on board
(18¼ x 21¼ in.; 46.0 x 54.0 cm)
Williams College Museum of Art, bequest of Mrs. Charles Prendergast (95.4.19)

INSCRIPTIONS
Unsigned

CR 376
RIDER AGAINST BLUE HILLS ca. 1914–15
Rider Against Blue Hills II
Oil on canvas
(20 x 30¼ in.; 50.8 x 76.8 cm)
Williams College Museum of Art, gift of Mrs. Charles Prendergast (86.18.10)

INSCRIPTIONS
l.l. in brown: Prendergast

BIBLIOGRAPHY
Wattenmaker 1990 (p. 38)

EXHIBITIONS
1983a Williams College (#26, ill.); 1985b Williams College (no #); 1986 Williams College (no #); 1989b Williams College (#19); 1989c Williams College (no #); 1990c Williams College (#94, ABCD); 1991a Williams College (no #); 1991b Williams College (no #); 1992 Williams College (no #); 1993 Williams College (no #); 1994a Williams College (no #)

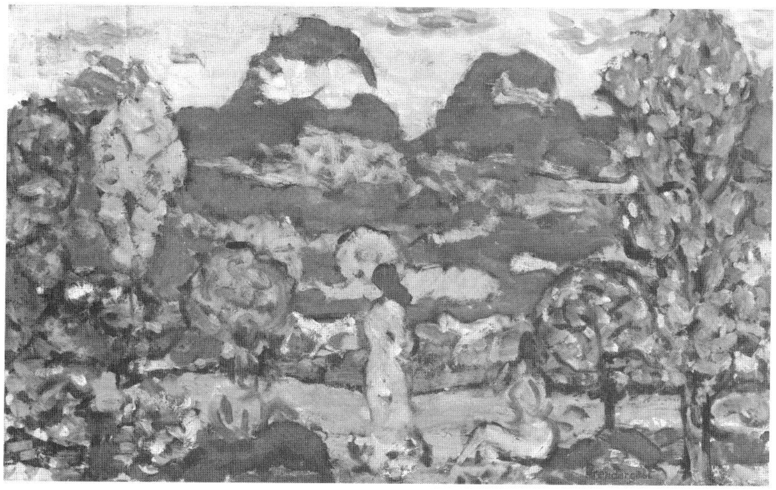

CR 377

CR 377
BLUE MOUNTAINS ca. 1914–15
Frame by Charles Prendergast
Oil on canvas
(16¼ x 25⅝ in.; 41.3 x 65.1 cm)
Williams College Museum of Art, gift of Mrs. Charles Prendergast (91.18.2)

INSCRIPTIONS
l.r. in red: Prendergast

BIBLIOGRAPHY
Mathews 1990 (p. 138; ill.); Wattenmaker 1990 (p. 38)

EXHIBITIONS
1990c Williams College (#93, ABCD); 1991b Williams College (no #); 1993 Williams College (no #); 1994a Williams College (no #); 1995b Williams College (no #)

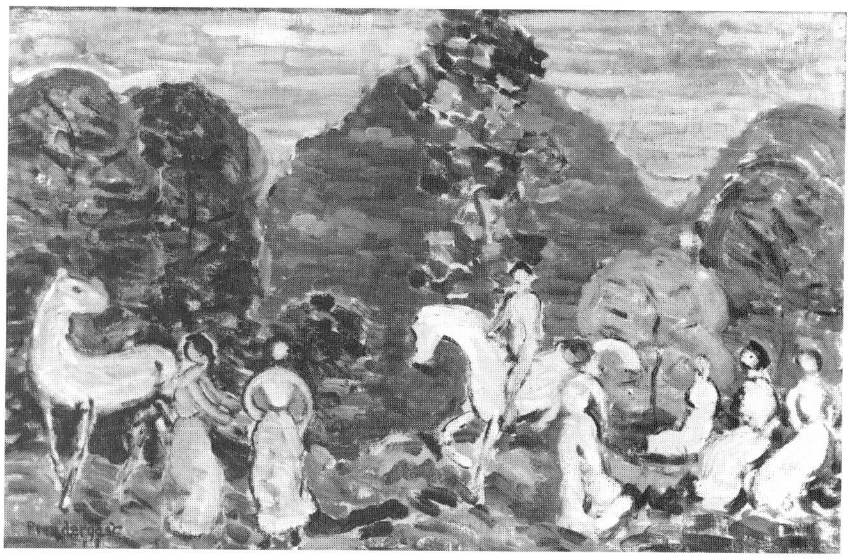

CR 376

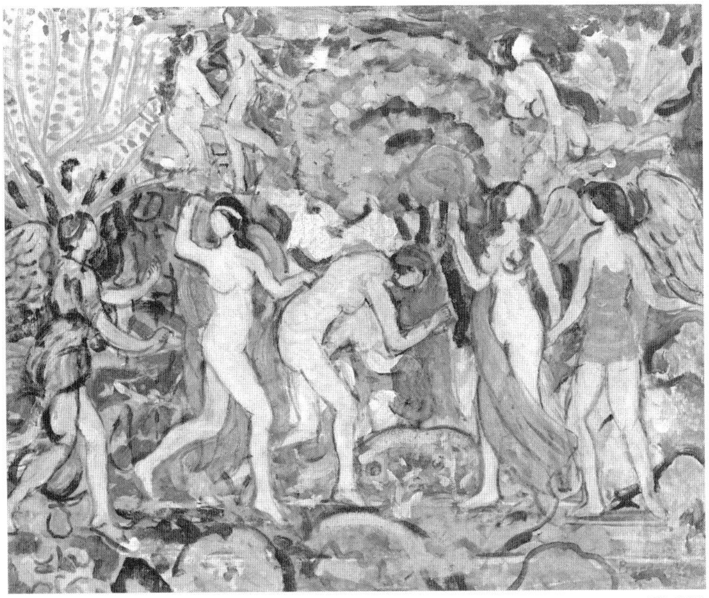

CR 385

CR 394

ST. MALO ca. 1907–10; REPAINTED ca. 1914–15
Oil on canvas
(20¼ x 24 in.; 51.4 x 61.0 cm)
Williams College Museum of Art, gift of Mrs. Charles Prendergast (86.18.36)

INSCRIPTIONS
l.r. in black ink (partially covered by green paint): Prendergast

BIBLIOGRAPHY
Lauzon 1989 (pp. E: 1, 4)

EXHIBITIONS
1986 Williams College (no #); 1989b Williams College (#12); 1989d Williams College (no #); 1990b Williams College (no #); 1990f Williams College (no #); 1992 Williams College (no #); 1993 Williams College (no #)

NOTE
This work appears to have the compositional elements of Prendergast's style around 1907–10, but the "mosiac-like" brushstrokes throughout suggest that it was repainted ca. 1914–15.

CR 385

FANTASY ca. 1914–15
Oil on panel
(22 x 26 in.; 55.8 x 66.0 cm)
Williams College Museum of Art, gift of Mrs. Charles Prendergast (85.45)

INSCRIPTIONS
l.r. in red: Prendergast

BIBLIOGRAPHY
Nemser 1966 (p. 65; ill.); Sawyer 1966 (n.p.); Spencer 1985 (p. 24); *New England Monthly* 1986 (p. 96); Isaacs 1990; Mathews 1990 (p. 137; ill.); Perlman 1990; Wattenmaker 1990 (p. 38)

EXHIBITIONS
1966a Knoedler (#43, ill.); 1982 Smithsonian SITES (#48, ill.); 1983c Williams College (#13, ill.); 1985b Williams College (no #); 1986 Williams College (no #); 1988a Williams College (no #); 1989b Williams College (#10); 1989c Williams College (no #); 1990c Williams College (#92, ABCD); 1991b Williams College (no #); 1992 Williams College (no #); 1993 Williams College (no #); 1995a Williams College (no #)

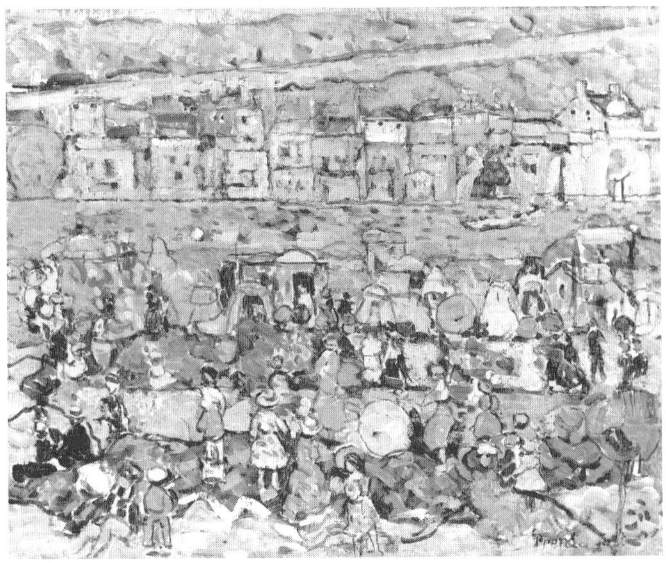

CR 394

CR 393

ST. SERVAN ca. 1914–15
La Tour Solidor
Oil on canvas
(17¼ x 23⅜ in.; 43.8 x 59.4 cm)
Williams College Museum of Art, bequest of Mrs. Charles Prendergast (95.4.71)

INSCRIPTIONS
l.r. in red: Prendergast

EXHIBITIONS
? 1940 Kraushaar (#14); 1977d Whitney (no #); 1983a Williams College (#6, ill.); 1995d Williams College (no #)

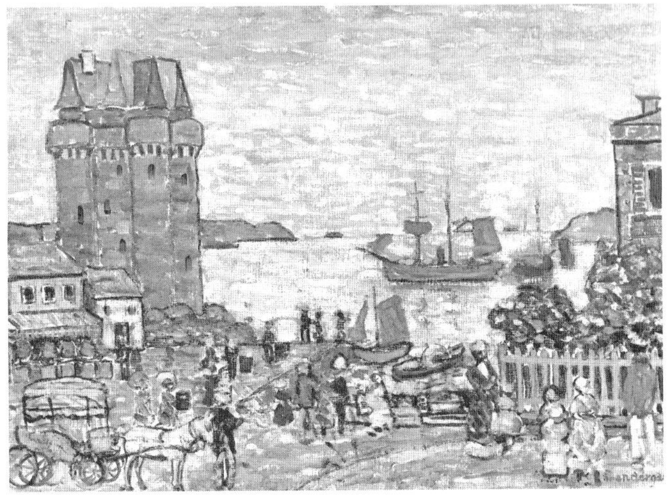

CR 393

CR 395
SUMMER HOTEL, MAINE ca. 1914–15
Passamaquoddy House
Oil on panel
(14 x 18½ in.; 35.6 x 47.0 cm)
Williams College Museum of Art, gift of Mrs. Charles Prendergast (86.18.65)

INSCRIPTIONS
l.l. in red: Prendergast

BIBLIOGRAPHY
Art Journal 1964b (p. 48; ill.); Huntington 1964 (p. 11; ill.); Bowen 1974 (pp. 104–05; ill., listed as by Charles Prendergast)

EXHIBITIONS
1964a Colby College; 1983a Williams College (#24, ill., as *Passamaquoddy House*); 1986 Williams College (no #); 1989b Williams College (#23); 1991a Williams College (no #); 1991b Williams College (no #); 1993 Williams College (no #); 1994a Williams College (no #)
Color plate, p. 40

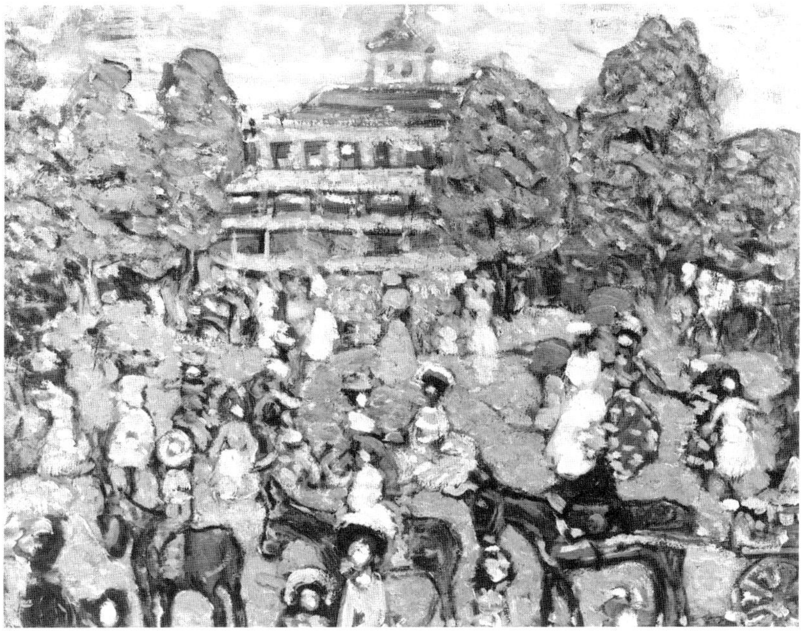

CR 395

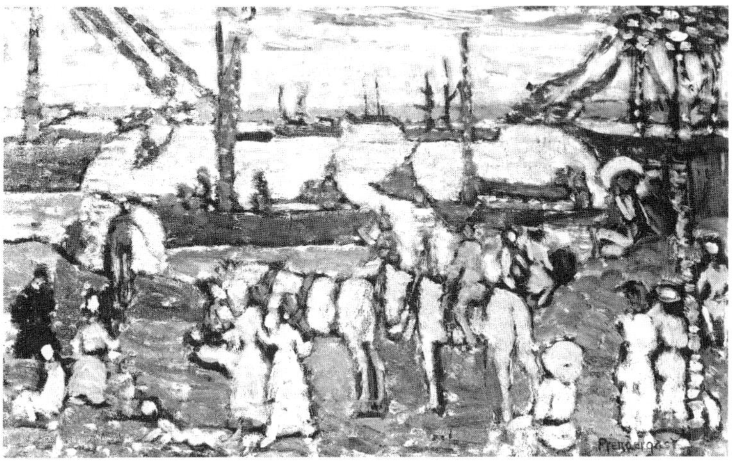

CR 397

CR 397
SUNSET, BOSTON HARBOR ca. 1914–15
Oil on panel
(13⅝ x 21⅝ in.; 34.6 x 54.9 cm)
Williams College Museum of Art, bequest of Mrs. Charles Prendergast (95.4.68)

INSCRIPTIONS
l.r. in brown: Prendergast

BIBLIOGRAPHY
Sawyer 1966 (n.p.)

EXHIBITIONS
1966a Knoedler (#42, ill.); 1995b Williams College (no #)

CR 398
GIRLS IN THE PARK ca. 1914–15
Oil on canvas
(28¼ x 39¾ in.; 71.8 x 101.0 cm)
Williams College Museum of Art, gift of Mrs. Charles Prendergast (86.18.7)

INSCRIPTIONS
l.l. in brown: Prendergast

BIBLIOGRAPHY
Ledes 1990 (p. 1272; ill.); Lingemann 1990 (pp. 116–17; ill.; as *Madchen in Park*); Mathews 1990 (p. 153; ill.); Mathews 1990a (ill.); Lewis 1991 (p. G: 1); DeWeese-Wehen 1991 (ill.); *SF Examiner* 1991 (ill.); Wilson, W. 1991 (p. F: 1; ill.)

EXHIBITIONS
1982 Smithsonian SITES (#49, ill.); 1983a Williams College (#20, ill.); 1985b Williams College (no #); 1986 Williams College (no #); 1990c Williams College (#108, ABCD); 1991b Williams College (no #); 1992 Williams College (no #); 1994a Williams College (no #); 1995b Williams College (no #)
Color plate, p. 44

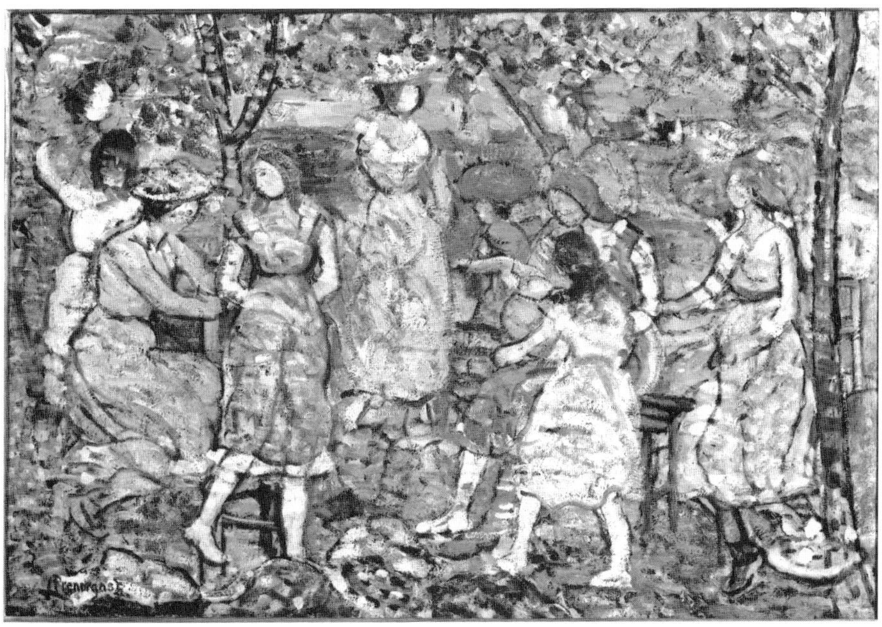

CR 398

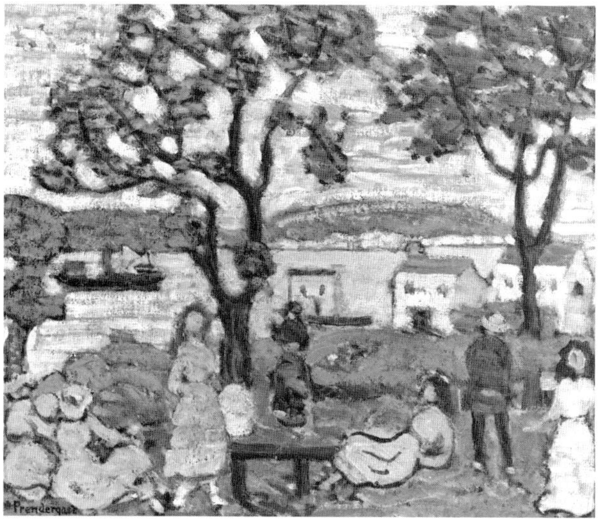

CR 407

CR 407

MAINE WATERWAY ca. 1914–15
Oil on canvas
(18 x 21 in.; 45.7 x 53.3 cm)
Williams College Museum of Art, bequest of Mrs. Charles Prendergast (95.4.112)

INSCRIPTIONS
l.l. in brown: Prendergast

EXHIBITIONS
1994a Williams College (no #)

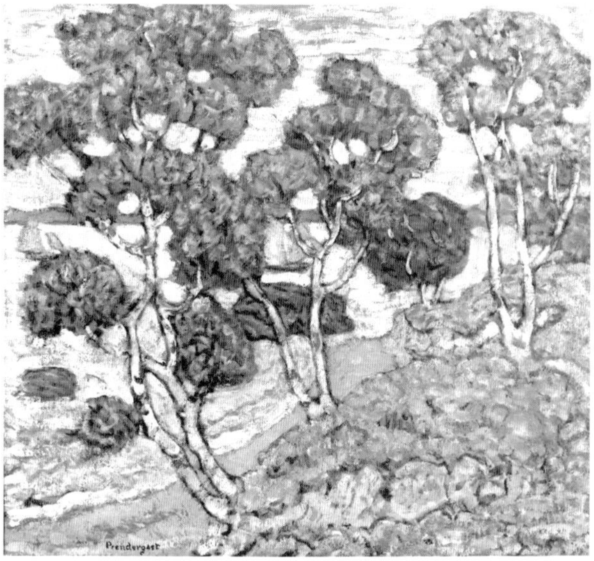

CR 408

CR 408

THE BIRCHES ca. 1914–15
Oil on canvas
(26⅛ x 28⅛ in.; 66.4 x 71.4 cm)
Williams College Museum of Art, gift of Mrs. Charles Prendergast (85.33)

INSCRIPTIONS
l.l. in green: Prendergast

BIBLIOGRAPHY
Barter 1989 (n.p.); Lauzon 1989 (pp. E: 1, 4); *American Art Review* 1993 (p. 90; ill.)

EXHIBITIONS
1986 Williams College (no #); 1988a Williams College (no #); 1989 Mead Art Museum (#59); 1990d Williams College (no #); 1990f Williams College (no #); 1991a Williams College (no #); 1991b Williams College (no #); 1993 Williams College (no #); 1994a Williams College (no #); 1995b Williams College (no #)

CR 413

PARK BY THE SEA ca. 1914–15
Oil on canvas
(26 x 32 in.; 66.0 x 81.3 cm)
Williams College Museum of Art, gift of Mrs. Charles Prendergast (86.18.39)

INSCRIPTIONS
l.l. in brown: Prendergast

BIBLIOGRAPHY
Kane 1992 (p. 1; ill.); Nassau County 1996 (p. 52; ill.)

EXHIBITIONS
1986 Williams College (no #); Williams College 1989b (#22); 1990f Williams College (no #); 1991a Williams College (no #); 1991b Williams College (no #); 1992 Williams College (no #); 1993 Williams College (no #); 1996 Nassau County Museum (no #, p. 52, ill.)

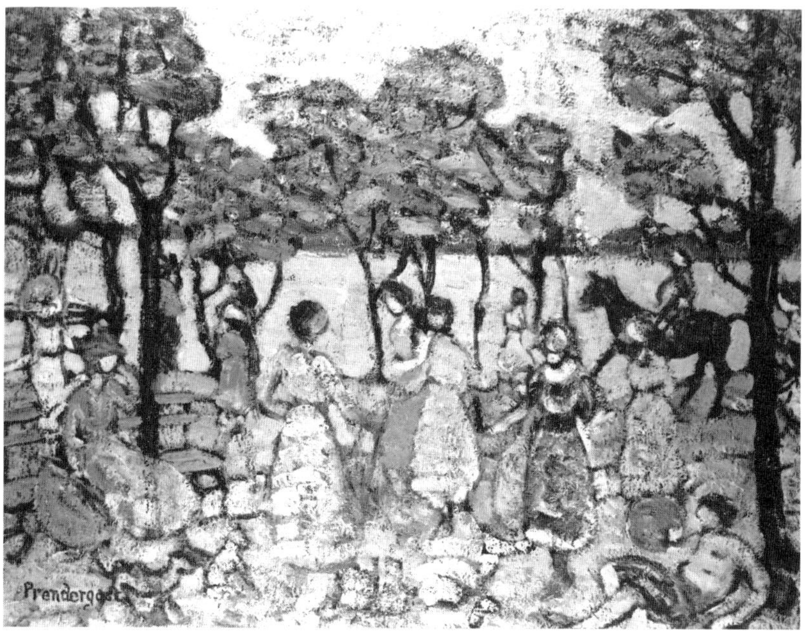

CR 413

CR 419
A DAY IN THE COUNTRY ca. 1914–15
Oil on canvas
(18¼ x 27 in.; 46.4 x 68.6 cm)
Williams College Museum of Art, gift of Mrs. Charles Prendergast (91.18.1)

INSCRIPTIONS
l.r. of center in black: Prendergast

BIBLIOGRAPHY
Kramer 1966 (p. D: 31; ill.); Sawyer 1966 (n.p.); Glavin 1976 (p. 76); Isaacs 1990; Smith, R. 1990

EXHIBITIONS
1966a Knoedler (#45, ill.); 1990c Williams College (#103, ABCD); 1991b Williams College (no #); 1993 Williams College (no #); 1994a Williams College (no #)

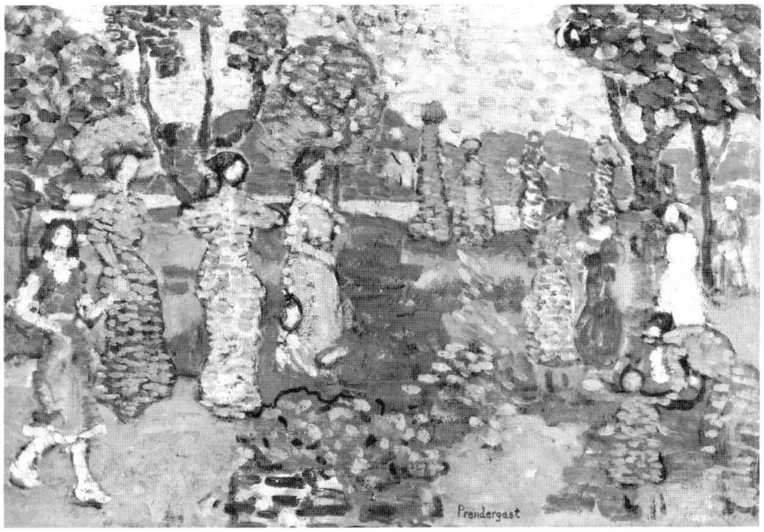

CR 419

CR 436
SUMMER DAY, SALEM ca. 1915–18
Frame by Charles Prendergast
Oil on canvas
(18 x 28¼ in.; 45.7 x 71.8 cm)
Williams College Museum of Art, gift of Mrs. Charles Prendergast (86.18.80)

INSCRIPTIONS
l.l. in brown: Prendergast

BIBLIOGRAPHY
Lauzon 1989 (pp. E: 1, 4)

EXHIBITIONS
1934a Whitney (#48); 1986 Williams College (no #); 1988b Williams College (frame for *Summer Day, Salem* by Charles Prendergast, #75); 1989c Williams College (no #); 1989d Williams College (no #); 1990f Williams College (no #); 1991a Williams College (no #); 1991b Williams College (no #); 1993 Williams College (no #); 1994a Williams College (no #); 1995b Williams College (no #)
Color plate, p. 46

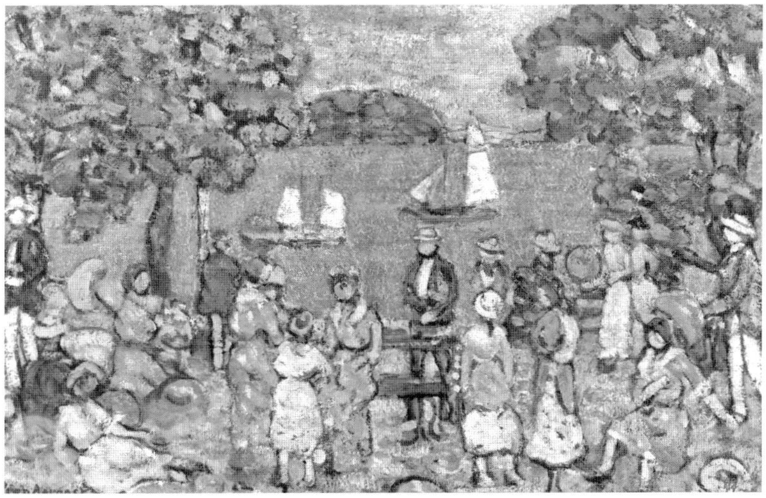
CR 436

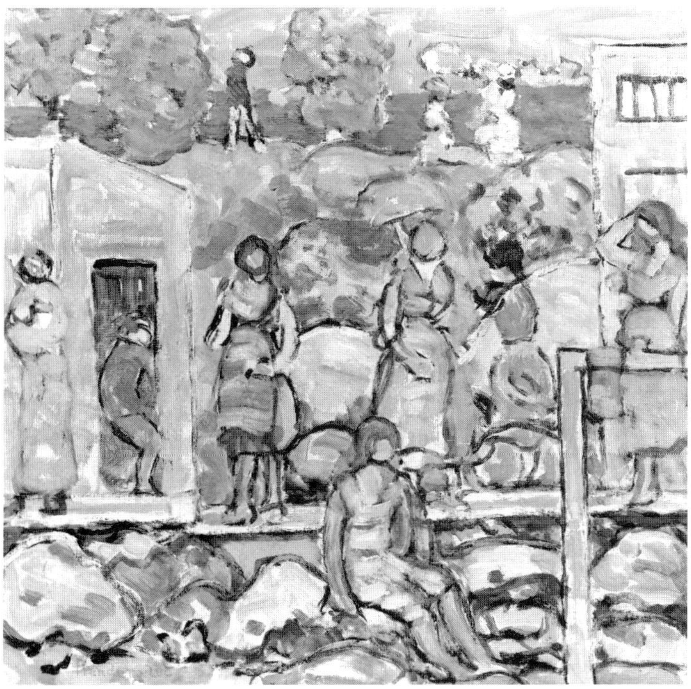
CR 455

CR 455
BATH HOUSES, ANNISQUAM ca. 1919
Frame by Charles Prendergast
Oil on canvas
(18 x 18½ in.; 45.7 x 47.0 cm)
Williams College Museum of Art, gift of Mrs. Charles Prendergast (86.18.67)

INSCRIPTIONS
l.l. in red: Prendergast

BIBLIOGRAPHY
Lauzon 1989 (pp. E: 1, 4; as *Bathhouse, Annisquam*)

EXHIBITIONS
1986 Williams College (no #); 1988a Williams College (no #); 1989c Williams College (no #); 1989d Williams College (no #); 1990b Williams College (no #); 1990f Williams College (no #); 1991a Williams College (no #); 1991b Williams College (no #); 1995b Williams College (no #)
Cf. the related watercolor, *Annisquam* (CR 1317), which is signed and dated 1919.

Watercolors

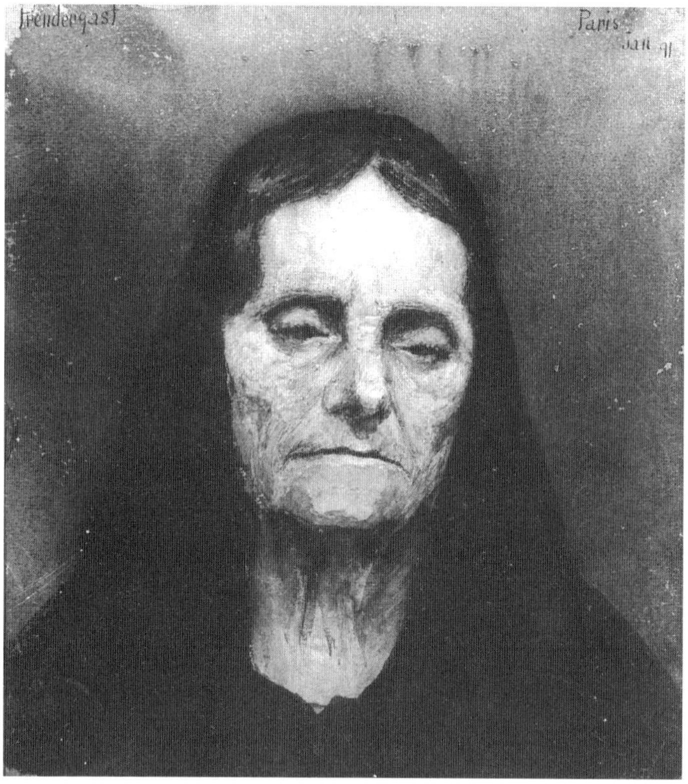

CR 517

CR 517
OLD WOMAN, PARIS 1891
Watercolor and pencil on paper
(10⅝ x 9⅜ in.; 27.0 x 23.8 cm)
Williams College Museum of Art, gift of Mrs. Charles Prendergast (86.18.1)

INSCRIPTIONS
u.l. in black ink: Prendergast
u.r. in black ink: Paris/Jan/91

BIBLIOGRAPHY
Rhys 1960 (p. 22); Dorais 1980 (p. 56); Langdale 1984 (p. 10)

EXHIBITIONS
1960 Boston MFA (#50, ill.); 1983a Williams College (#1); 1984b Williams College (#1); 1988a Williams College (no #); 1989c Williams College (no #); 1991a Williams College (no #); 1992 Williams College (no #)

CR 518
GIRL IN COSTUME 1891
Watercolor and pencil on paper
(8⅞ x 9¼ in.; 22.5 x 23.5 cm)
Williams College Museum of Art, gift of Mrs. Charles Prendergast (85.21.5)

INSCRIPTIONS
u.l. in black ink: Prendergast
u.r. in black ink: Paris./91

EXHIBITIONS
1988a Williams College (no #); 1989c Williams College (no #); 1991a Williams College (no #); 1993 Williams College (no #); 1995c Williams College (no #)

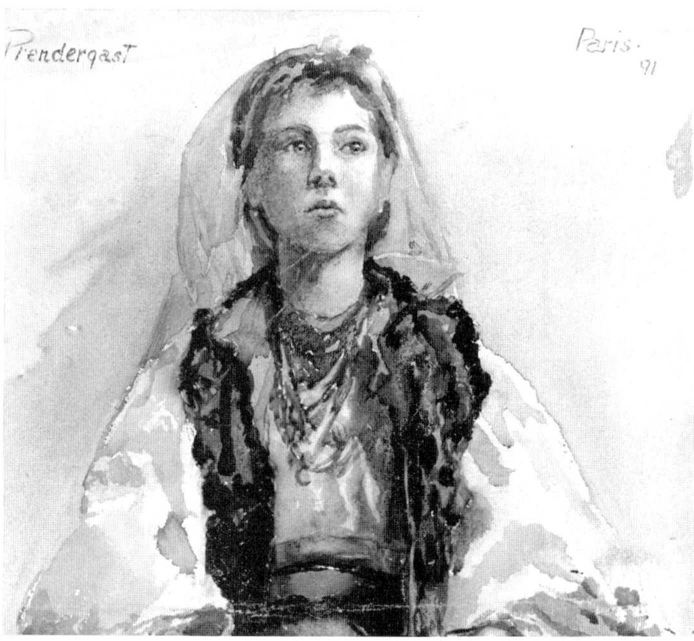

CR 518

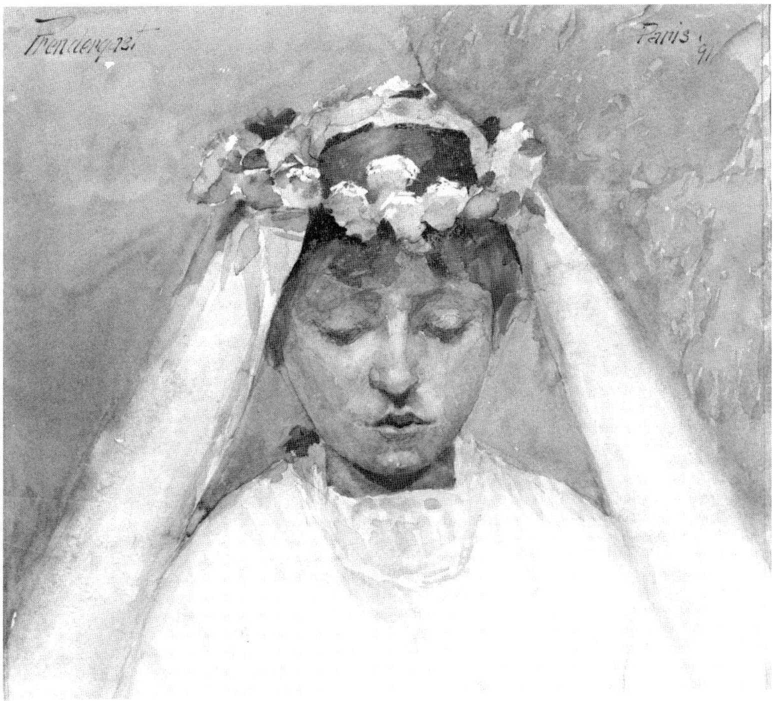

CR 519

CR 519

FIRST COMMUNION 1891
Watercolor and pencil on paper
(8⅞ x 9¼ in.; 22.5 x 23.5 cm)
Williams College Museum of Art, gift of Mrs. Charles Prendergast (85.21.6)

INSCRIPTIONS
u.l. in black ink: Prendergast
u.r. in black ink: Paris/'91

EXHIBITIONS
1988a Williams College (no #); 1989c Williams College (no #); 1991a Williams College (no #); 1993 Williams College (no #)

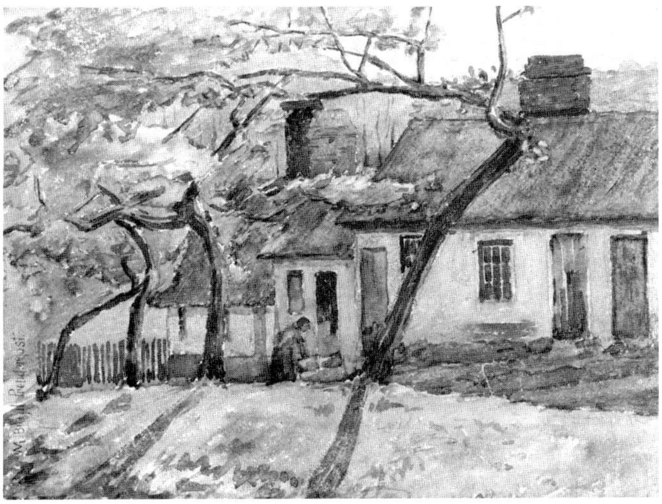

CR 520

CR 520

SUNLIGHT STUDY OF A COTTAGE AT EU, FRANCE ca. 1891
Watercolor and pencil on paper
(9 x 12 in.; 22.9 x 30.5 cm)
Williams College Museum of Art, bequest of Mrs. Charles Prendergast (95.4.100)

INSCRIPTIONS
l.l. in black ink (vertically): M. Brazil Prendergast.

BIBLIOGRAPHY
Wattenmaker 1994 (p. 23 as watercolor, p. 150 fn 29 as CR 520)

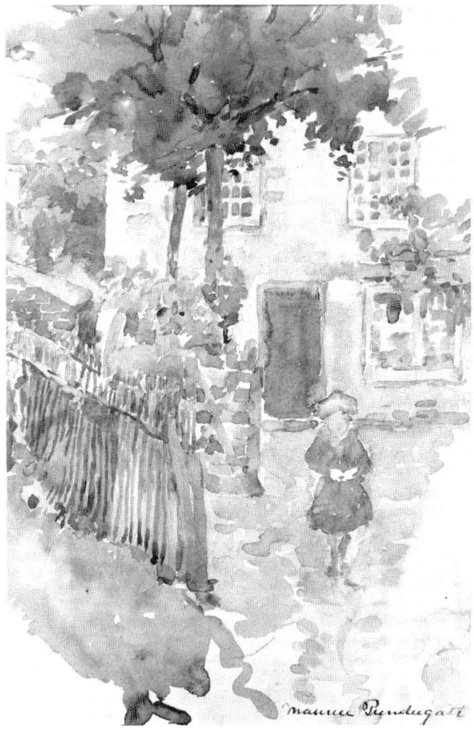

CR 523

CR 523

LITTLE GIRL IN RED, FRANCE
ca. 1891–94
Watercolor and pencil on paper
(14⅛ x 8½ in.; 35.9 x 21.6 cm)
Williams College Museum of Art, gift of Mrs. Charles Prendergast (86.18.53)

INSCRIPTIONS
l.r. in black ink: Maurice Prendergast
verso, l.r. in pencil: France 1894

EXHIBITIONS
1986 Williams College (no #); 1988b Williams College (#25); 1991a Williams College (no #); 1994a Williams College (no #)

CR 531
LE TREPORT 1892
Sunset, Low Tide
Watercolor and pencil on paper
(7¾ x 8¾ in.; 19.7 x 22.2 cm)
Williams College Museum of Art, gift of Mrs. Charles Prendergast (85.21.4)

INSCRIPTIONS
l.l. in black ink: MBP[monogram]rendergast/'92
verso, l.l. in pencil: Sunset/Low Tide

EXHIBITIONS
? 1934a Whitney (#143); ? 1935 Macbeth (no #); 1988a Williams College (no #); 1989d Williams College (no #); 1991a Williams College (no #)

CR 531 verso

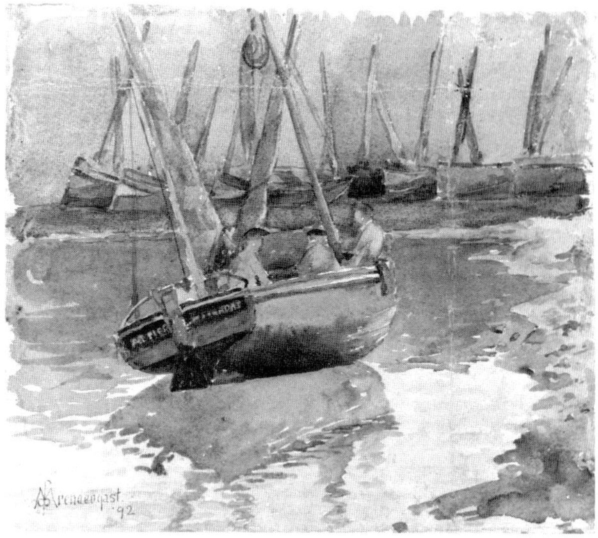
CR 531

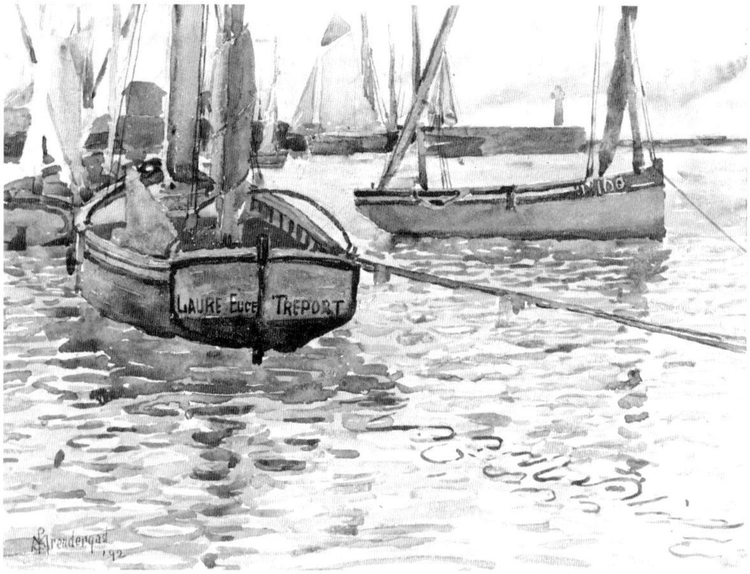
CR 532

CR 531 verso
SKETCHES: WOMEN, ONE MAN, SAILBOATS IN HARBOR, AND MONOGRAMS
Pencil

CR 532
THE LAURE EUCE-TREPORT 1892
Frame by Charles Prendergast
Watercolor and pencil on paper
(9 x 12 in.; 22.9 x 30.5 cm)
Williams College Museum of Art, bequest of Mrs. Charles Prendergast (95.4.101)

INSCRIPTIONS
l.l. in black ink: MBP[monogram]rendergast/'92

EXHIBITIONS
1988b Williams College (frame for *The Laure-Euce, Treport* by Charles Prendergast, #47); 1995c Williams College (no #)

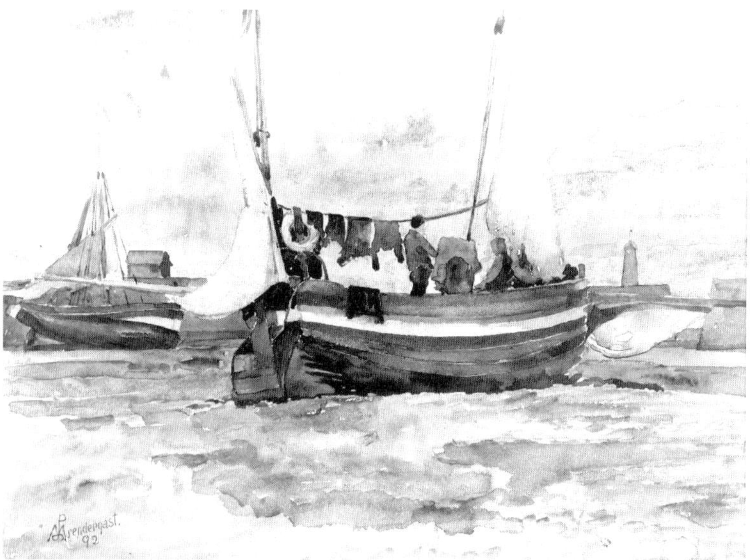
CR 533

CR 533
FISHING BOATS, NORMANDY 1892
Low Tide Early Morning at Treport; Low Tide Treport
Watercolor and pencil on paper
(9⅜ x 12⅝ in.; 23.8 x 32.1 cm)
Williams College Museum of Art, gift of Mrs. Charles Prendergast (86.18.50)

INSCRIPTIONS
l.l. in black ink: MBP[monogram]rendergast./92
verso, u.c. in brown (in Charles Prendergast's hand): 1892/Low Tide Treport

BIBLIOGRAPHY
Rhys 1952 (p. 28); Sawyer 1966 (n.p.); Langdale 1975 (n.p.); Dorais 1980 (p. 59)

EXHIBITIONS
1897 Malden C.O. Elliett (#48, as *Low Tide Treport*); 1944b Kraushaar (#25, as *Low Tide, Treport*); 1966a Knoedler (#1, ill.); 1988a Williams College (no #); 1989d Williams College (no #); 1991a Williams College (no #); 1993 Williams College (no #)

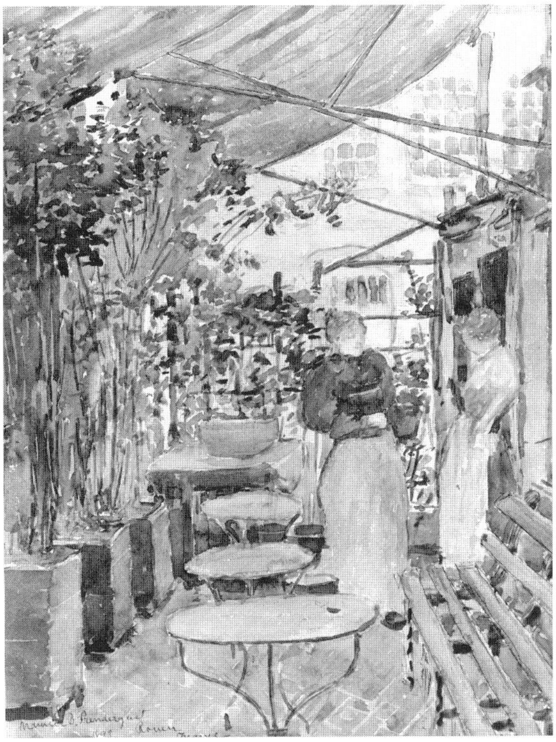

CR 540

CR 540

ROUEN 1893
Frame by Charles Prendergast
Watercolor, pencil, and ink on paper
(13½ x 9⅞ in.; 34.3 x 25.1 cm)
Williams College Museum of Art, gift of Mrs. Charles Prendergast (86.18.72)

INSCRIPTIONS
l.l. in ink: Maurice B. Prendergast/Rouen/1893/France

EXHIBITIONS
1986 Williams College (no #); 1991a Williams College (no #)

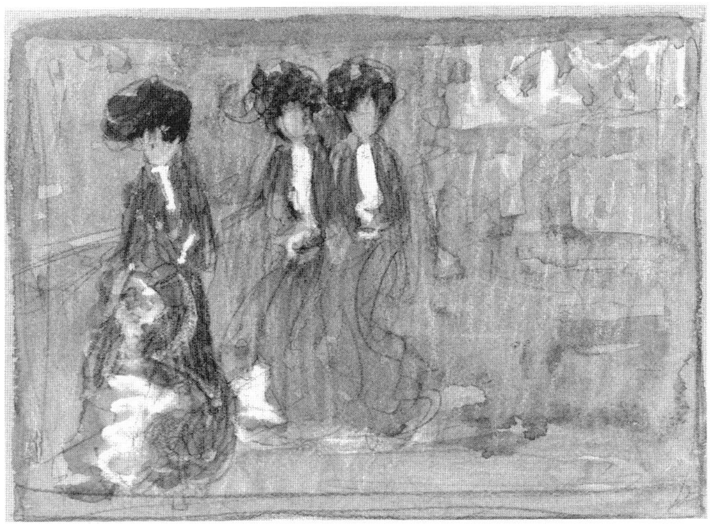

CR 554

CR 554

PARIS ca. 1893–94
Watercolor, pencil, and pastel on colored paper
(5½ x 7⅝ in.; 14.0 x 19.4 cm)
Williams College Museum of Art, bequest of Mrs. Charles Prendergast (95.4.96)

INSCRIPTIONS
l.r. in red pencil: MBP [monogram]

BIBLIOGRAPHY
Brady 1962 (n.p.)

EXHIBITIONS
1963a Davis Galleries (#9)

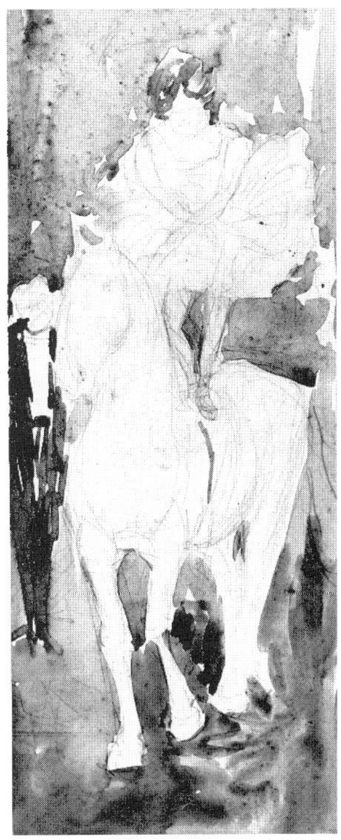

CR 593

CR 593

THE WHITE HORSE AND CIRCUS RIDER
ca. 1893–95
Frame by Charles Prendergast
Watercolor and pencil on paper
(9¼ x 4⅜ in.; 23.5 x 11.1 cm)
Williams College Museum of Art, bequest of Mrs. Charles Prendergast (95.4.92)

INSCRIPTIONS
Unsigned

EXHIBITIONS
1988b Williams College (frame for *The White Horse and Circus Rider* by Charles Prendergast, #53)

CR 593 verso

SKETCHES OF ROOSTERS, CHICKEN, DUCK
Pencil
(Too faint to reproduce)

NOTE
Cf. related pencil sketch on p. 33 of the Large Boston Public Garden Sketchbook (CR 1477) and related monotypes, *Bareback Rider* (CRs 1593, 1596, 1597).

CR 640
LOW TIDE, NANTASKET ca. 1896–97
Watercolor and pencil on paper
(20⅛ x 14 in.; 51.1 x 35.6 cm)
Williams College Museum of Art, gift of Mrs. Charles Prendergast (86.18.2)

INSCRIPTIONS
l.r. in blue: Prendergast

BIBLIOGRAPHY
Ferber 1982 (p. 85; ill.); Grant 1990b; Lauzon 1990 (p. 28); Mathews 1990 (p. 59; ill.)

EXHIBITIONS
1982 Smithsonian SITES (#42, ill.); 1983a Williams College (#2); 1985b Williams College (no #); 1986 Williams College (no #); 1989c Williams College (no #); 1990c Williams College (#14, CD); 1993 Williams College (no #)
Color plate, p. 20

CR 643
LOW TIDE ca. 1896–97
Watercolor and pencil on paper
(14 x 10 in.; 35.6 x 25.4 cm)
Williams College Museum of Art, gift of Mrs. Charles Prendergast (86.18.55)

INSCRIPTIONS
l.l. in red pencil: Prendergast
verso, u.l. in pencil (in Charles Prendergast's hand): Low Tide 1897

BIBLIOGRAPHY
Mathews 1990 (p. 60; ill.)

EXHIBITIONS
1986 Williams College (no #); 1989c Williams College (no #); 1990c Williams College (#15, CD); 1993 Williams College (no #)

CR 643 verso
LOW TIDE
Watercolor and pencil

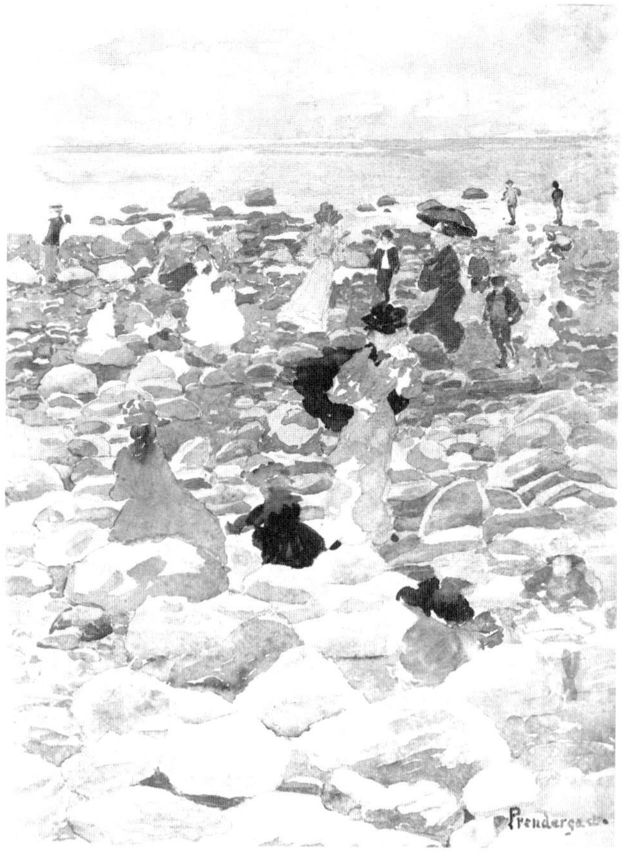

CR 640

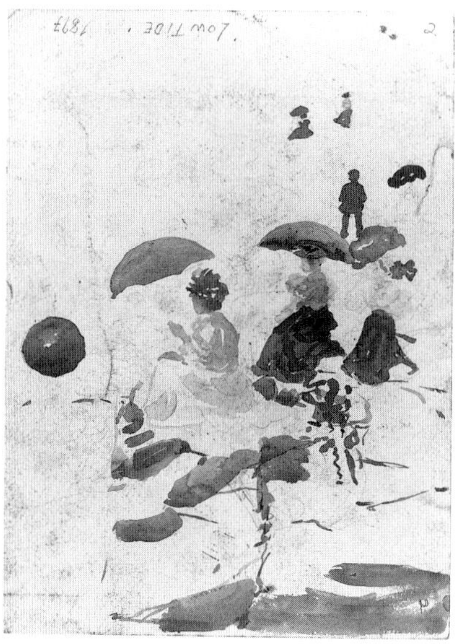
CR 643 verso

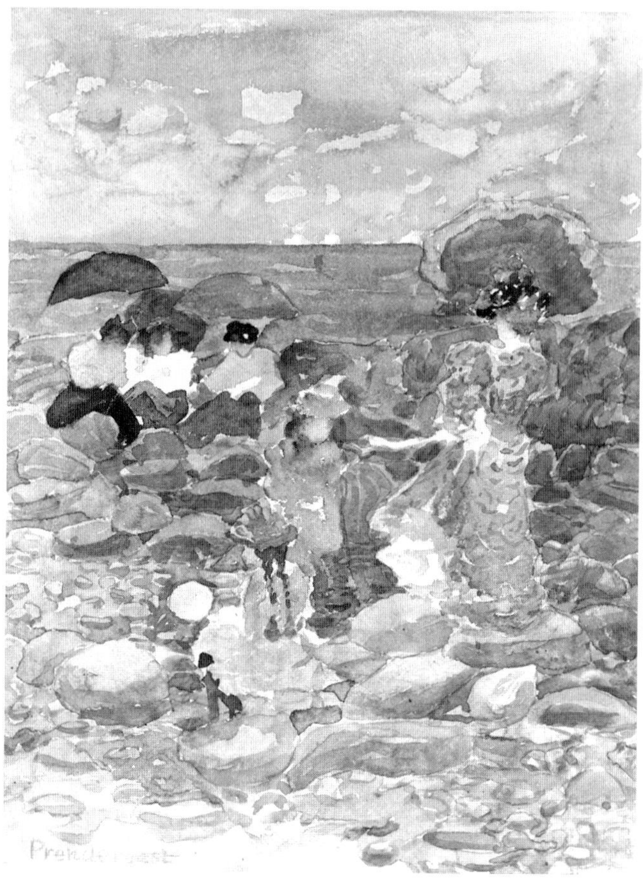
CR 643

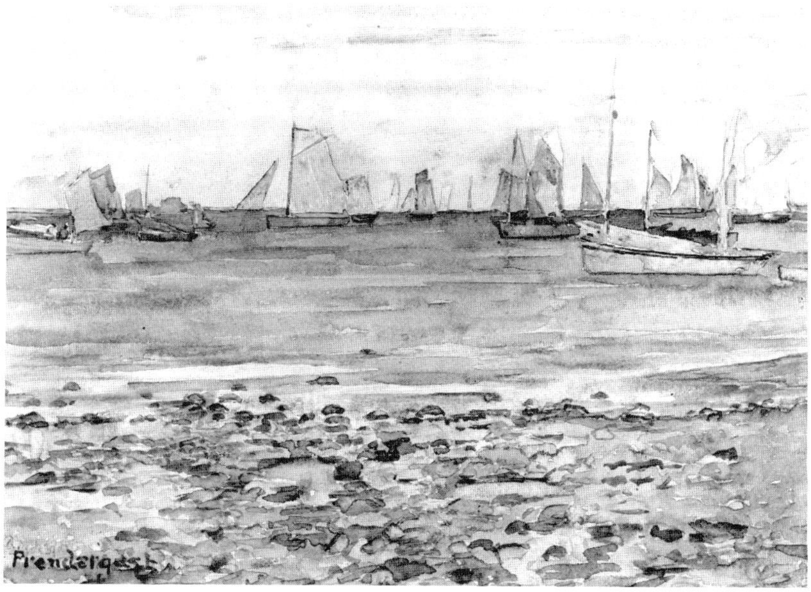

CR 665

CR 665
SUNNY MORNING, LOW TIDE AT THE BEACH ca. 1896–97
Watercolor and pencil on paper
(9 x 12½ in.; 22.9 x 31.7 cm)
Williams College Museum of Art, bequest of Mrs. Charles Prendergast (95.4.97)

INSCRIPTIONS
l.l. in pencil: Prendergast
l.l. in brown watercolor: Prendergast

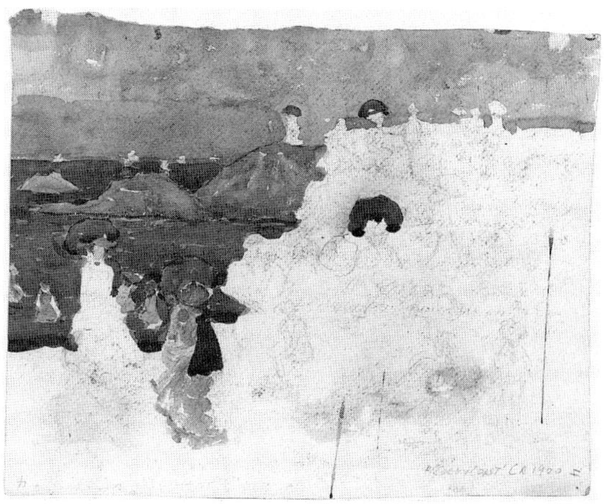

CR 667 verso

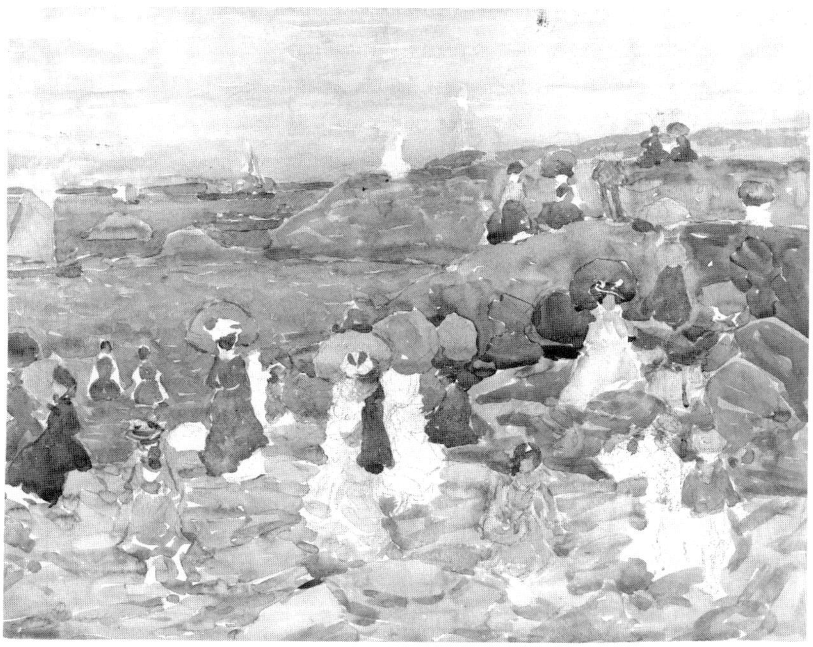

CR 667

CR 667
ROCKY COAST ca. 1896–97
Watercolor and pencil on paper
(14½ x 18 in.; 36.8 x 45.7 cm)
Williams College Museum of Art, gift of Mrs. Charles Prendergast (91.18.18)

INSCRIPTIONS
l.l. in pencil: Prendergast
l.r. in pencil (in another hand): Rocky Coast ca. 1900

EXHIBITIONS
1989d Williams College (no #); 1993 Williams College (no #); 1994a Williams College (no #)

CR 667 verso
ROCKY COAST SCENE
Watercolor and pencil

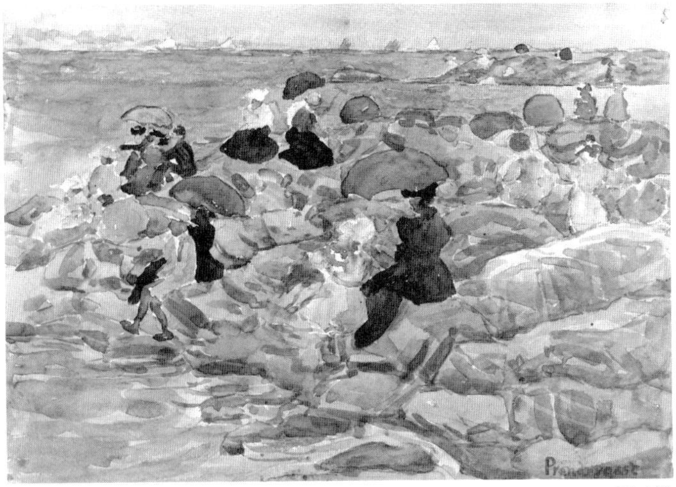

CR 669

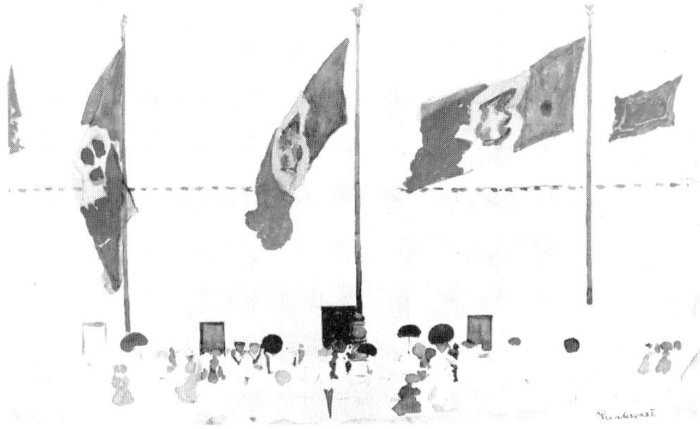

CR 678

CR 669

ROCKY POINT ca. 1896–97
Watercolor and pencil on paper
(10 x 14 in.; 25.4 x 35.6 cm)
Williams College Museum of Art, gift of Mrs. Charles Prendergast (86.18.56)

INSCRIPTIONS
l.r. in pencil: render
l.r. in blue: Prendergast

EXHIBITIONS
1986 Williams College (no #); 1989d Williams College (no #); 1991a Williams College (no #); 1993 Williams College (no #); 1995a Williams College (no #)

CR 678

VENICE ca. 1898–99
Watercolor and pencil on paper
(14⅛ x 20¾ in.; 35.9 x 52.7 cm)
Williams College Museum of Art, gift of Mrs. Charles Prendergast (86.18.61)

INSCRIPTIONS
l.r. in ink: Prendergast
verso, l.c. in pencil: Venice 1898

BIBLIOGRAPHY
Perlman 1990; Agar 1994 (p. 42; ill.)

EXHIBITIONS
1986 Williams College (no #); 1990c Williams College (#22, BCD); 1993 Williams College (no #); 1994b Williams College (#56)

NOTE
This is a view of the flags in front of San Marco.

CR 678 verso

NUDE BATHERS IN A LANDSCAPE
ca. 1913–15
Pencil

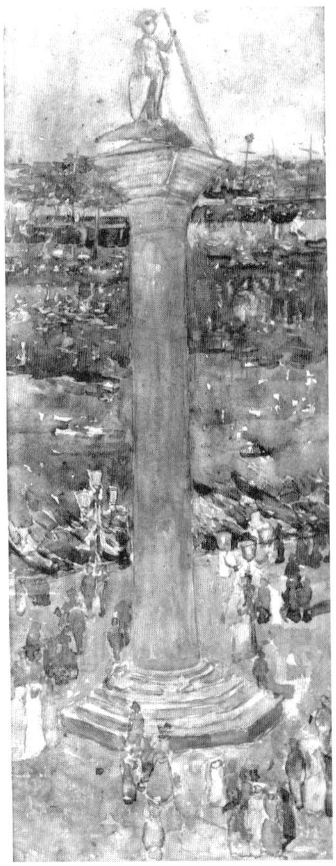

CR 693

CR 678 verso

CR 693

COLUMN OF ST. THEODORE ca. 1898–99
Column of St. George (Venice)
Frame by Charles Prendergast
Watercolor and pencil on paper
(15¼ x 5⅞ in.; 38.7 x 14.9 cm)
Williams College Museum of Art, bequest of Mrs. Charles Prendergast (95.4.93)

INSCRIPTIONS
l.l. in pencil: Prendergast
verso, u.c. in pencil: the Column of/St. George-Venice $45/47/[in another hand] #9

EXHIBITIONS
? 1901 Detroit (#23, as *Column of St. George (Venice))*; 1995c Williams College (no #)

CR 712

GRAND CANAL, VENICE ca. 1898–99
Watercolor and pencil on paper
(9¾ x 13⅝ in.; 24.8 x 34.6 cm)
Williams College Museum of Art, gift of Mrs. Charles Prendergast (91.18.6)

INSCRIPTIONS
l.l. in black ink: Prendergast

BIBLIOGRAPHY
Mathews 1990 (p. 73; ill.)

EXHIBITIONS
1990c Williams College (#28, ABCD); 1992 Williams College (no #); 1993 Williams College (no #)

NOTE
This view from the steps of the Dogana shows the former Bucintoro Rowing Club to the right and buildings that are now hotels along the Grand Canal.
Color plate, p. 8

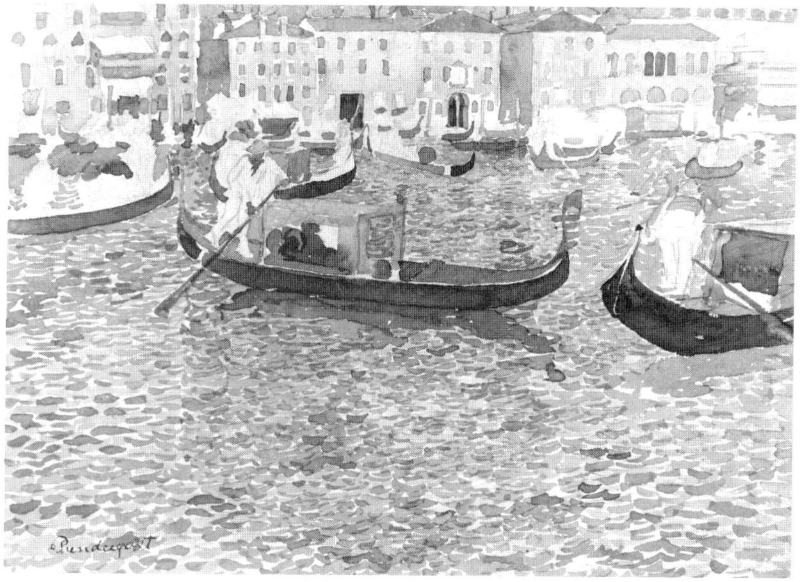

CR 712

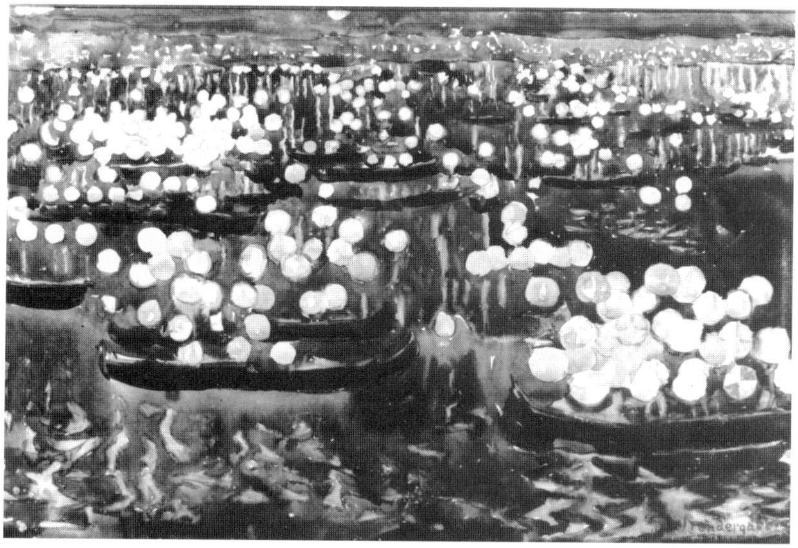

CR 724

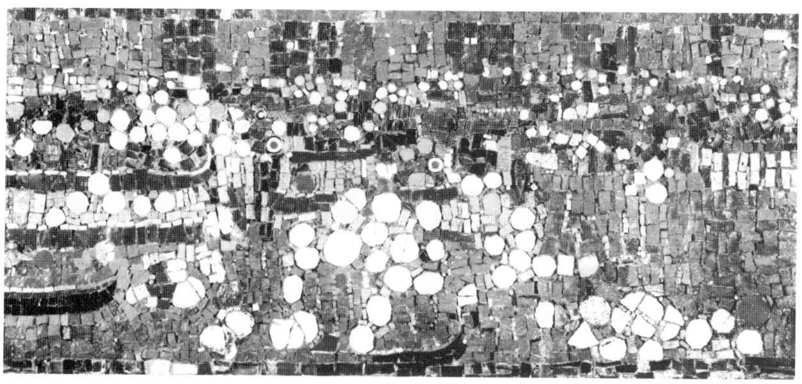

CR 725

CR 724

FESTA DEL REDENTORE ca. 1899
Festa della Redentore
Watercolor and pencil on paper
(11 x 17 in.; 27.9 x 43.2 cm)
Williams College Museum of Art, gift of Mrs. Charles Prendergast (91.18.5)

INSCRIPTIONS
l.r. in red: Prendergast

BIBLIOGRAPHY
Seldin 1983 (p. 21); Mathews 1990 (p. 74; ill.); Wilson, W. 1991 (p. F: 16; as *Fiesta del Redentore*)

EXHIBITIONS
1983 Coe Kerr (#58, ill., as *Festa della Redentore*); 1983a Williams College (#4, ill., as *Festa della Redentore*); 1990c Williams College (#29, CD); 1993 Williams College (no #)

NOTE
The Festa del Redentore takes place in the Giudecca canal on the third Sunday of July. Because Prendergast did not apply for a passport until 29 June 1898, it is likely that this is a scene of the 1899 Festa del Redentore.
Color plate, p. 26

CR 725

FIESTA GRAND CANAL, VENICE ca. 1899
Festa della Redentore; Mosaic, Venice
Glass and ceramic tiles in plaster
(11 x 23 in.; 27.9 x 58.4 cm)
Williams College Museum of Art, bequest of Mrs. Charles Prendergast (95.4.79)

BIBLIOGRAPHY
Wick 1960b (p. 85); Owens 1978 (p. 45); Langdale 1979a (p. 108); Langdale 1984 (p. 122); Wattenmaker 1994 (p. 52 as mosaic, p. 150 fn 46 as CR 725)

EXHIBITIONS
1983 Coe Kerr (#59, ill., as *Festa della Redentore*); 1983a Williams College (#5, ill., as *Mosaic, Venice*); See note, CR 724.

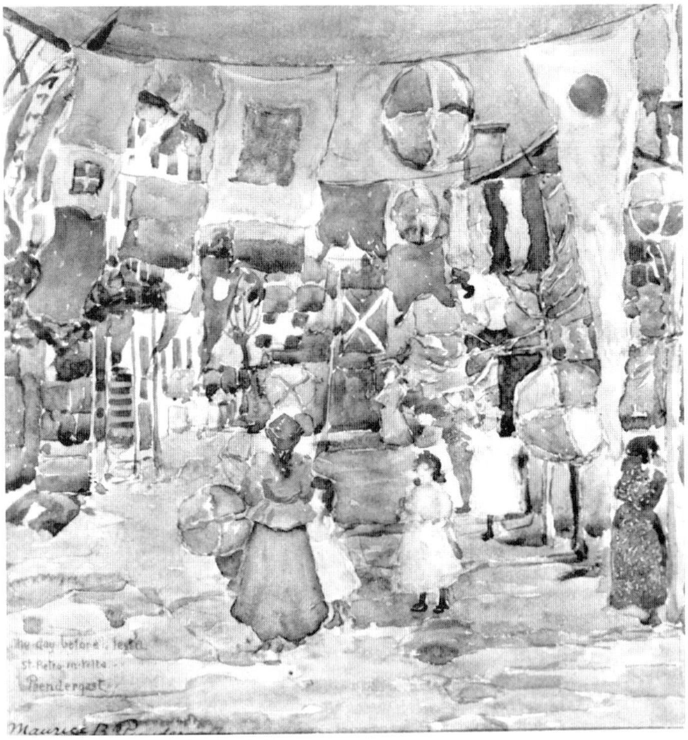

CR 729

CR 729

FIESTA-VENICE-S. PIETRO IN VOLTA ca. 1898–99

Day Before the Festa; The Day Before a Festa, St. Pietro in Volte

Frame by Charles Prendergast

Watercolor and pencil on paper

(13⅜ x 12½ in.; 34.0 x 31.7 cm)

Williams College Museum of Art, gift of Mrs. Charles Prendergast (86.18.76)

Inscriptions

l.l. in pencil: The day before festa/St. Pietro in Volta/Prendergast

l.l. in ink: Maurice B. Prendergast

Bibliography

Boston Evng Transcript 1900a (p. 11); Mathews 1990 (p. 70; ill.)

Exhibitions

1900 Chicago AIC (#76, as *The Day Before a Festa, St. Pietro in Volte*); 1986 Williams College (no #); 1990c Williams College (#25, ABCD); 1993 Williams College (no #)

Color plate, p. 24

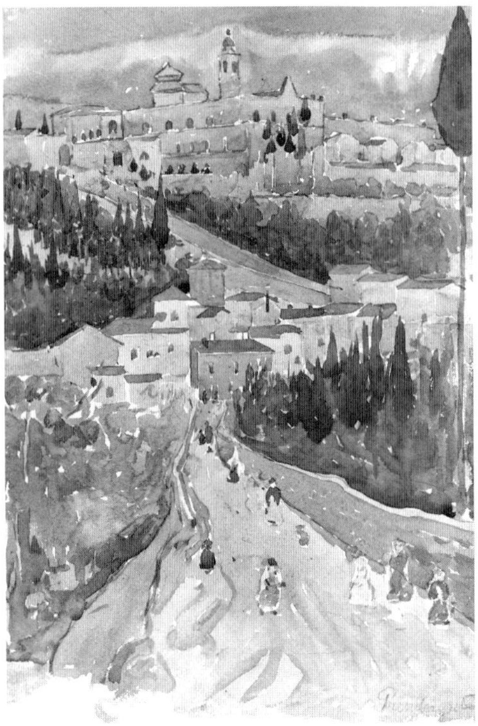

CR 743

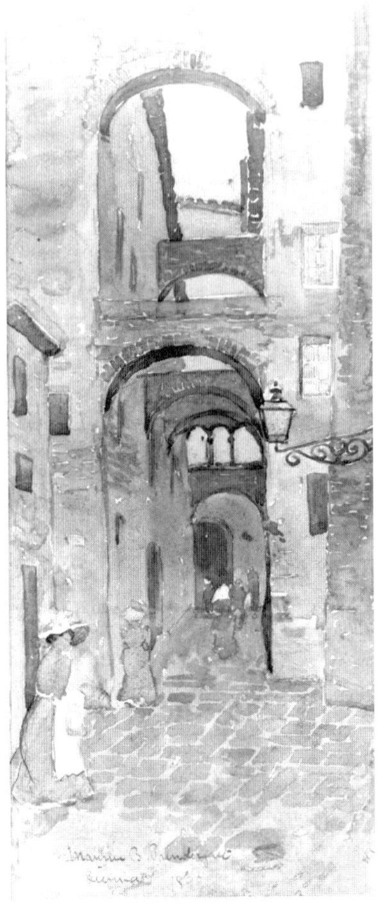

CR 738

CR 738

SIENA 1899

Frame by Charles Prendergast

Watercolor and pencil on paper

(14¼ x 5⅞ in.; 36.2 x 14.9 cm)

Williams College Museum of Art, gift of Mrs. Charles Prendergast (86.18.68)

Inscriptions

l.l. in brown ink: Maurice B. Prendergast/Sienna 1899

Exhibitions

1986 Williams College (no #); 1988b Williams College (Frame for *Siena* by Charles Prendergast, #49); 1991a Williams College (no #); 1992 Williams College (no #); 1995d Williams College (no #)

CR 743

ASSISI ca. 1898–99

Watercolor and pencil on paper

(15⅜ x 11 in.; 39.1 x 28 cm)

Williams College Museum of Art, gift of Mrs. Charles Prendergast (86.18.59)

Inscriptions

l.r. in pencil: Prendergast

Bibliography

Mathews 1990 (p. 75; ill.)

Exhibitions

1986 Williams College (no #); 1989b Williams College (#5); 1990c Williams College (#30, CD); 1992 Williams College (no #); 1993 Williams College (no #); 1995d Williams College (no #)

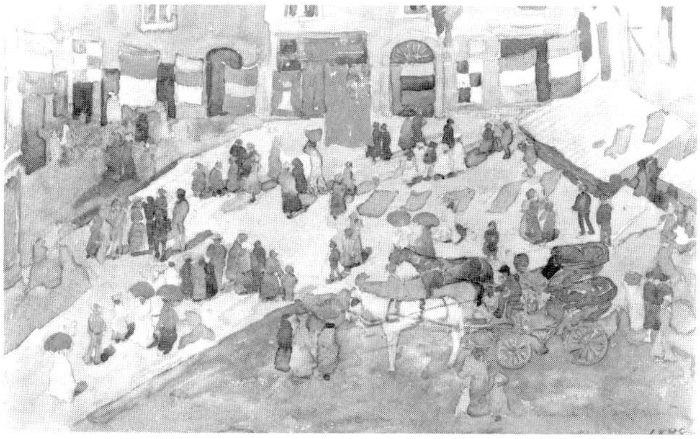

CR 751

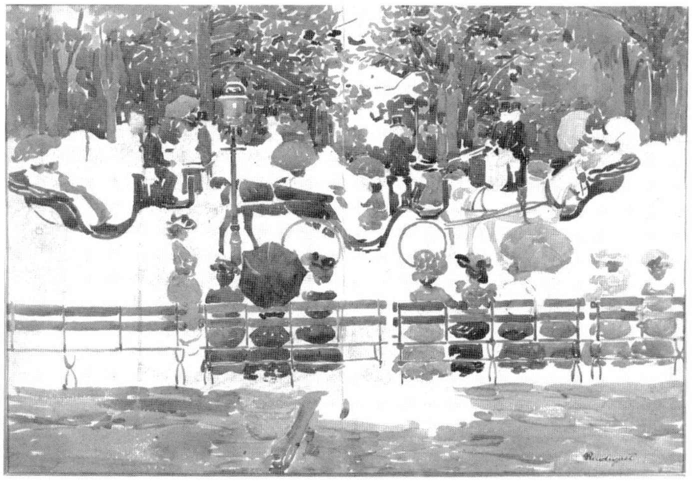

CR 774

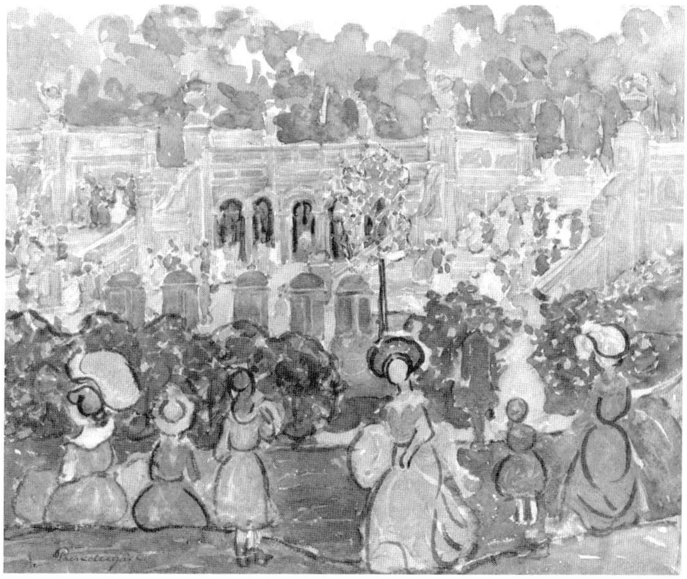

CR 783

CR 751
CAPRI ca. 1898–99
The Piazza, Capri
Frame by Charles Prendergast
Watercolor and pencil on paper
(9 x 14¼ in.; 22.9 x 36.2 cm)
Williams College Museum of Art, gift of Mrs. Charles Prendergast (86.18.73)

INSCRIPTIONS
l.r. in ink: Maurice B. Prendergast/1898
l.r. in ink: Prendergast
verso u.c. in pencil: the Piazza/Capri 1898/49/8

EXHIBITIONS
1901 Detroit (#27, as *The Piazza, Capri*); 1986 Williams College (no #); 1991a Williams College (no #); 1993 Williams College (no #)

CR 774
CENTRAL PARK ca. 1901
Central Park, New York City
Watercolor and pencil on paper
(15¼ x 22 in.; 38.7 x 55.9 cm)
Williams College Museum of Art, gift of Mrs. Charles Prendergast in memory of Maurice and Charles Prendergast, 1967 (67.13)

INSCRIPTIONS
l.r. in ink: Prendergast
verso: Central Park/New York City

BIBLIOGRAPHY
Faison 1979 (n.p., #48, ill.); Mathews 1990 (p. 82; ill.); Agar 1994 (p. 42; ill.)

EXHIBITIONS
1966 Colby College; 1978 Clark Art Institute (#12, ill.); 1990c Williams College (#37, ABCD)
Color plate, p. 28

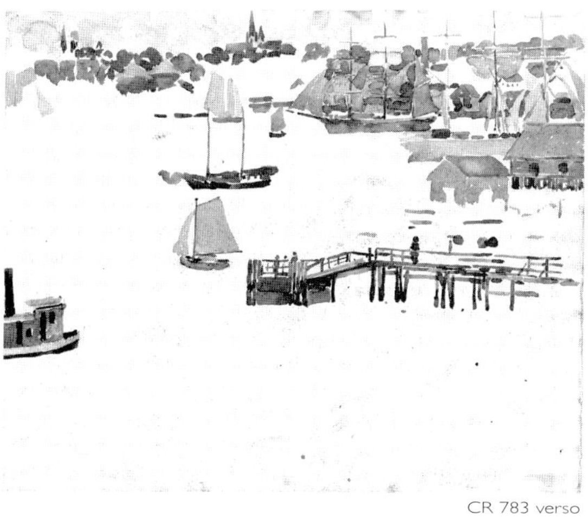

CR 783 verso

CR 783
CENTRAL PARK, NEW YORK ca. 1900–03;
REWORKED LATER
Watercolor, pencil, and gouache on paper
(12¾ x 15½ in.; 32.4 x 39.4 cm)
Williams College Museum of Art, gift of Mrs. Charles Prendergast (86.18.69)

INSCRIPTIONS
l.l. in ink: Prendergast

EXHIBITIONS
1982 Smithsonian SITES (#44, ill.); 1985b Williams College (no #); 1986 Williams College (no #); 1988b Williams College (#26); 1991a Williams College (no #); 1993 Williams College (no #); 1994a Williams College (no #)

CR 783 verso
HARBOR SCENE WITH PIER
Watercolor and pencil

CR 796

MAY DAY PICNIC, CENTRAL PARK 1902
ca. 1900–03
Frame by Charles Prendergast
Watercolor and pencil on paper
(11⅜ x 13¼ in.; 28.9 x 33.7 cm)
Private Collection and Williams College Museum of Art (93.13.1)

INSCRIPTIONS
l.l. in black: Prendergast
verso (in Charles Prendergast's hand): MAY-DAY PICNIC/CENTRAL PARK

PROVENANCE
The artist; to Charles Prendergast, 1924; to present collection, 1940; fractional interest to WCMA, 1993

EXHIBITIONS
1994a Williams College (no #)

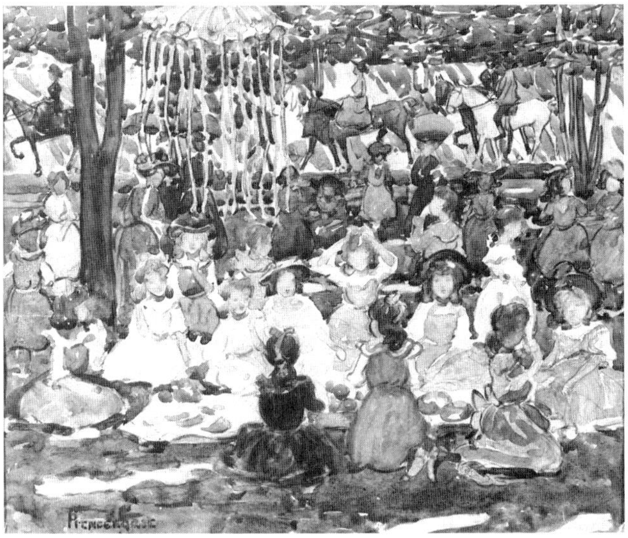

CR 796

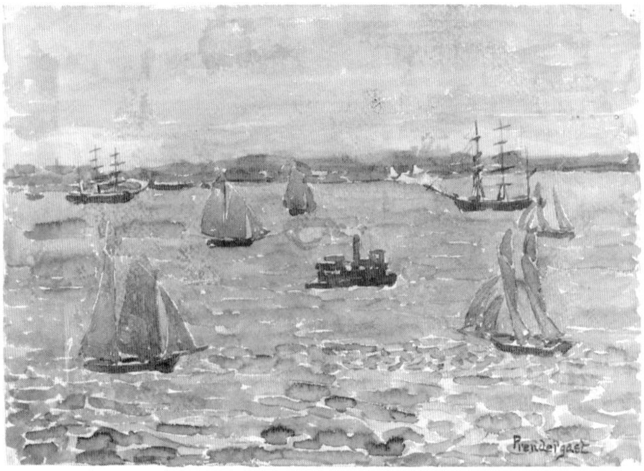

CR 820

CR 820

BOSTON HARBOR ca. 1900–05
Watercolor and pencil on paper
(11¼ x 16 in.; 28.6 x 40.6 cm)
Williams College Museum of Art, gift of Mrs. Charles Prendergast (91.18.15)

INSCRIPTIONS
l.r. in black: Prendergast
l.l. in brown: Prendergast
u.l. in pencil: Sky Paynes grey/vermil-lion/ochre/water figures grey/

EXHIBITIONS
1989d Williams College (no #); 1990b Williams College (no #); 1993 Williams College (no #)

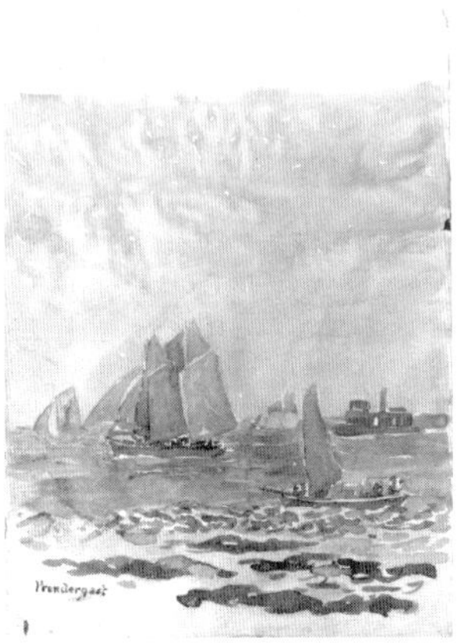

CR 820 verso

CR 820 verso

BOSTON HARBOR
Watercolor and pencil

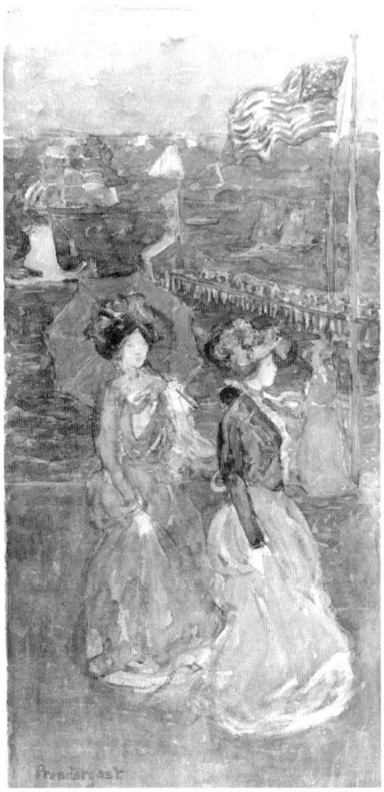

CR 825

CR 825

FIGURES UNDER THE FLAG ca. 1900–05
Frame by Charles Prendergast
Watercolor and pencil on paper
(20½ x 10¼ in.; 52.1 x 26.0 cm)
Williams College Museum of Art, gift of Mrs. Charles Prendergast (86.18.70)

INSCRIPTIONS
l.l. in black: Prendergast

BIBLIOGRAPHY
Drawing 1987 (p. 111; ill.); Lauzon 1989 (pp. E: 1, 4; as *Under the Flag*); Mathews 1990 (p. 62; ill.)

EXHIBITIONS
1986 Williams College (no #); 1989c Williams College (no #); 1990c Williams College (#17, CD); 1993 Williams College (no #)
Cf. related monotype, *On the Pier* (CR 1724).

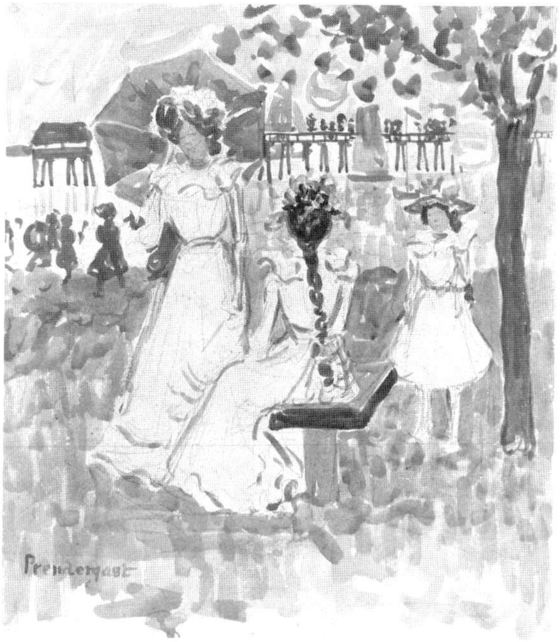

CR 827

CR 827

THE PIER ca. 1900–05
Watercolor and pencil on paper
(14½ x 12⅜ in.; 36.8 x 31.4 cm)
Williams College Museum of Art, gift of
Mrs. Charles Prendergast (86.18.77)

INSCRIPTIONS
l.l. in blue: Prendergast

BIBLIOGRAPHY
Sawyer 1966 (n.p.); *Antiques Arts Weekly* 1986 (p. 113; ill.)

EXHIBITIONS
1966a Knoedler (#7, ill.); 1970 Knoedler (#5); 1986 Williams College (no #); 1988b Williams College (#27); 1989c Williams College (no #); 1994a Williams College (no #)

CR 834

SURF, NANTASKET ca. 1900–05
Watercolor and pencil on paper
(15⅜ x 11⅛ in.; 39.1 x 28.3 cm)
Williams College Museum of Art, gift of
Mrs. Charles Prendergast (86.18.60)

INSCRIPTIONS
l.r. in black ink: Prendergast

BIBLIOGRAPHY
Lingemann 1990 (p. 114; ill.; as *Brandung Nantasket*); Mathews 1990a (ill.); Rappaport 1990 (cover; ill.); Wattenmaker 1990 (p. 39); Wolff 1990 (ill.); Wright 1990 (ill.); Zeaman 1990 (p. E: 1; ill.); *Americana* 1991 (ill.); DeWeese-Wehen 1991 (ill.); *Travel Holiday* 1991 (ill.)

EXHIBITIONS
1986 Williams College (no #); 1989c Williams College (no #); 1990c Williams College (#45, ABCD); 1993 Williams College (no #); 1995a Williams College (no #)
Color plate, p. 23

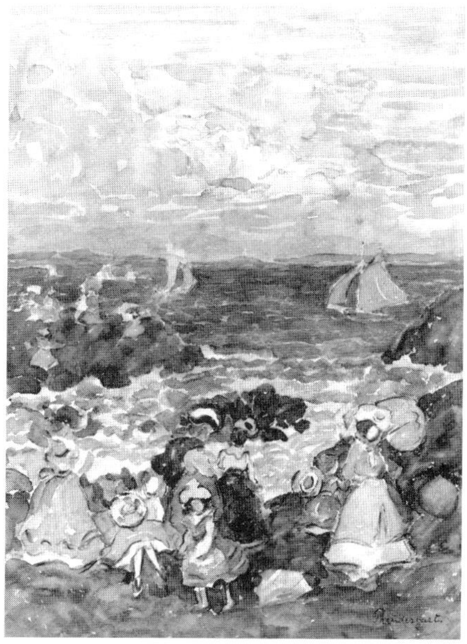

CR 834

CR 834 verso

CR 834 verso

UNTITLED SKETCH
Watercolor and pencil

CR 841

SURF, COHASSET ca. 1900–05
Watercolor and pencil on paper
(10⅝ x 14⅞ in.; 27.9 x 38.7 cm)
Williams College Museum of Art, gift of
Mrs. Charles Prendergast (91.18.9)

INSCRIPTIONS
l.r. in yellow pastel: Prendergast

BIBLIOGRAPHY
Antiques Arts Weekly 1990b; *Antiques Arts Weekly* 1990c

EXHIBITIONS
1982 Smithsonian SITES (#45, ill.); 1990c Williams College (#44, ABCD); 1993 Williams College (no #)

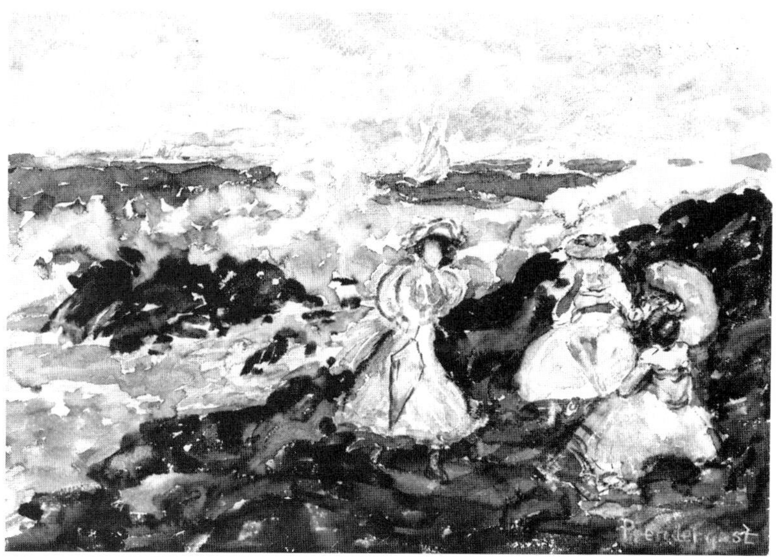

CR 841

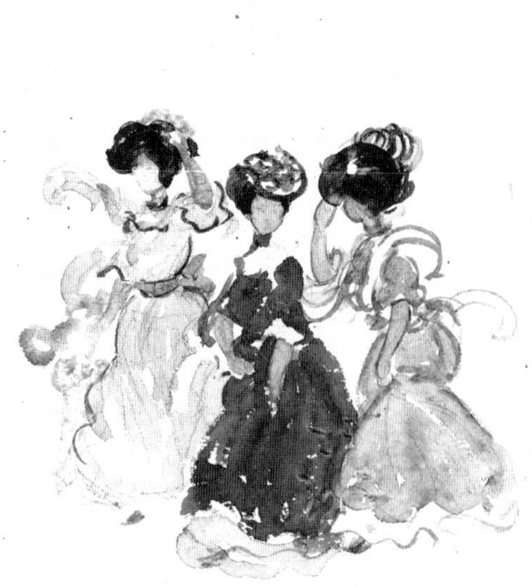

CR 856

CR 856
THREE WOMEN ca. 1905–07
Three Ladies
Frame by Charles Prendergast
Watercolor and pencil on paper
(8⅝ x 7½ in.; 21.9 x 19.0 cm)
Williams College Museum of Art, bequest of Mrs. Charles Prendergast (95.4.109)

INSCRIPTIONS
l.l.: MBP [monogram]

EXHIBITIONS
1963a Davis Galleries (#38)

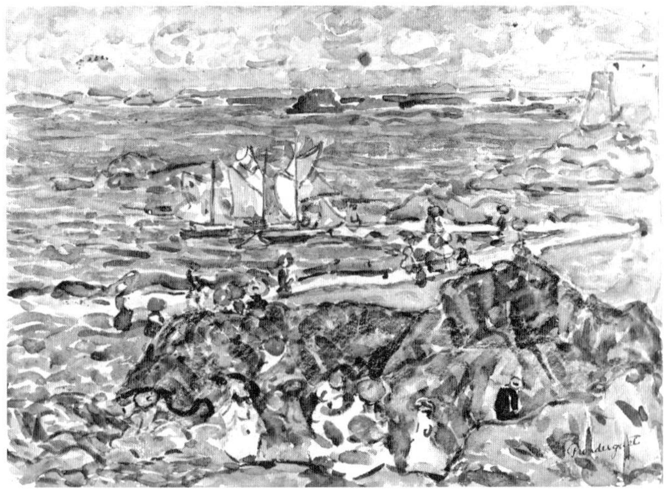

CR 866

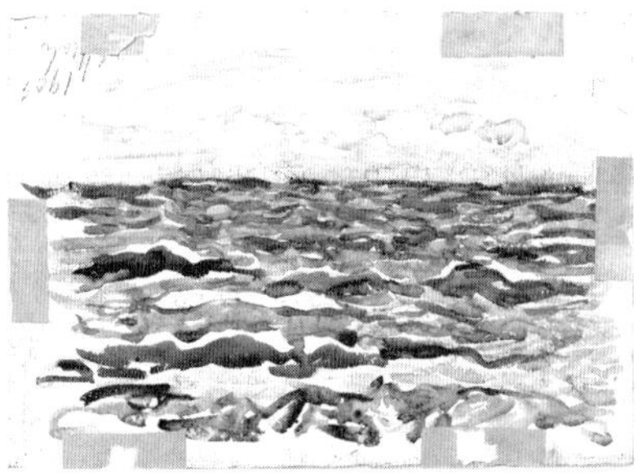

CR 866 verso

CR 866
ST. MALO ca. 1907
Watercolor and pencil on paper
(11 x 15 in.; 27.9 x 38.1 cm)
Williams College Museum of Art, gift of Mrs. Charles Prendergast (91.18.17)

INSCRIPTIONS
l.r. in black ink: Prendergast
verso, u.r. in pencil: 1909/St. Malo

EXHIBITIONS
1989d Williams College (no #); 1993 Williams College (no #)

CR 866 verso
STUDY OF SEA AND SKY
Watercolor and pencil

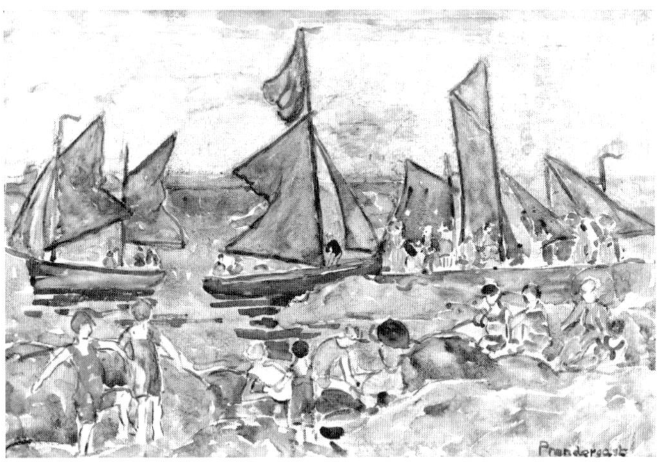

CR 867

CR 867
FISHING BOATS, LE TREPORT ca. 1907
Fishing Boats, Treport
Frame by Charles Prendergast
Watercolor and pencil on paper
(13¼ x 19⅜ in.; 33.7 x 49.2 cm)
Williams College Museum of Art, bequest of Mrs. Charles Prendergast (95.4.85)

INSCRIPTIONS
l.c. in pencil: Prendergast
l.r. in blue: Prendergast

EXHIBITIONS
1944b Kraushaar (#20, as *Fishing Boats, Treport*)

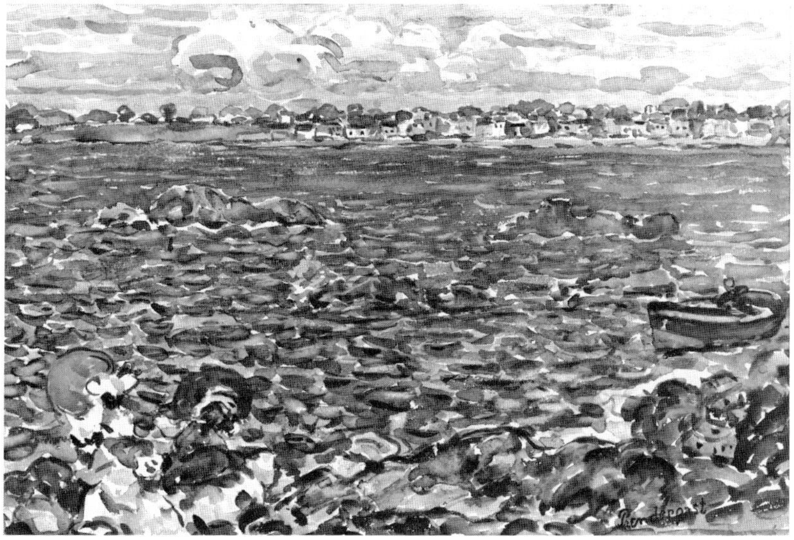

CR 873

CR 873

GLOUCESTER HARBOR ca. 1907
Frame by Charles Prendergast
Watercolor and pencil on paper
(13 x 19¼ in.; 33.0 x 48.9 cm)
Williams College Museum of Art, bequest of Mrs. Charles Prendergast (95.4.81)

INSCRIPTIONS
l.r. in black: Prendergast

EXHIBITIONS
? 1934a Whitney (#147); 1995c Williams College (no #)

CR 883

ST. MALO ca. 1907
Watercolor and pencil on paper
(11¼ x 15¼ in.; 28.6 x 38.7 cm)
Williams College Museum of Art, gift of Mrs. Charles Prendergast (86.18.75)

INSCRIPTIONS
l.r. in black: Prendergast

BIBLIOGRAPHY
Allen & Hanburys 1993 (n.p.; ill. July)

EXHIBITIONS
1986 Williams College (no #); 1989c Williams College (no #); 1990c Williams College (#59, ABCD); 1992 Williams College (no #); 1993 Williams College (no #)

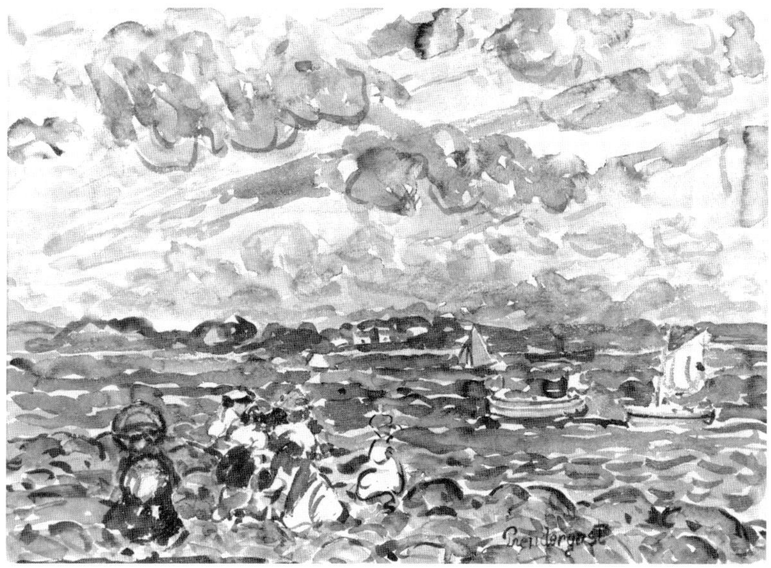

CR 883

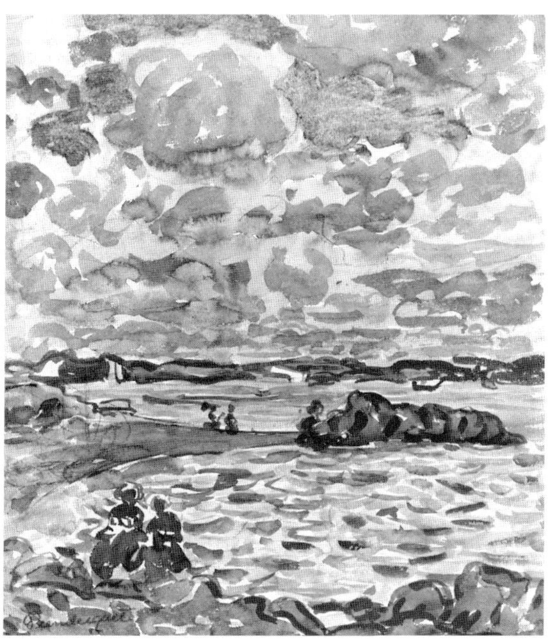

CR 885

CR 885

ST. MALO ca. 1907
Watercolor, charcoal, and pencil on paper
(14¾ x 12¾ in.; 37.5 x 32.4 cm)
Williams College Museum of Art, bequest of Mrs. Charles Prendergast (95.4.89)

INSCRIPTIONS
l.l. in pencil: Prendergast

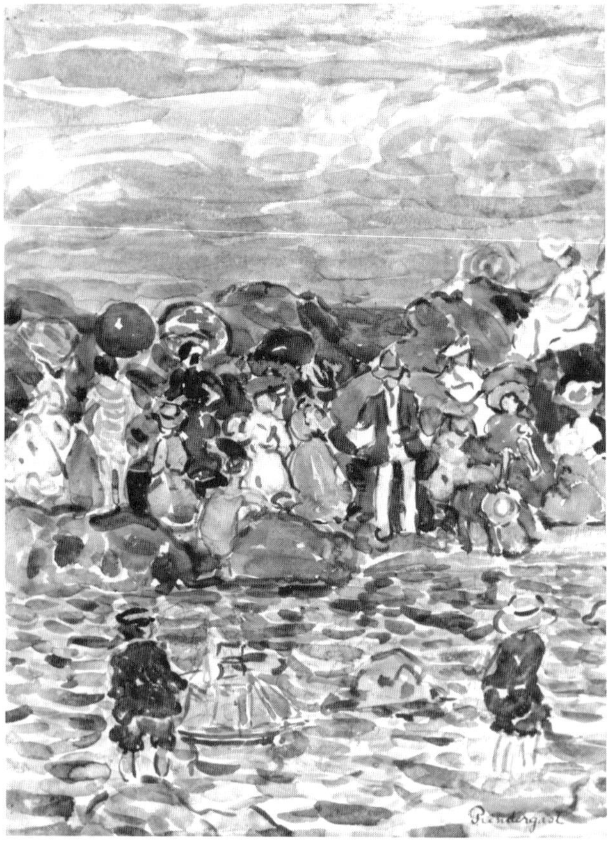

CR 896

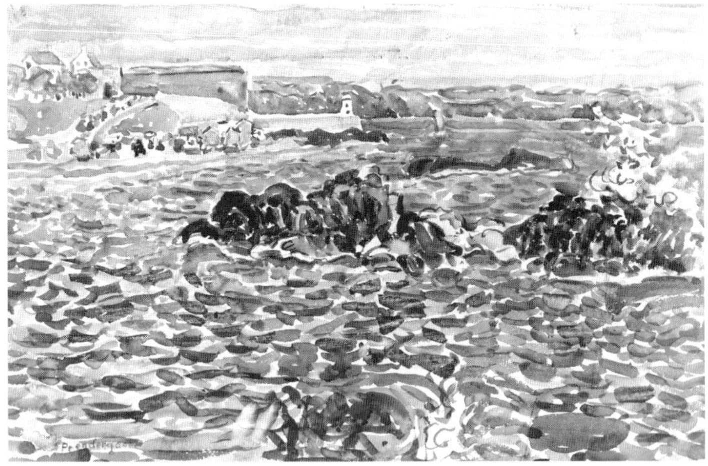

CR 901

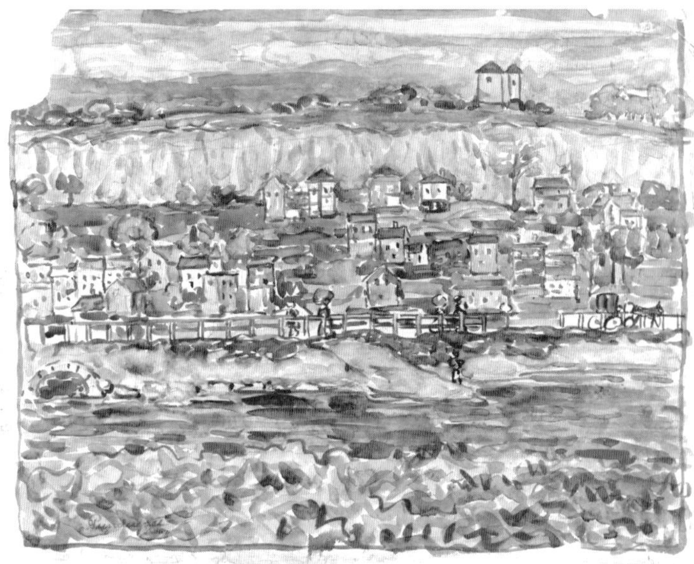

CR 904

CR 896

ST. MALO ca. 1907
Watercolor, pencil, and gouache on paper
(15¼ x 11 in.; 38.7 x 27.9 cm)
Williams College Museum of Art, gift of
Mrs. Charles Prendergast (86.18.74)

Inscriptions
l.r. in ink: Prendergast
verso in pencil: St Malo/1909

Exhibitions
1986 Williams College (no #); 1990c Williams College (#58, CD); 1993 Williams College (no #)

Note
Although later inscribed 1909, this work more likely dates from the artist's 1907 trip to St.-Malo.
Color plate, p. 14

CR 901

GLOUCESTER HARBOR ca. 1907
Frame by Charles Prendergast
Watercolor and pencil on paper
(13⅜ x 20 in.; 34.0 x 50.8 cm)
Williams College Museum of Art, gift of
Mrs. Charles Prendergast (86.18.49)

Inscriptions
l.l. in blue watercolor over pencil: Prendergast

Bibliography
Sawyer 1966 (n.p.); Lauzon 1989 (pp. E: 1, 4)

Exhibitions
1966a Knoedler (#46, ill.); 1970 Knoedler (#9); 1986 Williams College (no #); 1989d Williams College (no #); 1990b Williams College (no #)

Note
Although the title identifies the setting as the New England coast, the lighthouse on a pier and the bathing tents suggest that the subject is St.-Malo.

CR 904

ST. MALO ca. 1907
Watercolor and pencil on paper
(13¼ x 16⅞ in.; 33.7 x 42.9 cm)
Williams College Museum of Art, gift of
Mrs. Charles Prendergast (91.28.1)

Inscriptions
l.l. in pencil: Prendergast

Exhibitions
1993 Williams College (no #); 1995d Williams College (no #)

CR 910
FRANCE ca. 1907
Watercolor and pencil on paper
(12½ x 19½ in.; 31.7 x 49.5 cm)
Williams College Museum of Art, gift of Mrs. Charles Prendergast (86.18.57)

INSCRIPTIONS
verso u.l. in pencil (in Charles Prendergast's hand): France

EXHIBITIONS
1986 Williams College (no #); 1990b Williams College (no #); 1991a Williams College (no #)

CR 910 verso
FIGURE STUDIES
Pencil
(Too faint to reproduce)

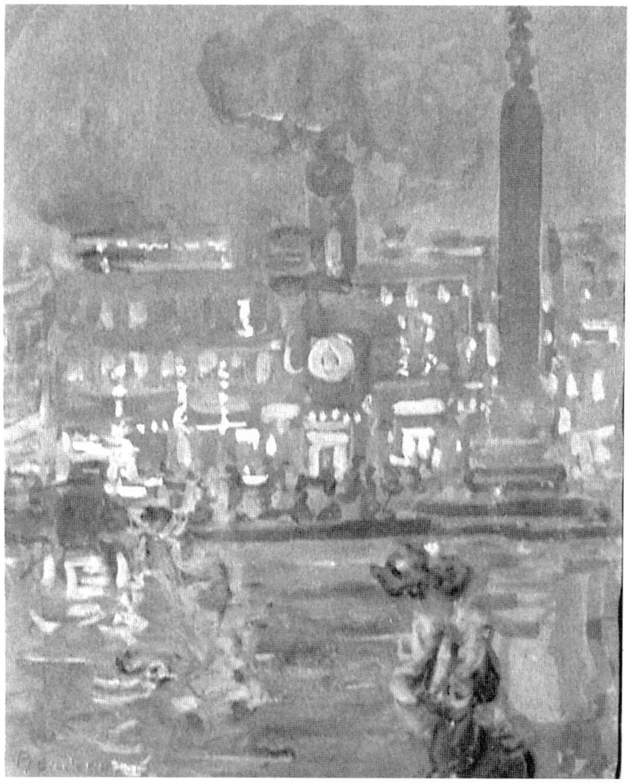
CR 918

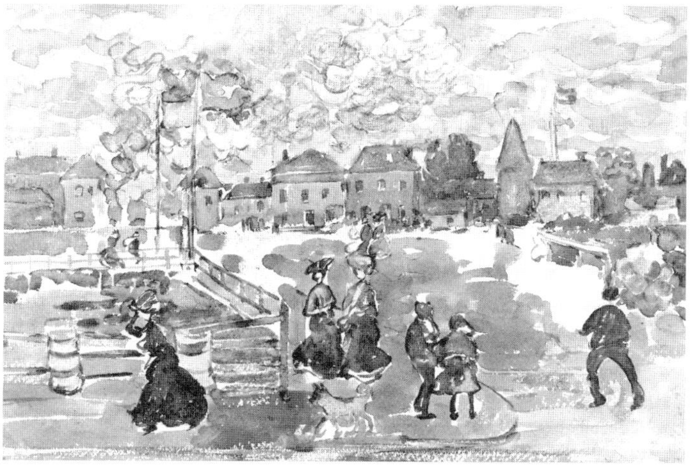
CR 910

CR 918
PARIS ca. 1907
Nocturne; Place Vendome
Watercolor and gouache on blue paper
(12¼ x 9¾ in.; 31.1 x 24.8 cm)
Williams College Museum of Art, gift of Mrs. Charles Prendergast (91.18.7)

INSCRIPTIONS
l.l. in pencil: Prendergast

EXHIBITIONS
1990c Williams College (#48, ABCD); 1995c Williams College (no #); 1995d Williams College (no #)

CR 929
QUEEN, LUXEMBOURG GARDENS ca. 1907
Frame by Charles Prendergast
Watercolor and pencil on paper
(13 x 19 in.; 33.0 x 48.3 cm)
Williams College Museum of Art, bequest of Mrs. Charles Prendergast (95.4.107)

INSCRIPTIONS
l.l. in ink: Prendergast

EXHIBITIONS
1944b Kraushaar (#28)

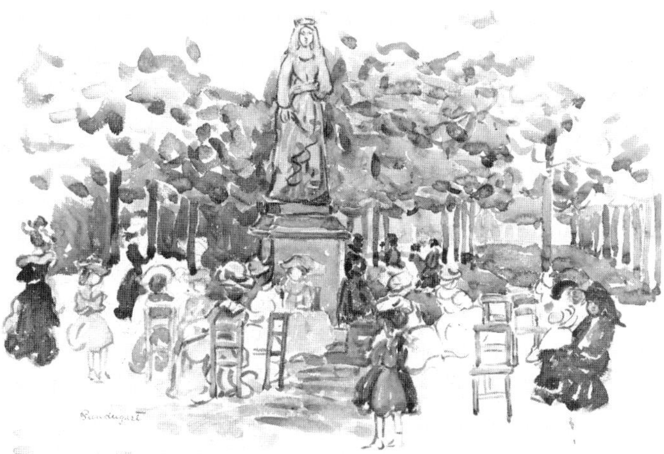
CR 929

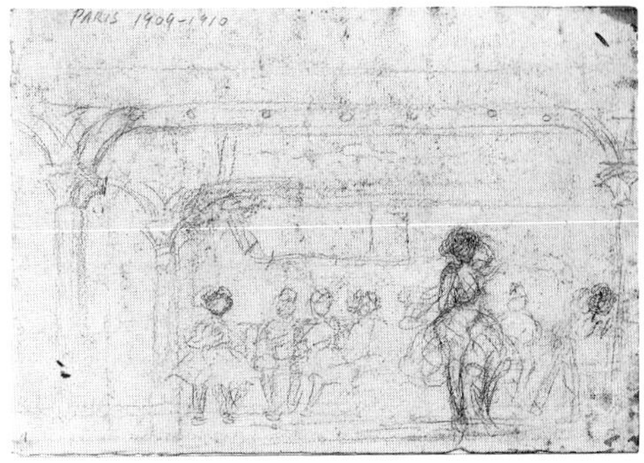

CR 930 verso

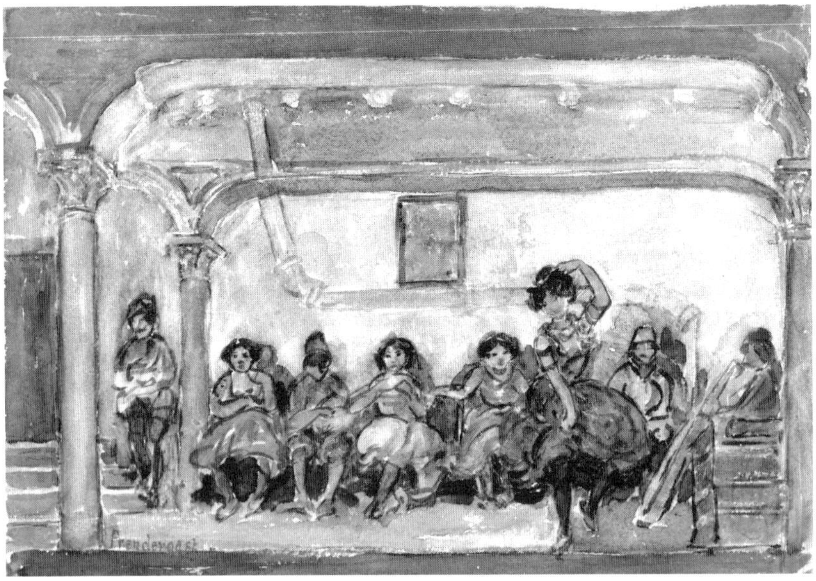

CR 930

CR 930
LA VIE MODERNE ca. 1907
Watercolor and pencil on paper
(11 x 15½ in.; 27.9 x 39.4 cm)
Williams College Museum of Art, gift of
Mrs. Charles Prendergast (85.21.8)

INSCRIPTIONS
l.l. in red: Prendergast

EXHIBITIONS
1988a Williams College (no #); 1989b Williams College (#8); 1991a Williams College (no #); 1992 Williams College (no #)

CR 930 verso
LA VIE MODERNE SKETCH
Pencil

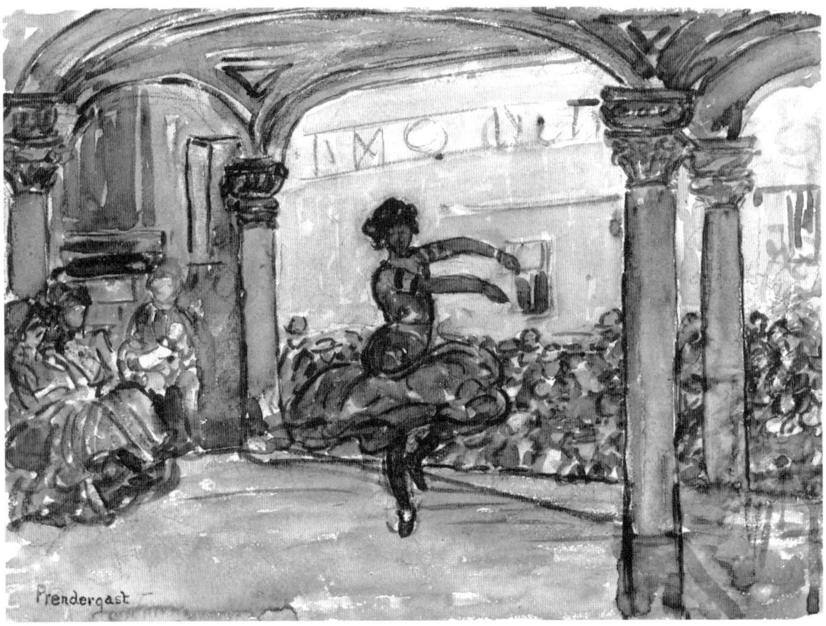

CR 931

CR 931
CABARET ca. 1907
Watercolor and pencil on paper
(11⅛ x 15¼ in.; 28.3 x 38.7 cm)
Williams College Museum of Art, gift of
Mrs. Charles Prendergast (85.21.7)

INSCRIPTIONS
l.l. in black: Prendergast

BIBLIOGRAPHY
Mathews 1990 (p. 33; ill.)

EXHIBITIONS
1988a Williams College (no #); 1989b Williams College (#7); 1992 Williams College (no #)

CR 931 verso
CABARET SKETCH
Pencil

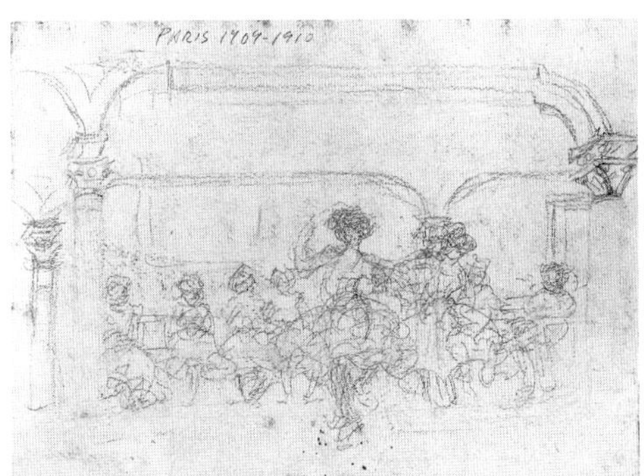

CR 931 verso

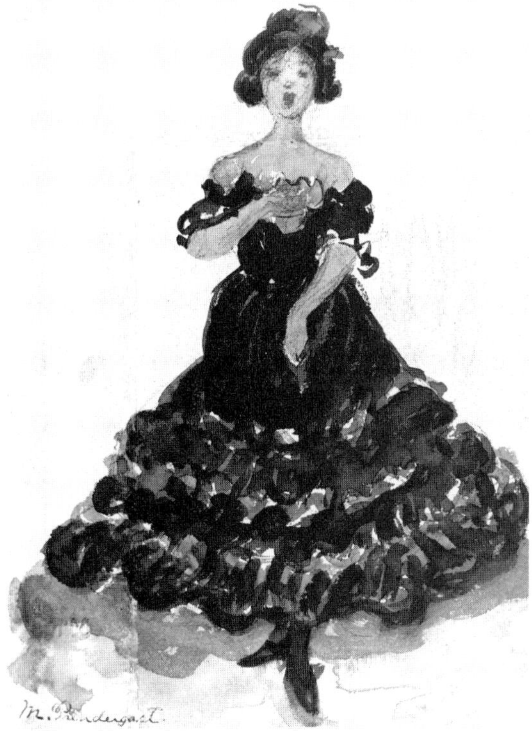

CR 932

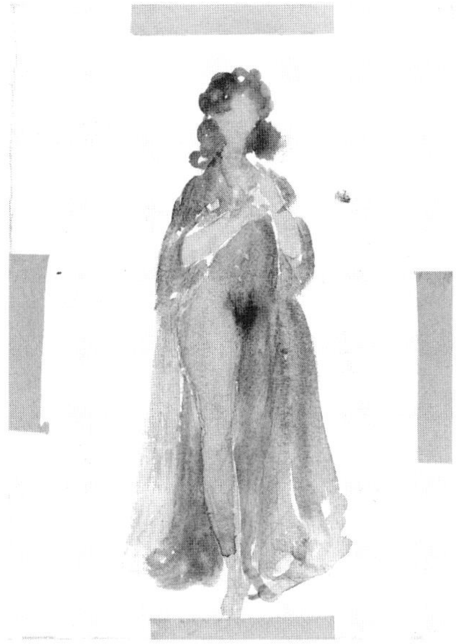

CR 932 verso

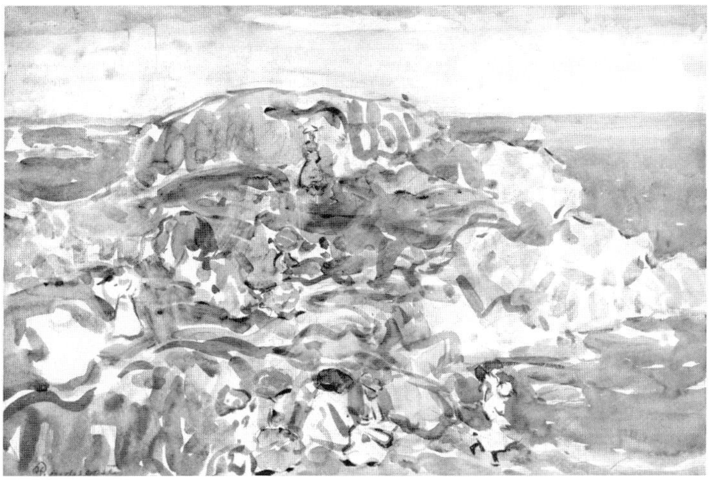

CR 945

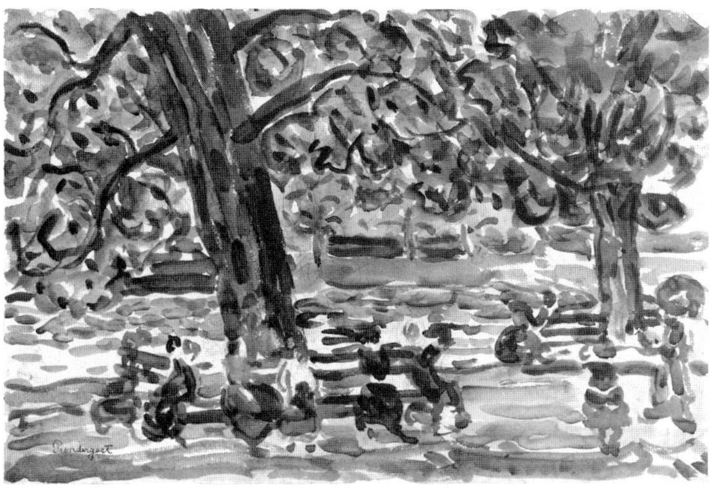

CR 955

CR 932
CAFÉ CONCERT SINGER ca. 1907
Watercolor and pencil on paper
(10⅛ x 7 in.; 25.7 x 17.8 cm)
Williams College Museum of Art, gift of Mrs. Charles Prendergast (85.21.9)

INSCRIPTIONS
l.l. in black ink: M. Prendergast.

EXHIBITIONS
1988a Williams College (no #); 1989c Williams College (no #); 1991a Williams College (no #)

CR 932 verso
NUDE WITH DRAPE

CR 945
ROCKY POINT ca. 1907–10
Watercolor and pencil on paper
(14⅝ x 20¾ in.; 37.1 x 52.7 cm)
Williams College Museum of Art, gift of Mrs. Charles Prendergast (86.18.52)

INSCRIPTIONS
l.l. in pencil: Prendergast

EXHIBITIONS
1990b Williams College (no #); 1991b Williams College (no #)

CR 955
PARK BENCHES ca. 1907–10
Watercolor and pencil on paper
(12 x 17⅞ in.; 30.5 x 45.4 cm)
Williams College Museum of Art, gift of Mrs. Charles Prendergast (91.28.16)

INSCRIPTIONS
l.l. in black ink: Prendergast

EXHIBITIONS
1993 Williams College (no #)

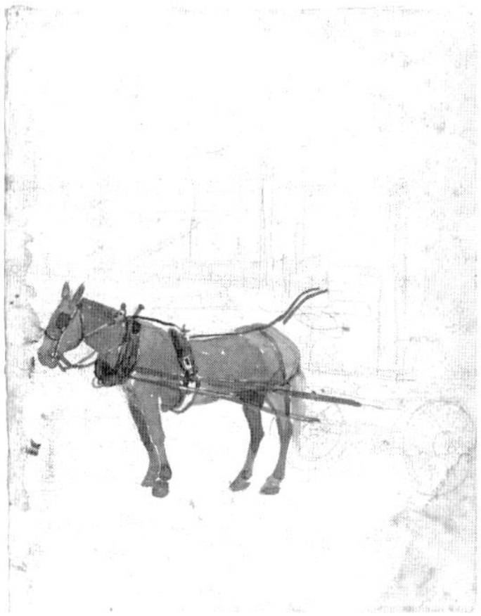

CR 960 verso

CR 960
SEASIDE PARK WITH SAILBOAT ca. 1907–10
Watercolor and pencil on paper
(11 x 14⅜ in.; 27.9 x 36.5 cm)
Williams College Museum of Art, gift of Mrs. Charles Prendergast in honor of Linda Shearer, Director, Williams College Museum of Art (91.28.2)

INSCRIPTIONS
l.r. in pencil: Prendergast/Prendergast

EXHIBITIONS
1993 Williams College (no #)

CR 960 verso
HORSE
Watercolor and pencil

CR 971
NEW ENGLAND HOLIDAY ca. 1910–11
Vacation in New England
Watercolor and pencil on paper
(14¾ x 21½ in.; 37.5 x 54.7 cm)
Williams College Museum of Art, gift of Mrs. Charles Prendergast (86.18.3)

INSCRIPTIONS
l.l. in black chalk: Prendergast

EXHIBITIONS
1982 Smithsonian SITES (#47, ill.); 1983a Williams College (#11, ill.); 1985b Williams College (no #); 1986 Williams College (no #); 1989c Williams College (no #); 1990b Williams College (no #); 1993 Williams College (no #)

CR 976
SPRING PROMENADE ca. 1910–11
Watercolor and pencil on paper
(21⅝ x 14⅞ in.; 54.9 x 37.8 cm)
Williams College Museum of Art, gift of Mrs. Charles Prendergast (86.18.6)

INSCRIPTIONS
l.l. in pencil: Prendergast

EXHIBITIONS
1982 Smithsonian SITES (#50, ill.); 1983a Williams College (#19, ill.); 1985b Williams College (no #); 1986 Williams College (no #); 1988a Williams College (no #); 1988b Williams College (#28); 1990c Williams College (#67, ABCD); 1993 Williams College (no #); 1994a Williams College (no #)
Color plate, p. 38

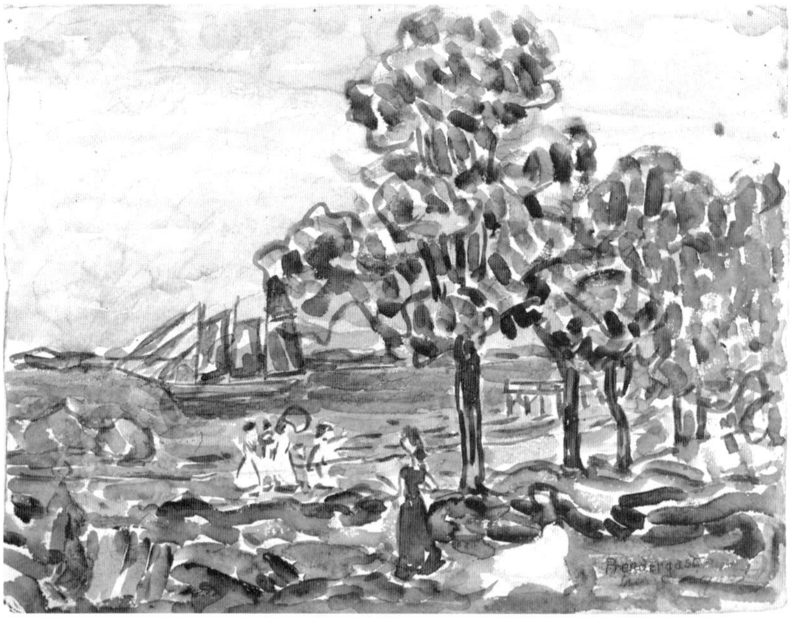

CR 960

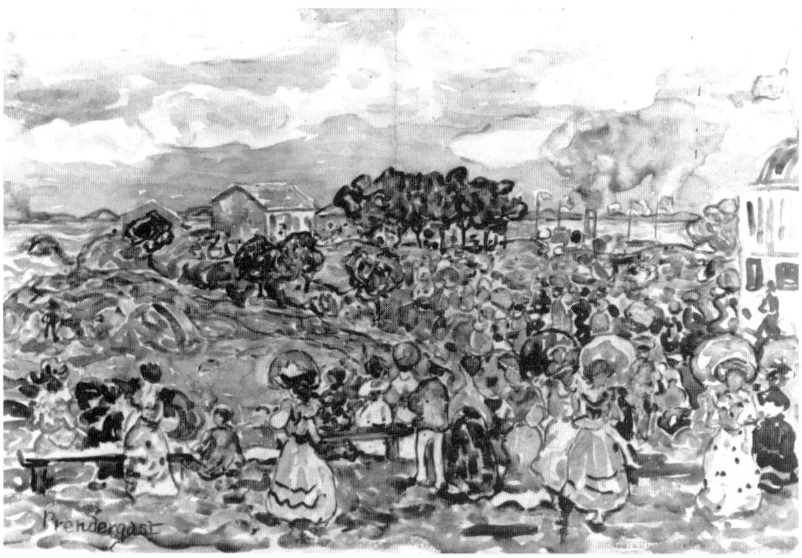

CR 971

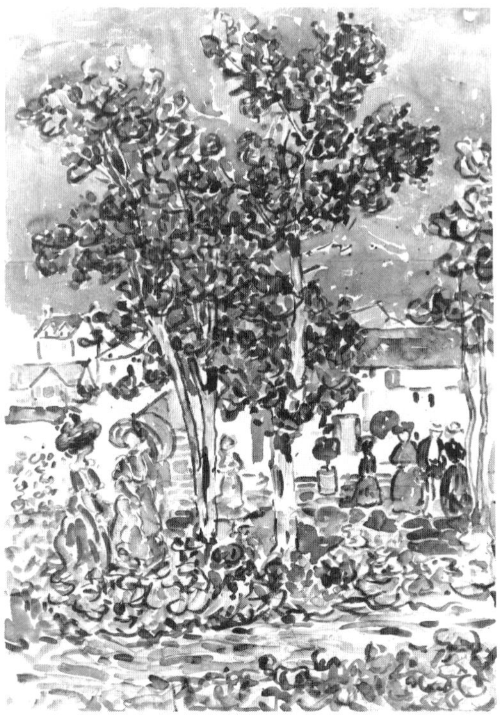

CR 976

CR 999
STUDY OF TREE AT THE SHORE ca. 1910–11
Watercolor and pencil on paper
(21¾ x 15¼ in.; 55.2 x 38.7 cm)
Collection of Williams College, gift of Mrs. Charles Prendergast (91.28.3)

INSCRIPTIONS
l.r. in black chalk: Prendergast

EXHIBITIONS
1993 Williams College (no #); 1994a Williams College (no #)

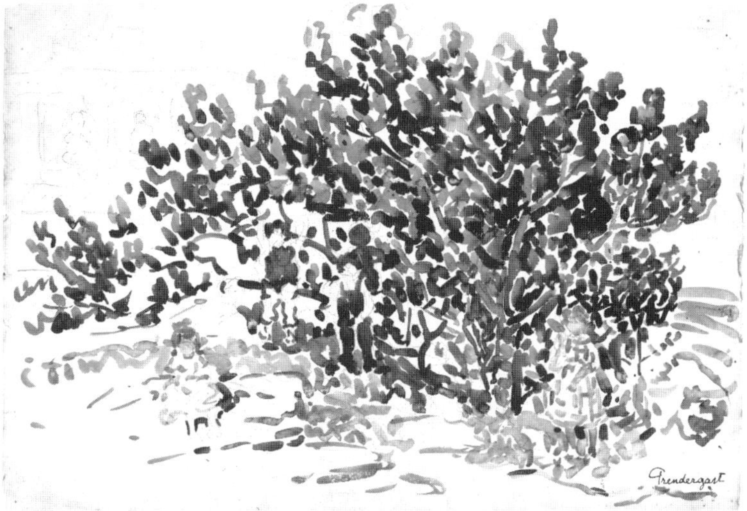

CR 1000

CR 1000
CHILDREN IN THE TREE ca. 1910–11
Watercolor and pencil on paper
(15⅛ x 22¼ in.; 38.4 x 56.5 cm)
Williams College Museum of Art, gift of Mrs. Charles Prendergast (91.18.3)

INSCRIPTIONS
l.r. in black ink: Prendergast

BIBLIOGRAPHY
Mathews 1990 (p. 113; ill.)

EXHIBITIONS
1988a Williams College (no #); 1990c Williams College (#68, ABCD); 1993 Williams College (no #); 1994a Williams College (no #)

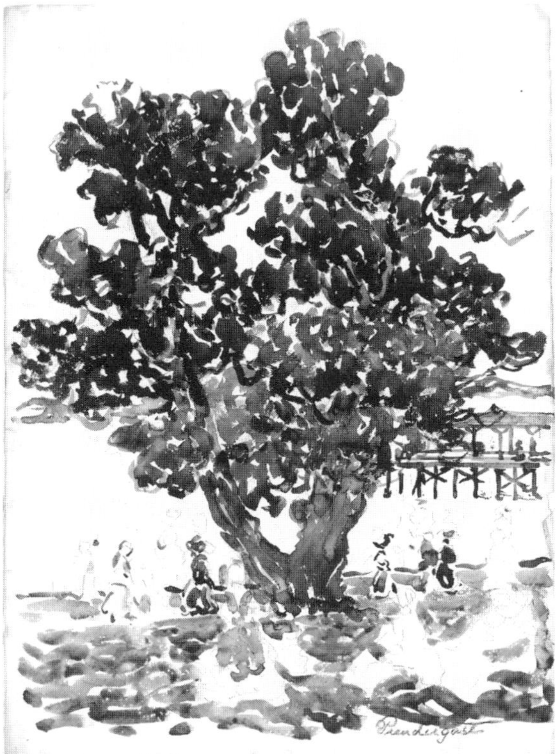

CR 999

CR 1000 verso
SKETCH FOR CHILDREN IN THE TREE
Pencil
(Too faint to reproduce)

CR 1002
STRAWBERRY HILL ca. 1910–11
Watercolor and pencil on paper
(14¼ x 11 in.; 36.2 x 27.9 cm)
Williams College Museum of Art, bequest of Mrs. Charles Prendergast (95.4.110)

INSCRIPTIONS
l.r. in gray: Prendergast

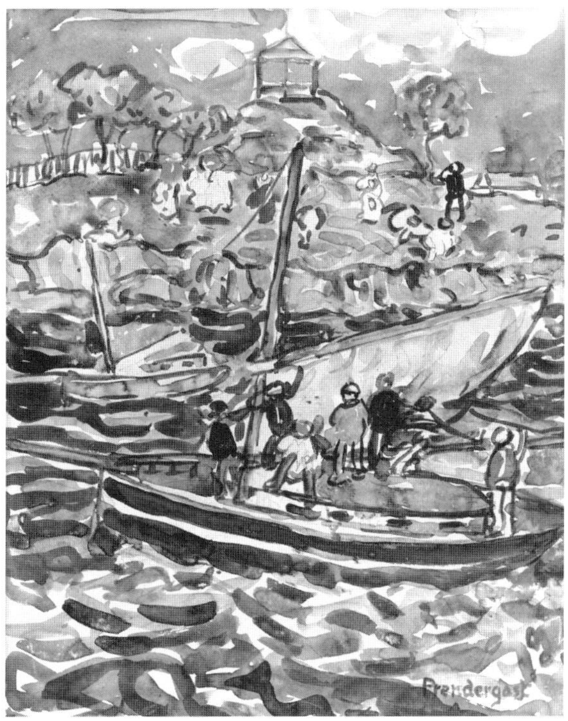

CR 1002

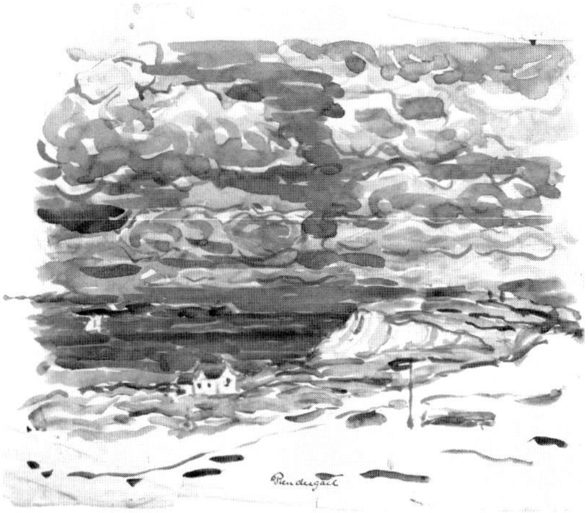

CR 1007

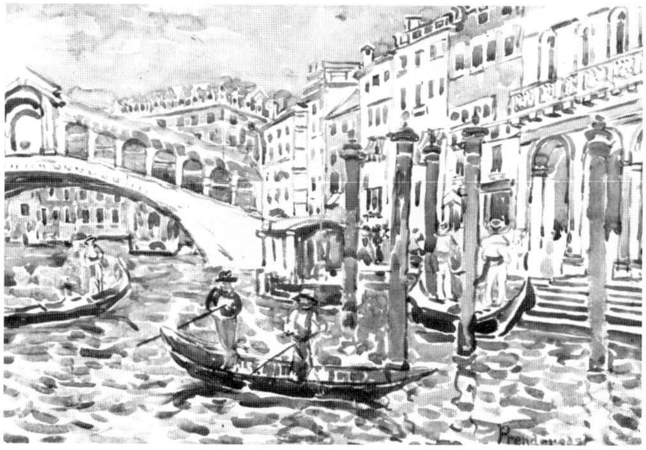

CR 1010

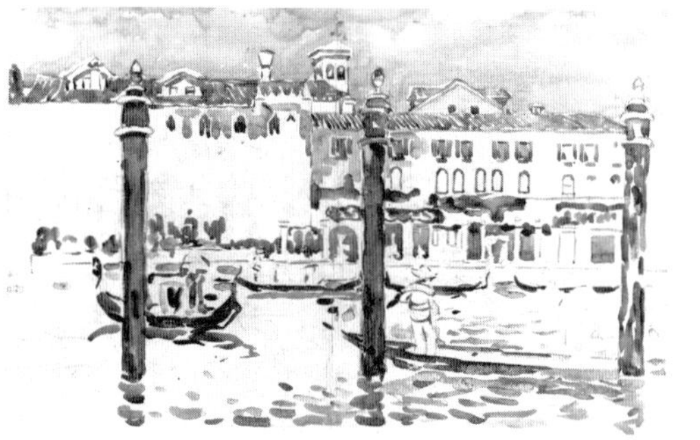

CR 1010 verso

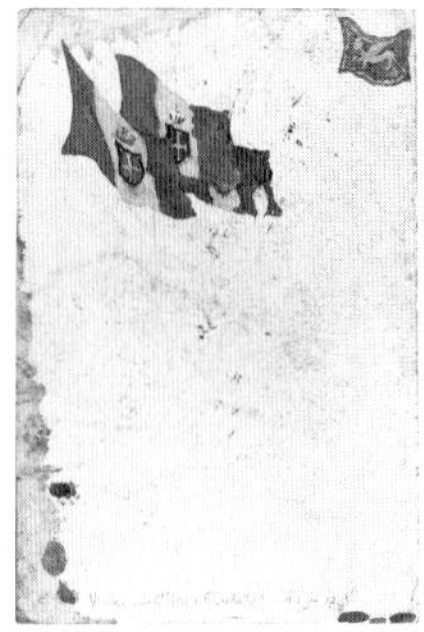

CR 1023 verso

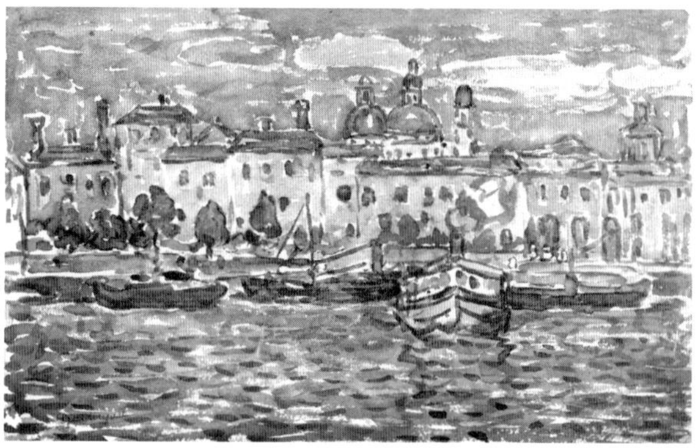

CR 1023

CR 1007

ST. MALO ca. 1910–11
Watercolor and pencil on paper
(13½ x 16 in.; 34.3 x 40.6 cm)
Williams College Museum of Art, gift of Mrs. Charles Prendergast (91.28.4)

INSCRIPTIONS
l.c. in black ink: Prendergast
verso in pencil: San Malo

EXHIBITIONS
1993 Williams College (no #)

NOTE
Although later titled *St. Malo,* this watercolor was likely painted after Prendergast returned from France.

CR 1010

RIALTO, VENICE ca. 1911–12
Watercolor and pencil on paper
(14⅞ x 21⅝ in.; 38.1 x 55.9 cm)
Williams College Museum of Art, gift of Mrs. Charles Prendergast (86.18.79)

INSCRIPTIONS
l.r. in brown: Prendergast

BIBLIOGRAPHY
Albertazzi 1990 (ill.); Andre 1990 (ill.); Baker 1990 (p. 14; ill.); *Issue* 1990 (ill.); Perlman 1990 (ill.)

EXHIBITIONS
? 1928 Anderson Galleries (#28); 1977d Whitney (no #); 1983 Coe Kerr (#65, 66, ill.); 1983a Williams College (# 8, 9, ill.); 1986 Williams College (no #); 1990c Williams College (#72, ABCD); 1993 Williams College (no #); 1995d Williams College (no #)

NOTE
This is a view of the Grand Canal from Riva del Carbon.

CR 1010 verso

RIALTO, VENICE
Watercolor and pencil

CR 1023

VENICE: THE ZATTERE ca. 1911–12
Watercolor and pencil on paper
(12½ x 19¼ in.; 31.7 x 48.9 cm)
Williams College Museum of Art, gift of Mrs. Charles Prendergast (91.28.6)

INSCRIPTIONS
l.l. in black ink: Prendergast

EXHIBITIONS
1993 Williams College (no #); 1995d Williams College (no #)

NOTE
This is a view along the Zattere, looking across the Giudecca canal with S. Maria della Salute in the distance.

CR 1023 verso

FLAGS IN PIAZZA SAN MARCO ca. 1898–99
Watercolor and pencil

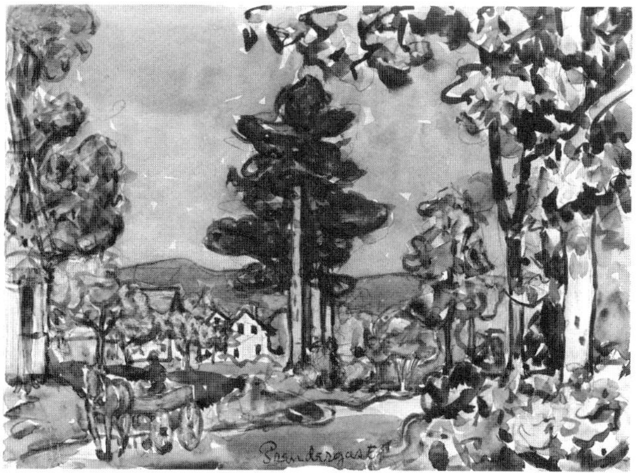

CR 1035

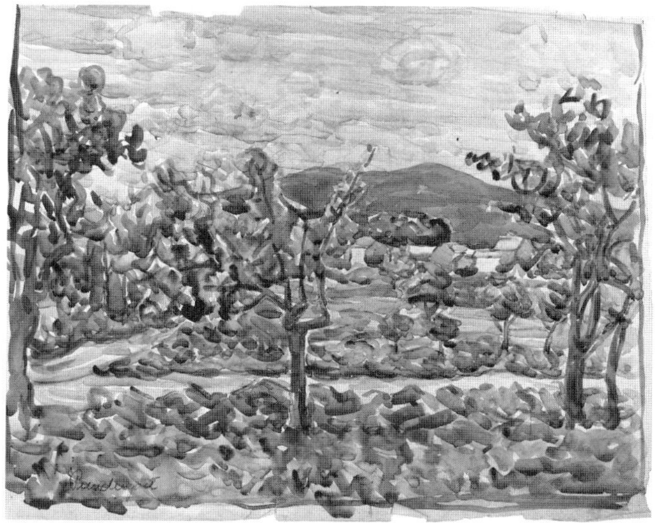

CR 1051

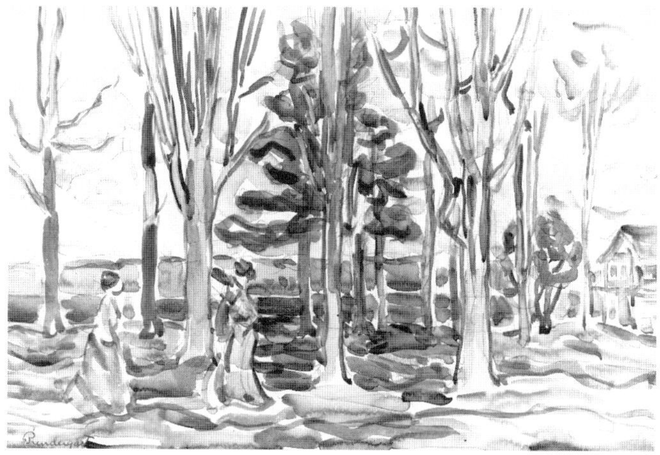

CR 1056

CR 1035
NEW HAMPSHIRE VILLAGE ca. 1910–13
Frame by Charles Prendergast
Watercolor, pastel, and pencil on paper
(8⅞ x 11¾ in.; 22.5 x 29.8 cm)
Williams College Museum of Art, bequest of Mrs. Charles Prendergast (95.4.104)

INSCRIPTIONS
l.c. in ink: Prendergast

CR 1046
LANDSCAPE, NEW HAMPSHIRE ca. 1910–13
Landscape
Watercolor, pencil, and pastel on paper
(12 x 17⅞ in.; 30.5 x 45.4 cm)
Williams College Museum of Art, Museum Purchase (41.1)

INSCRIPTIONS
l.r. in pencil: Prendergast

PROVENANCE
(Macbeth); to present collection, 1941

BIBLIOGRAPHY
Owens 1978 (p. 22, as *Landscape*); Spencer 1985 (p. 18)

EXHIBITIONS
1941 Williams College (#14, as *Landscape*); 1963 Southern Vermont (#59, as *Landscape*); 1978 Clark Art Institute (#16, ill.); 1983a Williams College (#15); 1985b Williams College (no #); 1990b Williams College (no #); 1991c Williams College (no #); 1993 Williams College (no #)

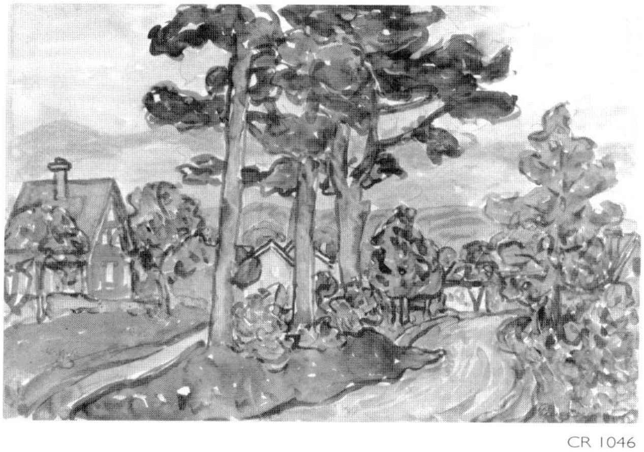

CR 1046

CR 1051
FARMLAND ca. 1910–13
Watercolor and pencil on paper
(13¼ x 16¾ in.; 33.7 x 42.5 cm)
Williams College Museum of Art, bequest of Mrs. Charles Prendergast (95.4.4)

INSCRIPTIONS
l.l. in pencil: Prendergast

CR 1056
FALL DAY ca. 1910–13
Watercolor and pencil on paper
(12 x 17¾ in.; 30.5 x 45.1 cm)
Williams College Museum of Art, gift of Mrs. Charles Prendergast (86.18.41)

INSCRIPTIONS
l.l. in ink: Prendergast

EXHIBITIONS
1990b Williams College (no #); 1991b Williams College (no #)

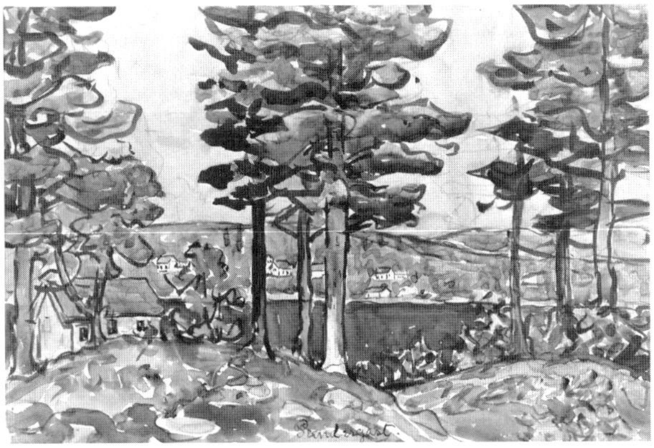

CR 1065

CR 1065

LAKE OSSIPEE, NEW HAMPSHIRE
ca. 1910–13
Frame by Charles Prendergast
Watercolor and pencil on paper
(12 x 17⅞ in.; 30.5 x 45.4 cm)
Williams College Museum of Art, gift of Mrs. Charles Prendergast (86.18.54)

INSCRIPTIONS
l.c. in black ink: Prendergast

BIBLIOGRAPHY
Williams College 1991 (n.p.; ill.)

EXHIBITIONS
1930 Kraushaar (#9); 1938 Addison Gallery (#47); 1986 Williams College (no #); 1990b Williams College (no #)

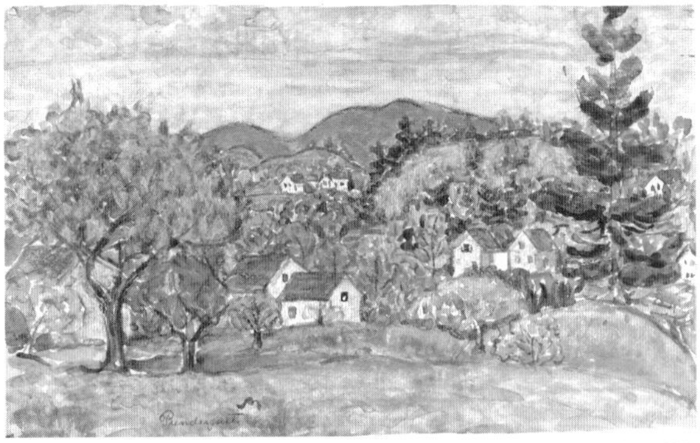

CR 1083

CR 1083

AUTUMN IN MAINE ca. 1910–13
Watercolor, pastel, and pencil on paper
(13½ x 22 in.; 34.3 x 55.9 cm)
Williams College Museum of Art, gift of Mrs. Charles Prendergast (91.18.21)

INSCRIPTIONS
l.l. in pencil: Prendergast/Prendergast

EXHIBITIONS
1990b Williams College (no #); 1991b Williams College (no #)

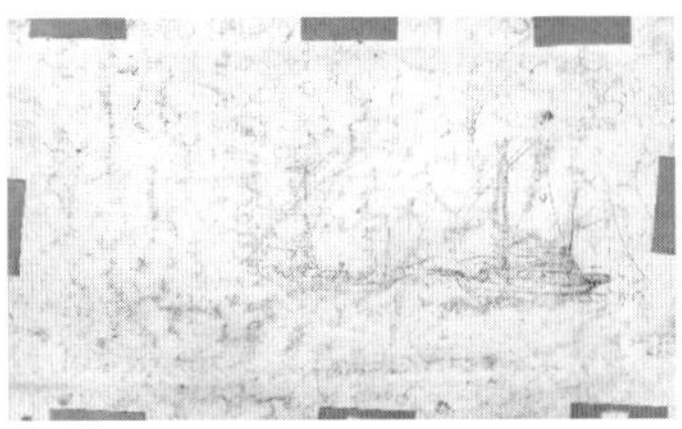

CR 1083 verso

CR 1083 verso

SAILBOATS
Pencil

CR 1088

ROAD TO THE VILLAGE ca. 1910–13
Watercolor and pencil on paper
(8¾ x 11¾ in.; 22.2 x 29.8 cm)
Williams College Museum of Art, gift of Mrs. Charles Prendergast in honor of Nancy Mowll Mathews, Prendergast Curator (91.28.5)

INSCRIPTIONS
l.r. in black ink: Prendergast

EXHIBITIONS
1993 Williams College (no #); 1995d Williams College (no #)

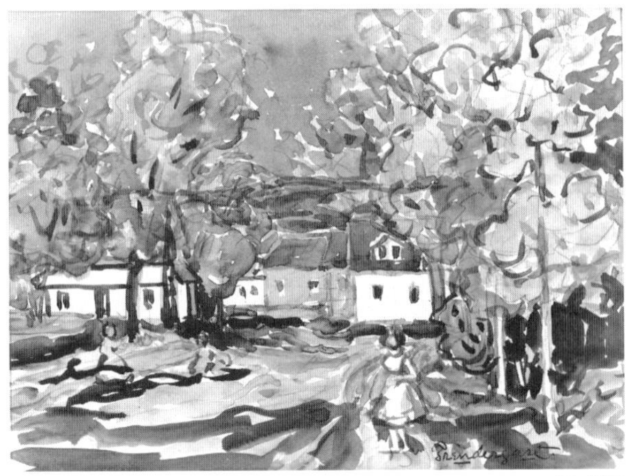

CR 1088

CR 1098

APPLE TREE ca. 1910–13
Watercolor and pencil on paper
(15 x 22 in.; 38.1 x 55.9 cm)
Williams College Museum of Art, gift of Mrs. Charles Prendergast (91.28.7)

INSCRIPTIONS
l.l. in pencil: Prendergast

EXHIBITIONS
1993 Williams College (no #)

CR 1098 verso

LANDSCAPE
Pencil
(Too faint to reproduce)

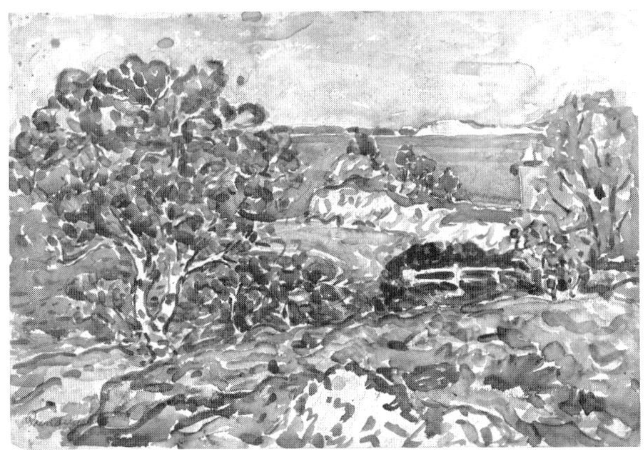

CR 1098

CR 1100

BIRCHES ca. 1910–13
Watercolor, pastel, and pencil on paper
(15 x 21½ in.; 38.1 x 54.6 cm)
Williams College Museum of Art, gift of
Mrs. Charles Prendergast (86.18.35)

INSCRIPTIONS
l.r. in ink: Prendergast

BIBLIOGRAPHY
Sawyer 1966 (n.p.)

EXHIBITIONS
1966a Knoedler (#50, ill.); 1970 Knoedler (#4); 1986 Williams College (no #); 1988a Williams College (no #); 1991b Williams College (no #); 1993 Williams College (no #)

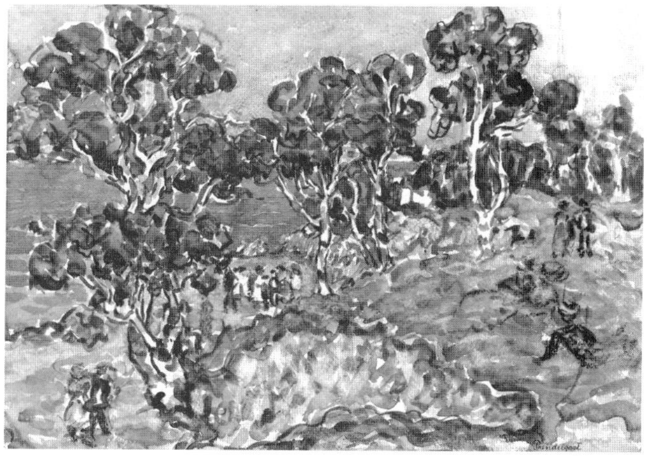

CR 1100

CR 1101

THE BIRCHES ca. 1910–13
Watercolor, pencil, and pastel on paper
(13¾ x 18⅝ in.; 33.7 x 47.3 cm)
Williams College Museum of Art, bequest of
Mrs. Charles Prendergast (95.4.18)

INSCRIPTIONS
l.r. in green pencil: Prendergast

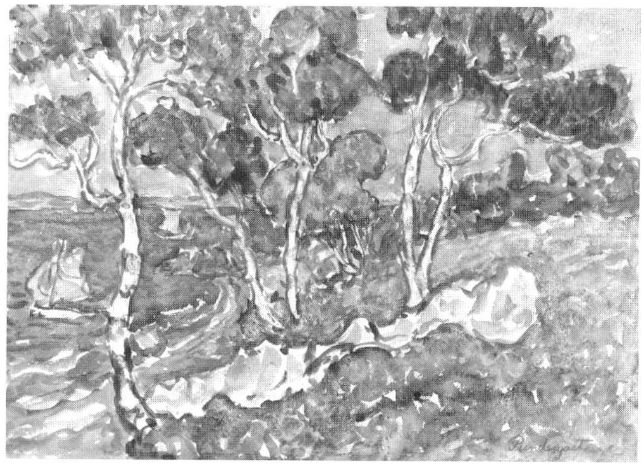

CR 1101

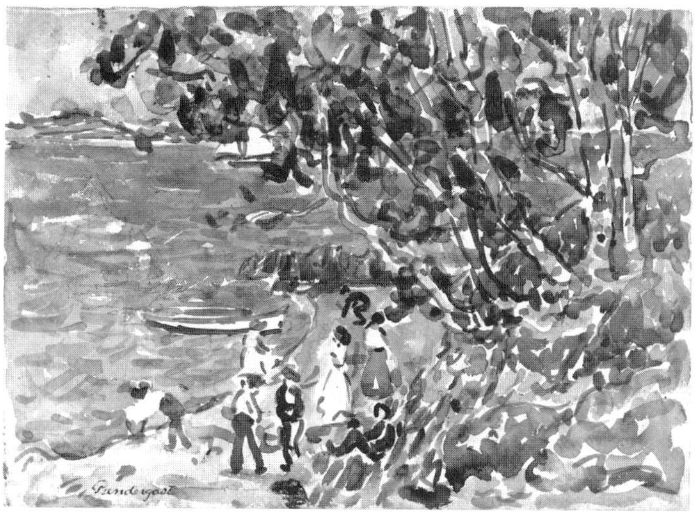

CR 1104

CR 1104

BIRCHES NEAR A COVE ca. 1910–13
Watercolor and pencil on paper
(11⅛ x 15¼ in.; 28.3 x 38.7 cm)
Williams College Museum of Art, gift of
Mrs. Charles Prendergast in honor of Francis
Oakley, President, Williams College (91.28.8)

INSCRIPTIONS
l.l. in black ink: Prendergast

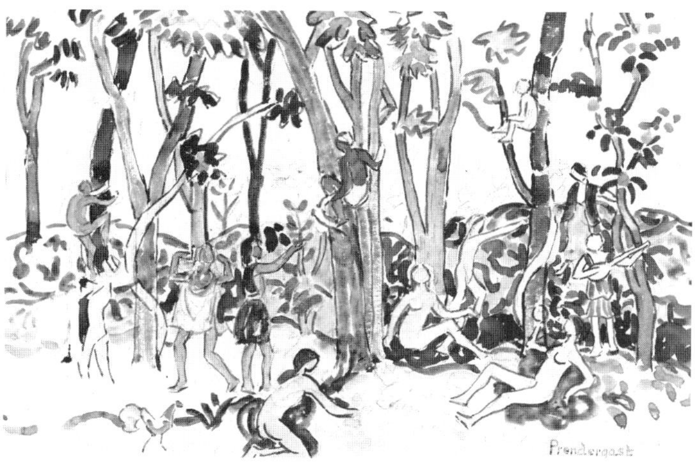

CR 1110

CR 1110

JUNGLE FANTASY ca. 1910–13
Watercolor and pencil on paper
(11½ x 17⅝ in.; 29.2 x 44.8 cm)
Williams College Museum of Art, bequest of
Mrs. Charles Prendergast (95.4.64)

INSCRIPTIONS
l.r. in blue: Prendergast

BIBLIOGRAPHY
Goldin 1976b (p. 63; ill.)

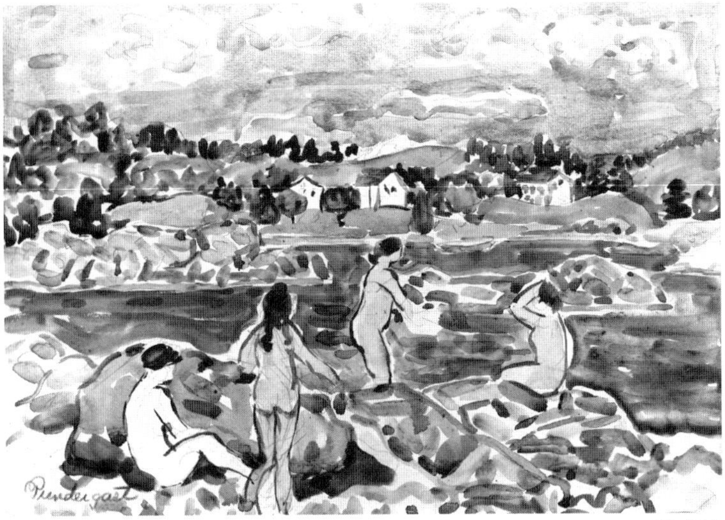

CR 1115

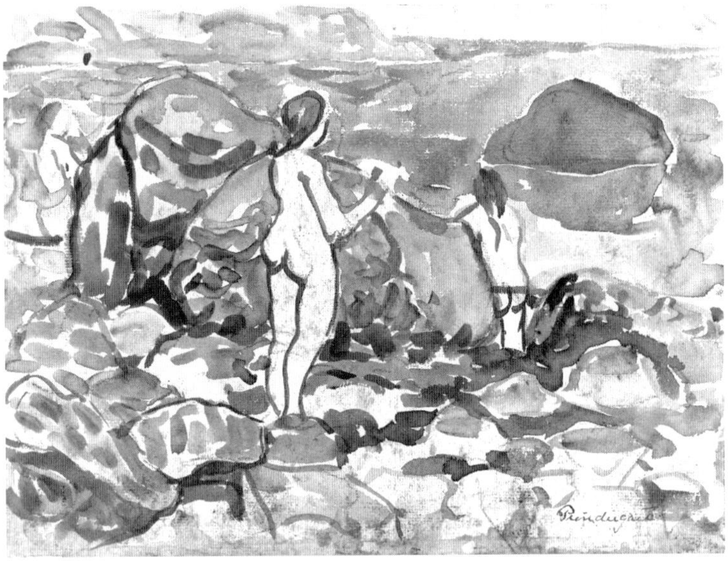

CR 1116

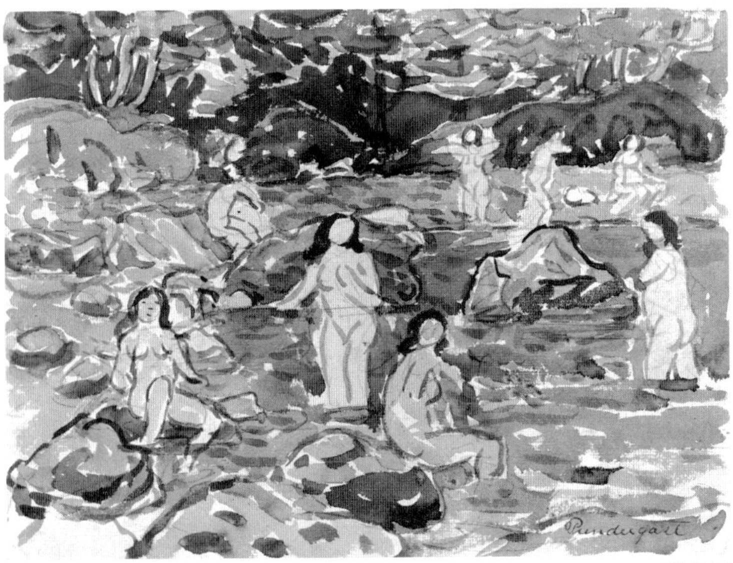

CR 1117

CR 1115
BATHERS AT PASSAMAQUODDY BAY
ca. 1910–13
Frame by Charles Prendergast
Watercolor and pencil on paper
(9⅝ x 13⅝ in.; 24.4 x 34.6 cm)
Williams College Museum of Art, bequest of Mrs. Charles Prendergast (95.4.66)

INSCRIPTIONS
l.l. in pencil: Prendergast

CR 1116
ROCKY SHORE WITH BATHERS
ca. 1910–13
Watercolor and pencil on paper
(9 x 12 in.; 22.9 x 30.5 cm)
Williams College Museum of Art, bequest of Mrs. Charles Prendergast (95.4.2)

INSCRIPTIONS
l.r. in black ink: Prendergast

EXHIBITIONS
1995c Williams College (no #)

CR 1117
EIGHT BATHERS IN A COVE ca. 1910–13
Watercolor and pencil on paper
(9⅛ x 12 in.; 23.2 x 30.5 cm)
Williams College Museum of Art, gift of Mrs. Charles Prendergast (91.28.9)

INSCRIPTIONS
l.r. in black ink: Prendergast

EXHIBITIONS
1993 Williams College (no #)

CR 1121
MODERN NUDE ca. 1910–13
Watercolor, pencil, and pastel on paper
(19⅞ x 14 in.; 50.5 x 35.6 cm)
Williams College Museum of Art, bequest of Mrs. Charles Prendergast (95.4.7)

INSCRIPTIONS
l.r. in red: M.B.P./Prendergast.

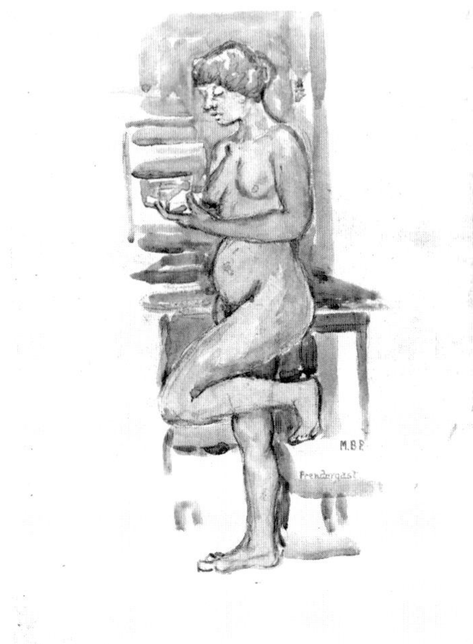

CR 1121

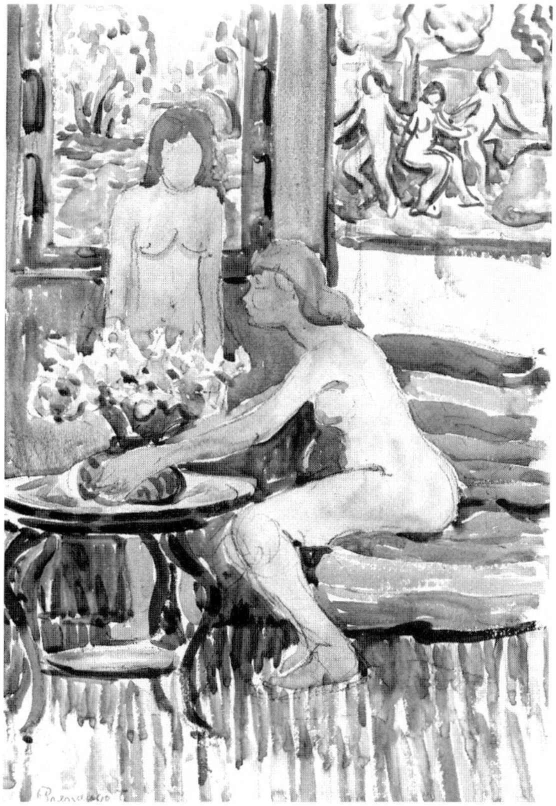

CR 1123

CR 1123
NUDES WITH JONQUILS ca. 1910–13
Jonquils
Frame by Charles Prendergast
Watercolor and pencil on paper
(11½ x 17½ in.; 22.9 x 44.5 cm)
Williams College Museum of Art, gift of
Mrs. Charles Prendergast (86.18.66)

INSCRIPTIONS
l.l. in red pencil: Prendergast

EXHIBITIONS
1930 Kraushaar (#10); 1986 Williams College (no #); 1989c Williams College (no #); 1991b Williams College (no #); 1991c Williams College (no #)

CR 1124
NARCISSUS ca. 1910–13
Watercolor and pencil on paper
(21 x 14¼ in.; 53.3 x 36.2 cm)
Williams College Museum of Art, bequest of
Mrs. Charles Prendergast (95.4.6)

INSCRIPTIONS
l.r. in blue: Prendergast

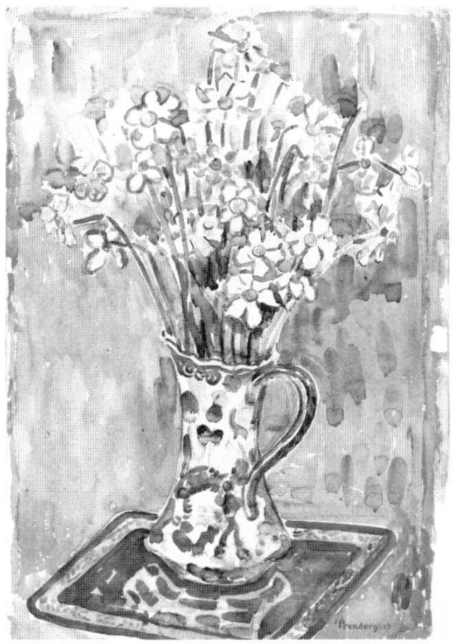

CR 1124

CR 1124 verso

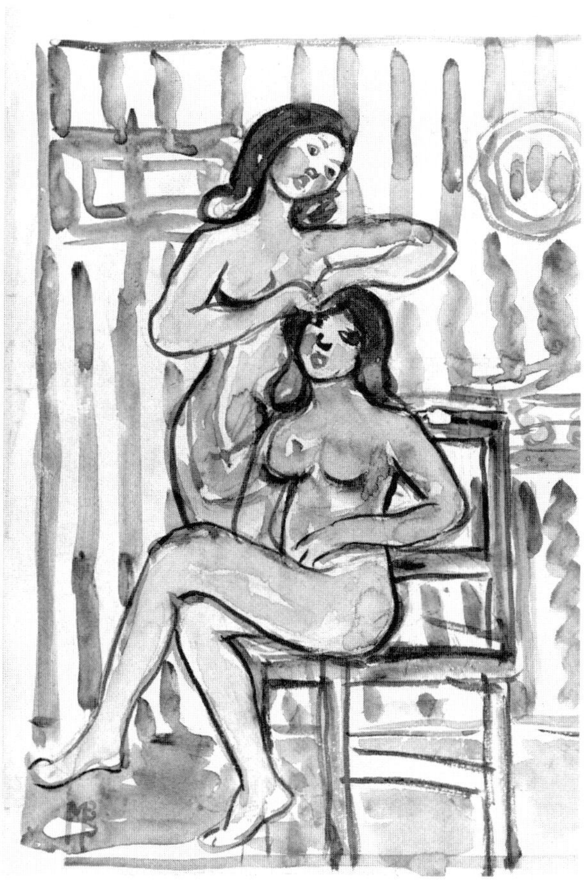

CR 1125

CR 1124 verso
VENICE ca. 1898–99
Watercolor and pencil
l.r. in pencil: Venice
u.r. vertically in pencil: M Imp. Nex

CR 1125
TWO NUDES ca. 1910–13
Watercolor and pencil on paper
(15⅜ x 9⅝ in.; 39.1 x 24.4 cm)
Williams College Museum of Art, bequest of
Mrs. Charles Prendergast (95.4.22)

INSCRIPTIONS
l.l. in green: MBP [monogram]
Cf. related studies in sketchbook CR 1509.

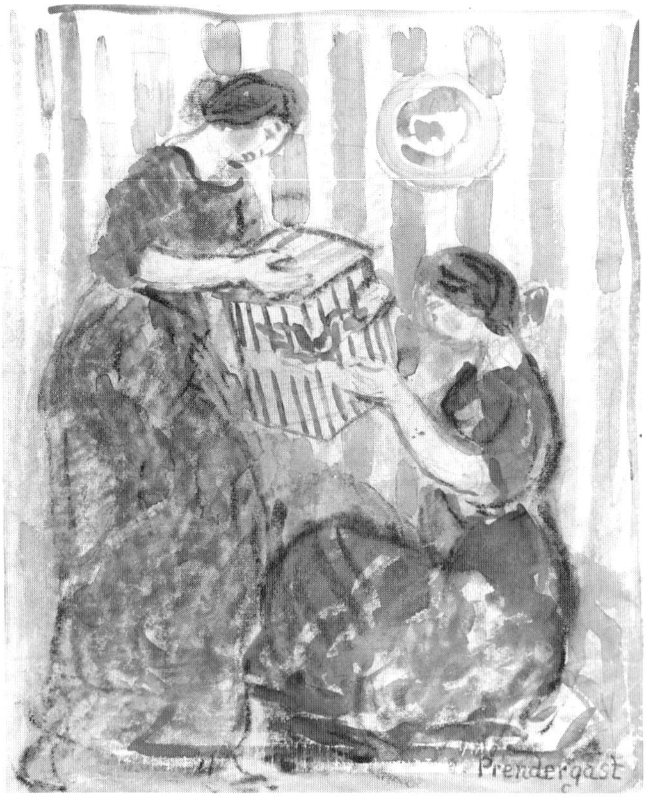

CR 1126

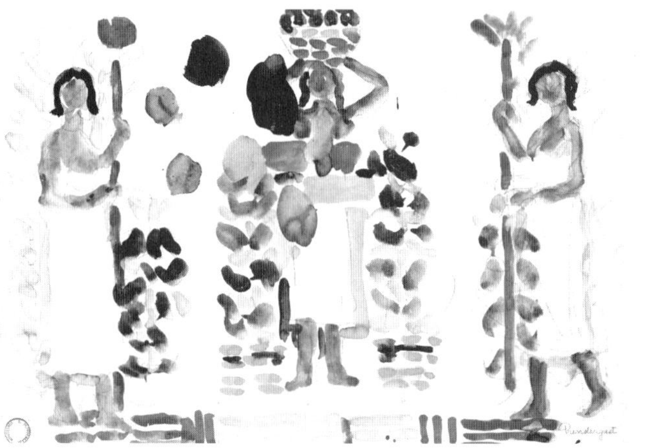

CR 1127

CR 1126
THE BIRD CAGE ca. 1910–13
Watercolor, pastel, and pencil on paper
(15½ x 12½ in.; 39.4 x 31.7 cm)
Williams College Museum of Art, bequest of
Mrs. Charles Prendergast (95.4.94)

INSCRIPTIONS
l.r. in blue: Prendergast

BIBLIOGRAPHY
Owens 1978 (pp. 7, 12)

EXHIBITIONS
1978 Clark Art Institute (#27, ill.)

CR 1127
THE OFFERING ca. 1910–13
Exotic Ceremony; Three Figures
Watercolor and pencil on paper
(12 x 18 in.; 30.5 x 45.7 cm)
Williams College Museum of Art, gift of
Mrs. Charles Prendergast (87.1.2)

INSCRIPTIONS
l.r. in pencil: Prendergast

EXHIBITIONS
1963a Davis Galleries (#3, as *Three Figures*); 1989b Williams College (#9); 1991a Williams College (no #)

CR 1128
THREE FIGURES WITH PARASOL ca. 1910–13
Figures with Parasol
Frame by Charles Prendergast
Watercolor, pastel, charcoal, and pencil on paper
(13¼ x 16⅝ in.; 33.7 x 42.2 cm)
Williams College Museum of Art, bequest of
Mrs. Charles Prendergast (95.4.111)

INSCRIPTIONS
l.l. in pencil: Prendergast
l.r. in black ink: Prendergast

CR 1128 verso
UNTITLED: SKETCH OF FOUR NUDES
Watercolor and pencil

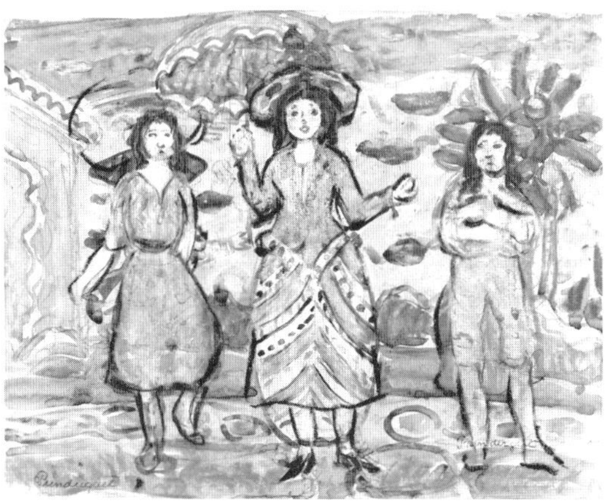

CR 1128

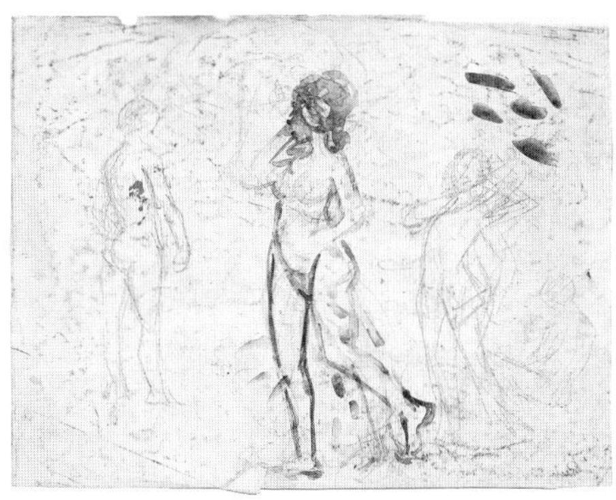

CR 1128 verso

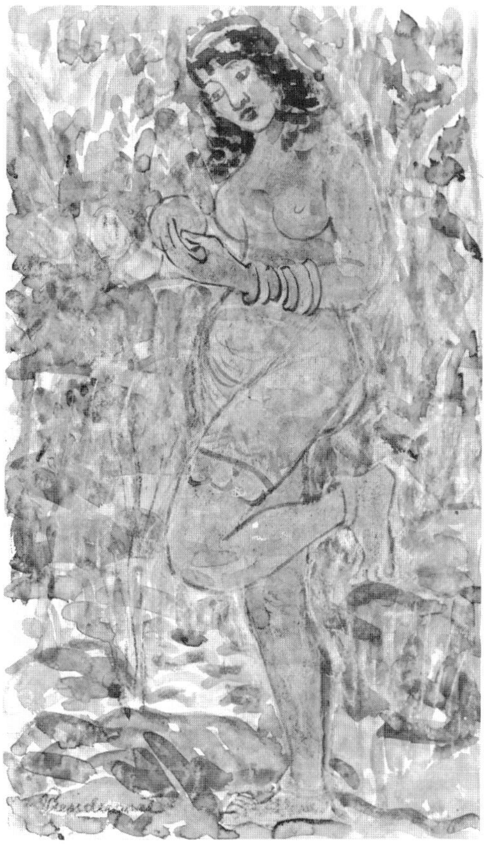

CR 1129

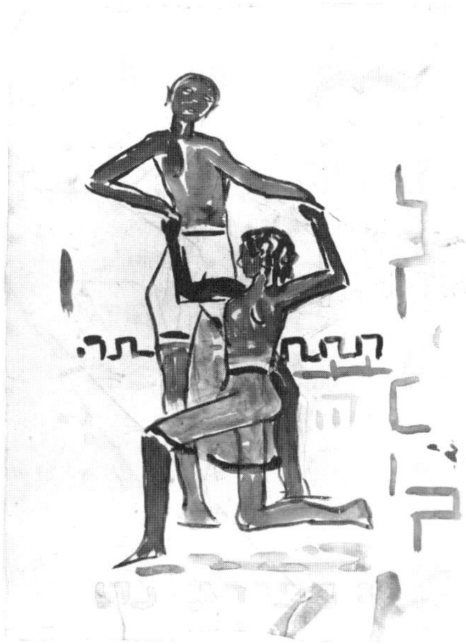

CR 1130

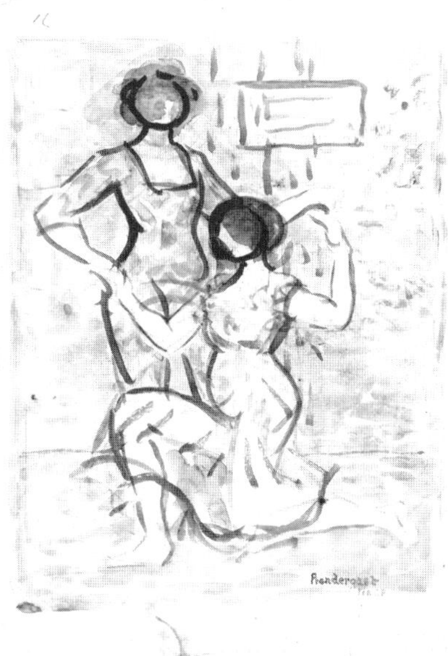

CR 1130 verso

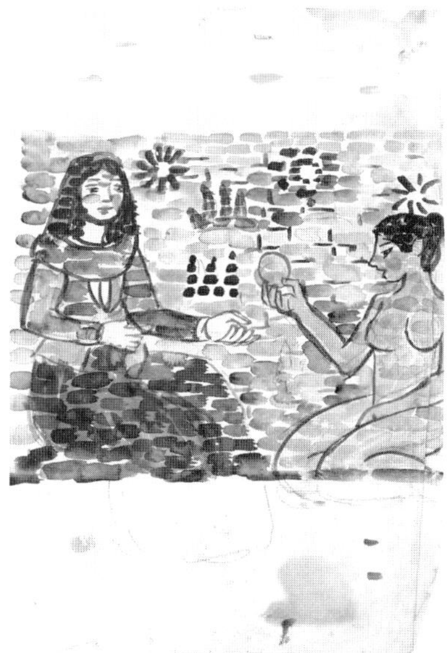

CR 1131

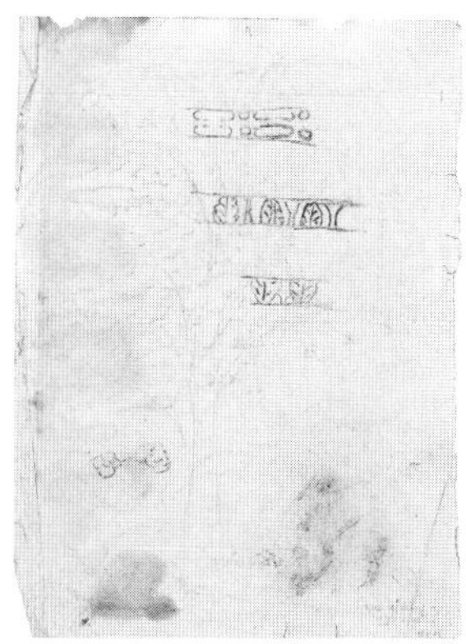

CR 1131 verso

CR 1129
EXOTIC NUDE ca. 1910–13
Watercolor, pencil, and pastel on paper
(18 x 11⅞ in.; 45.7 x 30.2 cm)
Williams College Museum of Art, gift of Mrs. Charles Prendergast (91.28.10)

INSCRIPTIONS
l.l. in black chalk: Prendergast

EXHIBITIONS
1992 Williams College (no #); 1993 Williams College (no #)

CR 1130
EGYPTIAN DANCERS ca. 1910–13
Watercolor and pencil on paper
(13¾ x 9¾ in.; 34.9 x 24.8 cm)
Williams College Museum of Art, bequest of Mrs. Charles Prendergast (95.4.13)

INSCRIPTIONS
unsigned

CR 1130 verso
MODERN DANCERS
Watercolor and pencil
Cf. related sketch in sketchbook CR 1503.

CR 1131
THE OFFERING ca. 1910–13
Watercolor and pencil on paper
(15⅜ x 11 in.; 39.1 x 27.9 cm)
Williams College Museum of Art, bequest of Mrs. Charles Prendergast (95.4.24)

INSCRIPTIONS
Unsigned

EXHIBITIONS
1989c Williams College (no #)

CR 1131 verso
TREE AND FRAME MOLDINGS
Pencil

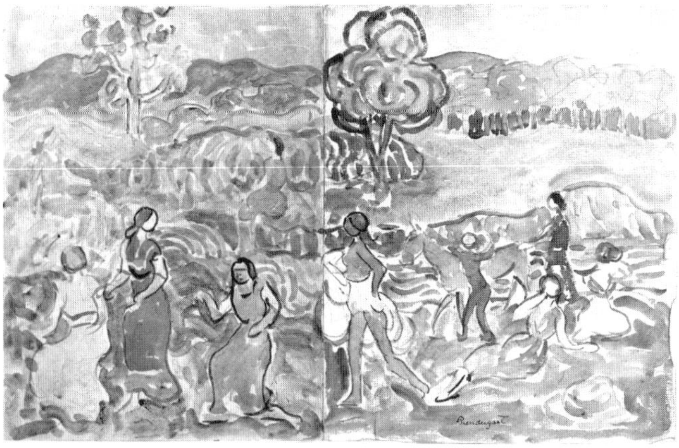

CR 1138

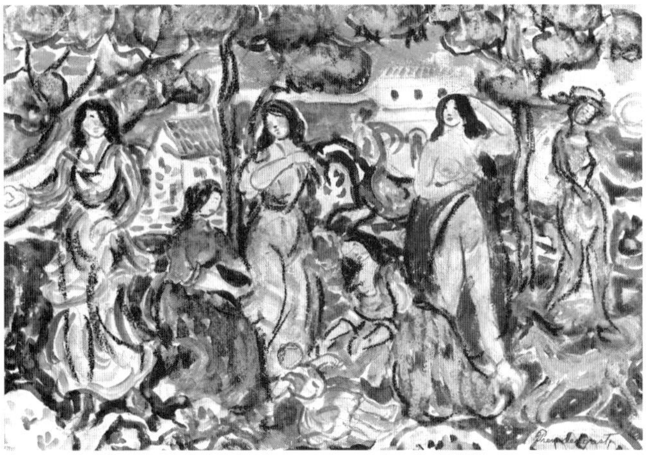

CR 1142

CR 1138
PASTORAL LANDSCAPE ca. 1912–15
Watercolor and pencil on pieced paper
(12 x 19 in.; 30.5 x 48.3 cm)
Williams College Museum of Art, bequest of
Mrs. Charles Prendergast (95.4.3)

INSCRIPTIONS
l.r. in black ink: Prendergast

CR 1142
FIGURES IN LANDSCAPE ca. 1912–15
Watercolor, charcoal, pastel, and pencil on paper
(13½ x 19½ in.; 34.3 x 49.5 cm;)
Williams College Museum of Art, gift of
Mrs. Charles Prendergast (91.18.10)

INSCRIPTIONS
l.r. in pencil: Prendergast

BIBLIOGRAPHY
Mathews 1990 (p. 130; ill.)

EXHIBITIONS
1990c Williams College (#85, ABCD); 1993
Williams College (no #); 1995c Williams
College (no #)

CR 1146
BATHERS ca. 1912–15
Watercolor and pastel on paper
(14½ x 18½ in.; 36.8 x 47.0 cm)
Williams College Museum of Art, gift of
Mrs. Charles Prendergast (86.18.9)

INSCRIPTIONS
l.c. in pencil: Prendergast

BIBLIOGRAPHY
Isaacs 1990; Mathews 1990 (p. 127; ill.); *L.A. County* 1991b

EXHIBITIONS
1966a Knoedler (#53, ill.); 1983a Williams
College (#25); 1985b Williams College (no #);
1989c Williams College (no #); 1990c
Williams College (#82, ABCD); 1993
Williams College (no #)

CR 1146 verso
FOUR GIRLS ca. 1900–03
Watercolor
Cf. related study in sketchbook CR 1498.

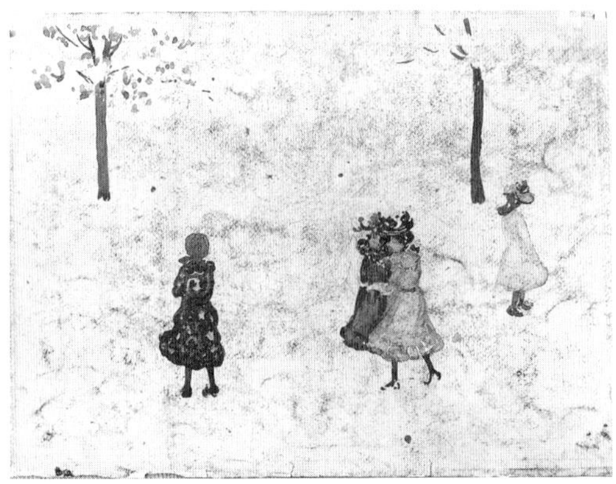

CR 1146 verso

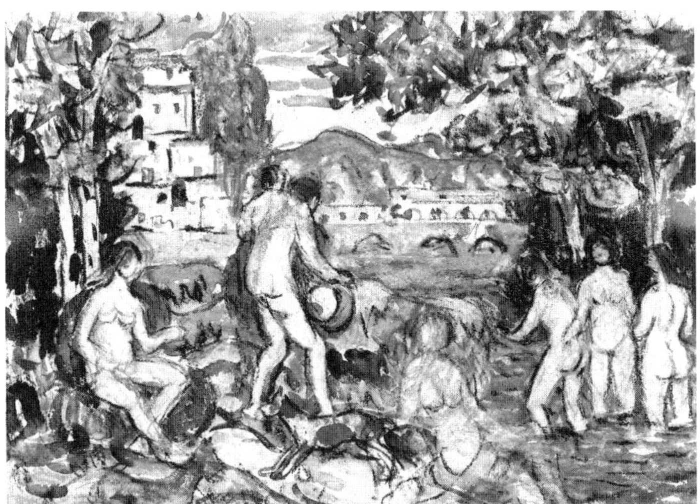

CR 1146

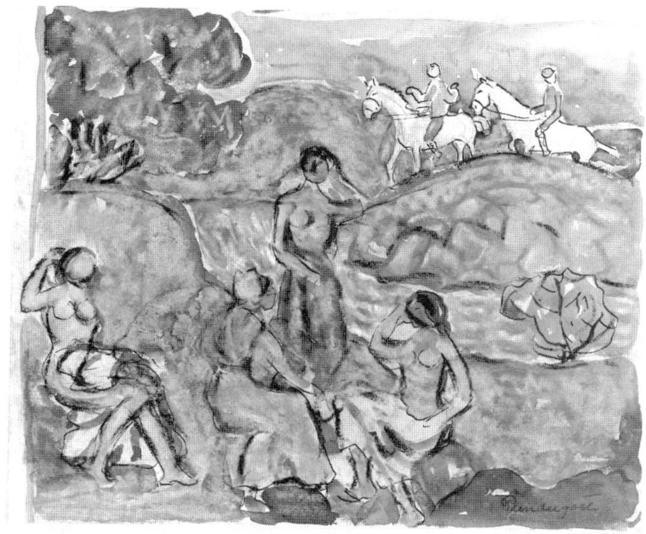

CR 1147

CR 1147
HUNTERS ca. 1912–15
Watercolor, pastel, ink, and pencil on paper (12 x 14⅞ in.; 30.5 x 37.8 cm)
Williams College Museum of Art, gift of Mrs. Charles Prendergast (91.28.11)

INSCRIPTIONS
l.r. in pencil: Prendergast

EXHIBITIONS
Williams College 1989b (#21); Williams College 1991a (no #)
Cf. related sketch in sketchbook CR 1502.

CR 1155
FOUR DANCERS ca. 1912–15
Watercolor and pencil on paper (8¾ x 11⅝ in.; 22.2 x 29.5 cm)
Williams College Museum of Art, bequest of Mrs. Charles Prendergast (95.4.91)

INSCRIPTIONS
l.l. in ink: Prendergast

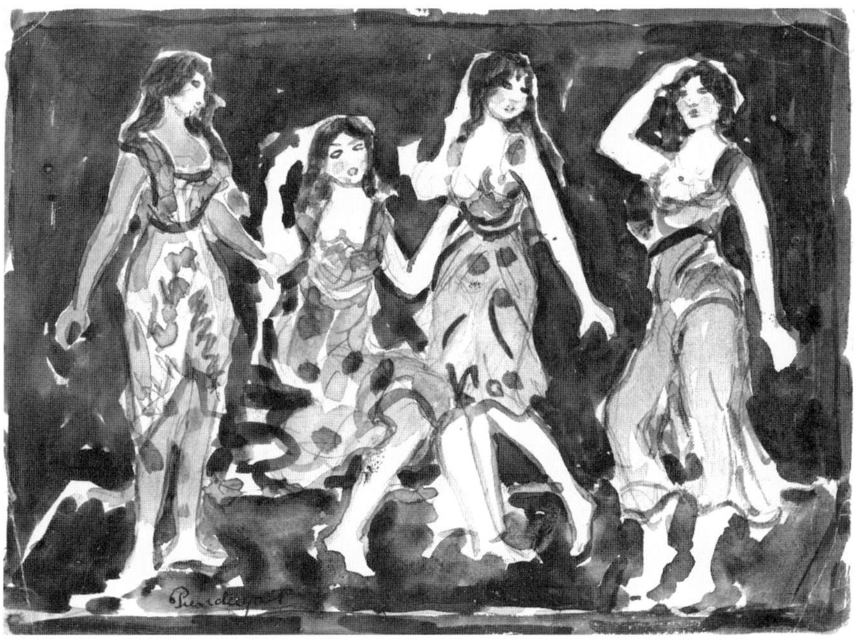

CR 1155

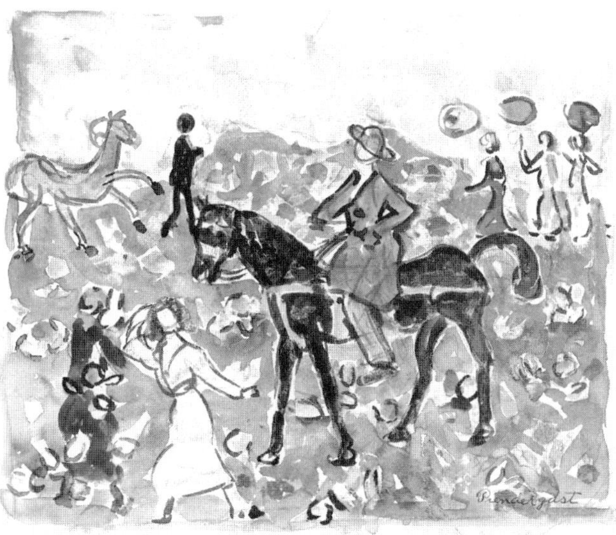

CR 1158

CR 1158
FANTASY WITH HORSEBACK RIDER
ca. 1912–15
Watercolor and pencil on paper, laid down on cardboard (12 x 13⅝ in.; 30.5 x 34.6 cm)
Williams College Museum of Art, bequest of Mrs. Charles Prendergast (95.4.25)

INSCRIPTIONS
l.r. in black ink: Prendergast
Cf. related sketch in sketchbook CR 1502.

CR 1159

HORSEBACK RIDER ca. 1912–15
Man on Horse
Frame by Charles Prendergast
Watercolor, pastel, and pencil on paper
(11⅝ x 16⅛ in.; 29.5 x 41.0 cm)
Williams College Museum of Art, gift of Mrs. Charles Prendergast (86.18.47)

INSCRIPTIONS
l.l. in black ink: Prendergast

BIBLIOGRAPHY
Rhys 1952 (pp. 136, 138)

EXHIBITIONS
1950 Kraushaar (#33); 1988a Williams College (no #); 1989b Williams College (#18); 1991a Williams College (no #)

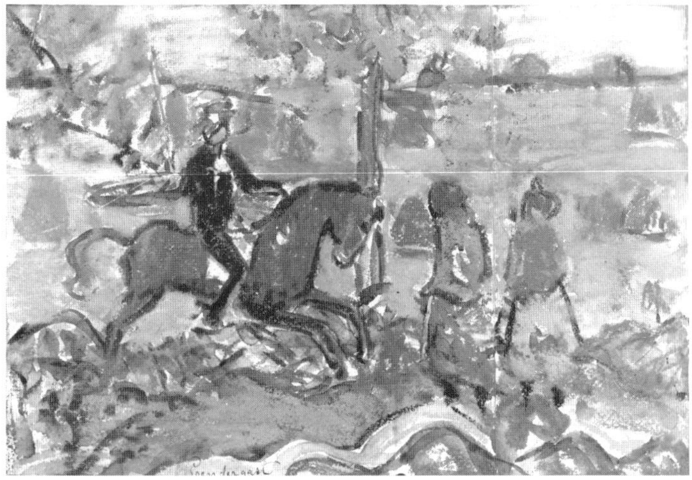

CR 1159

CR 1159 verso

GONDOLAS ON THE GRAND CANAL, VENICE ca. 1911–12
Pencil and watercolor

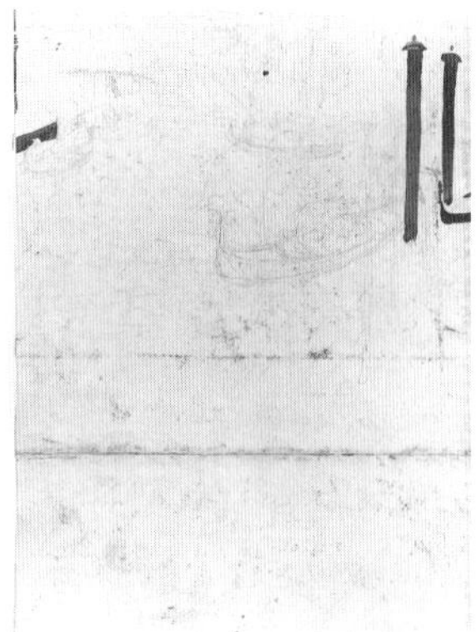

CR 1159 verso

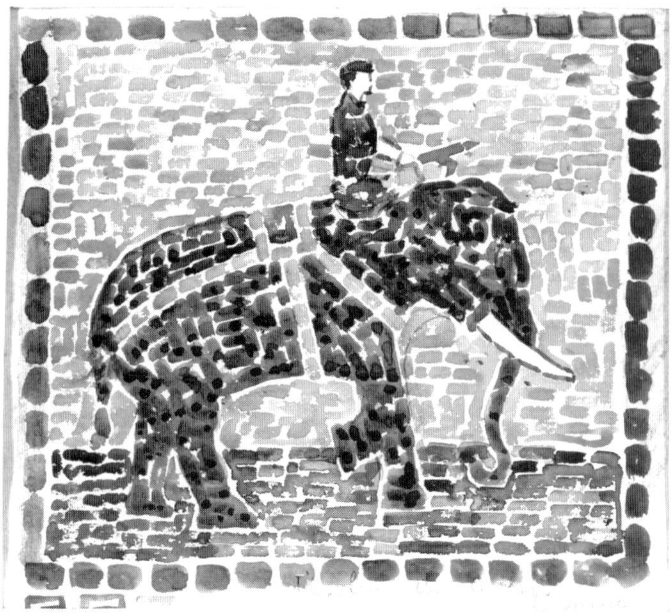

CR 1162

CR 1162

ELEPHANT ca. 1912–15
Watercolor and pencil on paper
(10⅜ x 11½ in.; 26.4 x 29.2 cm)
Williams College Museum of Art, gift of Mrs. Charles Prendergast (91.18.4)

INSCRIPTIONS
l.r. in pencil: tile from the Ceylon/Prendergast

BIBLIOGRAPHY
Mathews 1990 (p. 147; ill.)

EXHIBITIONS
1983a Williams College (#10, ill.); 1990c Williams College (#102, ABCD); 1992 Williams College (no #); 1993 Williams College (no #)

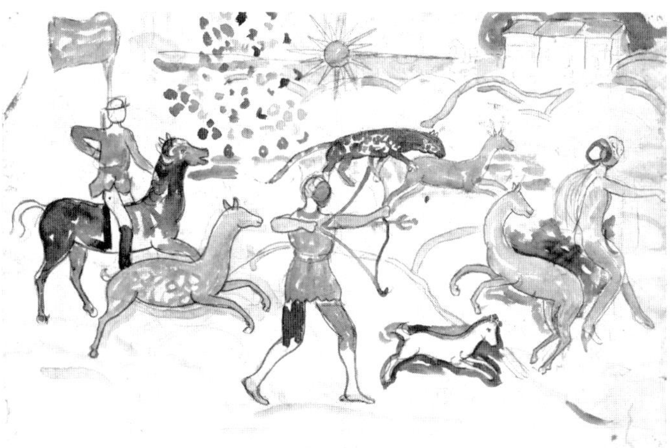

CR 1163

CR 1163

DEER HUNT ca. 1912–15
Watercolor and pencil on paper
(12⅛ x 18¾ in.; 30.8 x 47.6 cm)
Williams College Museum of Art, gift of Mrs. Charles Prendergast (91.18.23)

INSCRIPTIONS
Unsigned

EXHIBITIONS
1989b Williams College (#20); 1991a Williams College (no #)
Cf. Charles Prendergast's *Bounding Deer* (CR 2278).

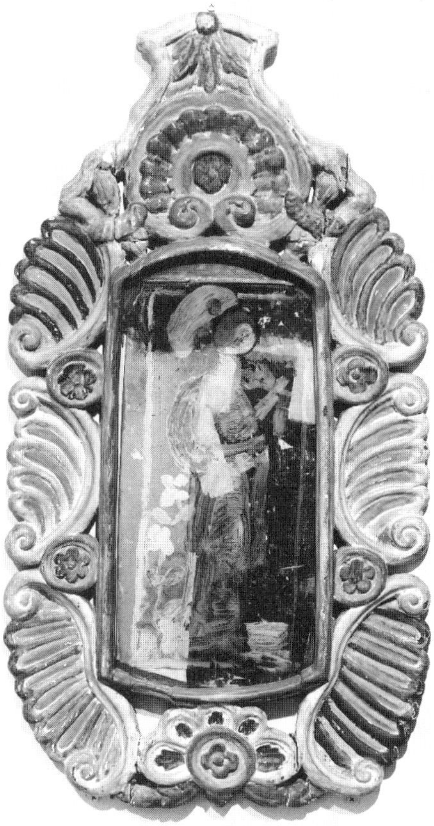

CR 1167

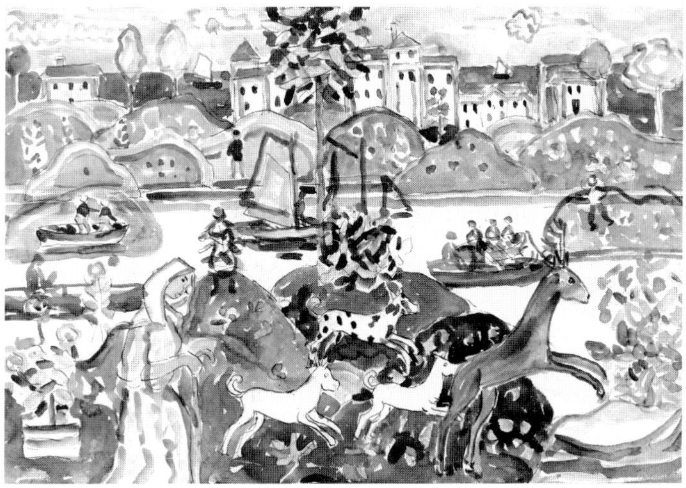

CR 1166

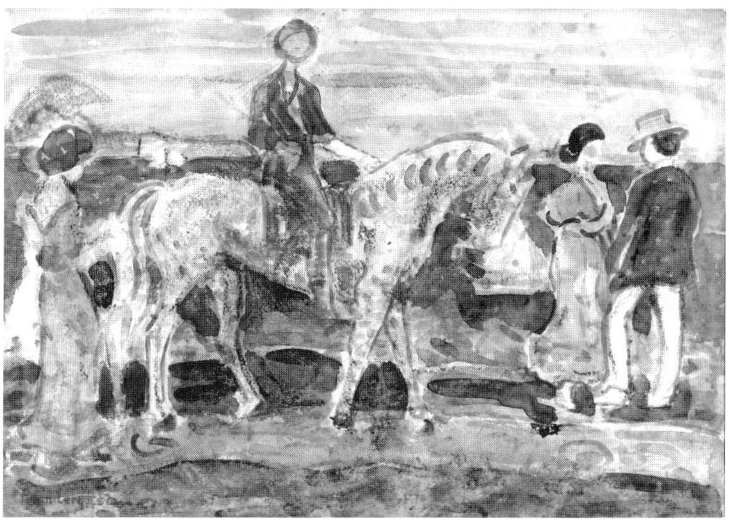

CR 1165

CR 1165
BLUE HORSE ca. 1912–15
Frame by Charles Prendergast
Watercolor and pastel on paper
(22½ x 28½ in.; 51.2 x 72.4 cm)
Williams College Museum of Art, gift of
Mrs. Charles Prendergast (86.18.46)

Inscriptions
l.l. in red: Prendergast

Exhibitions
1988a Williams College (no #); 1989b Williams College (#17); 1989c Williams College (no #)

CR 1166
FANTASY ca. 1912–15
Watercolor, pencil, and ink on paper
(13¾ x 19½ in.; 34.9 x 49.5 cm)
Williams College Museum of Art, gift of
Mrs. Charles Prendergast (83.20.2)

Inscriptions
Unsigned

Bibliography
Mathews 1990 (p. 142; ill.)

Exhibitions
1983a Williams College (#12, ill.); 1985b Williams College (no #); 1986 Williams College (no #); 1988a Williams College (no #); 1990a Williams College (#97, ABCD); 1993 Williams College (no #)
Cf. Charles Prendergast's *Deer Hunt* (CR 2275).

CR 1167
PAINTING ON GLASS ca. 1912–17
Frame by Charles Prendergast
(21¼ x 11½ in.; 54.0 x 29.2 cm)
Williams College Museum of Art, gift of
Mrs. Charles Prendergast (86.18.21)

Inscriptions
Unsigned

Exhibitions
1968 Rutgers University (#80, ill.)

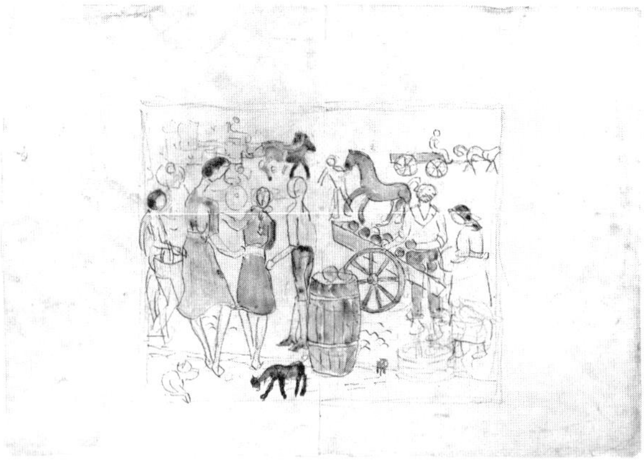

CR 1168

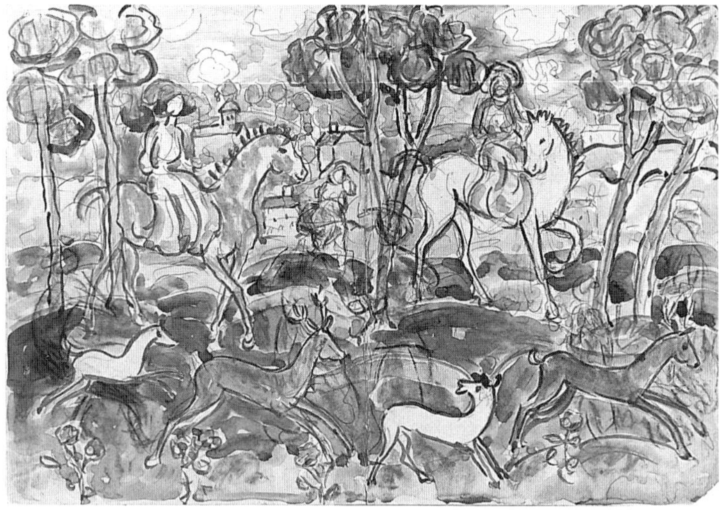

CR 1170

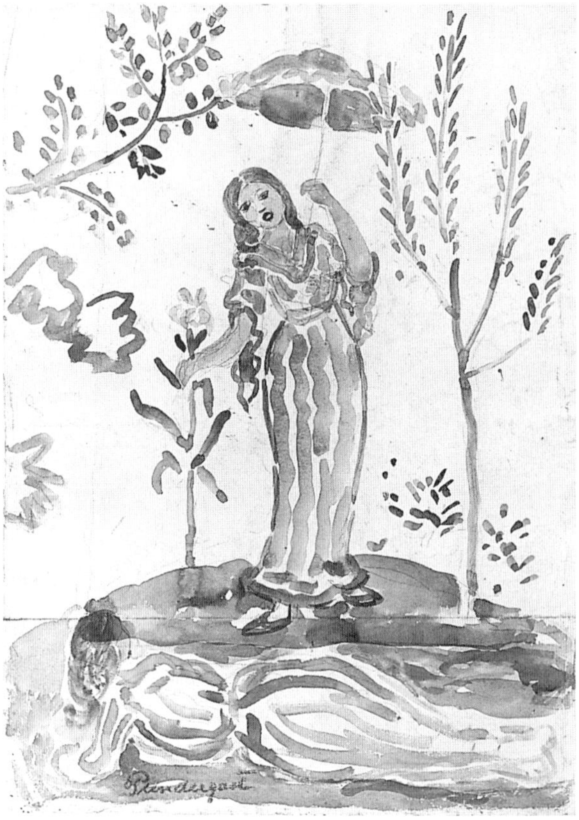

CR 1172

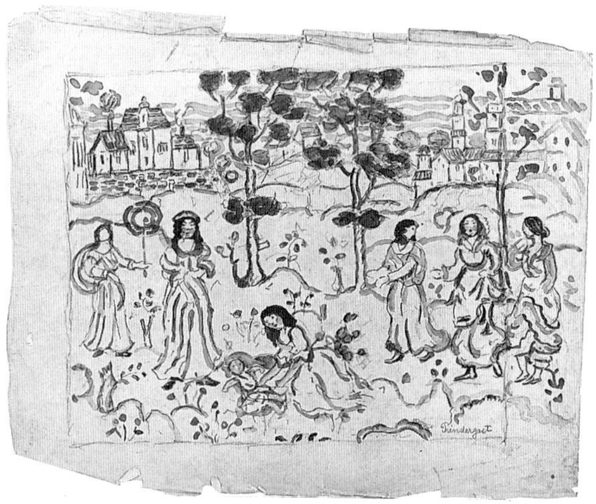

CR 1174

CR 1168
MARKET PLACE ca. 1912–15
Watercolor, pencil, ink, and pastel on paper
(13½ x 19¼ in.; 34.3 x 48.9 cm)
Williams College Museum of Art, bequest of
Mrs. Charles Prendergast (95.4.26)

INSCRIPTIONS
l.r. in pink: MBP [monogram]
Cf. Charles Prendergast's Market Day
(CR 2276).

CR 1170
THE RIDERS ca. 1912–15
Watercolor, pencil, and pastel on paper
(13½ x 19½ in.; 34.3 x 49.5 cm)
Williams College Museum of Art, bequest of
Mrs. Charles Prendergast (95.4.28)

INSCRIPTIONS
verso, in pencil: The Riders

CR 1172
PINK AND BLUE ca. 1913–15
Watercolor and pencil on paper
(17 x 11¾ in.; 43.2 x 29.8 cm)
Williams College Museum of Art, bequest of
Mrs. Charles Prendergast (95.4.1)

INSCRIPTIONS
l.l. in pencil: Prendergast

CR 1174
PASTORALE ca. 1913–15
Watercolor and pencil on paper
(16 x 18⅜ in.; 40.7 x 46.5 cm)
Williams College Museum of Art, bequest of
Mrs. Charles Prendergast (95.4.27)

INSCRIPTIONS
l.r. in pencil: Prendergast

BIBLIOGRAPHY
Breuning 1931 (p. 13)

CR 1174 verso
SKETCH OF A RIDER
Pencil
(Too faint to reproduce)

CR 1176
FEEDING THE SWANS ca. 1913–15
Watercolor and pencil on paper
(18⅛ x 21¼ in.; 46.0 x 54.0 cm)
Williams College Museum of Art, bequest of
Mrs. Charles Prendergast (95.4.17)

INSCRIPTIONS
l.r. in pencil: Prendergast

CR 1177
FIGURES WITH PARASOLS UNDER TREES
ca. 1913–15
Watercolor and pencil on gessoed paper
(9¼ x 13 in.; 23.5 x 33.0 cm)
Williams College Museum of Art, bequest of
Mrs. Charles Prendergast (95.4.102)

INSCRIPTIONS
l.r.: Prendergast

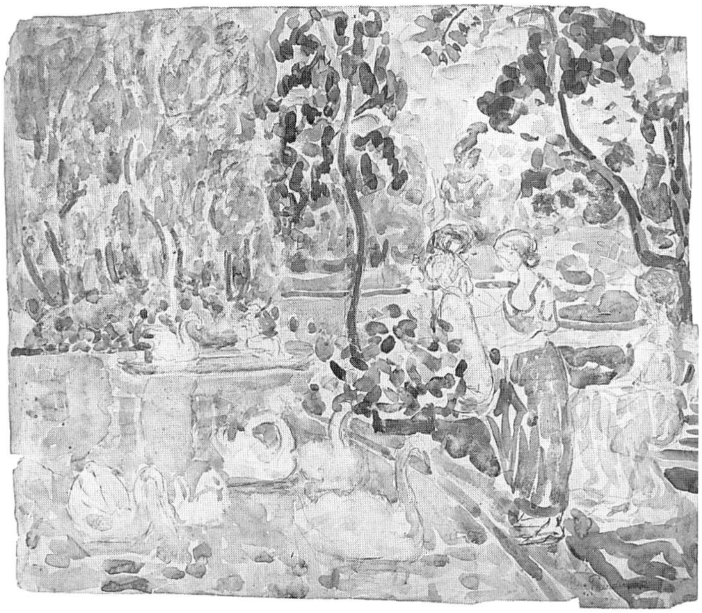

CR 1176

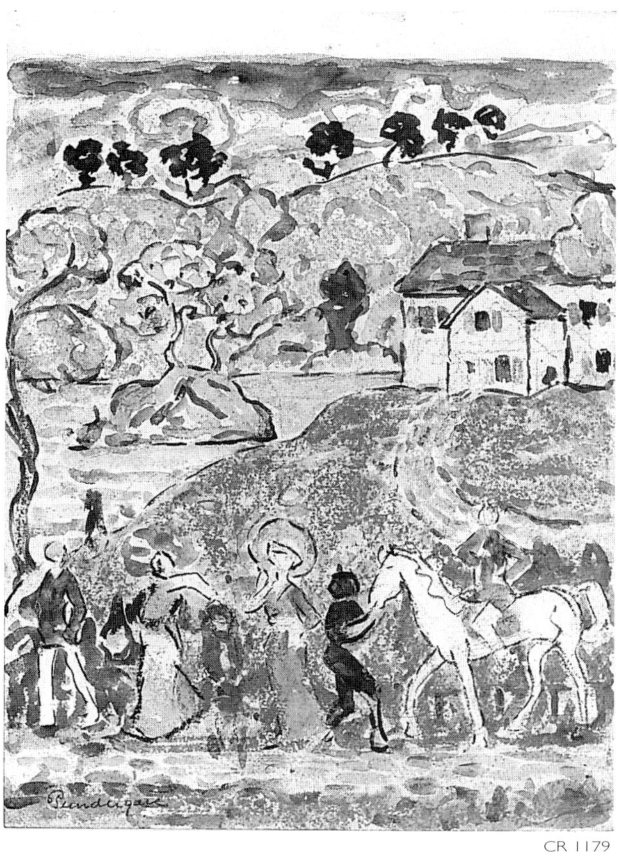

CR 1179

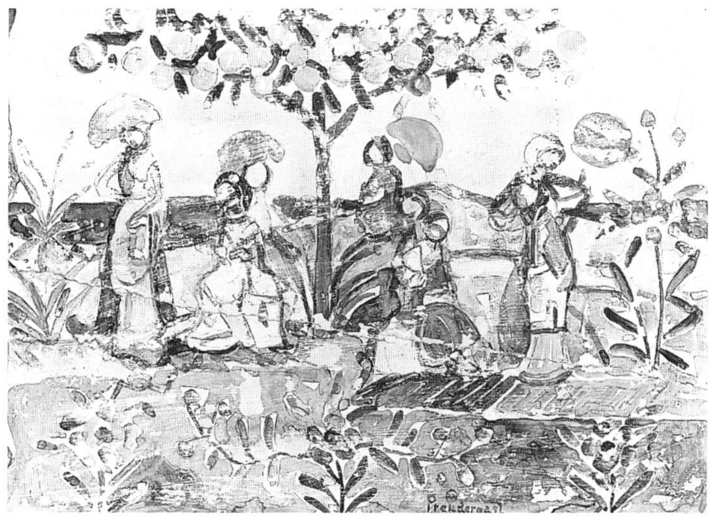

CR 1177

CR 1179
RIDER ON WHITE HORSE ca. 1913–15
Frame by Charles Prendergast
Watercolor, pencil, and pastel on paper
(14 x 10 in.; 35.6 x 25.4 cm)
Williams College Museum of Art, bequest of
Mrs. Charles Prendergast (95.4.98)

INSCRIPTIONS
l.l.: Prendergast

CR 1179 verso
SKETCH OF VENETIAN BRIDGE
Pencil
(Too faint to reproduce)

CR 1181

THE INLET GLOUCESTER ca. 1913–15
Watercolor, pencil, and black chalk on paper
(11½ x 12½ in.; 29.2 x 31.7 cm)
Williams College Museum of Art, bequest of
Mrs. Charles Prendergast (95.4.65)

INSCRIPTIONS
l.r. in black ink: Prendergast

CR 1182

GUIDING THE COWS ca. 1913–15
Watercolor, pencil, and crayon on paper
(14⅛ x 22½ in.; 35.9 x 57.1 cm)
Williams College Museum of Art, gift of
Mrs. Charles Prendergast (91.18.24)

INSCRIPTIONS
l.r. in black: Prendergast

EXHIBITIONS
1989b Williams College (#4); 1991a Williams College (no #); 1992 Williams College (no #)

CR 1182 verso

SKETCH OF GIRLS AND STREET SCENE
ca. 1900–03
Watercolor and pencil

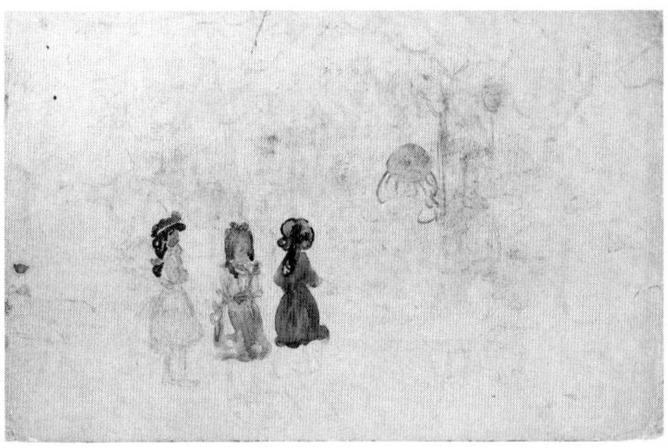

CR 1182 verso

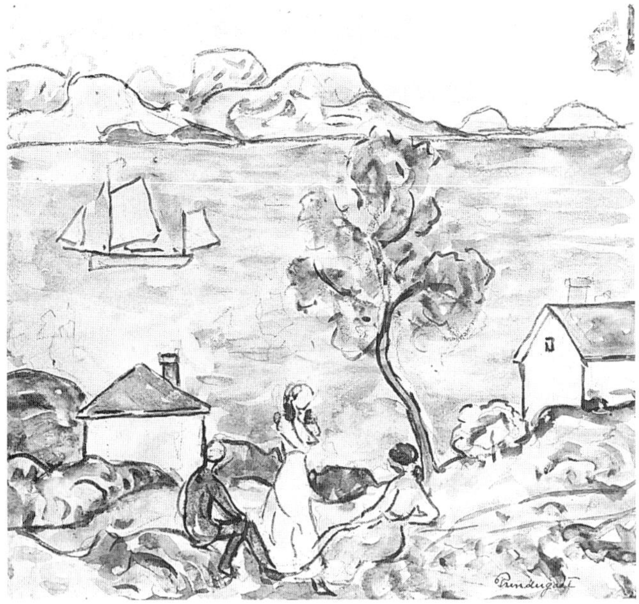

CR 1181

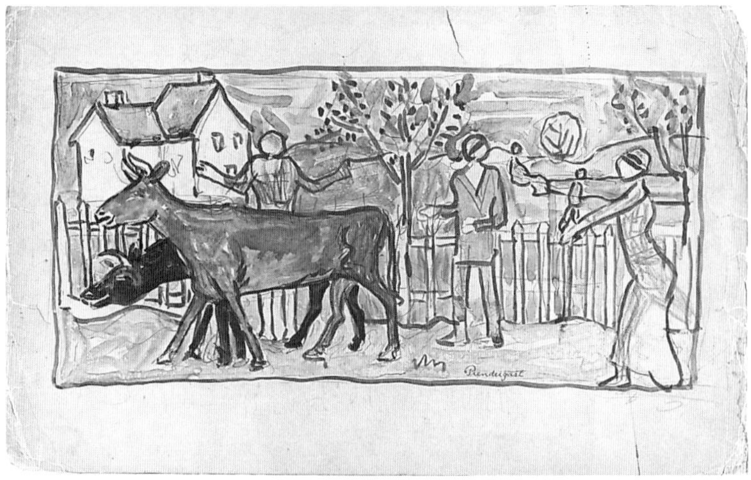

CR 1182

CR 1201

MARBLEHEAD ca. 1914–15
Frame by Charles Prendergast
Watercolor, pencil, charcoal, and pastel on paper
(11½ x 18 in.; 29.2 x 45.7 cm)
Williams College Museum of Art, gift of
Mrs. Charles Prendergast (86.18.5)

INSCRIPTIONS
l.r. in black ink over pencil: Prendergast

BIBLIOGRAPHY
Dooley 1938b (p. 7; ill.); Rhys 1952 (p. 185); Lauzon 1990 (p. 28); Mathews 1990 (p. 125; ill.); Mathews 1990a (ill.); Agar 1994 (p. 44; ill.)

EXHIBITIONS
? 1934a Whitney (#82); 1938 Addison Gallery (#48); 1939 Fogg Museum (#23); ? 1950 Kraushaar (#31); 1966a Knoedler (#47, ill.); 1983a Williams College (#16, ill.); 1985b Williams College (no #); 1986 Williams College (no #); 1990c Williams College (#80, ABCD); 1993 Williams College (no #); 1994a Williams College (no #)
Color plate, p. 2

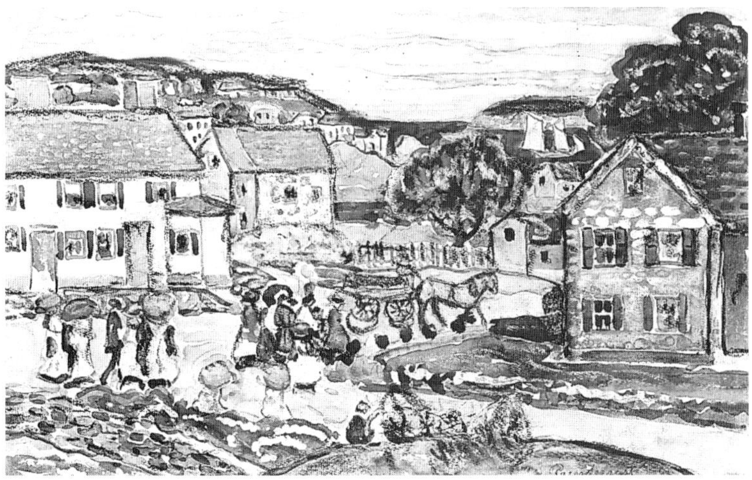

CR 1201

CR 1204

HAY HARVESTING, MAINE 1913–15
Watercolor and pastel on paper
(12¼ x 16¾ in.; 31.1 x 42.5 cm)
Williams College Museum of Art, gift of
Mrs. Charles Prendergast (91.18.16)

INSCRIPTIONS
l.l. in pencil: Prendergast [P reinforced in ink]

EXHIBITIONS
1990b Williams College (no #); 1991c Williams College (no #)

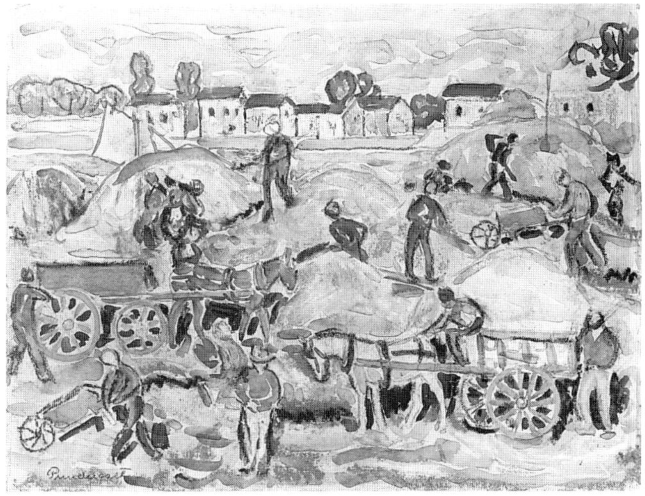

CR 1204

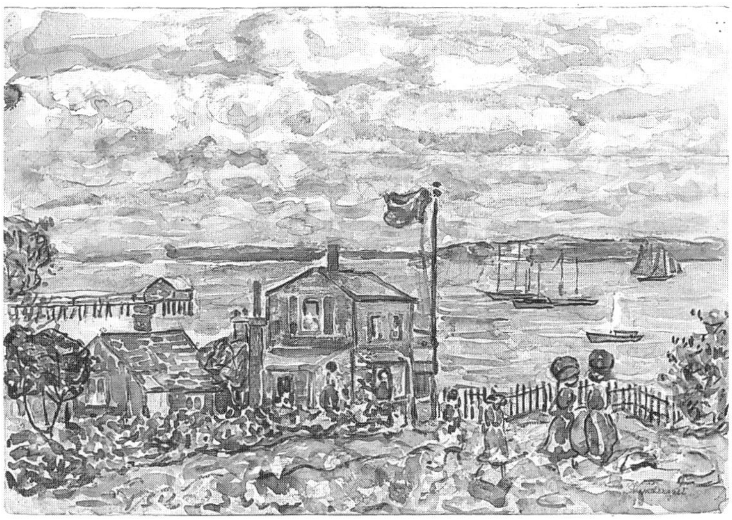

CR 1207

CR 1207 verso

CR 1207

HOUSES BY THE HARBOR 1913–15
Watercolor and pencil on paper
(15⅛ x 21¾ in.; 38.4 x 55.2 cm)
Williams College Museum of Art, gift of
Mrs. Charles Prendergast (91.28.12)

INSCRIPTIONS
l.r. in pencil: Prendergast

EXHIBITIONS
1993 Williams College (no #); 1995d Williams College (no #)

CR 1207 verso

UNTITLED: CARROUSEL
Pencil

CR 1209

MARBLEHEAD ca. 1913–15
? Marblehead No. 2
Frame by Charles Prendergast
Watercolor, pastel, charcoal, and pencil on paper
(13 x 19¼ in.; 33.0 x 48.9 cm)
Williams College Museum of Art, bequest of
Mrs. Charles Prendergast (95.4.108)

INSCRIPTIONS
l.l. in ink: Prendergast

EXHIBITIONS
? 1934a Whitney (#88, as *Marblehead No. 2*)

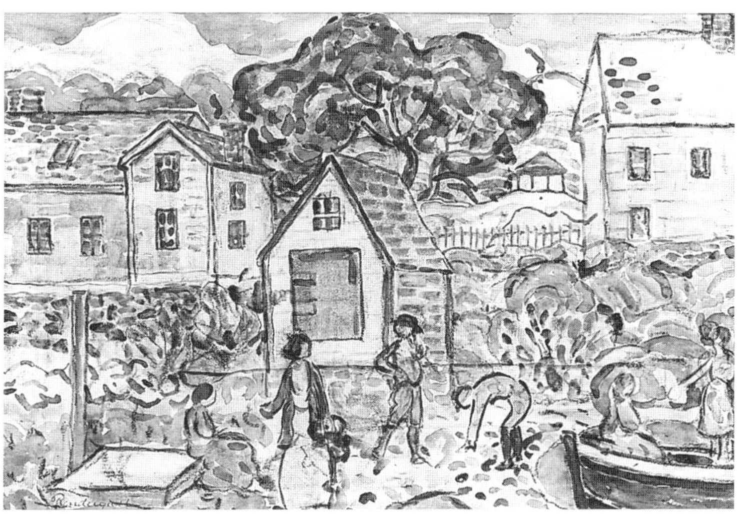

CR 1209

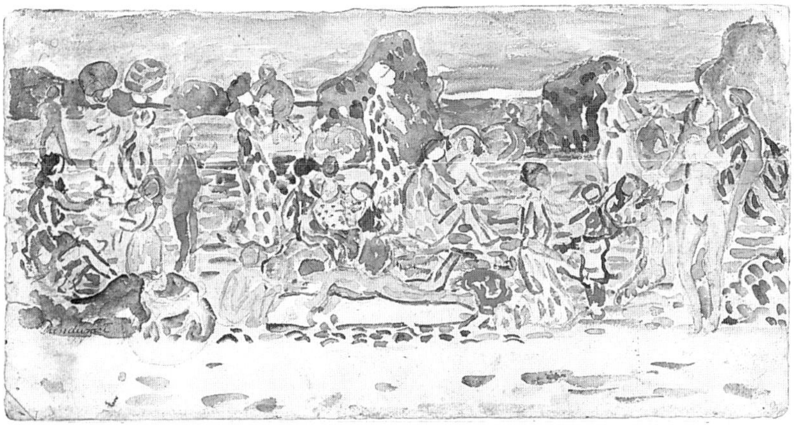

CR 1211

CR 1211

SUMMER DAY ca. 1913–15
Frame by Charles Prendergast
Watercolor on paper
(9⅞ x 19⅛ in.; 25.1 x 48.6 cm)
Williams College Museum of Art, gift of
Mrs. Charles Prendergast (86.18.42)

INSCRIPTIONS
l.l. in ink: Prendergast

BIBLIOGRAPHY
Sawyer 1966 (n.p.); Wattenmaker 1976 (p. 191); Lauzon 1989 (pp. E: 1, 4)

EXHIBITIONS
1966a Knoedler (#48, ill.); 1988a Williams College (no #); 1988b Williams College (frame for *Summer Day* by Charles Prendergast, #81); 1989d Williams College (no #); 1990b Williams College (no #)

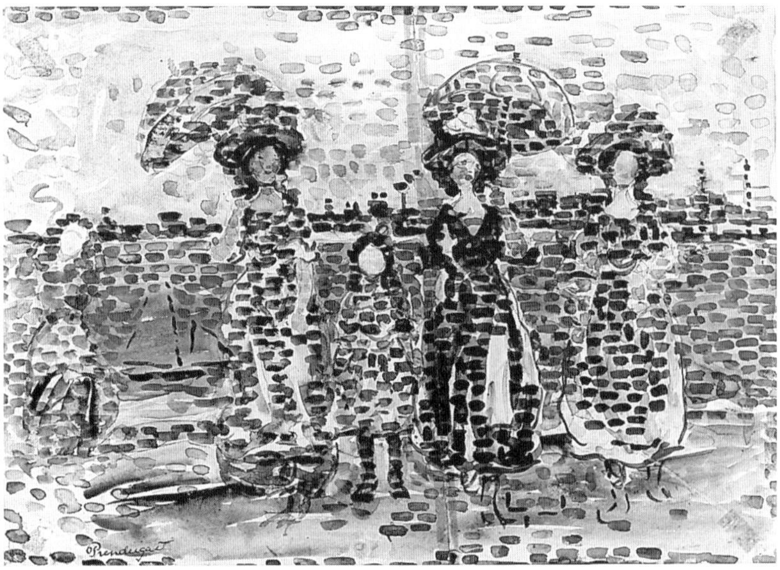

CR 1213

CR 1213

PROMENADE WITH FIVE FIGURES
ca. 1913–15
Watercolor and pencil on paper
(13 x 18¼ in.; 33.0 x 46.4 cm)
Williams College Museum of Art, bequest of
Mrs. Charles Prendergast (95.4.78)

INSCRIPTIONS
l.l in ink: Prendergast

CR 1218

BOAT LANDING, DINARD ca. 1914
Landing, Dinard
Frame by Charles Prendergast
Watercolor, gouache, and charcoal on paper
(15¼ x 22¼ in.; 38.7 x 57.1 cm)
Williams College Museum of Art, gift of
Mrs. Charles Prendergast (86.18.71)

INSCRIPTIONS
l.r.: Prendergast
verso in pencil: St. Malo/1909

BIBLIOGRAPHY
Mathews 1990 (p. 124; ill.)

EXHIBITIONS
1938 Addison Gallery (#43); 1960 Boston MFA (#103, ill.); 1968 Rutgers University (#78, ill.); 1986 Williams College (no #); 1988b Williams College (frame for *Boat Landing, Dinard* by Charles Prendergast, #70); 1990c Williams College (#79, ABCD); 1993 Williams College (no #); 1994a Williams College (no #)
Color plate, p. 42

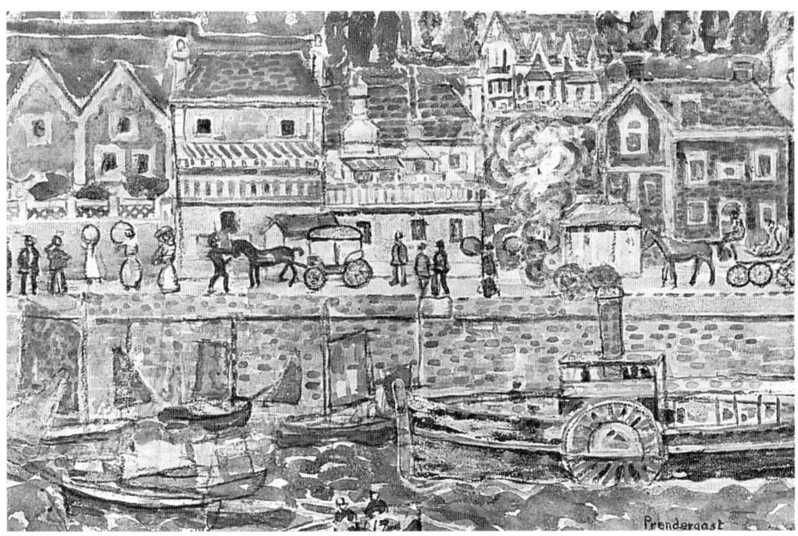

CR 1218

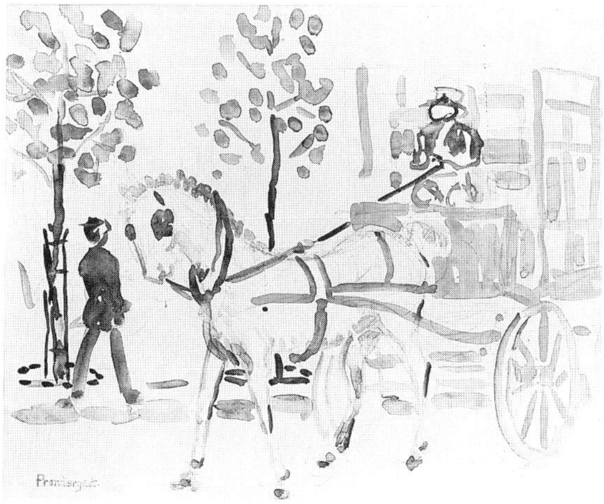

CR 1222

CR 1222
HORSE AND WAGON ca. 1914–15
Frame by Charles Prendergast
Watercolor and pencil on paper
(11¼ x 13¾ in.; 28.6 x 34.9 cm)
Williams College Museum of Art, bequest of
Mrs. Charles Prendergast (95.4.88)

Inscriptions
l.l. in red: Prendergast

Bibliography
Christian Science 1960b (p. 8; ill.)

Exhibitions
1960 Boston MFA (#118, ill.)

CR 1225
SUMMER HOTEL, MAINE ca. 1914–15
Pasmaquady House, Nahant; Passamaquoddy House
Frame by Charles Prendergast
Watercolor and pencil on paper
(11½ x 17¾ in.; 29.2 x 45.1 cm)
Williams College Museum of Art, bequest of
Mrs. Charles Prendergast (95.4.70)

Inscriptions
l.r. in ink: Prendergast

Exhibitions
1930 Kraushaar (#21, as *Pasmaquady House, Nahant*); 1983a Williams College (#22, ill., as *Passamaquoddy House*)

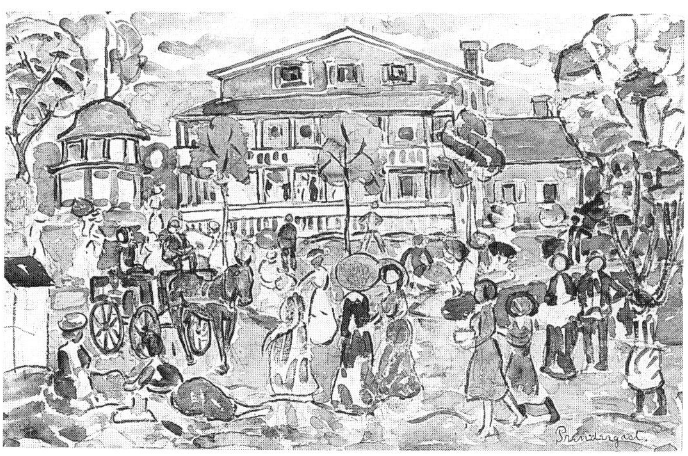

CR 1225

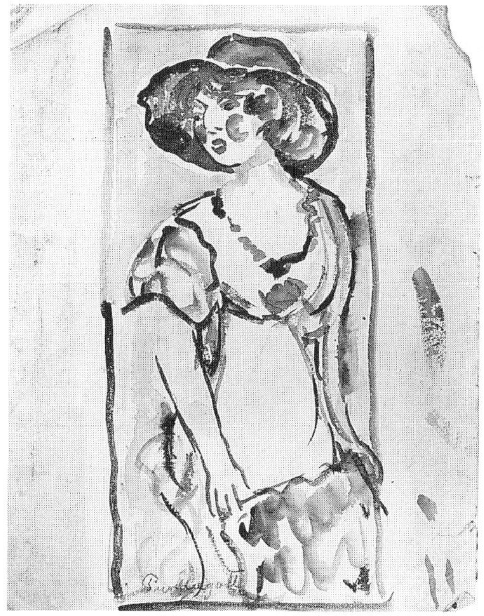

CR 1234

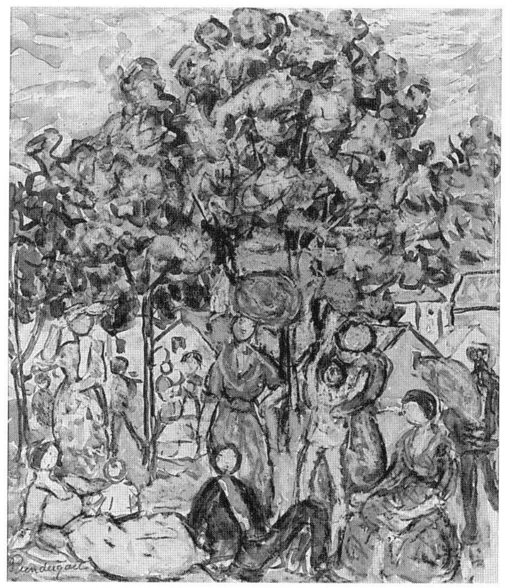

CR 1239

CR 1234
WOMAN WITH LARGE BLUE HAT ca. 1915–16
Watercolor on paper
(12 x 9 in.; 30.5 x 22.9 cm)
Williams College Museum of Art, bequest of
Mrs. Charles Prendergast (95.4.23)

Inscriptions
l.l. in pencil: Prendergast

Exhibitions
1995c Williams College (no #)

CR 1239
FAMILY GROUP ca. 1915–16
Frame by Charles Prendergast
Watercolor, pastel, and pencil on paper
(15¾ x 13 in.; 40.0 x 33.0 cm)
Williams College Museum of Art, bequest of
Mrs. Charles Prendergast (95.4.86)

Inscriptions
l.l. in pencil: Prendergast

CR 1241
IN THE PARK ca. 1915–16
Watercolor and pencil on paper
(9¾ x 17 in.; 24.8 x 43.2 cm)
Williams College Museum of Art, bequest of Mrs. Charles Prendergast (95.4.84)

INSCRIPTIONS
l.l. in brown: Prendergast

CR 1263
HARBOR VILLAGE ca. 1916–19
Watercolor and pencil on paper
(12 x 17⅞ in.; 30.5 x 45.4 cm)
Williams College Museum of Art, gift of Mrs. Charles Prendergast (91.28.13)

INSCRIPTIONS
l.r. in black chalk: Prendergast

EXHIBITIONS
1993 Williams College (no #); 1995d Williams College (no #)

CR 1266
NEW HAMPSHIRE ca. 1916–19
Houses, New Hampshire
Watercolor, pastel, and pencil on paper
(11¼ x 15⅛ in.; 28.6 x 38.4 cm)
Williams College Museum of Art, gift of Bernard Heineman Jr. '45 (73.43)

INSCRIPTIONS
l.r. in watercolor over pencil: Prendergast
l.l. in pencil: Prendergast

PROVENANCE
The artist; to Charles Prendergast, 1924; to Mrs. Charles Prendergast, 1948; to (Kraushaar); to (Downtown), 1954; to Bernard Heineman Jr., 1960; to present collection, 1973

BIBLIOGRAPHY
Owens 1978 (p. 40, as *Houses, New Hampshire*)

EXHIBITIONS
1930b Cleveland (#75); 1978 Clark Art Institute (#14, ill., as *Houses, New Hampshire*); 1990b Williams College (no #); 1991c Williams College (no #); 1993 Williams College (no #); 1995d Williams College (no #)
Cf. related pencil sketch in sketchbook CR 1549.

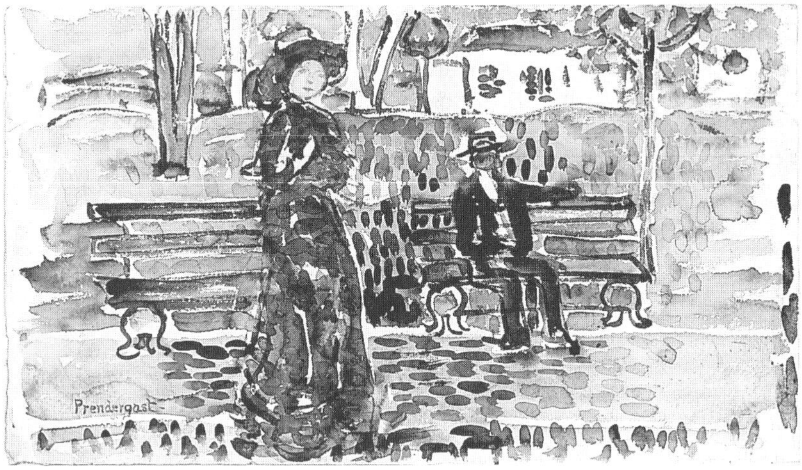

CR 1241

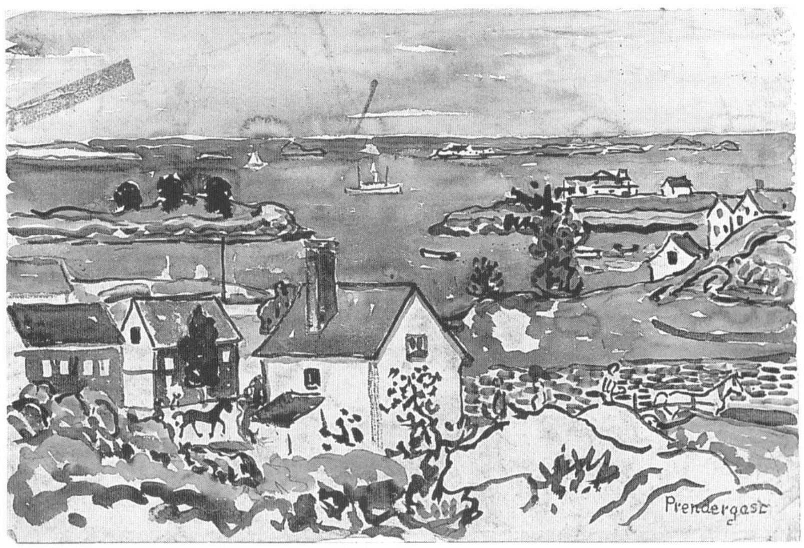

CR 1263

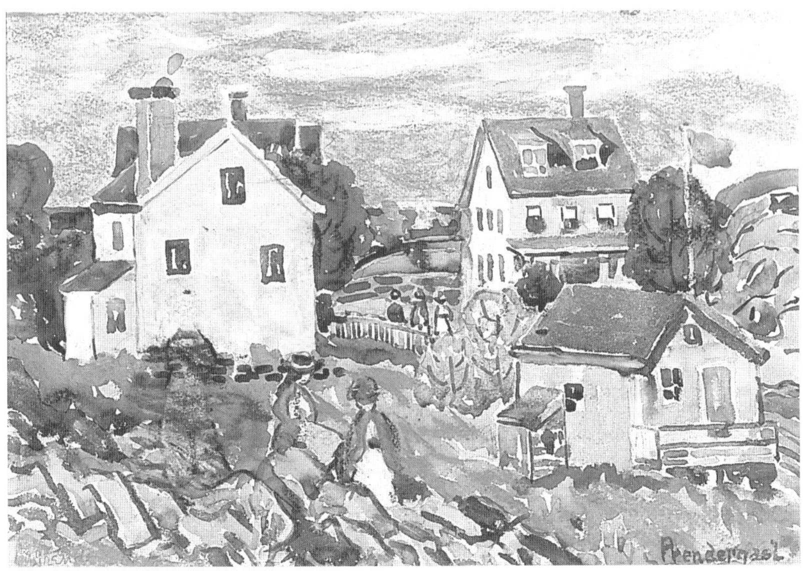

CR 1266

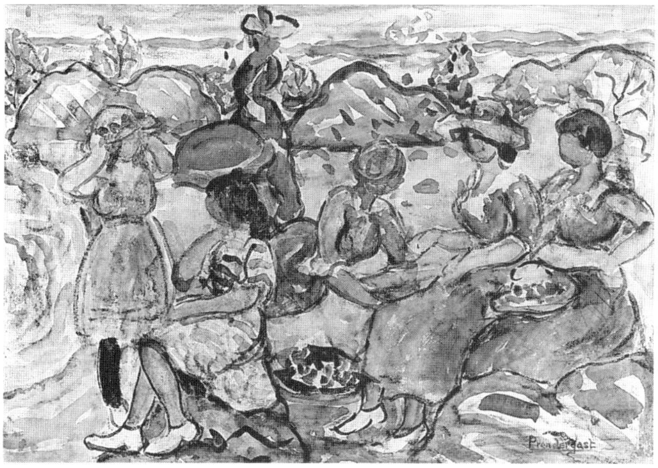

CR 1290

CR 1290
SIX GIRLS ca. 1916–19
Watercolor and pastel on paper
(13½ x 19½ in.; 34.3 x 49.5 cm)
Williams College Museum of Art, gift of Mrs. Charles Prendergast (86.18.38)

INSCRIPTIONS
l.r. in red: Prendergast

BIBLIOGRAPHY
Sawyer 1966 (n.p.); Goethals 1991 (cover; ill.)

EXHIBITIONS
1963 Southern Vermont (#54); 1966a Knoedler (#58); 1970 Knoedler (#8); 1988a Williams College (no #); 1989c Williams College (no #); 1991a Williams College (no #); 1993 Williams College (no #)

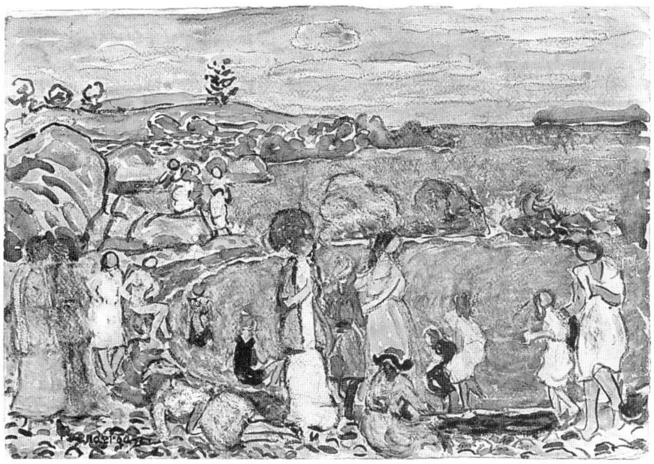

CR 1310

CR 1310
NORTH SHORE, MASS. ca. 1916–19
Watercolor, pencil, pastel, and gouache on paper
(15½ x 22⅜ in.; 39.3 x 56.8 cm)
Williams College Museum of Art, gift of Mrs. Charles Prendergast in honor of President John W. Chandler (85.16.2)

INSCRIPTIONS
l.l. in blue: Prendergast

EXHIBITIONS
1985b Williams College (no #); 1988a Williams College (no #); 1989d Williams College (no #); 1991a Williams College (no #)

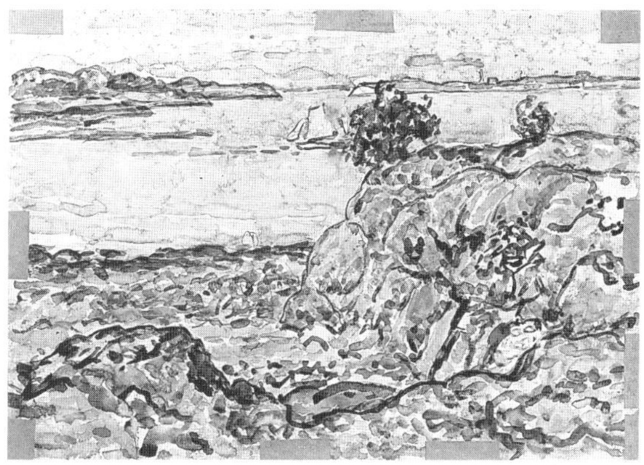

CR 1315 verso

CR 1315
A DAY IN JUNE ca. 1916–19
Watercolor, pastel, and pencil on paper
(13¾ x 19¾ in.; 34.9 x 50.2 cm)
Williams College Museum of Art, gift of Mrs. Charles Prendergast (91.18.13)

INSCRIPTIONS
l.r. in charcoal: Prendergast

BIBLIOGRAPHY
Lauzon 1989 (pp. E: 1, 4)

EXHIBITIONS
1989d Williams College (no #); 1991a Williams College (no #); 1993 Williams College (no #)

CR 1315 verso
ROCKY SHORE
Watercolor and pencil

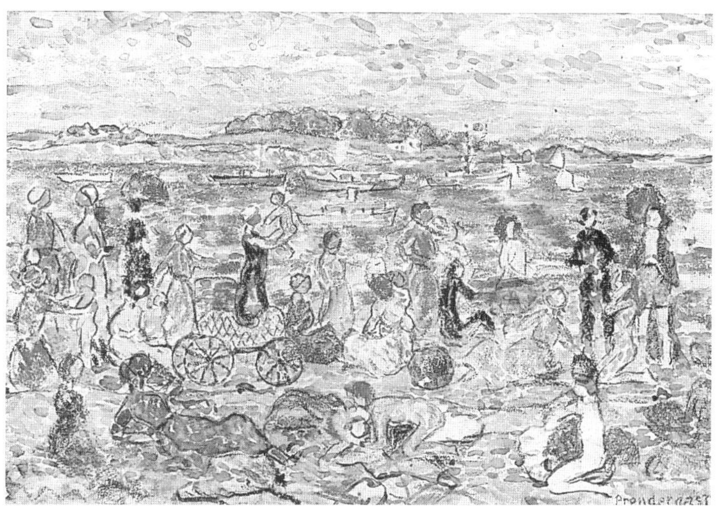

CR 1315

CR 1317

ANNISQUAM 1919
Watercolor, pastel, and pencil on paper
(14 x 20 in.; 35.6 x 50.8 cm;)
Williams College Museum of Art, gift of Mrs. Charles Prendergast (91.18.11)

INSCRIPTIONS
l.l. in black ink: Prendergast/1919

BIBLIOGRAPHY
Lauzon 1989 (pp. E: 1, 4)

EXHIBITIONS
1989d Williams College (no #); 1991a Williams College (no #); 1993 Williams College (no #)
Cf. related studies in sketchbook CR 1551.

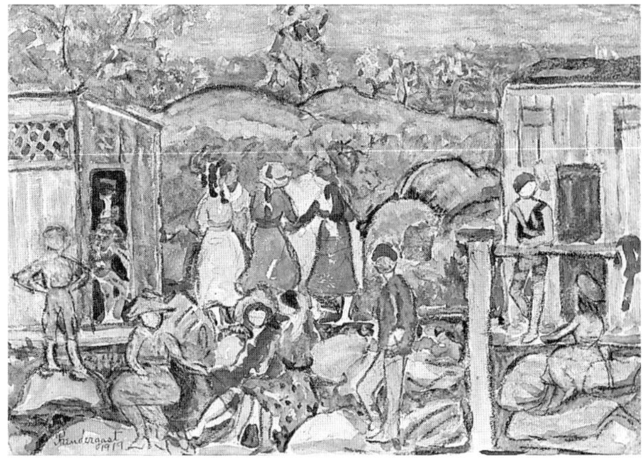

CR 1317

CR 1319

BEACH RESORT ca. 1919
Watercolor, pastel, and pencil on paper
(13⅞ x 19⅞ in.; 35.2 x 50.5 cm)
Williams College Museum of Art, gift of Mrs. Charles Prendergast (86.18.58)

INSCRIPTIONS
l.r. in pencil: Prendergast

BIBLIOGRAPHY
Lauzon 1989 (pp. E: 1, 4)

EXHIBITIONS
1986 Williams College (no #); 1988a Williams College (no #); 1989d Williams College (no #); 1990b Williams College (no #); 1993 Williams College (no #)
Cf. related studies in sketchbook CR 1551.

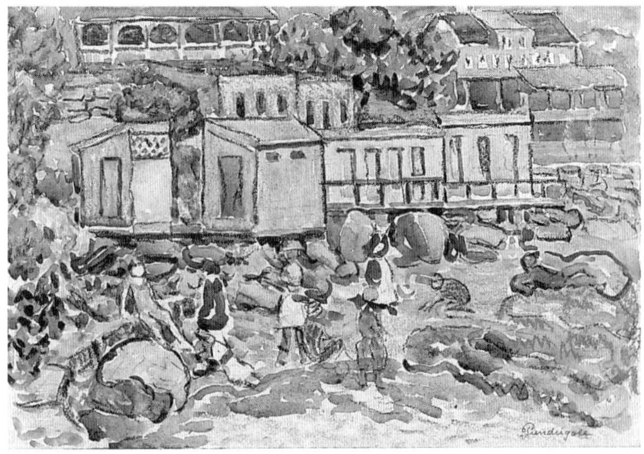

CR 1319

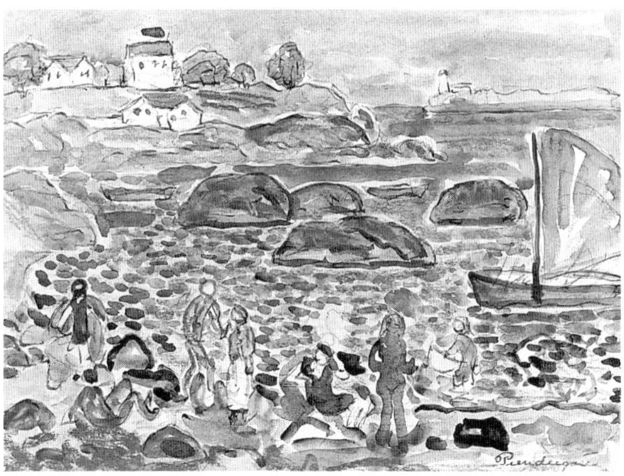

CR 1327

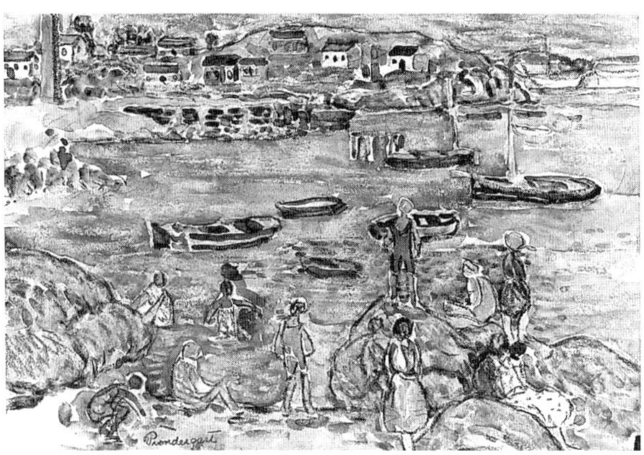

CR 1333

CR 1327

LIGHTHOUSE, THE INLET, GLOUCESTER
ca. 1920–23
Watercolor, pencil, pastel, and ink on paper
(9¾ x 13⅜ in.; 24.8 x 34.0 cm)
Williams College Museum of Art, bequest of Mrs. Charles Prendergast (95.4.95)

INSCRIPTIONS
l.r. in pencil: Prendergast

CR 1333

GLOUCESTER BEACH ca. 1920–23
Watercolor, charcoal, pencil, and pastel on paper
(13¾ x 19¾ in.; 34.6 x 50.2 cm)
Williams College Museum of Art, bequest of Mrs. Charles Prendergast (95.4.82)

INSCRIPTIONS
l.l. in pencil: Prendergast

BIBLIOGRAPHY
Wattenmaker 1994 (p. 141 as watercolor of Gloucester, p. 152 fn 137 as CR 1333, *Gloucester Beach*); 1996 Spanierman (#22 ill. p. 11, p. 12).

EXHIBITIONS
1965 Knoedler (no #); 1966a Knoedler (no #); 1970 Knoedler (#7); 1982 Smithsonian SITES (#51, ill.); 1996 Spanierman (#22, ill.)

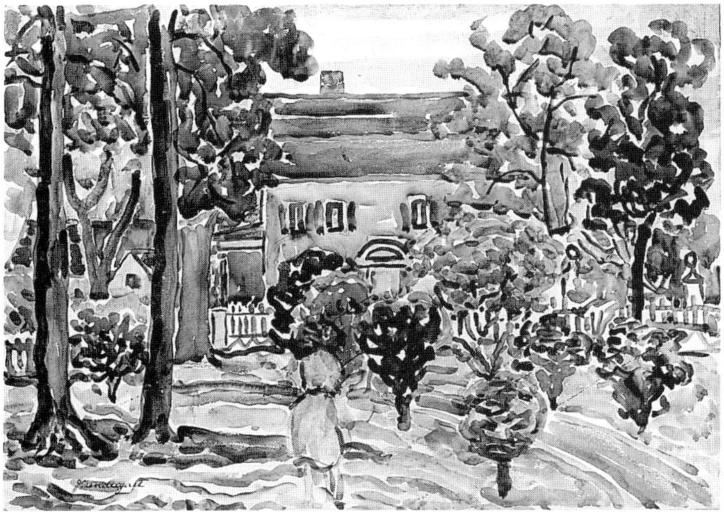

CR 1358

CR 1358

SPRINGTIME ca. 1920–23
Watercolor and pencil on paper
(13⅞ x 19⅞ in.; 35.2 x 50.5 cm)
Williams College Museum of Art, gift of Mrs. Charles Prendergast (91.18.12)

INSCRIPTIONS
l.l. in black ink: Prendergast

EXHIBITIONS
1988a Williams College (no #); 1990b Williams College (no #); 1991c Williams College (no #); 1994a Williams College (no #)

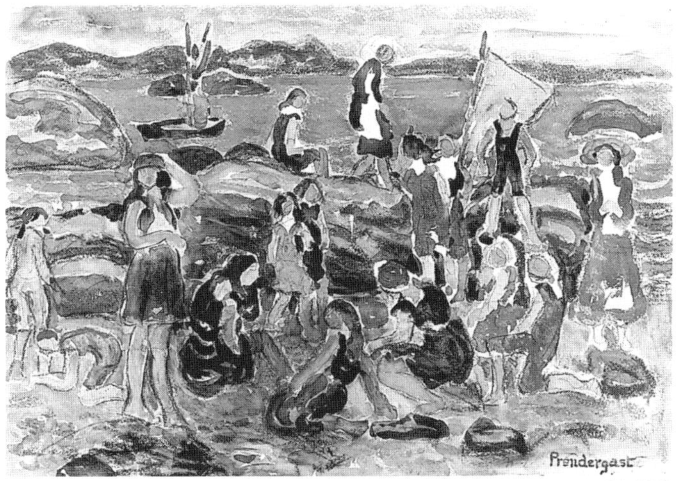

CR 1380

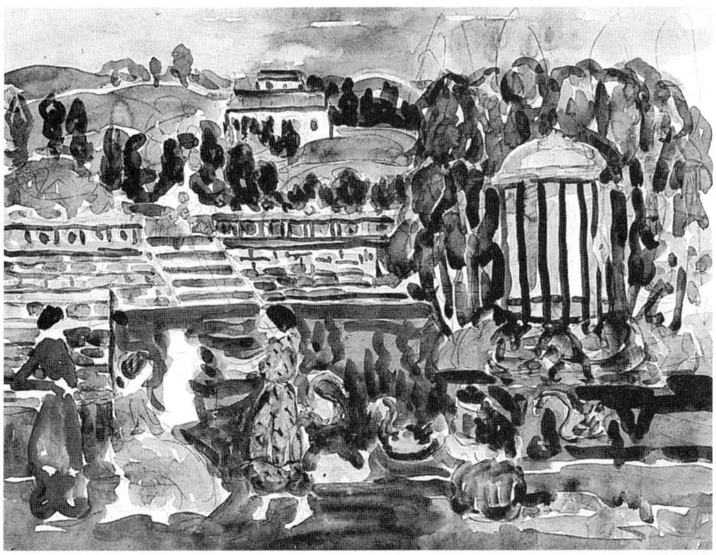

CR 1369

CR 1369

LAKE PAVILION ca. 1920–23
Summer House on the Lake
Watercolor and pencil on paper
(17 x 22 in.; 43.2 x 55.9 cm)
Williams College Museum of Art, bequest of Mrs. Charles Prendergast (95.4.75)

INSCRIPTIONS
Unsigned

CR 1380

CROWDED BEACH ca. 1920–23
Watercolor, pastel, and pencil on paper
(14 x 20 in.; 35.6 x 50.8 cm;)
Williams College Museum of Art, gift of Mrs. Charles Prendergast (91.18.19)

INSCRIPTIONS
l.r. in purple: Prendergast

EXHIBITIONS
1988a Williams College (no #); 1989d Williams College (no #); 1991c Williams College (no #)

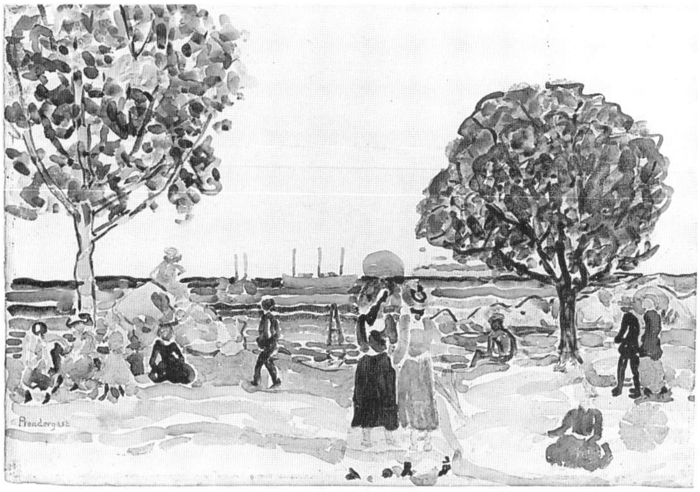

CR 1381

CR 1381
SEA SCENE WITH TREES ca. 1920–23
Beach
Watercolor and pencil on paper
(15¼ x 22 in.; 38.7 x 55.9 cm)
Williams College Museum of Art, bequest of Mrs. Charles Prendergast (95.4.67)

INSCRIPTIONS
l.l. in red: Prendergast

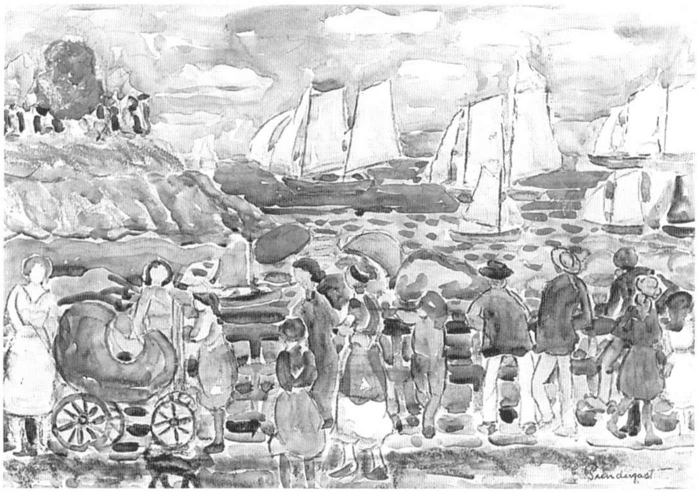

CR 1382

CR 1382
YACHT RACE ca. 1920–23
Frame by Charles Prendergast
Watercolor, pastel, and pencil on paper
(13½ x 19½ in.; 34.3 x 49.5 cm)
Williams College Museum of Art, bequest of Mrs. Charles Prendergast (95.4.99)

INSCRIPTIONS
l.r.: Prendergast

BIBLIOGRAPHY
Art News 1938a (p. 15; ill.); Rhys 1952 (p. 188)

EXHIBITIONS
? 1921 Brooklyn (#241); 1934a Whitney (#150); 1938 Addison (#58, ill.)

CR 1383 verso

CR 1383
THE COVE, GLOUCESTER, MASS. ca. 1920–23
Watercolor, pastel, and charcoal on paper
(13⅞ x 19⅞ in.; 35.2 x 50.5 cm)
Williams College Museum of Art, gift of Mrs. Charles Prendergast in honor of President John W. Chandler (85.16.1)

INSCRIPTIONS
l.r.: Prendergast

EXHIBITIONS
1985b Williams College (no #); 1988a Williams College (no #); 1989c Williams College (no #); 1991a Williams College (no #)

CR 1383 verso
THE COVE
Pencil

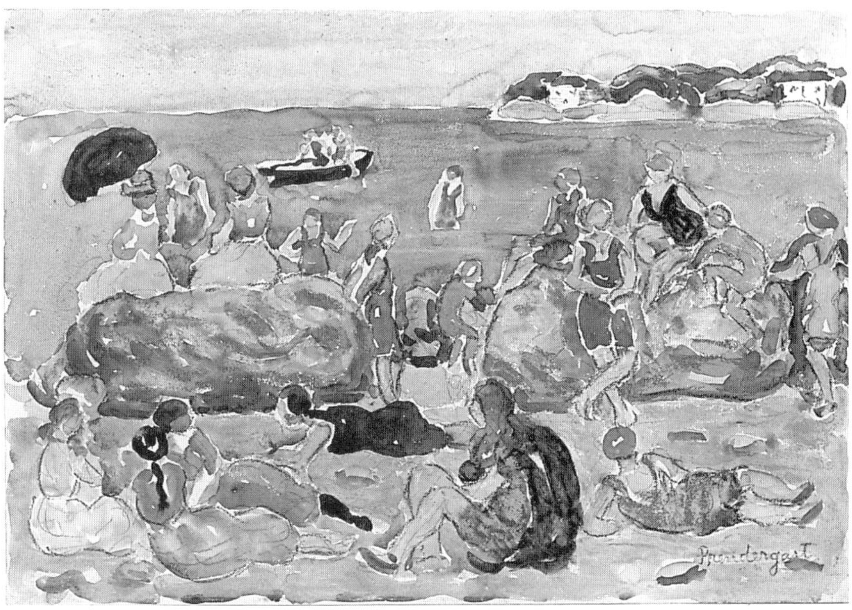

CR 1383

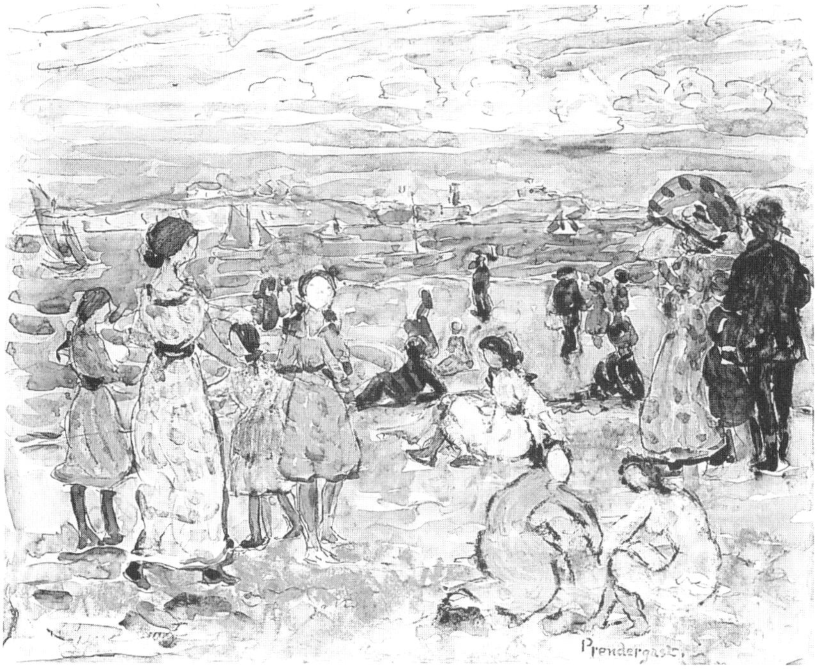

CR 1387

CR 1387

BEACH SCENE ca. 1920–23
Watercolor, pencil, pastel, and ink on paper
(13¾ x 16¾ in.; 34.9 x 42.5 cm)
Williams College Museum of Art, bequest of
Mrs. Charles Prendergast (95.4.69)

INSCRIPTIONS
l.r. in black: Prendergast
l.l. in pencil (faint): Prendergast

BIBLIOGRAPHY
Sawyer 1966 (n.p.)

EXHIBITIONS
1966 Knoedler (#51, ill.)

CR 1393

BASS ROCKS, GLOUCESTER ca. 1920–23
Watercolor and pencil on paper
(13⅞ x 19⅞ in.; 35.2 x 50.5 cm)
Williams College Museum of Art, gift of
Mrs. Charles Prendergast (91.28.14)

INSCRIPTIONS
l.l. in red: Prendergast
verso in pencil (in Charles Prendergast's hand):
Bass Rocks./Gloucester

BIBLIOGRAPHY
Lauzon 1989 (pp. E: 1, 4)

EXHIBITIONS
1989d Williams College (no #); 1991a Williams College (no #); 1996 Spanierman (no #)

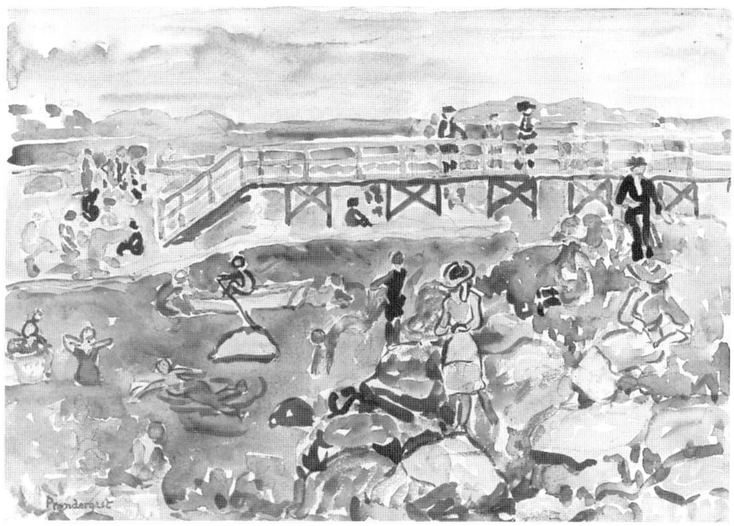

CR 1393

CR 1396

GLOUCESTER ca. 1920–23
Watercolor and pencil on paper
(14⅜ x 20½ in.; 36.5 x 52.1 cm)
Williams College Museum of Art, gift of Mrs.
Charles Prendergast (91.18.20)

INSCRIPTIONS
l.r. in black ink: Prendergast

EXHIBITIONS
1989d Williams College (no #); 1990b Williams College (no #)

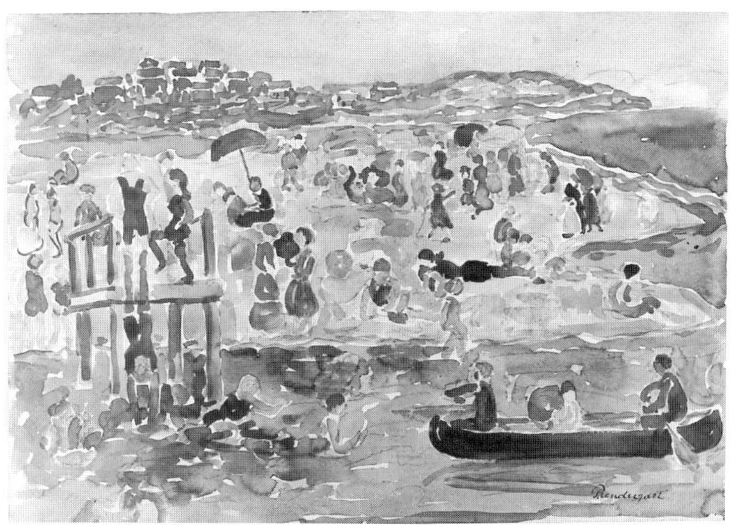

CR 1396

Drawings

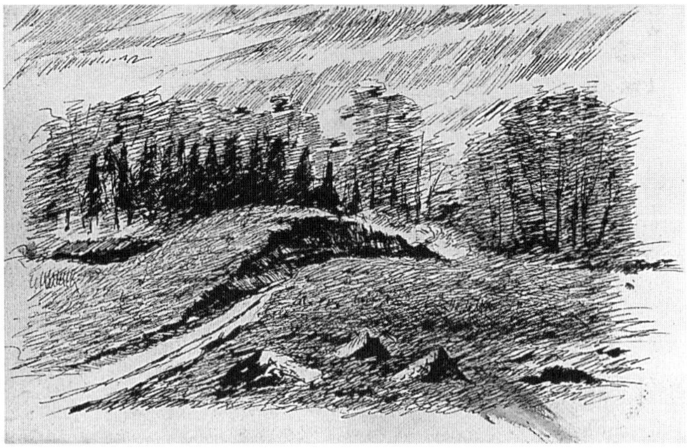

CR 1400

CR 1400
LANDSCAPE ca. 1887
Blue ink on paper
(4¾ x 7½ in.; 12.1 x 19.0 cm)
Williams College Museum of Art, gift of Mrs. Charles Prendergast (85.22.1)

INSCRIPTIONS
Unsigned

BIBLIOGRAPHY
Brady 1962 (n.p.)

EXHIBITIONS
1963a Davis Galleries (#24); 1988a Williams College (no #); 1990f Williams College (no #)

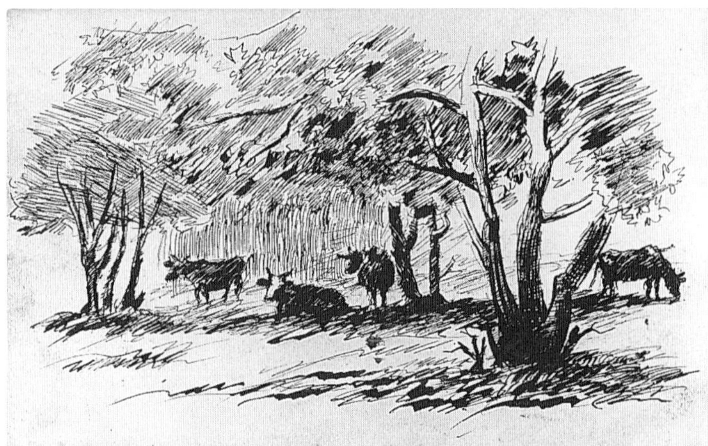

CR 1401

CR 1401
COWS ca. 1887
Blue ink on paper
(4⅝ x 7½ in.; 11.7 x 19.0 cm)
Williams College Museum of Art, gift of Mrs. Charles Prendergast (85.22.3)

INSCRIPTIONS
Unsigned

BIBLIOGRAPHY
Brady 1962 (n.p.)

EXHIBITIONS
1963a Davis Galleries (#23); 1988a Williams College (no #)

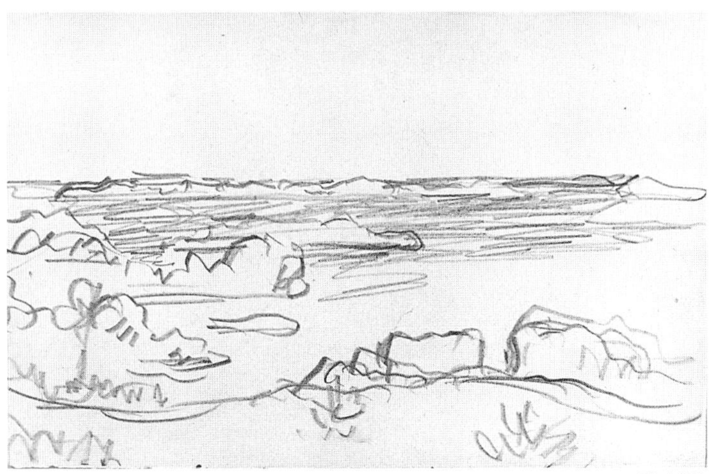

CR 1407

CR 1407
SKETCHBOOK PAGE ca. 1907–10
Pencil on paper
(5⅛ x 7⅞ in.; 13.0 x 20.0 cm)
Williams College Museum of Art, gift of Mrs. Charles Prendergast (85.26.21)

INSCRIPTIONS
Unsigned

EXHIBITIONS
1989d Williams College (no #); 1990f Williams College (no #); 1991b Williams College (no #); 1991c Williams College (no #)

CR 1408

SKETCHBOOK PAGE ca. 1907–10
Pencil on paper
(5⅛ x 7⅞ in.; 13.0 x 20.0 cm)
Williams College Museum of Art, gift of
Mrs. Charles Prendergast (85.26.23)

INSCRIPTIONS
Unsigned

EXHIBITIONS
1989d Williams College (no #); 1990f Williams College (no #); 1991b Williams College (no #); 1991c Williams College (no #)

CR 1408 verso

SKETCH OF ROCKY COAST
Pencil

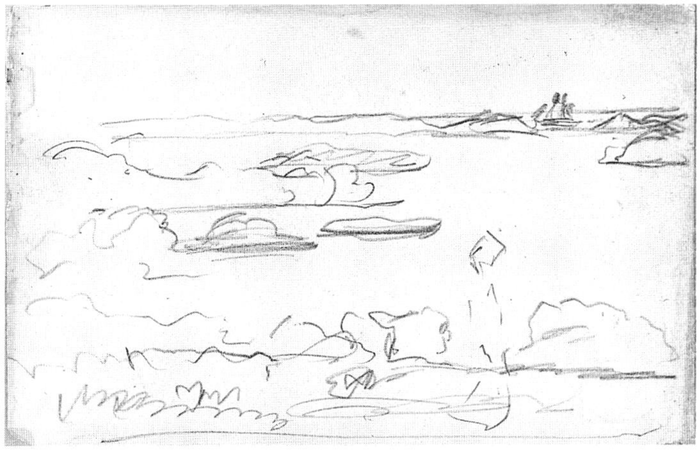

CR 1408

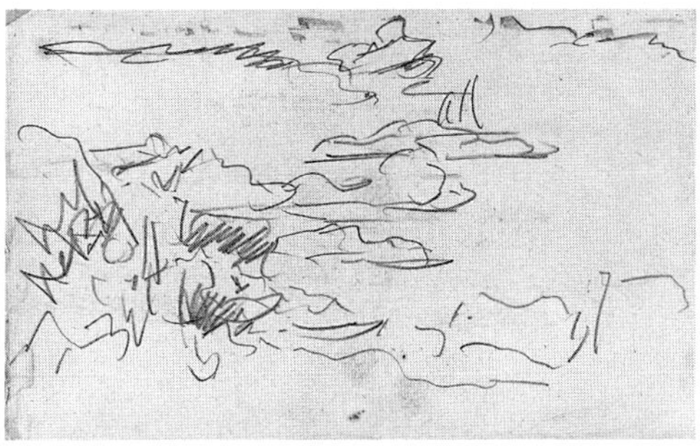

CR 1408 Verso

CR 1411

SKETCHBOOK PAGE ca. 1907–10
Pencil on paper
(5⅛ x 7⅞ in.; 13.0 x 20.0 cm)
Williams College Museum of Art, gift of
Mrs. Charles Prendergast (85.26.22)

INSCRIPTIONS
Unsigned

EXHIBITIONS
1989d Williams College (no #); 1990f Williams College (no #); 1991b Williams College (no #); 1991c Williams College (no #)

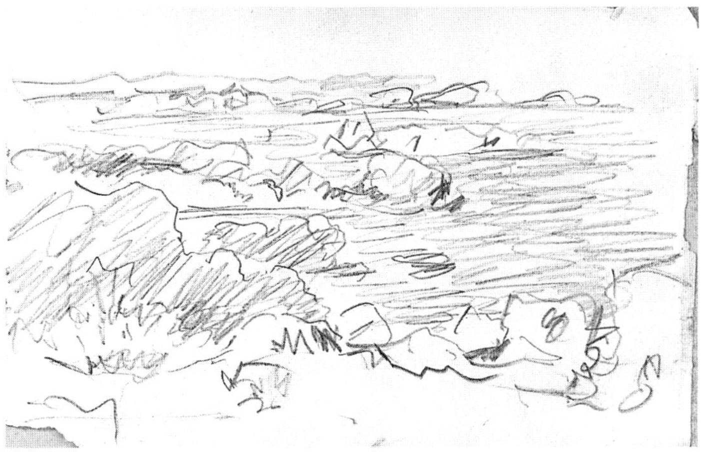

CR 1411

CR 1412

SKETCHBOOK PAGE ca. 1907–10
Pencil on paper
(5⅛ x 7⅞ in.; 13.0 x 20.0 cm)
Williams College Museum of Art, gift of
Mrs. Charles Prendergast (85.26.13)

INSCRIPTIONS
Unsigned

EXHIBITIONS
1989d Williams College (no #)

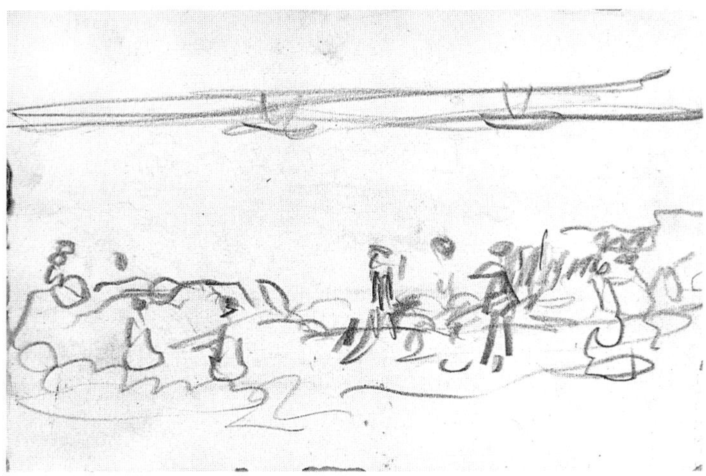

CR 1412

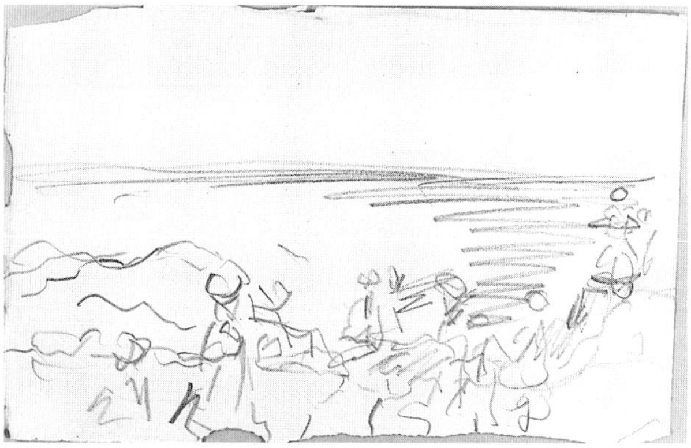

CR 1413

CR 1413
SKETCHBOOK PAGE ca. 1907–10
Pencil on paper
(5⅛ x 7⅞ in.; 13.0 x 20.0 cm)
Williams College Museum of Art, gift of Mrs. Charles Prendergast (85.26.12)

INSCRIPTIONS
Unsigned

EXHIBITIONS
1989c Williams College (no #)

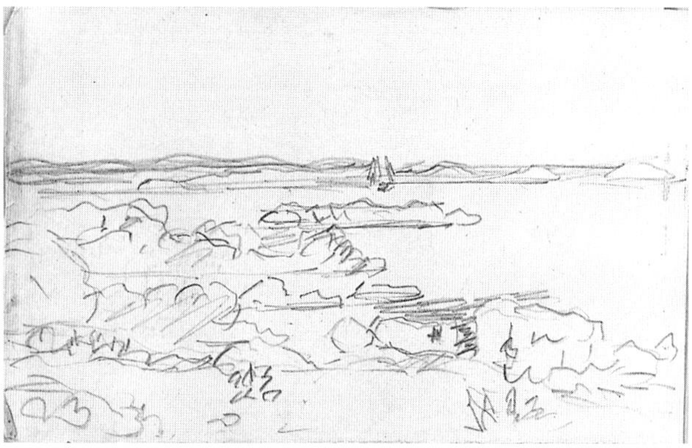

CR 1414

CR 1414
SKETCHBOOK PAGE ca. 1907–10
Pencil on paper
(5⅛ x 7⅞ in.; 13.0 x 20.0 cm)
Williams College Museum of Art, gift of Mrs. Charles Prendergast (85.26.11)

INSCRIPTIONS
Unsigned

BIBLIOGRAPHY
AAA Newsletter 1986 (p. 5)

EXHIBITIONS
1989d Williams College (no #); 1990f Williams College (no #)

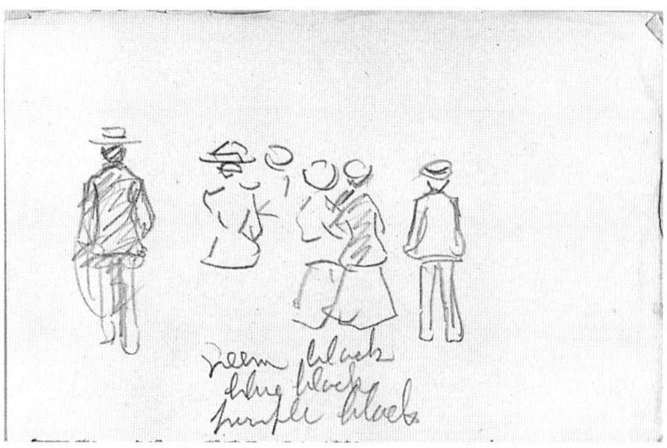

CR 1414 verso

CR 1414 verso
SKETCH OF FIGURES
Pencil

INSCRIPTIONS
l.c.: green black/blue black/purple black

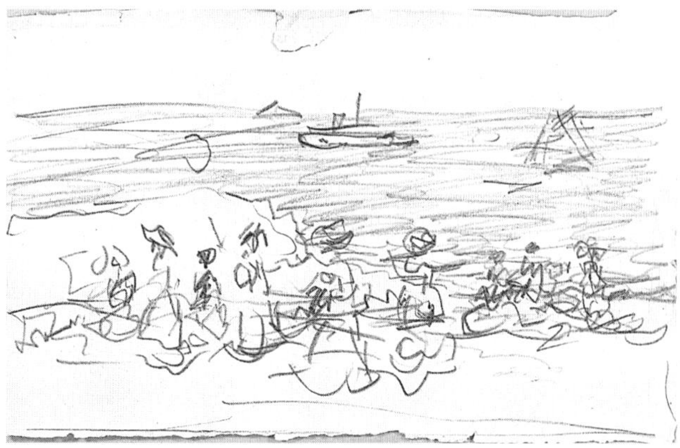

CR 1415

CR 1415
SKETCHBOOK PAGE ca. 1907–10
Pencil on paper
(5⅛ x 7⅞ in.; 13.0 x 20.0 cm)
Williams College Museum of Art, gift of Mrs. Charles Prendergast (85.26.16)

INSCRIPTIONS
Unsigned

EXHIBITIONS
1989c Williams College (no #) verso; 1989d Williams College (no #); 1990f Williams College (no #)

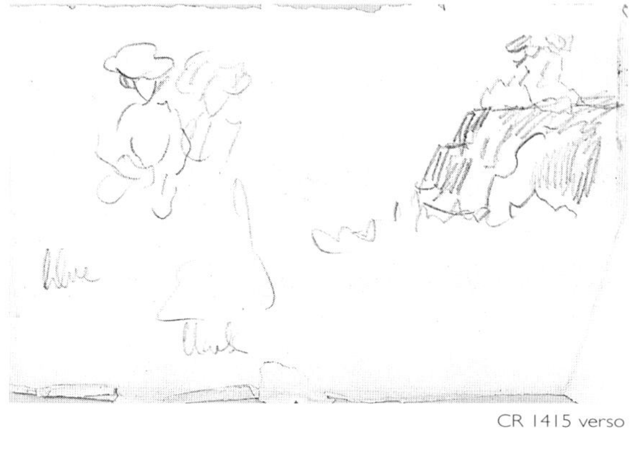

CR 1415 verso

CR 1415 verso
SKETCH OF FIGURES AND ROCKS
Pencil

INSCRIPTIONS
l.l.: blue/black

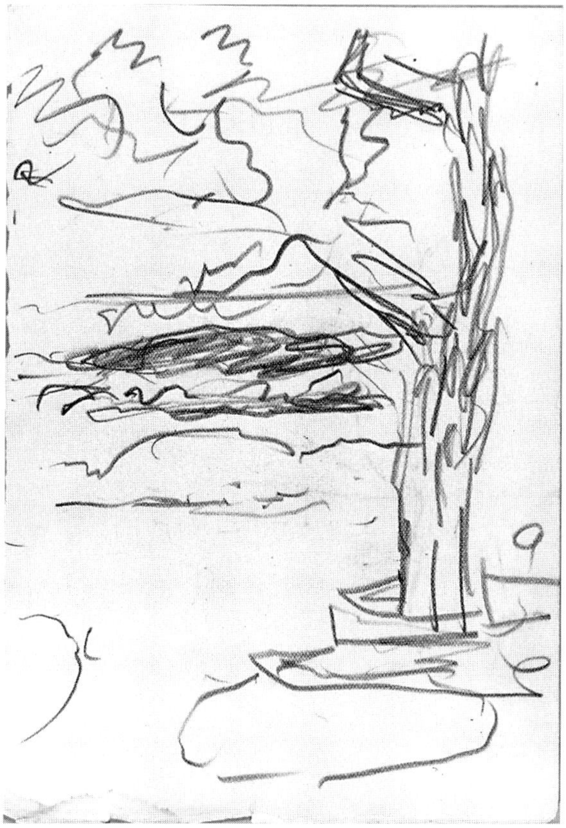

CR 1416

CR 1416
SKETCHBOOK PAGE ca. 1907–10
Pencil on paper
(7⅞ x 5⅛ in.; 20.0 x 13.0 cm)
Williams College Museum of Art, gift of Mrs. Charles Prendergast (85.26.14)

INSCRIPTIONS
Unsigned

EXHIBITIONS
1990f Williams College (no #); 1991b Williams College (no #)

CR 1416 verso
SKETCH OF PARK SCENE
Pencil

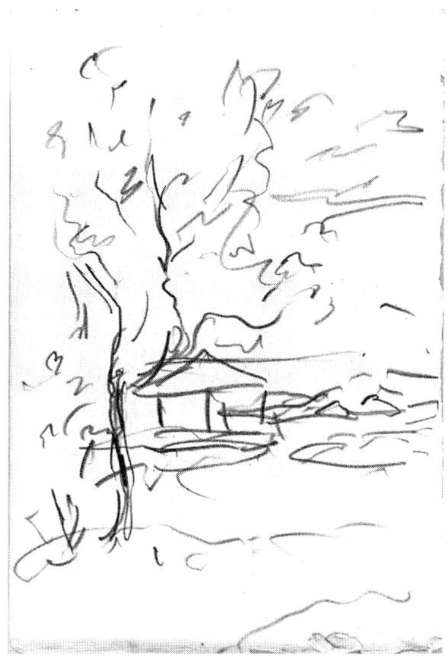

CR 1416 verso

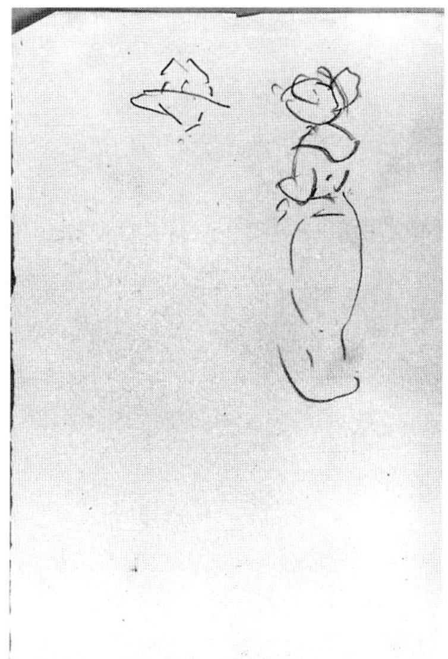

CR 1417 verso

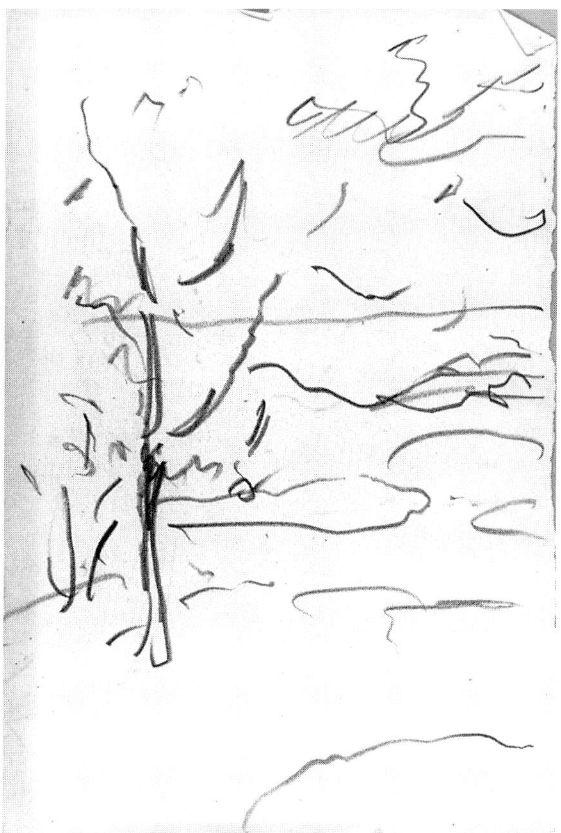

CR 1417

CR 1417
SKETCHBOOK PAGE ca. 1907–10
Pencil on paper
(7⅞ x 5⅛ in.; 20.0 x 13.0 cm)
Williams College Museum of Art, gift of Mrs. Charles Prendergast (85.26.19)

INSCRIPTIONS
Unsigned

EXHIBITIONS
1989c Williams College (no #) verso; 1990f Williams College (no #); 1991b Williams College (no #)

CR 1417 verso
SKETCH OF FIGURES
Pencil

CR 1418

SKETCHBOOK PAGE ca. 1907–10
Pencil on paper
(7⅞ x 5⅛ in.; 20.0 x 13.0 cm)
Williams College Museum of Art, gift of Mrs. Charles Prendergast (85.26.20)

INSCRIPTIONS
Unsigned

EXHIBITIONS
1990f Williams College (no #); 1991b Williams College (no #)

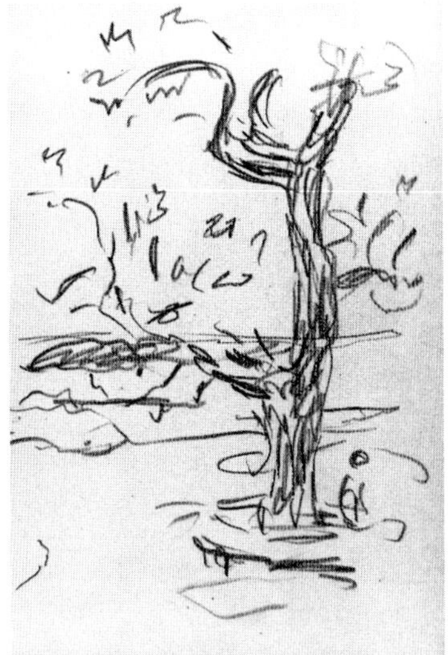

CR 1418

CR 1419

SKETCHBOOK PAGE ca. 1907–10
Pencil on paper
(7⅞ x 5⅛ in.; 20.0 x 13.0 cm)
Williams College Museum of Art, gift of Mrs. Charles Prendergast (85.26.15)

INSCRIPTIONS
Unsigned

EXHIBITIONS
1990f Williams College (no #) verso; 1991b Williams College (no #)

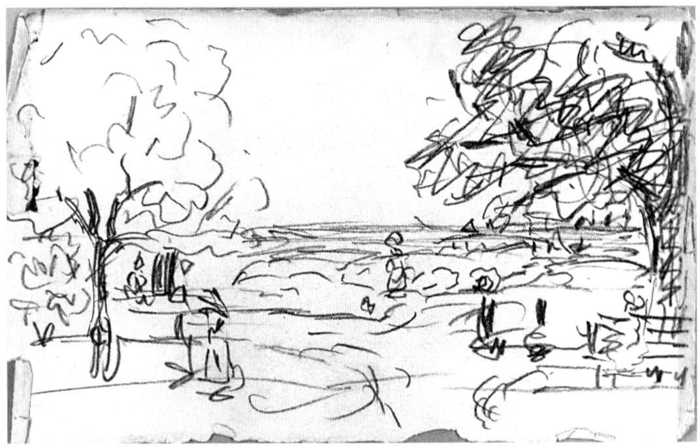

CR 1419

CR 1421

SKETCHBOOK PAGE ca. 1910–15
Pencil on paper
(5⅛ x 7⅞ in.; 13.0 x 20.0 cm)
Williams College Museum of Art, gift of Mrs. Charles Prendergast (85.26.10)

INSCRIPTIONS
u.r.: grey
l.r.: grey

BIBLIOGRAPHY
AAA Newsletter 1986 (p. 5)

EXHIBITIONS
1989c Williams College (no #) verso

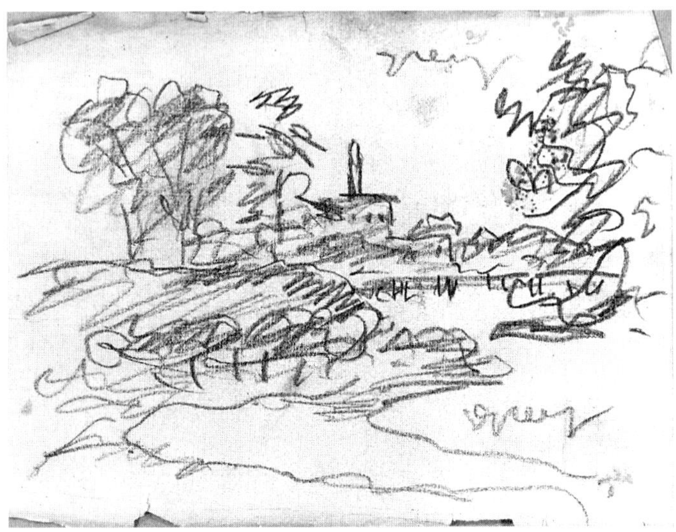

CR 1421

CR 1421 verso

SKETCH OF WOMAN
Pencil

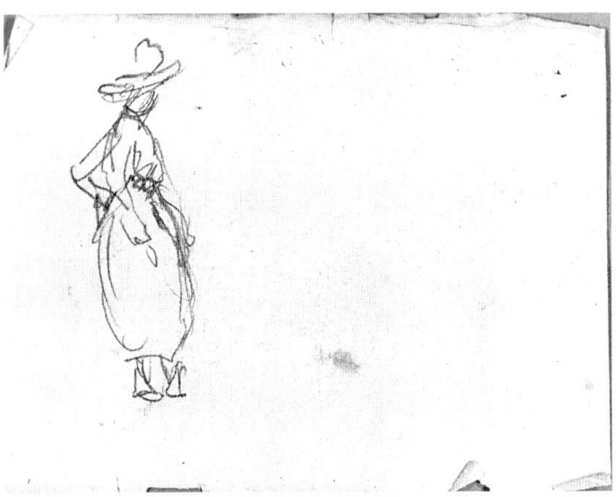

CR 1421 verso

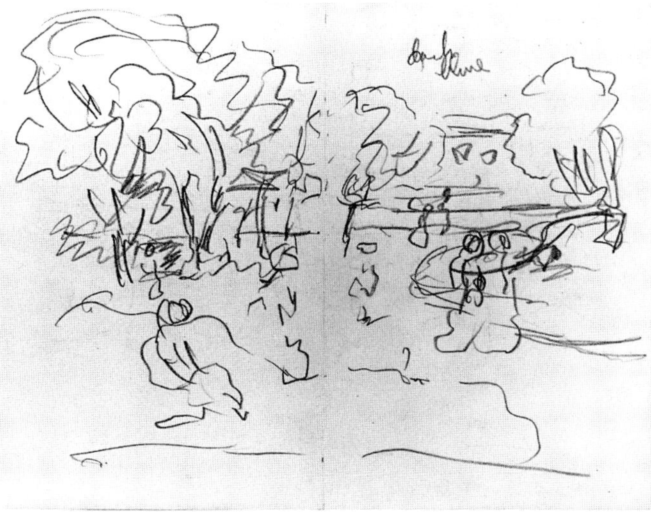

CR 1427

CR 1427
LANDSCAPE ca. 1910–15
Pencil on paper
(7¾ x 10 in.; 19.7 x 25.4 cm)
Williams College Museum of Art, gift of Mrs. Charles Prendergast (85.22.2)

INSCRIPTIONS
u.l.: dark/blue

BIBLIOGRAPHY
Brady 1962 (n.p.)

EXHIBITIONS
1963a Davis Galleries (#35, recto and verso)

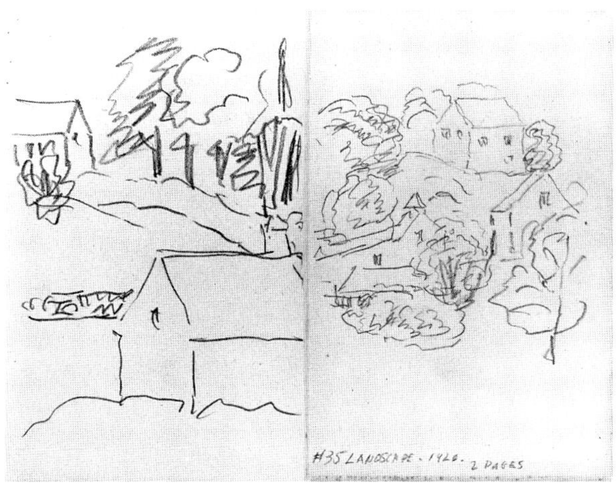

CR 1427 verso

CR 1427 verso
TWO LANDSCAPE SKETCHES
Pencil

CR 1435
THREE WOMEN ca. 1912–15
Pencil and crayon on paper
(9⅞ x 6½ in.; 25.1 x 16.5 cm)
Williams College Museum of Art, bequest of Mrs. Charles Prendergast (95.4.90)

INSCRIPTIONS
l.r. in pencil: M.B.P.

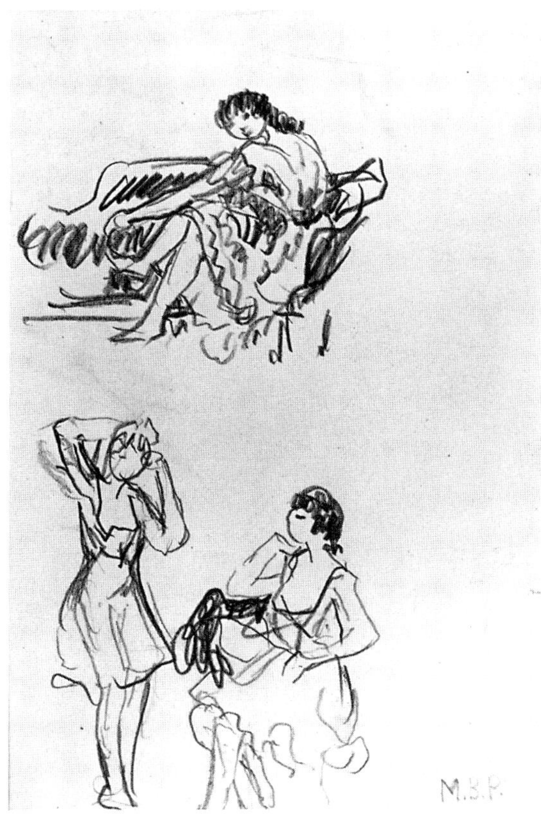

CR 1435

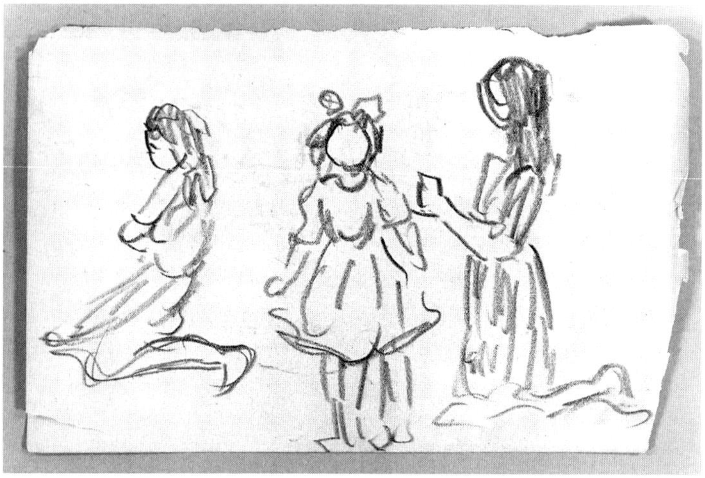

CR 1444

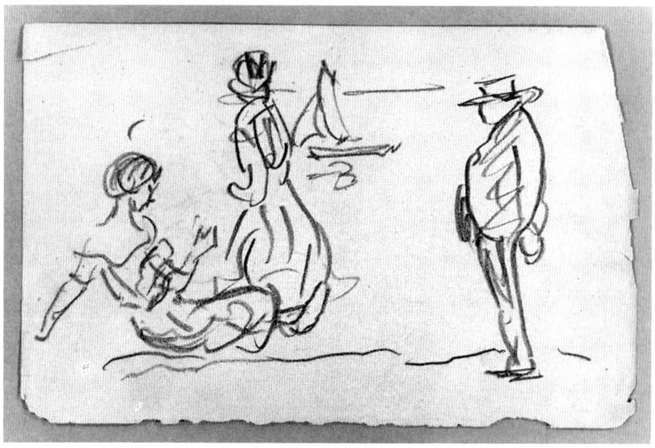

CR 1444 verso

CR 1444
SKETCHBOOK PAGE ca. 1912–15
Pencil on paper
(5⅛ x 7⅞ in.; 13.0 x 20.0 cm)
Williams College Museum of Art, gift of Mrs. Charles Prendergast (85.26.17)

EXHIBITIONS
1989c Williams College (no #); 1990f Williams College (no #)

CR 1444 verso
SKETCH OF FIGURES ON BEACH
Pencil

CR 1445
WOMAN IN BLUE DRESS ca. 1912–15
Watercolor and pencil on paper
(12½ x 11⅜ in.; 31.7 x 28.9 cm)
Williams College Museum of Art, gift of Mrs. Charles Prendergast (89.2)

INSCRIPTIONS
l.r. in pencil (in a late hand): Prendergast

EXHIBITIONS
1963a Davis Galleries (#5, recto and verso); 1991a Williams College (no #)

CR 1445 verso
SEATED WOMAN
Pencil

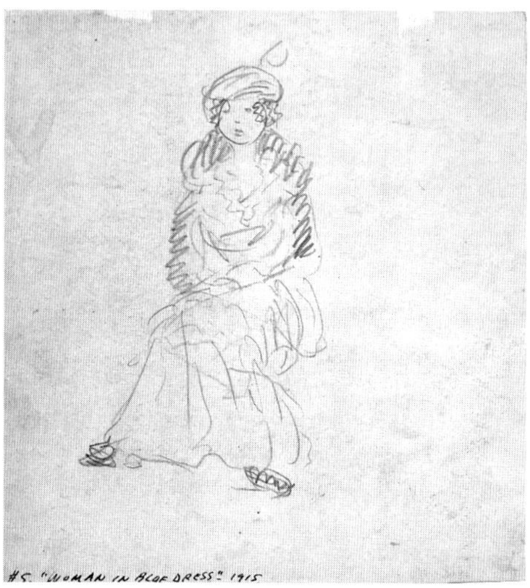

CR 1445 verso

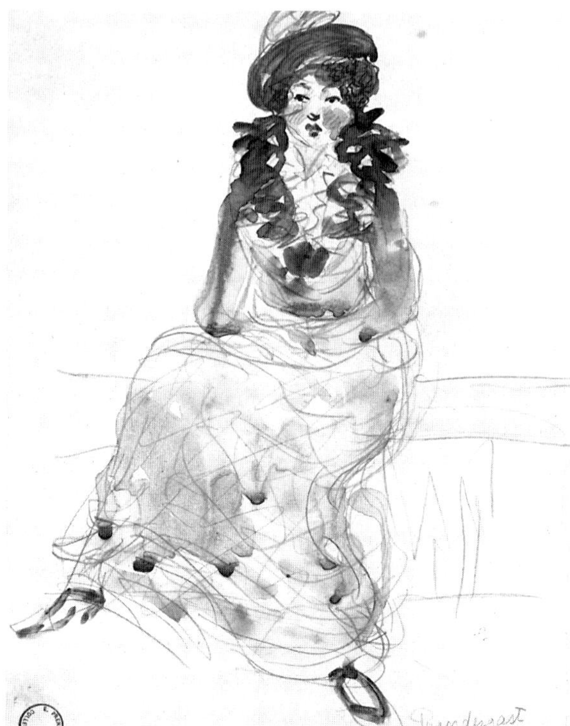

CR 1445

CR 1447

STANDING NUDE ca. 1912–15
Pencil and crayon on paper
(12½ x 9¼ in.; 31.8 x 23.5 cm)
Williams College Museum of Art, gift of Mrs. Charles Prendergast (85.22.5)

INSCRIPTIONS
Unsigned

EXHIBITIONS
1963a Davis Galleries (#16); 1990a Williams College (no #); 1991b Williams College (no #); 1991c Williams College (no #)

CR 1449

STANDING NUDE ca. 1912–15
Pencil on paper
(12¼ x 9⅜ in.; 31.1 x 23.6 cm)
Williams College Museum of Art, gift of Mrs. Charles Prendergast (85.22.10)

INSCRIPTIONS
Unsigned

EXHIBITIONS
1990a Williams College (no #); 1991b Williams College (no #)

CR 1449 verso

SEATED NUDE
Pencil

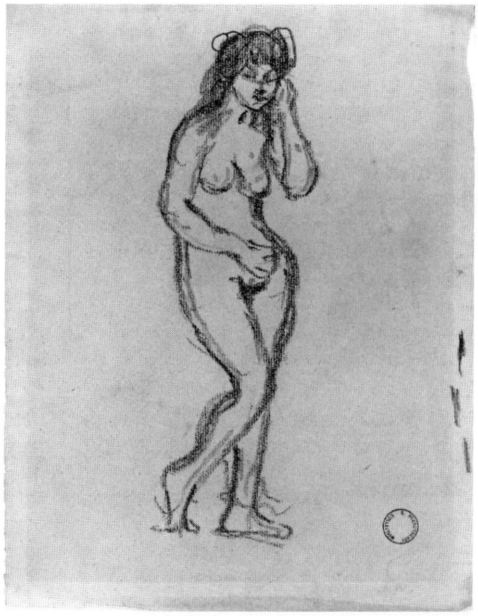

CR 1447

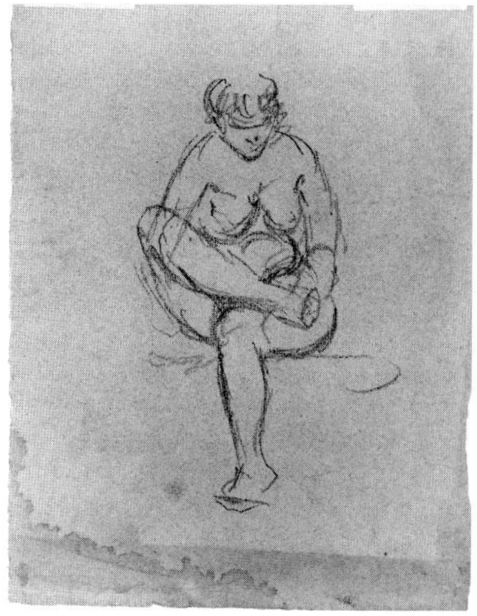

CR 1449 verso

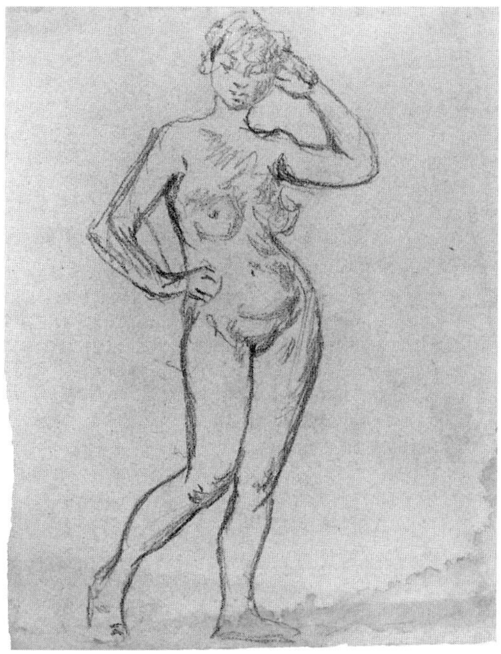

CR 1449

CR 1450

SEATED NUDE ca. 1912–15
Pencil on paper
(12⅜ x 9½ in.; 31.4 x 24.1 cm)
Williams College Museum of Art, gift of Mrs. Charles Prendergast (85.22.6)

INSCRIPTIONS
Unsigned

EXHIBITIONS
1963a Davis Galleries (#15); 1990a Williams College (no #); 1991b Williams College (no #)

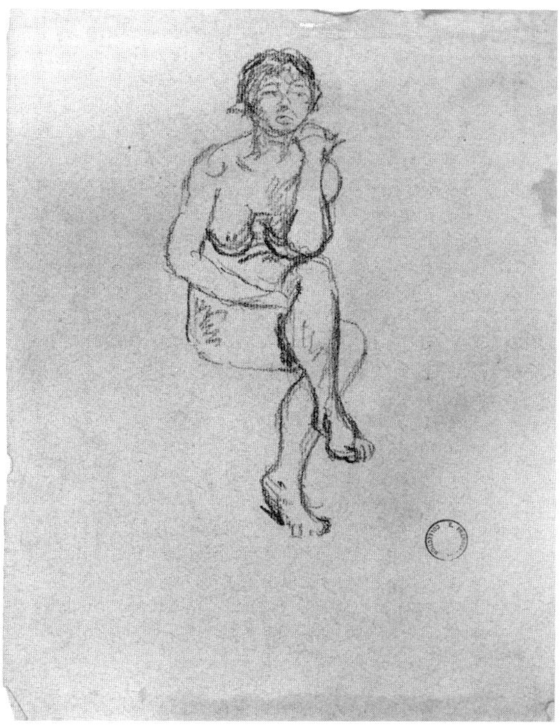

CR 1450

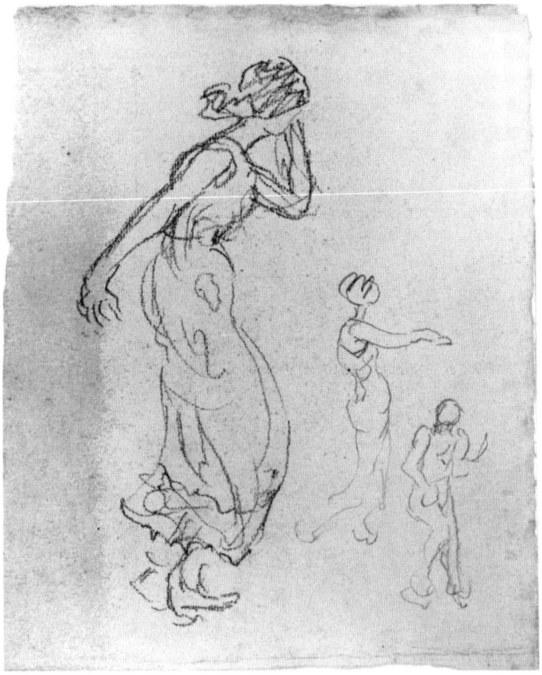

CR 1452

CR 1452

THREE FIGURES ca. 1912–15
Pencil on paper
(12⅜ x 9¾ in.; 31.4 x 24.8 cm)
Williams College Museum of Art, gift of
Mrs. Charles Prendergast (85.22.8)

INSCRIPTIONS
Unsigned

EXHIBITIONS
1988a Williams College (no #); 1990a Williams College (no #); 1993 Williams College (no #)

CR 1452 verso

FIGURE STUDIES
Pencil

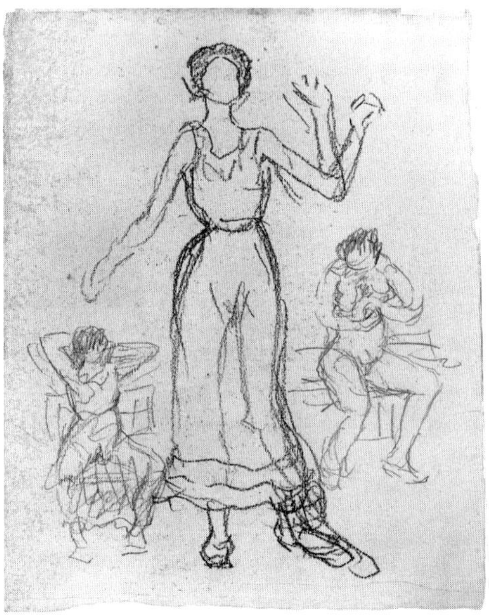

CR 1452 verso

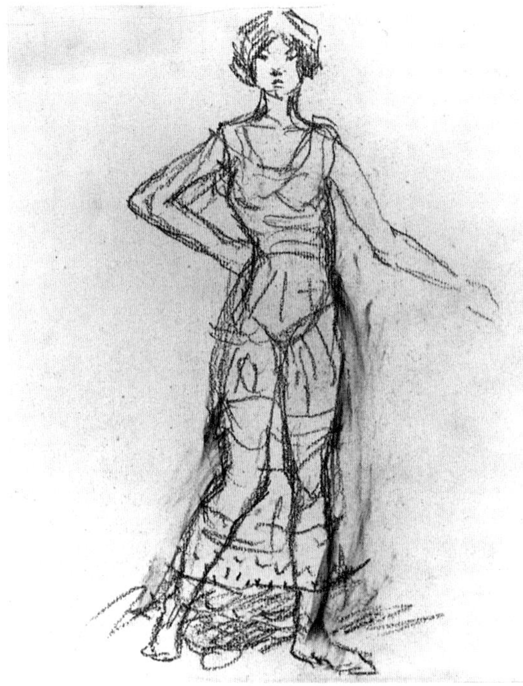

CR 1453

CR 1453

STANDING WOMAN ca. 1912–15
Pencil on paper
(12¾ x 9⅝ in.; 32.4 x 24.4 cm)
Williams College Museum of Art, gift of
Mrs. Charles Prendergast (85.22.11)

INSCRIPTIONS
Unsigned

EXHIBITIONS
1988a Williams College (no #); 1990a Williams College (no #)

CR 1453 verso

DANCER
Pencil

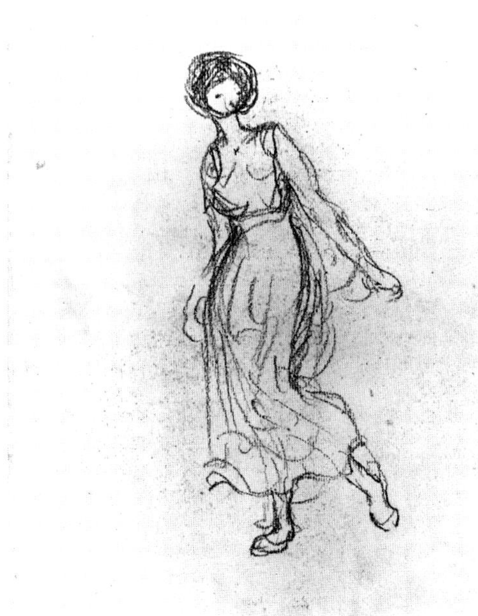

CR 1453 verso

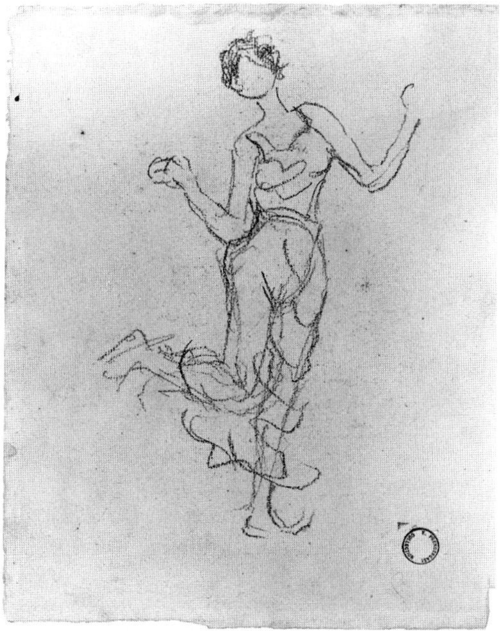

CR 1454

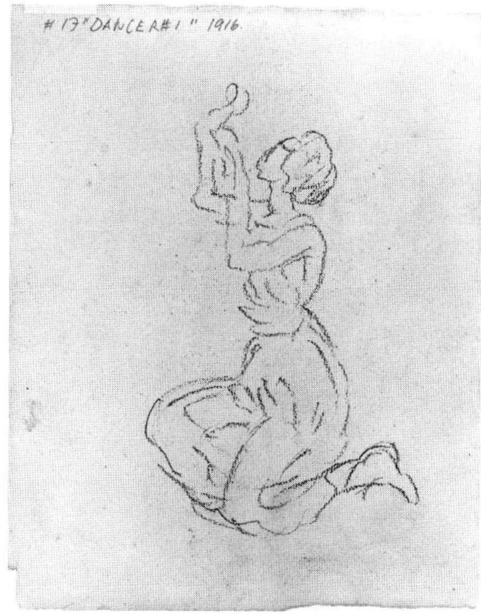

CR 1454 verso

CR 1454
DANCER #1 ca. 1912–15
Pencil on paper
(12 x 9½ in.; 30.5 x 24.1 cm)
Williams College Museum of Art, gift of
Mrs. Charles Prendergast (85.22.7)

INSCRIPTIONS
Unsigned

BIBLIOGRAPHY
Brady 1962 (n.p.)

EXHIBITIONS
1963a Davis Galleries (#17, recto and verso, recto ill.); 1988a Williams College (no #); 1989b Williams College (#14); 1990a Williams College (no #); 1991c Williams College (no #)

CR 1454 verso
KNEELING WOMAN
Pencil

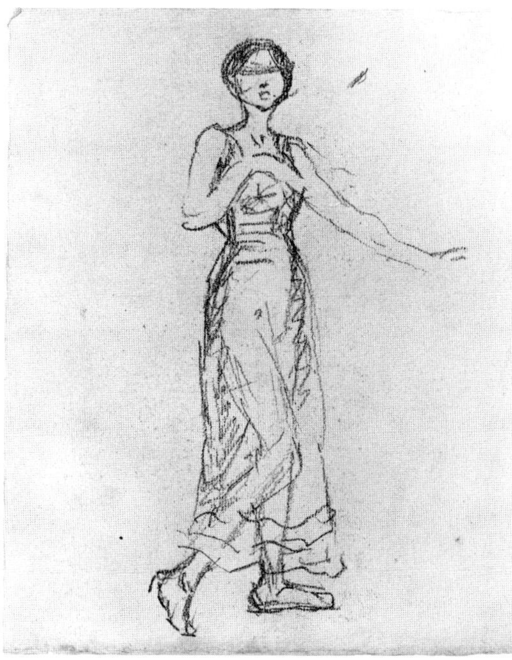

CR 1455

CR 1455
STANDING WOMAN ca. 1912–15
Pencil on paper
(12⅛ x 9½ in.; 30.8 x 24.1 cm)
Williams College Museum of Art, gift of
Mrs. Charles Prendergast (85.22.9)

INSCRIPTIONS
Unsigned

EXHIBITIONS
1988a Williams College (no #); 1990a Williams College (no #)

CR 1455 verso
SEATED WOMAN
Pencil

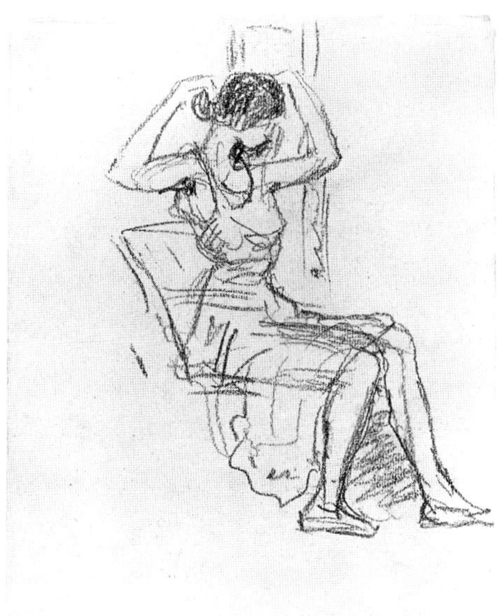

CR 1455 verso

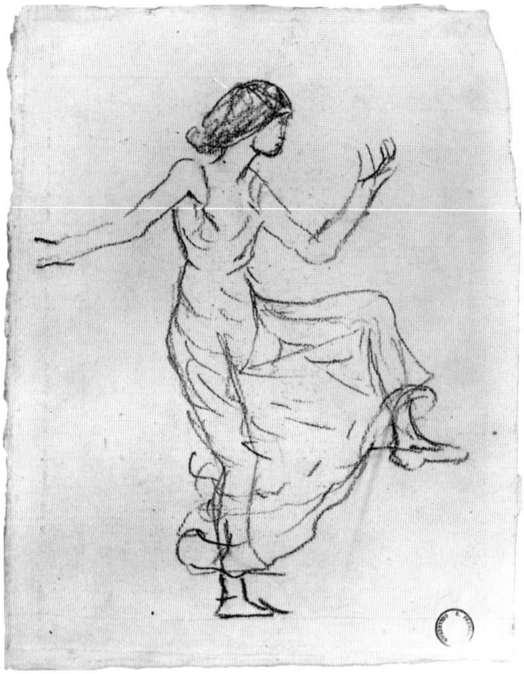

CR 1456

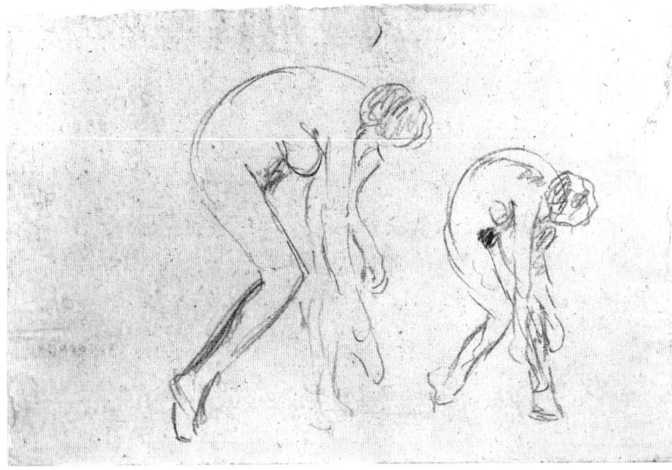

CR 1458

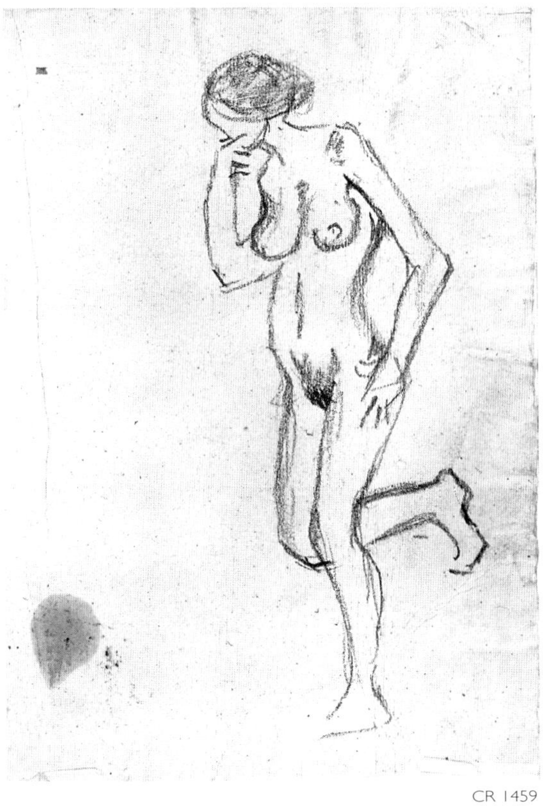

CR 1459

CR 1456
DANCER #3 ca. 1912–15
Pencil on paper
(12¼ x 9⅜ in.; 31.1 x 23.6 cm)
Williams College Museum of Art, gift of Mrs. Charles Prendergast (85.22.4)

INSCRIPTIONS
Unsigned

BIBLIOGRAPHY
Brady 1962 (n.p.); Mathews 1990 (p. 34; ill.)

EXHIBITIONS
1963a Davis Galleries (#19); 1988a Williams College (no #); 1990a Williams College (no #); 1992 Williams College (no #)

CR 1458
TWO STUDIES OF A NUDE BENDING
ca. 1912–15
Pencil on paper
(7¾ x 11⅜ in.; 19.7 x 28.9 cm)
Williams College Museum of Art, gift of Mrs. Charles Prendergast (87.5.1)

INSCRIPTIONS
Unsigned

EXHIBITIONS
1988a Williams College (no #); 1990a Williams College (no #); 1991b Williams College (no #); 1993 Williams College (no #)

CR 1459
STUDY OF A NUDE ca. 1912–15
Pencil on paper
(11⅜ x 7⅞ in.; 28.9 x 20.0 cm)
Williams College Museum of Art, gift of Mrs. Charles Prendergast (87.5.2)

INSCRIPTIONS
Unsigned

EXHIBITIONS
1988a Williams College (no #); 1990a Williams College (no #); 1991b Williams College (no #)

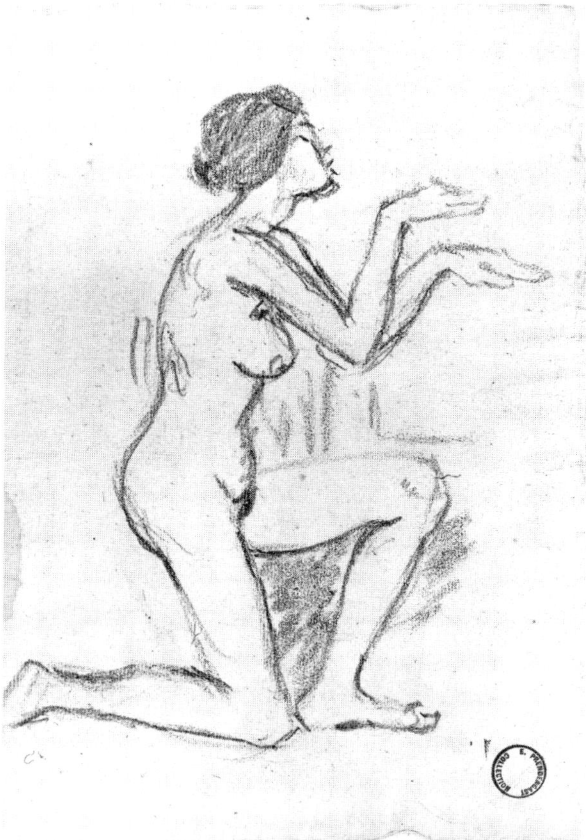

CR 1460

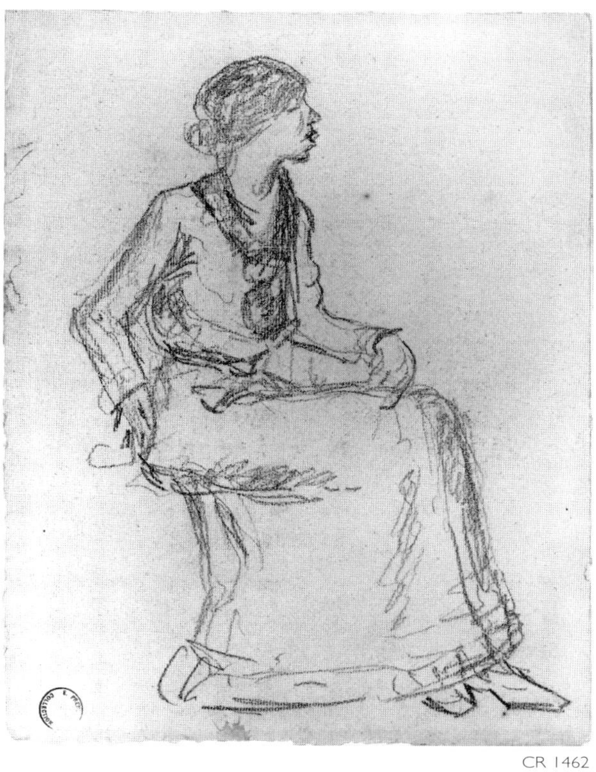

CR 1462

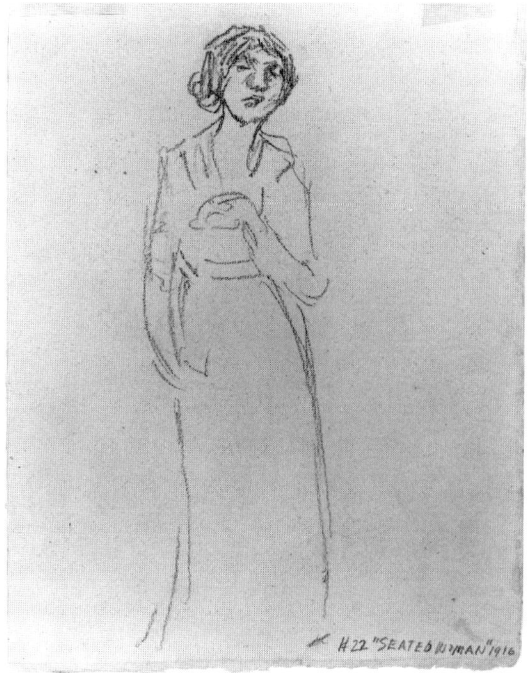

CR 1462 verso

CR 1460
KNEELING NUDE ca. 1912–15
Woman Kneeling
Pencil on paper
(11½ x 7⅞ in.; 29.2 x 20.0 cm)
Williams College Museum of Art, gift of Mrs. Charles Prendergast (86.18.48)

INSCRIPTIONS
Unsigned

EXHIBITIONS
1963a Davis Galleries (#21); 1990a Williams College (no #); 1991b Williams College (no #)

CR 1462
SEATED WOMAN ca. 1912–15
Pencil on paper
(12⅜ x 9⅜ in.; 31.4 x 23.6 cm)
Williams College Museum of Art, gift of Mrs. Charles Prendergast (86.18.45)

INSCRIPTIONS
Unsigned

EXHIBITIONS
1963a Davis Galleries (#22, recto and verso); 1988a Williams College (no #)

CR 1462 verso
STANDING WOMAN
Pencil

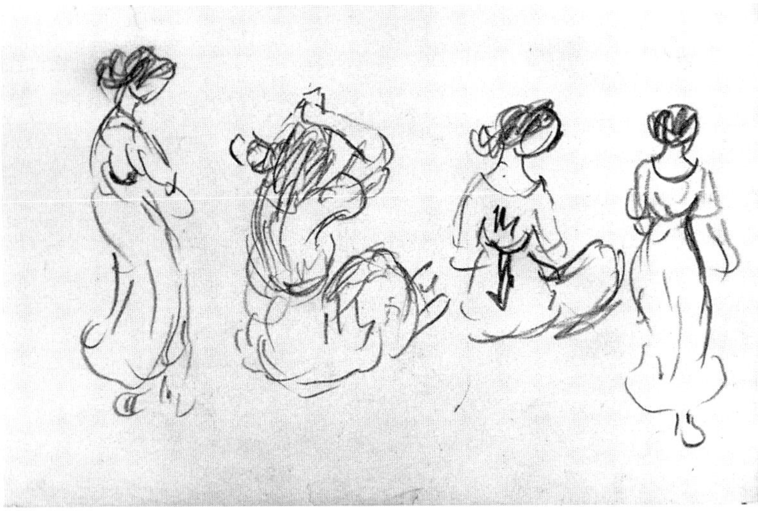

CR 1463

CR 1463
SKETCHBOOK PAGE ca. 1912–15
Pencil on paper
(5⅛ x 7⅞ in.; 13.0 x 20.0 cm)
Williams College Museum of Art, gift of Mrs. Charles Prendergast (85.26.18)

EXHIBITIONS
1989c Williams College (no #); 1990f Williams College (no #)

CR 1463 verso
TWO STANDING WOMEN
Pencil

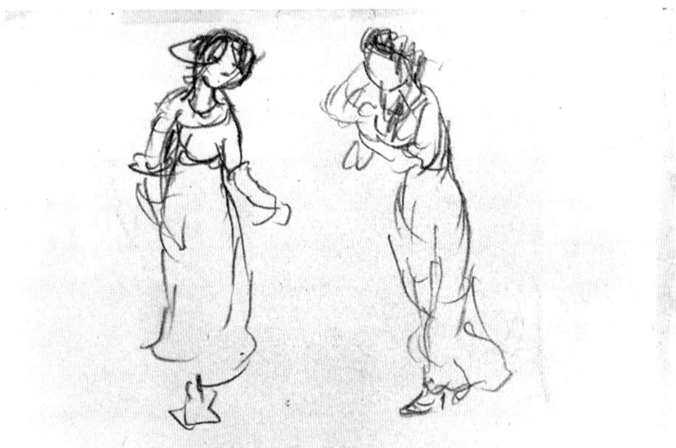

CR 1463 verso

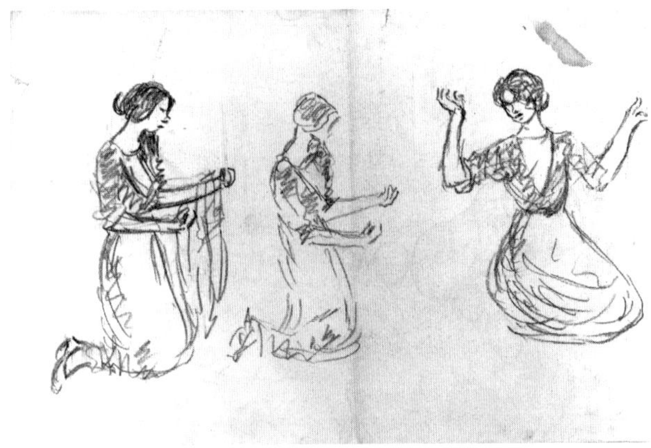

CR 1465 verso

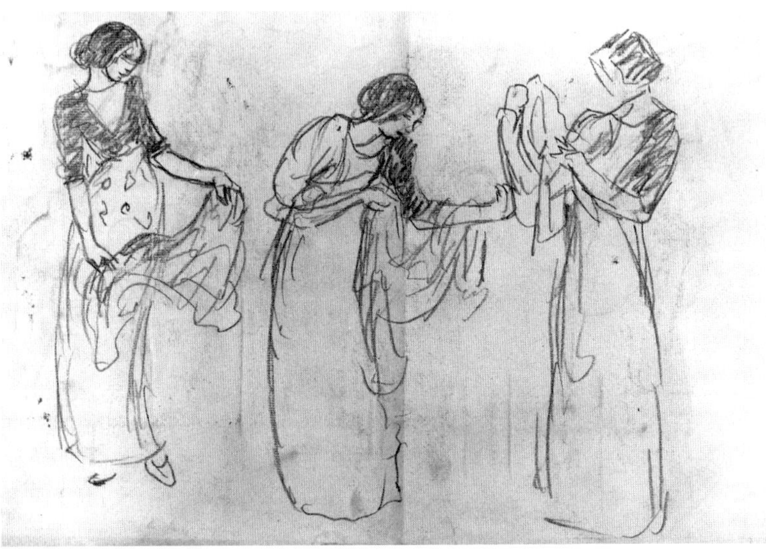

CR 1465

CR 1465
STUDY OF THREE GIRLS WITH SCARVES
ca. 1912–15
Pencil on paper
(12¾ x 19⅛ in.; 32.4 x 48.6 cm)
Williams College Museum of Art, gift of Mrs. Charles Prendergast (86.18.44)

INSCRIPTIONS
Unsigned

EXHIBITIONS
1960 Boston MFA (#145, ill.); 1988a Williams College (no #); 1991c Williams College (no #)

CR 1465 verso
THREE GIRLS KNEELING, ONE WITH SCARF
Pencil

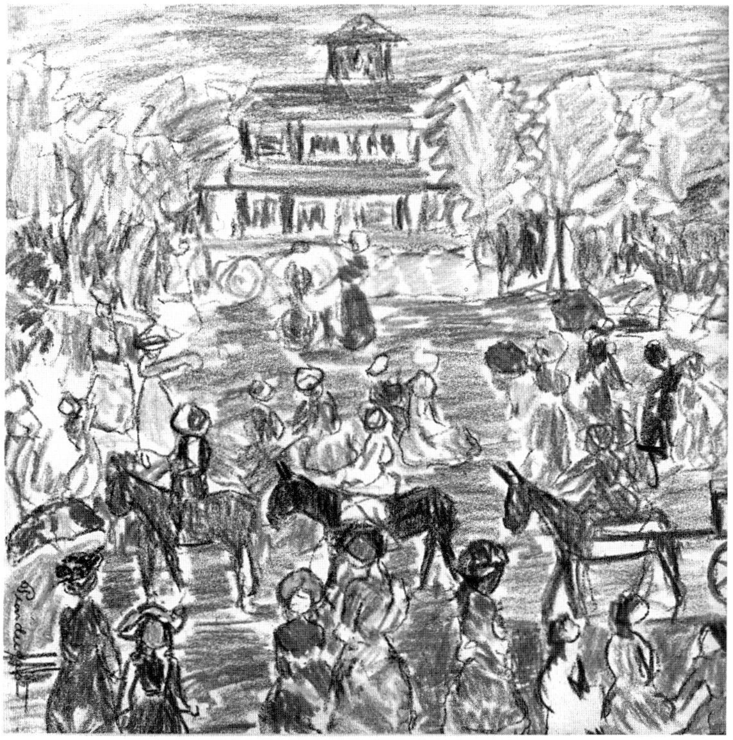

CR 1466

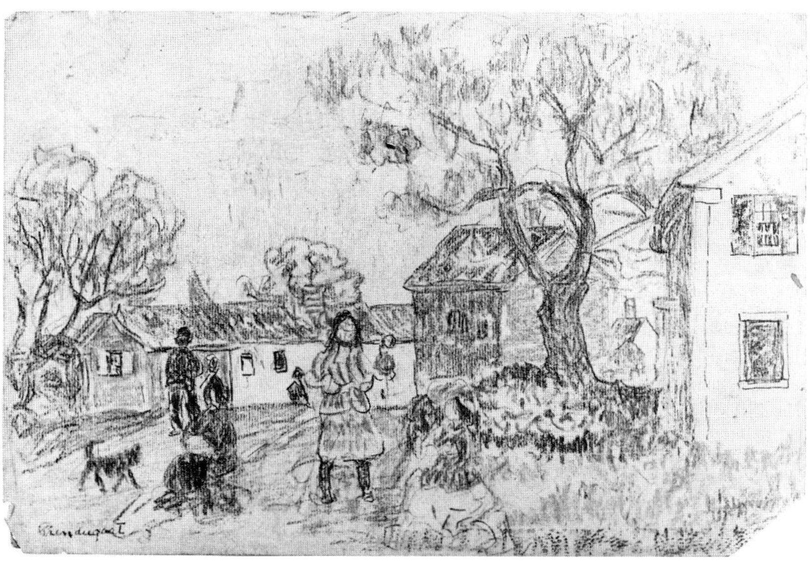

CR 1470

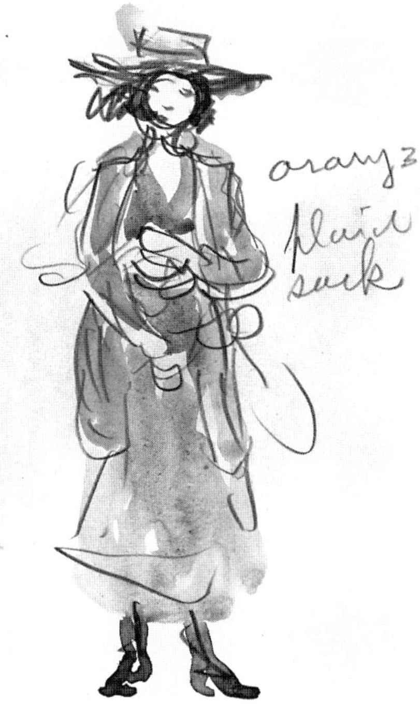

CR 1472

CR 1466

SUMMER HOTEL, MAINE ca. 1914–15
Passamaquoddy House
Colored pencil or crayon on paper
(13 x 13 in.; 33.0 x 33.0 cm)
Williams College Museum of Art, bequest of Mrs. Charles Prendergast (95.4.72)

INSCRIPTIONS
l.l. in pencil: Prendergast

EXHIBITIONS
1983a Williams College (#22, ill., as *Passamaquoddy House*)

CR 1470

VILLAGE IN SUMMER ca. 1915
Crayon and pencil on paper
(10½ x 15⅜ in.; 26.7 x 39.1 cm)
Williams College Museum of Art, bequest of Mrs. Charles Prendergast (95.4.5)

INSCRIPTIONS
l.l. in black ink: Prendergast

CR 1472

STUDY OF A WOMAN ca. 1915–20
Watercolor and pencil on paper
(7½ x 4⅞ in.; 19.0 x 12.4 cm)
Williams College Museum of Art, bequest of Mrs. Charles Prendergast (95.4.106)

INSCRIPTIONS
u.r.: orange/plaid/sack

EXHIBITIONS
1963a Davis Galleries (#45)

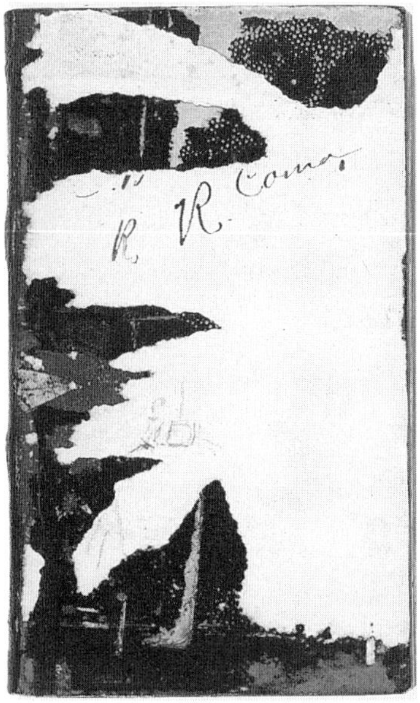

CR 1481

CR 1481

SKETCHBOOK ca. 1900–05
(SKETCHBOOK OF FRAME STUDIES)
Sketchbook, 95 pencil drawings on lined paper
(6⅞ x 4 in.; 17.5 x 10.2 cm)
Williams College Museum of Art, gift of Mrs. Charles Prendergast (85.26.9)

BIBLIOGRAPHY
AAA Newsletter 1986 (p. 5)

EXHIBITIONS
1988b Williams College (#94); 1989b Williams College (#1); 1989c Williams College (no #); 1993 Williams College (no #)

NOTES
Ninety-five pages of pencil drawings, which may have been done in Venice, mostly frame studies with more than his usual care for their descriptive quality, showing molding ornaments and sections. There are also a few studies of horses in profile and four or five human figures; there is one manuscript note of three pages that is difficult to decipher but seems to read as advice to some studio intruder, somewhat as follows: "I am working. My mind is virtually set to compose, to which everything else is secondary, that is, which interferes with my work. You cannot come around working on your frames and pictures; do them at your house, you have plenty of room." (AAA 3583)

CR 1507

SKETCHBOOK ca. 1912–15
(PARIS SKETCHBOOK)
Sketchbook, 89 pencil, pen-and-ink, and wash drawings
(8¼ x 6¾ in.; 20.6 x 17.1 cm)
Williams College Museum of Art, gift of Mrs. Charles Prendergast (85.26.1)

INSCRIPTIONS
inside cover per EP: Maurice B. Prendergast/66 pages pencil drawings

BIBLIOGRAPHY
AAA Newsletter 1986 (p. 5)

EXHIBITIONS
1988a Williams College (no #); 1989c Williams College (no #); 1989d Williams College (no #); 1990c Williams College (no #, CD); 1990f Williams College (no #); 1991b Williams College (no #); 1993 Williams College (no #)

NOTES
Seventy pages of pencil drawings, nineteen pages of pen-and-ink drawings, and an ink wash drawing, all from Paris, of female figures in various poses, clothed and nude, children, classical and mythological figures, a male model in various poses, several line framed compositions from paintings, including landscapes, and some naively designed landscapes with figures and studies of separate trees, all in the style of Charles Prendergast but likely by Maurice, studies of an archaic Greek figure sculpture, dog, swans, and duck; three book titles, *L'art decoratif,* Fernand Roches, 4 rue de Gaff, Paris, *The Childhood of Art* [H. G. Spearing, 1913?], and *Art in Egypt,* an incomplete statement, are to be found in private collections and museums, and one name with address, Henry Fitch Taylor, La Tourette, Richmond, Staten Island, N.Y. [Taylor, manager of the Madison Gallery, New York, was one of the sixteen founders of the Association of American Painters and Sculptors, who organized the Armory Show of 1913]. (AAA 3583)
Cf. related works, *Four Girls in Meadow* (CR 1235), *Head of a Girl* (CR 327), and *Portrait of a Young Girl* (CR 332).

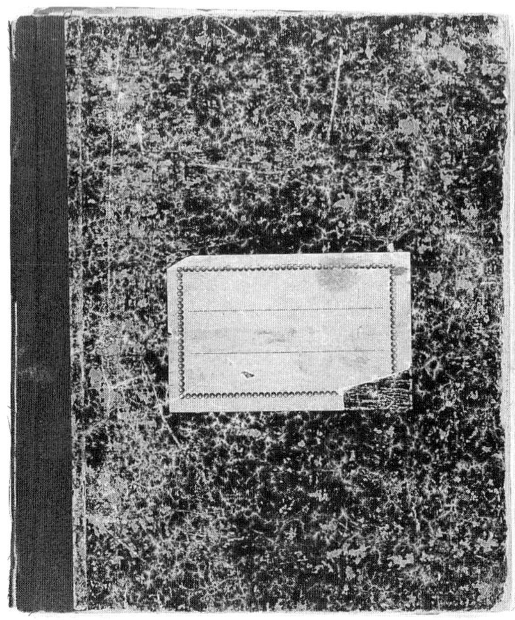

CR 1507

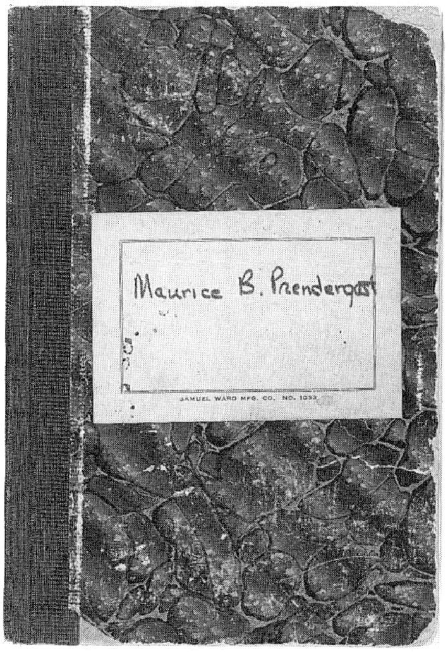

CR 1559

CR 1559

SKETCHBOOK ca. 1920–23
Sketchbook, 21 pencil, watercolor, and crayon drawings
(7¾ x 5¼ in.; 19.7 x 9.5 cm)
Williams College Museum of Art, gift of Mrs. Charles Prendergast in honor of John W. Chandler, President of Williams College, 1973–85 (85.11.2)

INSCRIPTIONS
on cover: Maurice B. Prendergast (hand?)
first page: Maurice B. Prendergast

BIBLIOGRAPHY
AAA Newsletter 1986 (p. 5)

EXHIBITIONS
1988a Williams College (no #); 1988b Williams College (#95); 1989c Williams College (no #); 1989d Williams College (no #); 1990c Williams College (no #, CD); 1990f Williams College (no #); 1991b Williams College (no #); 1995c Williams College (no #)

NOTES
Fifteen pencil drawings, six watercolors, and a crayon drawing of unidentified locations on the New England coast with harbors, distant points with villages, islands, boats and rocky shores, figure studies of women clothed and nude, a page with four comic heads and two pages of frame studies; manuscript notes other than color notations consist of Maurice's signature and two comments on the temperature. (AAA 3583)
Cf. related works, *Fishing Village* (CR 1264), *Rockport* (CR 1362), and *Bay Side Marblehead* (CR 1353).

CR 1561

SKETCHBOOK ca. 1920–23
Sketchbook, 82 pencil, watercolor, and crayon drawings
(7¾ x 5¼ in.; 19.7 x 13.3 cm)
Williams College Museum of Art, gift of Mrs. Charles Prendergast (85.26.2)

INSCRIPTIONS
on cover: Maurice B. Prendergast/130 Bowdoin St./Boston Mass.

BIBLIOGRAPHY
AAA Newsletter 1986 (p. 5)

EXHIBITIONS
1988a Williams College (no #); 1989c Williams College (no #); 1989d Williams College (no #); 1990c Williams College (no #, CD); 1990f Williams College (no #); 1991b Williams College (no #)

NOTES
Sixty-six pages of pencil drawings, nine watercolors, and two crayon drawings done on Cape Ann, vicinity of Gloucester, Salem (and Annisquam?), of single and group figure studies, nude male figures, nude female figures, rocky harbors and village scenes with and without figures, a distinctive two-story cubic building with a sign on a mansard roof (resort hotel?), a line framed village view in crayon, seaside parks with figures, wagons, sun shelters, a distinctive distant village with one tall chimney and a square tower, a park scene with distinctive hexagonal sun shelter; manuscript notes show two addresses for Maurice Prendergast: 130 Bowdoin St., Boston, and 50 S. Washington. (AAA 3583)
Cf. related works, *Beach Gathering* (CR 1386) and *Figures in a Cove* (CR 1378).

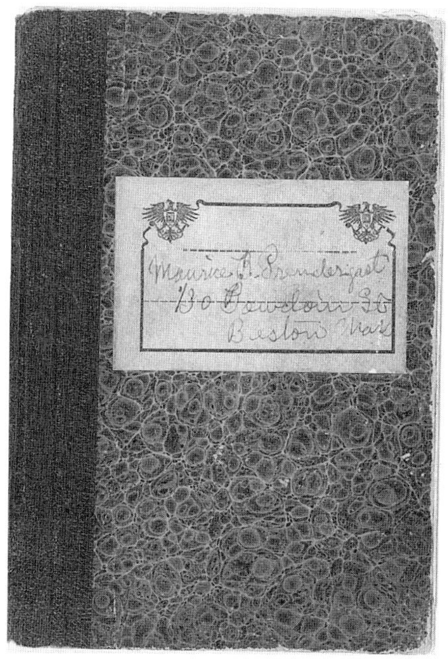

CR 1561

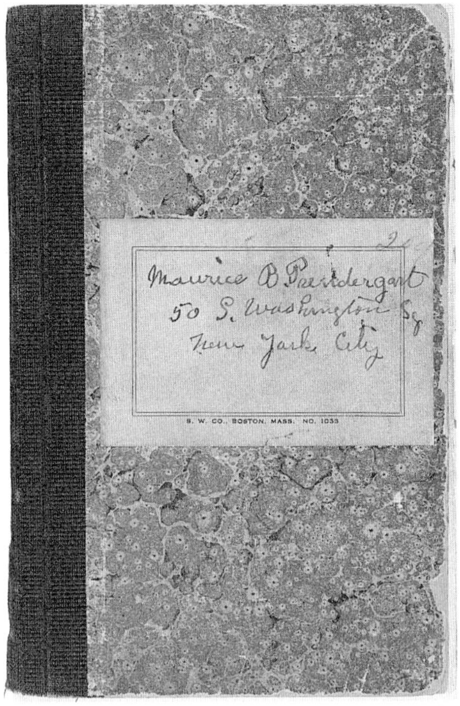

CR 1562

CR 1562

SKETCHBOOK ca. 1920–23
Sketchbook, 82 pencil and watercolor drawings (7¾ x 5 in.; 19.7 x 12.7 cm)
Williams College Museum of Art, gift of Mrs. Charles Prendergast in honor of John W. Chandler, President of Williams College, 1973–85 (85.11.1)

INSCRIPTIONS
on cover: Maurice B. Prendergast/50 S. Washington Sq./New York City

BIBLIOGRAPHY
AAA Newsletter 1986 (p. 5)

EXHIBITIONS
1988a Williams College (no #); 1989c Williams College (no #); 1989d Williams College (no #); 1990c Williams College (no #, CD); 1990f Williams College (no #); 1991b Williams College (no #); 1993 Williams College (no #); 1995c Williams College (no #)

NOTES
Eighty pages of pencil drawings and eleven watercolors done at various locations on Cape Ann (some labeled) of rocky coves, islands, seaside parks with and without figures, figures on the shore with donkeys, a motorboat with a sun canopy, sailboats, distinctive distant factories exhibiting three tall chimneys, studies of women and children, figure studies clothed and nude, church and spire with distinctive fourgored dome, seaside park with distinctive hexagonal sun shelter (Salem Willows?) and figures, rocky beach with bathhouses (Annisquam), pier with gangplank, float and boats; Maurice B. Prendergast, 50 S. Washington Sq., New York City [on cover], Maurice Prendergast, 54 Middle St. [on flyleaf], all gold, Salem [autumn park scene, suggesting the time around October 1], East Gloucester, Annisquam, I am going to Rocky Neck; I want to see an artist friend, Mr. Brown; here to Old Gloucester he is coming back 15 [October?]; I got a note from Pepper September [artist and writer Charles Hovey Pepper?]. He said that he will see me very shortly. He is in Maine with Cutler. [Carl Gordon Cutler, color expert, and joint author with Stephen C. Pepper of *Modern Color*, Harvard University Press, 1923.]
Cf. reference in CR 1503 (AAA 3583).
Cf. related works, *Long Beach* (CR 1392), *Beach* (CR 1323), and *In the Park* (CR 1344).

Monotypes

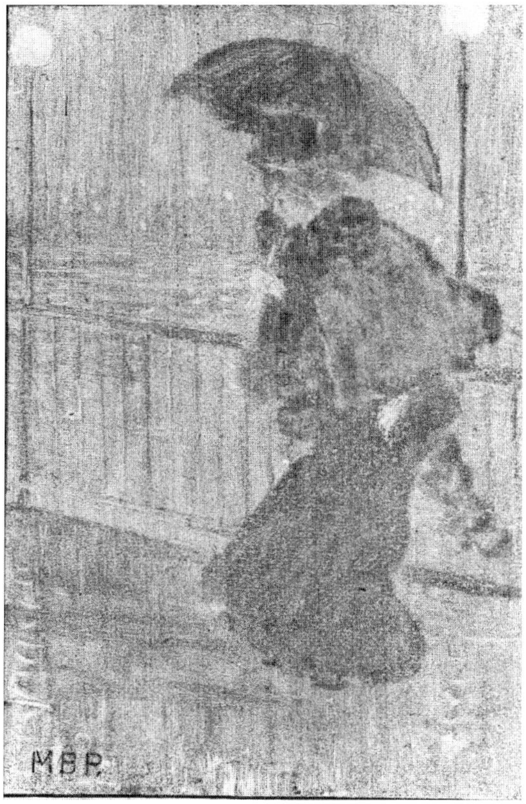

CR 1566

CR 1566
THE ESPLANADE, BOSTON ca. 1891–95
Monotype on paper
(8¾ x 5¾ in.; 22.2 x 14.6 cm; image)
Private collection and Williams College Museum of Art (93.13.3)

INSCRIPTIONS
l.l. in pencil (probably in another hand): MBP

EXHIBITIONS
1994a Williams College (no #)

CR 1597
BAREBACK RIDER ca. 1895
Monotype on paper
(7½ x 5¾ in., 19.1 x 14.6 cm; image)
Williams College Museum of Art, gift of Mrs. Charles Prendergast
(85.21.1)

INSCRIPTIONS
l.r. in plate: MBP

BIBLIOGRAPHY
Mathews 1990 (p. 43; ill.)

EXHIBITIONS
1989b Williams College (#6); 1991a Williams College (no #)
Cf. earlier pull, *Bareback Rider* (CR 1596).
Cf. also preparatory sketch for horse and rider, *The White Horse and Circus Rider* (CR 593), and p. 33 of the "Large Boston Public Garden Sketchbook" (CR 1477).

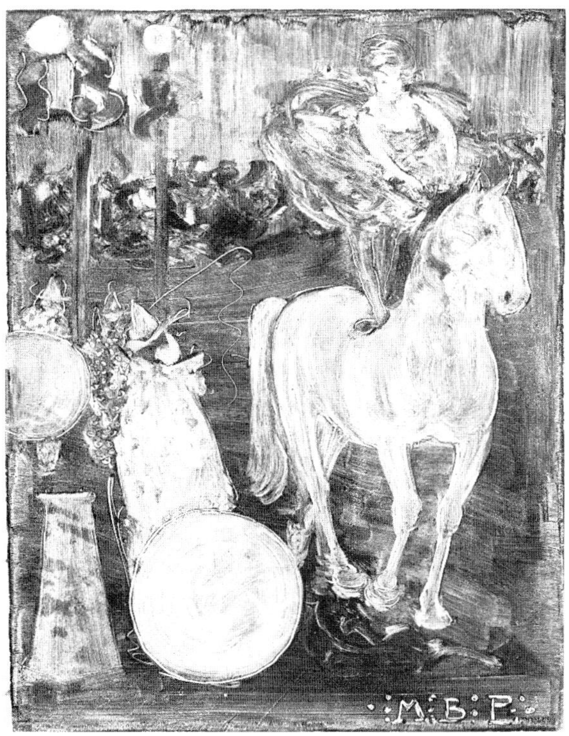

CR 1597

CR 1611

SKIPPING ROPE ca. 1895–97
Monotype on paper
(5⅝ x 4½ in.; 14.3 x 11.4 cm; image)
Williams College Museum of Art, gift of Mrs. Charles Prendergast (85.21.3)

INSCRIPTIONS
u.l. in plate: MBP [monogram]

EXHIBITIONS
1898 Boston Water Color Club (#87); 1991a Williams College (no #)

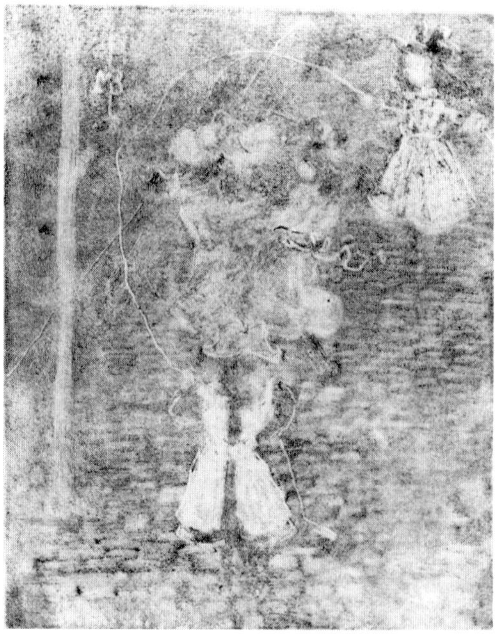

CR 1611

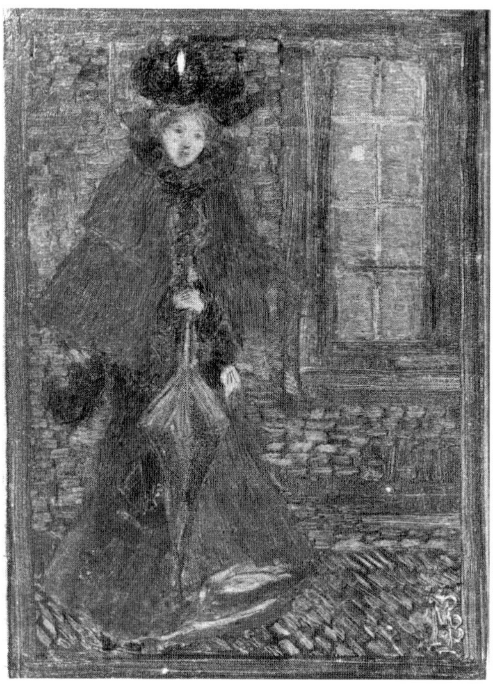

CR 1622

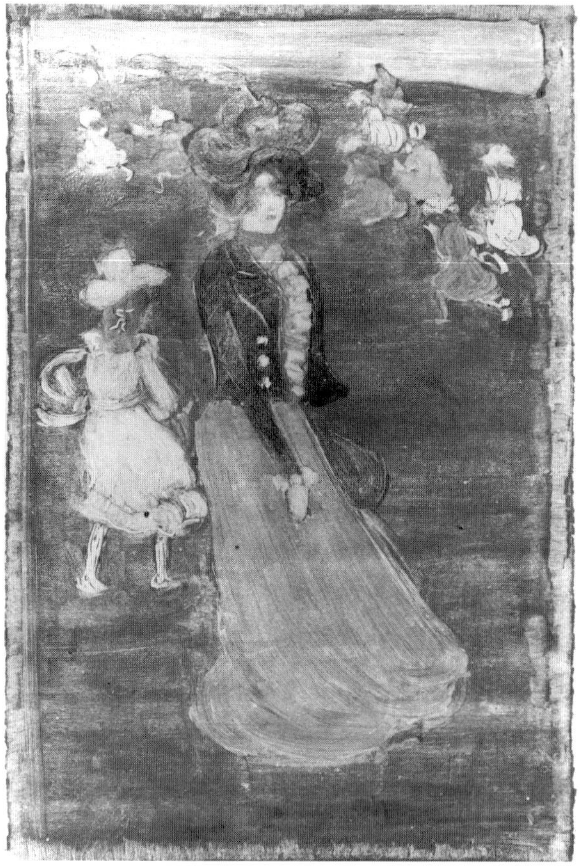

CR 1660

CR 1622

RED CLOAK WITH CAPE ca. 1895–1900
Frame by Charles Prendergast
Monotype on paper with pencil additions
(8¾ x 6¼ in.; 22.2 x 15.9 cm; image)
Williams College Museum of Art (97.00.00)

INSCRIPTIONS
l.r. in plate: MBP [monogram]

PROVENANCE
The artist; to Charles Prendergast, 1924; to private collection, 1941, from Mr. and Mrs. Charles Prendergast; to present collection, 1997

CR 1660

LADY IN PINK SKIRT ca. 1895–97
Lady with Pink Skirt
Monotype on paper
(15½ x 11 in.; 39.4 x 27.9 cm; sheet)
Williams College Museum of Art, gift of Mrs. Charles Prendergast (86.18.78)

INSCRIPTIONS
l.l. in gold crayon (probably in another hand): M/B/P

BIBLIOGRAPHY
Howat 1973 (p. 104); Mathews 1990 (p. 164; ill.)

EXHIBITIONS
1960 Boston MFA (#129, ill.); 1986 Williams College (no #); 1989c Williams College (no #); 1990c Williams College (#119. BCD); 1993 Williams College (no #); 1994a Williams College (no #)

NOTE
All Breezy Common compositions are based on a watercolor sketch on p. 43 of the "Boston Watercolor Sketchbook" (CR 1478).
Color plate, p. 17

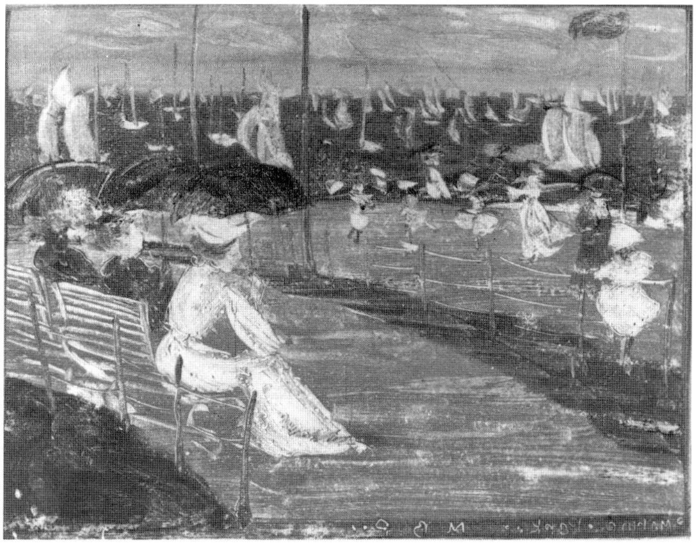

CR 1679

CR 1679

MARINE PARK, SOUTH BOSTON ca. 1895–97
Monotype on paper with pencil additions
(9⅞ x 12⅝ in.; 25.1 x 32.1 cm; sheet)
Williams College Museum of Art, gift of George and Wilhelmina Batchelder (98.2)

INSCRIPTIONS
l.r. in plate: MBP Marine Park [written backwards]

BIBLIOGRAPHY
Langdale 1979a (p. 89); Langdale 1984 (p. 110)

EXHIBITIONS
? 1936 Kraushaar (#24 as *Marine Park;* ? 1937 Corcoran (#5); 1967 Bard (#13 as *Marine Park*)

CR 1696

THE OPERA CLOAK ca. 1895–97
Monotype on paper
(10¼ x 5⅜ in.; 26.0 x 13.7 cm; image)
Williams College Museum of Art, bequest of Mrs. Charles Prendergast (95.4.103)

INSCRIPTIONS
across bottom in plate: The Opera Cloak MBP [monogram]

EXHIBITIONS
? 1898 Boston Water Color Club (#84); ? 1901 Detroit (#29); 1967 Bard College (#51)
Cf. possible other pull with changes, *Lady with Cape and Boa* (CR 1695).

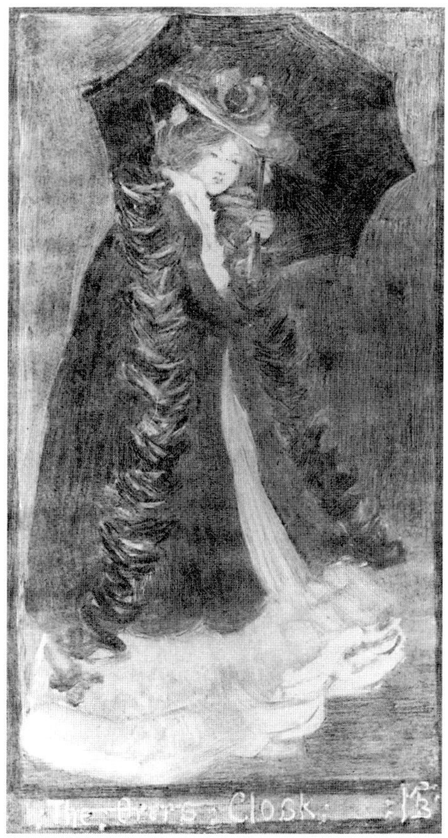

CR 1696

CR 1739

LADY IN BLUE WITH WHITE BOA 1901

Lady in Blue with Boa; ? Lady in Blue No. 1; ? Lady in Blue No. 2

Frame by Charles Prendergast
Monotype on paper with pencil additions
(9¼ x 5⅜ in.; 23.5 x 13.7 cm; image)
Private collection and Williams College Museum of Art (93.13.2)

INSCRIPTIONS
across bottom in plate: Blue 1901 1 col Print MBP [monogram]

PROVENANCE
The artist; to Charles Prendergast, 1924; to present collection, 1941; fractional interest to WCMA, 1993

EXHIBITIONS
? 1902 Boston Water Color Club (#103, as *Lady in Blue No. 1* or #104, as *Lady in Blue No. 2*); ? 1902 Chicago AIC (#402, as *Lady in Blue No. 1* or #403, as *Lady in Blue No. 2*); 1994a Williams College (no #)
Cf. another pull, *Lady in Blue* (CR 1738).

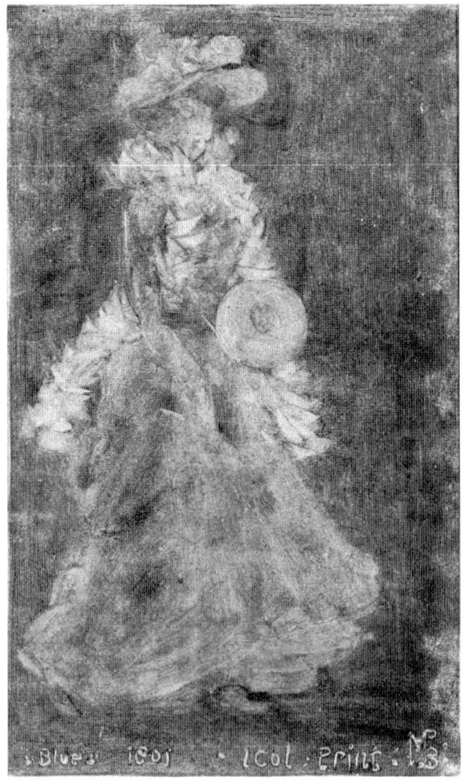

CR 1739

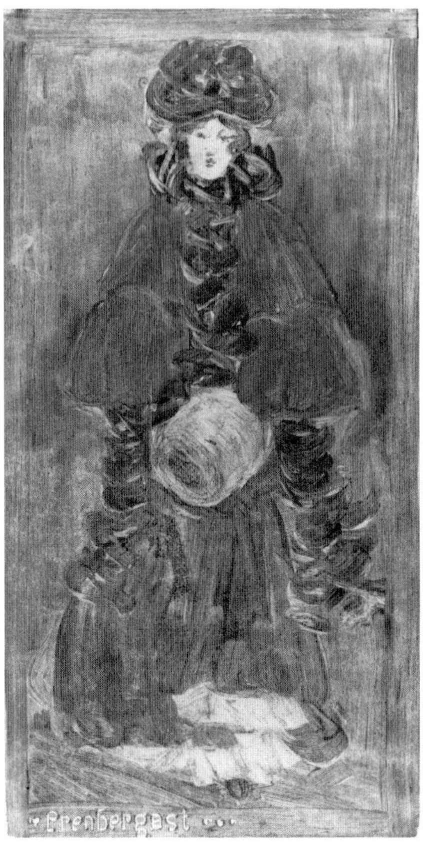

CR 1744

CR 1744

LADY WITH RED CAPE AND MUFF

ca. 1900–02
Monotype on paper
(9 15/16 x 4⅞ in.; 25.3 x 12.4 cm; image)
Williams College Museum of Art, gift of Mrs. Charles Prendergast (85.21.2)

INSCRIPTIONS
l.l. in plate: Prendergast

BIBLIOGRAPHY
Mathews 1990 (p. 161; ill.)

EXHIBITIONS
1986 Williams College (no #); 1989c Williams College (no #); 1990c Williams College (#116, ABCD); 1992 Williams College (no #); 1993 Williams College (no #); 1994a Williams College (no #)

Literature Cited

AAA NEWSLETTER 1986
"Special Projects." *Archives of American Art Newsletter* (spring 1986), p. 5.

AGAR 1994
Eunice Agar. "Maurice Brazil Prendergast's Pivotal Watercolors." *Watercolor '94* (spring 1994), pp. 40–45.

ALBERTAZZI 1990
Mario Albertazzi. "Un picnic continuo." *America Oggi Magazine* (29 July 1990).

ALLEN & HANBURYS 1993
Allen & Hanburys (Division of Glaxo Inc.). *The 1994 Allen & Hanburys Calendar of American Art.* Allen & Handburys, 1993.

AMERICAN ART REVIEW 1993
"Williamstown–Williams College Museum of Art: Maurice Prendergast." *American Art Review* V (summer 1993), p. 90.

AMERICANA 1991
"Prendergast: An American Original." Americana (February 1991).

ANDRE 1990
Mila Andre. "Prendergast, and plenty of it." *New York Daily News* (1 June 1990).

ANTIQUES ARTS WEEKLY 1986
"Williams College to Show Prendergast Collection." *Antiques & The Arts Weekly* (31 October 1986), p. 113.

ANTIQUES ARTS WEEKLY 1990b
"Definitive Exhibit of Works by Maurice Prendergast at the Whitney." *Antiques & The Arts Weekly* (6 July1990).

ANTIQUES ARTS WEEKLY 1990c
"At Williams College Museum of Art Six Years of Research Results in Definitive Maurice Prendergast Exhibition." *Antiques & The Arts Weekly* (23 November 1990).

ART JOURNAL 1964b
"Maine—100 Artists of the 20th Century." *Art Journal* 24 (fall 1964), p. 48.

ART NEWS 1938a
"The Brothers Prendergast in Review." *Art News* 37 (8 October 1938), pp. 14–15, 19.

BAKER 1990
Kenneth Baker. "The Two Faces of Modernism." San Francisco Examiner–*Chronicle* (15 July 1990), pp. 14–15.

BARTER 1989
Judith Barter. [essay in] *American Modernism from Amherst and Williams Colleges.* Amherst, MA: Mead Art Museum, Amherst College, 1991.

BASSO 1946a
Hamilton Basso. "Profiles: A Glimpse of Heaven-I." *New Yorker Magazine* 22 (27 July 1946), pp. 24–28, 30.

BASSO 1946b
"Profiles: A Glimpse of Heaven-II." *New Yorker Magazine* 22 (3 August 1946), pp. 28–32, 34, 36, 37.

BOSTON EVNG TRANSCRIPT 1900a
"The Murphy and Prendergast Exhibition in Chicago." *Boston Evening Transcript* (3 January 1900), p. 11.

BOWEN 1974
Louise de Koven Bowen. "Baymeuth." *Yankee* 38 (September 1974), pp. 102–110.

BRADY 1962
Robert Brady. *Drawings by Maurice B. Prendergast from 1887 to 1924.* New York, 1962.

BREUNING 1931
Margaret Breuning. *Maurice Prendergast.* New York, 1931.

BROOKS 1938
Van Wyck Brooks. "Anecdotes of Maurice Prendergast." *The Prendergasts: Retrospective Exhibition of the Works of Maurice and Charles Prendergast.* Addison Gallery of American Art, Phillips Academy. Andover MA, 1938.

BROWN 1963
Milton W. Brown. *The Story of the Armory Show.* New York, 1963.

CHRISTIAN SCIENCE 1960b
N.K. Untitled Article. *Christian Science Monitor* (14 November 1960), p. 8.

CR *or* CATALOGUE RAISONNÉ 1990
Carol Clark, Nancy Mowll Mathews, Gwendolyn Owens. *Maurice Brazil Prendergast, Charles Prendergast : A Catalogue Raisonné.* Williamstown and Munich, 1990.

DEWEESE-WEHEN 1991
Joy DeWeese-Wehen. "Prendergast: Master of Modernism." *Antique Monthly.*

DOOLEY 1938b
William Germain Dooley. "New England Honors Two Worthy Brothers (Andover's Museum Stages Pleasant, Colorful Exhibit by Prendergasts)." *Boston Evening Transcript* (24 September 1938), p. 7.

DORAIS 1980
Lucie Dorais. "James Wilson Morrice, Peintre Canadien (1865–1924). Les de Formation." Master's thesis, University of Montreal, 1980.

DRAWING 1987
"Drawings on Exhibition." *Drawing* 8 (January–February 1987), pp. 108–112.

EGLINGTON 1934
Laurie Eglington. "Prendergast Art in Fine Memorial." *Art News* 32 (3 March 1934), pp. 3–4.

FAISON 1979
S. Lane Faison Jr. *Williams College Museum of Art: Handbook of the Collection.* Williamstown, MA, 1979.

FERBER 1982
Linda S. Ferber. "The Domestication of Impressionism." *Art News* 81 (March 1982), pp. 84–88.

GENAUER 1961b
E.G[enauer]. "Tapestry of a Lonely Life." *New York Herald Tribune* (26 February 1961), p. 19.

GLACKENS 1957
Ira Glackens. *William Glackens and the Ashcan Group: The Emergence of Realism in American Art.* New York, 1957.

GLAVIN 1976
Ellen Glavin, S.N.D., and Eleanor Green. "Chronology." *Maurice Prendergast: Art of Impulse and Color.* University of Maryland Art Gallery, College Park, MD, 1976.

GLAVIN 1982
Ellen M. Glavin. "Maurice Prendergast: The Boston Experience." *Art & Antiques* 5 (July–August 1982), pp. 64–71.

GOETHALS 1991
Marion Goethals. *Maurice Prendergast Reviewed: The Theme of Decoration.* Williams College Museum of Art, Williamstown, MA, 1991.

GOLDIN 1976b
Amy Goldin. "How Are the Prendergasts Modern?" *Art in America* 64 (September 1976), pp. 60–67.

GRANT 1990B
Daniel Grant. "Williams Exhibit Puts Prendergast in Context." *Boston Herald* (3 November 1990).

GREEN 1977
Eleanor Green. "Maurice Prendergast, Myth, and Reality." *American Art Review* 4 (July 1977), pp. 89–103.

HITCHINGS 1989
Sinclair Hitchings. "The Prendergast's Boston." *The Prendergast's and the Arts and Crafts Movement.* Williams College. Williamstown, MA 1989.

HOWAT 1973
John K. Howat and Dianne H. Pilgrim, intro. *American Impressionist and Realist Paintings and Drawings from the Collection of Mr. and Mrs. Raymond J. Horowitz.* Catalogue by Dianne H. Pilgrim. New York, 1973.

HUNTINGTON 1964
Christopher Huntington, essay. *Maine: 100 Artists of the 20th Century.* Colby College Art Museum. Waterville, ME, 1964.

ISAACS 1990
Arlene B. Isaacs. "Maurice Prendergast: Charms of the Belle Epoch." *Upper East Side Resident* (16 July 1990).

ISSUE 1990
"Maurice Prendergast." *The Issue* (November 1990).

KANE 1992
Marie Louise Kane. "The Last Word." *Antiques & The Arts Weekly* (28 August 1992), pp. 1, 64–66.

KRAMER 1966
Hilton Kramer. "Prendergast: An American in the Camp of Cézanne." *New York Times* (6 November 1966), D: 31.

L.A. COUNTY 1991b
"Maurice Prendergast." *The Magazine of the Los Angeles County Museum of Art* (February 1991).

LANGDALE 1975
Cecily Langdale, intro. *Charles Conder, Robert Henri, James Morrice, Maurice Prendergast: The Formative Years, Paris 1890s.* New York: Davis & Long Company, 1975.

LANGDALE 1979a
Cecily Langdale, essay. 1979. *Monotypes by Maurice Prendergast: A Loan Exhibition.* New York: Davis & Long Company, 1979.

LANGDALE 1984
Cecily Langdale. *Monotypes by Maurice Prendergast in the Terra Museum of American Art.* Chicago, 1984.

LAUZON 1989
Lorraine Lauzon. "Tracing Prendergast's North Shore Trail." *Berkshire Eagle* (24 August 1989), E: 1, 4.

LAUZON 1990
Lorraine Lauzon. "Prendergast Exhibit Features Gentle World." *Catholic Observer* (2 November 1990), p. 28.

LEDES 1990
Allison Eckhardt Ledes. "Current and Coming: Maurice Prendergast–an American Modernist." I (June 1990), pp. 1272, 1274.

LEWIS 1991
Jo Ann Lewis. "In the Light of a Summer's Day: Maurice Prendergast's Sparkling Scenes of an Era, at the Phillips." *Washington Post* (18 May 1991), G: 1, G: 8.

LINGEMANN 1990
Susanne Lingemann. "New York: Maurice Prendergast: Der Central Park mit dem Charme von Montmartre." *art* (June 1990), pp. 114–117.

MATHEWS 1990
Nancy Mowll Mathews. *Maurice Prendergast.* Williamstown, MA: Williams College Museum of Art; and Munich: Prestel-Verlag, 1990.

MATHEWS 1990A
Nancy Mowll Mathews. "An American Progressive." *The Antique Collector* (July 1990), pp. 26–31.

MILLIKEN 1926b
William Mathewson Milliken. "Maurice Prendergast, American Artist." *The Arts* 9 (April 1926), pp. 180–182.

NASSAU COUNTY 1996
Nassau County Museum of Art. *Town and Country: In Pursuit of Life's Pleasures.* Roslyn Harbor, NY: Nassau County Museum of Art, 1996.

NEMSER 1966
C.N[emser]. "Maurice Prendergast." *Arts Magazine* 41 (December 1966), p. 65.

NEW ENGLAND MONTHLY 1986
"Art of Two Brothers." *New England Monthly* 3 (December 1986), p. 96.

NEWARK EVENING NEWS 1909a
"Widely Shown Exhibition of 'The Eight' American Artists at the Public Library." *Newark [N.J.] Evening News* (1 May 1909), p. 3.

OWENS 1978
Gwendolyn Owens. *Watercolors by Maurice Prendergast from New England Collections.* Williamstown, MA, 1978.

PEPPER 1910
Charles Hovey Pepper. "Is Drawing to Disappear in Artistic Individuality?" *World To-Day* 19 (July 1910), pp. 716–719.

PERLMAN 1990
Bennard Perlman. "American Original Remembered in Whitney's Prendergast Show." *Baltimore Record* (31 July 1990).

PORTER 1966
Fairfield Porter. "The Prendergast Anomaly." *Art News* 65 (November 1996), pp. 36–39, 78–79.

RAPPAPORT 1990
Susan S. Rappaport, ed. *1990 Traveler's Guide to Museum Exhibitions.* Washington, DC: Museum Guide Publications, Inc., 1990.

RHYS 1952
Hedley Howell Rhys. "Maurice Prendergast: The Sources and Development of His Style." Ph.D. diss., Harvard University, 1952.

RHYS 1960
Hedley Howell Rhys. "Maurice B. Prendergast." *Maurice Prendergast* 1859–1924. Boston, 1960.

SF EXAMINER 1991
"Modernism and a Billion Heir." *San Francisco Examiner* (12 March 1991).

SAWYER 1966
Charles H. Sawyer. "Maurice B. Prendergast." *Paintings and Watercolors by Maurice Prendergast.* C.W. Knoedler Art Galleries. New York, 1966.

SELDIN 1983
Donna Seldin, intro. *Americans in Venice: 1879–1913.* Coe Kerr Gallery. New York, 1983.

SIMS 1979
Patterson Sims. *Maurice B. Prendergast: A Concentration of Works from the Permanent Collection.* New York, 1979.

SMITH, R. 1990
Roberta Smith. "In the Sun-Dappled World of Maurice Prendergast." *New York Times* (15 June 1990).

SORIA 1982
Regina Soria. *Dictionary of Nineteenth-Century American Artists in Italy, 1760–1914.* London, 1982.

SPANIERMAN 1996
Spanierman. *Painters of Cape Ann, 1840–1940: One Hundred Years in Gloucester and Rockport.* New York: Spanierman Gallery, 1996.

SPENCER 1985
Harold Spencer. "On Some Works by Maurice Prendergast." *Bulletin 1985: William Benton Museum of Art, University of Connecticut,* no. 13 (1985).

TAMPA MUSEUM 1989
Tampa Museum of Art. *At the Water's Edge: 19th and 20th Century American Beach Scenes.* Tampa, FL: Tampa Museum of Art, 1989.

TRAVEL HOLIDAY 1991
"American Impressionist." *Travel Holiday* (March 1991).

WATTENMAKER 1976
Richard J. Wattenmaker. *Puvis de Chavannes and the Modern Tradition.* Ontario, 1975.

WATTENMAKER 1982
Richard J. Wattenmaker. "Maurice Prendergast." *Allen Memorial Art Museum Bulletin* 40 (1982–1983), pp. 25–37.

WATTENMAKER 1990
Richard J. Wattenmaker. "Maurice Prendergast at the Whitney." *New Criterion* (November 1990), pp. 33–40.

WATTENMAKER 1994
Richard J. Wattenmaker. *Maurice Prendergast.* New York: Harry N. Abrams, Inc. in association with The National Museum of American Art, Smithsonian Institution, 1994.

WICK 1960b
Peter A. Wick. Catalogue. *Maurice Prendergast 1859–1924.* Boston, 1960.

WILLIAMS COLLEGE 1991
Williams College Museum of Art. *Watercolors & Conservation: Turn-of-the-Century Materials & Techniques: Symposium.* Williamstown, MA: Williams College Museum of Art, 1991.

WILSON, W. 1991
William Wilson. "A Yankee Boulevardier." *Los Angeles Times* (22 February 1991), F: 1, F: 16.

WOLFF 1990
Theodore F. Wolff. "Prendergast Imbued Watercolors With Magic." *Christian Science Monitor* (26 June 1990).

WRIGHT 1990
Peg Churchill Wright. "Prendergast Exhibit at Williams May Be Season Highlight." *Schenectady [N.Y.] Daily Gazette* (21 September 1990).

ZEAMAN 1990
John Zeaman. "A Pilgrim's Steady Progress." *Hackensack [N.J.] Sunday Record* (10 June 1990), E: 1, 5.

Exhibitions Cited

1897 MALDEN C.O. ELLIETT
Artists' Exhibition and Sale. Malden, MA: Gallery of C.O. Elliett, 21 April–4 May 1897.

1898 BOSTON WATER COLOR CLUB
Water Color Club: Eleventh Annual Exhibition. Boston: Boston Art Club, 24 February–12 March.

1900 CHICAGO AIC
Catalogue of an Exhibition of the Works of Hermann Dudley Murphy and of the Works of Maurice B. Prendergast. Chicago: Art Institute of Chicago, 3–28 January 1900.

1901 DETROIT
Special Exhibition of Water Colors and Monotypes by Mr. Maurice B. Prendergast. Detroit: Detroit Museum of Art, November 1901, circulating.

1902 CHICAGO AIC
Catalogue of the Fourteenth Annual Exhibition of Watercolors, Pastels, and Miniatures by American Artists. Chicago: Art Institute of Chicago, 22 April–8 June 1902.

1908 MACBETH
Exhibition of Paintings by Arthur B. Davies, William J. Glackens, Robert Henri, Ernest Lawson, George Luks, Maurice B. Prendergast, Everett Shinn, John Sloan. New York: Macbeth Galleries, 3–15 February 1908, circulating with changes.

1921 BROOKLYN
Catalogue of a Group Exhibition of Watercolor Paintings by American Artists. Brooklyn, NY: Brooklyn Museum, 8 November–18 December 1921.

1925 KRAUSHAAR
Catalogue of a Memorial Exhibition of Paintings and Watercolors by Maurice Prendergast. New York: C.W. Kraushaar Art Galleries, 16 February–4 March 1925.

1925a CHICAGO AIC
Special Exhibitions: Sculpture by Nancy Cox-McCormack, Mural Paintings by Puvis de Chavannes, Albert Besnard and the National Society of Mural Painters, Decorative Paintings by Eduard Buk Ulreich, Drawings and Lithographs by C.O. Woodbury, Paintings by Maurice Prendergast. Chicago: Art Institute of Chicago, 17 March–24 April 1925.

1926a CLEVELAND
The Maurice Prendergast Memorial Exhibition. Cleveland, OH: Cleveland Museum of Art, 15 January–15 February 1926.

1928 ANDERSON GALLERIES
Works by American Artists Selected by the Associated Dealers in American Paintings. New York: Anderson Galleries, 21 February–10 March 1928.

1930 KRAUSHAAR
Exhibition of Paintings and Watercolors by Maurice Prendergast. New York: C.W. Kraushaar Art Galleries, 30 October–17 November 1930.

1930b CLEVELAND
Eighth Exhibition of Watercolors and Pastels. Cleveland, OH: Cleveland Museum of Art, 6 November–7 December 1930.

1934a WHITNEY
Maurice Prendergast Memorial Exhibition. New York: Whitney Museum of American Art, 21 February–22 March 1934.

1935 MACBETH
Exhibition of Watercolors and Pastels. New York: Macbeth Galleries, 14 May–3 June 1935.

1938 ADDISON GALLERY
The Prendergasts: Retrospective Exhibition of the Work of Maurice and Charles Prendergast. Andover, MA: Addison Gallery of American Art, Phillips Academy, 24 September–6 November 1938.

1939 FOGG MUSEUM
Art in New England: New England Genre. Cambridge, MA: William Hayes Fogg Art Museum, 15 May–1 September 1939.

1940 KRAUSHAAR
Paintings by Maurice Prendergast. New York: C.W. Kraushaar Art Galleries, 18 March–10 April 1940.

1941 WILLIAMS COLLEGE
Exhibition of Recent Accessions. Williamstown, MA: Lawrence Art Museum, Williams College, 7–30 October 1941.

1944b KRAUSHAAR
Maurice Prendergast: Paintings and Watercolors of Chartres, Dieppe, Dinard, Tréport, Paris, St.-Malo. New York: C.W. Kraushaar Art Galleries, 13 November–9 December 1944.

1950 DES MOINES
Paint: Materials and Techniques for Painting (Historical and Contemporary). Des Moines, IA: Des Moines Art Center, 10 October–7 November 1950, circulating.

1950 KRAUSHAAR
Maurice Prendergast: Retrospective Exhibition of Paintings, Water Colors, and Monotypes. New York: Kraushaar Galleries, 3–28 January 1950.

1960 BOSTON MFA
Maurice Prendergast 1859–1924. Boston: Museum of Fine Arts, 26 October–4 December 1960, circulating with changes.

1963 SOUTHERN VERMONT
"The Eight:" Fifty-five Years Later.

Manchester, VT: Southern Vermont Art Center, 22 June–7 July 1963.

1963a DAVIS GALLERIES
Drawings by Maurice Brazil Prendergast (1861–1924). New York: Davis Galleries, 5 February–2 March 1963.

1963b DAVIS GALLERIES
Charles Prendergast: Watercolors, Carvings, Panels. New York: Davis Galleries, 22 October–9 November 1963.

1964a COLBY COLLEGE
Maine: 100 Artists of the 20th Century. Waterville, ME: Colby College Art Museum, 25 June–30 September 1964.

1965 KNOEDLER
American Paintings and Sculpture: 18th, 19th, and 20th Century. New York: M. Knoedler and Company, summer 1965.

1966 COLBY COLLEGE
Art in the Making. Waterville, ME: Colby College Art Museum, 14 July–25 September 1966, circulating.

1966a KNOEDLER
Paintings and Watercolors by Maurice Prendergast: A Loan Exhibition. New York: Knoedler Galleries, 1–26 November 1966.

1967 BARD COLLEGE
Maurice Prendergast: The Monotypes. Annandale-on-Hudson, NY: William Cooper Procter Art Center, Bard College, 1–21 May 1967.

1968 RUTGERS UNIVERSITY
The Art of Charles Prendergast. New Brunswick, NJ: Rutgers University Art Gallery and the Museum of Fine Arts, Boston; MFA, Boston, 2 October–3 November 1968, circulating.

1969 KNOEDLER
American Paintings. New York: M. Knoedler and Company, 20 May–20 June 1969.

1970 KNOEDLER
American Water Colors, Drawings, and Graphics Exhibition. New York: M. Knoedler and Company, November 1970.

1976 UNIVERSITY OF MARYLAND
Maurice Prendergast: Art of Impulse and Color. College Park, MD: University of Maryland Art Gallery, 1 September–6 October 1976, circulating.

1977a DAVIS & LONG
Maurice Prendergast. New York: Davis & Long Company, 4–28 May 1977.

1977d WHITNEY
20th Century American Art from Friends' Collections. New York: Whitney Museum of American Art, 27 July–27 September 1977.

1978 CLARK ART INSTITUTE
Watercolors by Maurice Prendergast from New England Collections. Williamstown, MA: Sterling and Francine Clark Art Institute, 11 November–17 December 1978.

1982 SMITHSONIAN SITES
Impressionnistes Américains. Washington, DC: Smithsonian Institution Traveling Exhibiton Service; Musée du Petit Palais, Paris, 31 March–30 May 1982, circulating.

1983 COE KERR
Americans in Venice 1879–1913. New York: Coe Kerr Gallery, 19 October–16 November 1983, circulating.

1983a WILLIAMS COLLEGE
The Art of Maurice and Charles Prendergast. Williamstown, MA: Williams College Museum of Art, 11 September–4 December 1983.

1983c WILLIAMS COLLEGE
Recent Acquisitions. Williamstown, MA: Williams College Museum of Art, 11 September–15 October 1983.

1984b WILLIAMS COLLEGE
Portraits by the Prendergasts. Williamstown, MA: Williams College Museum of Art, 19 October 1984–24 March 1985.

1985b WILLIAMS COLLEGE
The Art of the Prendergasts. Williamstown, MA: Williams College Museum of Art, 6 June–8 September 1985.

1986 HIGH MUSEUM
The Advent of Modernism: Post Impressionism and North American Art, 1900–1918. Atlanta, GA: High Museum of Art, 4 March–11 May 1986.

1986 WILLIAMS COLLEGE
Maurice and Charles Prendergast. Williamstown, MA: Williams College Museum of Art, 19 October 1986–28 April 1987.

1988a WILLIAMS COLLEGE
The Artist's Eye: Maurice and Charles Prendergast. Williamstown, MA: Williams College Museum of Art, 7 May–18 September 1988.

1988b WILLIAMS COLLEGE
The Prendergasts and The Arts and Crafts Movement. Williamstown, MA: Williams College Museum of Art, 8 October 1988–8 January 1989.

1989 MEAD ART MUSEUM
American Modernism from Amherst and Williams Colleges. Amherst, MA: Mead Art Museum, Amherst College, 20 October–17 December 1989.

1989 TAMPA MUSEUM
At the Water's Edge: 19th and 20th Century American Beach Scenes. Tampa, FL: Tampa Art Museum, 9 December 1989–4 March 1990, circulating.

1989b WILLIAMS COLLEGE
Kindred Spirits: Maurice and Charles

Prendergast. Williamstown, MA: Williams College Museum of Art, 2 December 1989–18 March 1990.

1989c WILLIAMS COLLEGE
Maurice Prendergast's Women: Real & Ideal. Williamstown, MA: Williams College Museum of Art, 21 January–26 November 1989.

1989d WILLIAMS COLLEGE
Maurice Prendergast at the Beach. Williamstown, MA: Williams College Museum of Art, 22 July–26 November 1989.

1990a WILLIAMS COLLEGE
Maurice Prendergast: Figures and Movement. Williamstown, MA: Williams College Museum of Art, 31 March–26 August 1990.

1990b WILLIAMS COLLEGE
Maurice Prendergast's Landscapes. Williamstown, MA: Williams College Museum of Art, 31 March–26 August 1990.

1990c WILLIAMS COLLEGE
Maurice Prendergast. New York: Whitney Museum of American Art, 1 June–2 September 1990; Williamstown, MA: Williams College Museum of Art, 6 October–16 December 1990; Los Angeles: Los Angeles County Museum of Art, 21 February–22 April 1991; Washington DC: The Phillips Collection, 18 May–25 August 1991.

1990d WILLIAMS COLLEGE
Maurice Prendergast in Context: Selections from Regional Museums. Williamstown, MA: Williams College Museum of Art, 15 September–25 November 1990.

1990f WILLIAMS COLLEGE
Maurice Prendergast: Pieces of the Picture. Williamstown, MA: Williams College Museum of Art, 8 December 1990–12 April 1991.

1991a WILLIAMS COLLEGE
Maurice Prendergast Reviewed: The Theme of Decoration. Williamstown, MA: Williams College Museum of Art, 4 May–4 August 1991.

1991b WILLIAMS COLLEGE
Maurice Prendergast in the Teens. Williamstown, MA: Williams College Museum of Art, 17 August 1991–5 March 1992.

1991c WILLIAMS COLLEGE
Fugitive Colors and Other Lessons in Conservation. Williamstown, MA: Williams College Museum of Art, 24 August–3 November 1991.

1992 WILLIAMS COLLEGE
The Prendergasts and the History of Art. Williamstown, MA: Williams College Museum of Art, 25 April 1992–31 January 1993.

1993 WILLIAMS COLLEGE
Maurice Prendergast: Highlights from the Collection. Williamstown, MA: Williams College Museum of Art, 20 February–1 August 1993.

1994a WILLIAMS COLLEGE
Modernism!: European and American Art, 1900–1950. Williamstown, MA: Williams College Museum of Art, 29 January 1994–17 July 1995.

1994b WILLIAMS COLLEGE
Drawing Out: Works for Artists. Williamstown, MA: Williams College Museum of Art, 24 September–11 December 1994.

1995 AHI
Maurice Brazil Prendergast: Watercolors and Paintings. New York: AHI Gallery, 17 January–18 February 1995.

1995a WILLIAMS COLLEGE
The Wilderness Cult. Williamstown, MA: Williams College Museum of Art, 25 February–11 June 1995.

1995b WILLIAMS COLLEGE
Painting Changes: Prendergast and His Contemporaries. Williamstown, MA: Williams College Museum of Art, 5 August 1995–July 1997.

1995c WILLIAMS COLLEGE
The History of American Watercolors. Williamstown, MA: Williams College Museum of Art, 5 August–3 December 1995.

1995d WILLIAMS COLLEGE
Building Themes: Images of Architecture, 1870–1950, from the Permanent Collection. Williamstown, MA: Williams College Museum of Art, 16 December 1995–5 August 1996.

1996 NASSAU COUNTY MUSEUM
Town and Country: In Pursuit of Life's Pleasures. Roslyn Harbor, NY: Nassau County Museum of Art, 12 May–11 August 1986.

1996 SPANIERMAN
Painters of Cape Ann, 1840–1940: One Hundred Years in Gloucester and Rockport. New York: Spanierman Gallery, 13 April–22 June 1996.

Index of Works by Title

Index of Works by Accession Number

Sketch of Figures on Beach

85.26.18 *Sketchbook Page* CR 1463; verso: *Two Standing Women*

85.26.19 *Sketchbook Page* CR 1417; verso: *Sketch of Figures*

85.26.20 *Sketchbook Page* CR 1418

85.26.21 *Sketchbook Page* CR 1407

85.26.22 *Sketchbook Page* CR 1411

85.26.23 *Sketchbook Page* CR 1408; verso: *Sketch of Rocky Coast*

85.33 *The Birches* CR 408

85.45 *Fantasy* CR 385

86.18.1 *Old Woman, Paris* CR 517

86.18.2 *Low Tide, Nantasket* CR 640

86.18.3 *New England Holiday* CR 971

86.18.4 *Woman in Green Dress* CR 343

86.18.5 *Marblehead* CR 1201

86.18.6 *Spring Promenade* CR 976

86.18.7 *Girls in the Park* CR 397

86.18.8 *Bathers in a Cove* CR 366

86.18.9 *Bathers* CR 1146; verso: *Four Girls*

86.18.10 *Rider Against Blue Hills* CR 376

86.18.21 *Painting on Glass* CR 1167

86.18.29 *Profile of a Little Girl* CR 15

86.18.30 *Portrait of a Young Girl* CR 332 ; verso: *Portrait of a Blonde Girl*

86.18.31 *Italian Girl* CR 330

86.18.32 *Two Girls in Red - Venice* CR 331

86.18.33 *In the Library* CR 50

86.18.35 *Birches* CR 1100

86.18.36 *St. Malo* CR 394

86.18.37 *North Shore* CR 123; verso *Seaside Scene*

86.18.38 *Six Girls* CR 1290

86.18.39 *Park by the Sea* CR 413

86.18.40 *Low Tide CMO* CR 28

86.18.41 *Fall Day* CR 1056

86.18.42 *Summer Day* CR 1211

86.18.43 *Late Summer* CR 192

86.18.44 *Study of Three Girls with Scarves* CR 1465; verso: *Three Girls Kneeling, One with Scarf*

86.18.45 *Seated Woman* CR 1462; verso: *Standing Woman*

86.18.46 *Blue Horse* CR 1165

86.18.47 *Horseback Rider* CR 1159; verso: *Gondolas on the Grand Canal, Venice*

86.18.48 *Kneeling Nude* CR 1460

86.18.49 *Gloucester Harbor* CR 901; verso: *Scattered Watercolor Strokes*

86.18.50 *Fishing Boats, Normandie* CR 533

86.18.51 *Beach Scene, Maine* CR 366a

86.18.52 *Rocky Point* CR 945

86.18.53 *Little Girl in Red, France* CR 523

86.18.54 *Lake Ossippee, New Hampshire* CR 1065

86.18.55 *Low Tide* CR 643; verso: *low tide*

86.18.56 *Rocky Point* CR 669

86.18.57 *France* CR 910; verso: *Figure Studies*

86.18.58 *Beach Resort* CR 1319

86.18.59 *Assisi* CR 743

86.18.60 *Surf, Nantasket* CR 834; verso: *Untitled Sketch*

86.18.61 *Venice* CR 678; verso: *Nude Bathers in a Landscape*

86.18.62 *Sailboats, St. Malo* CR 369

86.18.64 *Poppies in a Blue Vase* CR 321

86.18.65 *Summer Hotel, Maine* CR 395

86.18.66 *Nudes with Jonquils* CR 1123

86.18.67 *Bath Houses, Annisquam* CR 455

86.18.68 *Siena* CR 738

86.18.69 *Central Park, New York* CR 783

86.18.70 *Figures Under the Flag* CR 825

86.18.71 *Boat Landing, Dinard* CR 1218

86.18.72 *Rouen* CR 540

86.18.73 *Capri* CR 751

86.18.74 *St. Malo* CR 896

86.18.75 *St. Malo* CR 883

86.18.76 *Fiesta-Venice-S. Pietro in Volta* CR 729

86.18.77 *The Pier* CR 827

86.18.78 *Lady in Pink Skirt* CR 1660

86.18.79 *Rialto, Venice* CR 1010; verso: *Rialto, Venice*

86.18.80 *Summer Day, Salem* CR 436

86.18.82 *Green Shore* CR 293

86.18.83 *Seated Nude Arranging Her Hair* CR 351

87.1.2 *The Offering* CR 1127

87.5.1 *Two Studies of a Nude Bending* CR 1458

87.5.2 *Study of a Nude* CR 1459

89.2 *Woman in Blue Dress* CR 1445; verso: *Seated Woman*

90.11.5 *Head of a Girl* CR 25

90.11.6 *Woman in Paris* CR 16

91.18.1 *A Day in the Country* CR 419

91.18.2 *Blue Mountains* CR 377

91.18.3 *Children in the Tree* CR 1000; verso: *Sketch for Children in the Tree*

91.18.4 *Elephant* CR 1162

91.18.5 *Festa del Redentore* CR 724

91.18.6 *Grand Canal, Venice* CR 712

91.18.7 *Paris* CR 918

91.18.8 *Study St. Malo, No. 12* CR 71

91.18.9 *Surf, Cohasset* CR 841

91.18.10 *Figures in Landscape* CR 1142

91.18.11 *Annisquam* CR 1317

91.18.12 *Springtime* CR 1358

91.18.13 *A Day in June* CR 1315; verso *Rocky Shore*

91.18.14 *Flowers* CR 319

91.18.15 *Boston Harbor* CR 820; verso: *Boston Harbor*

91.18.16 *Hay Harvesting, Maine* CR 1204

91.18.17 *St. Malo* CR 866; verso: *Study of Sea and Sky*

91.18.18 *Rocky Coast* CR 667; verso: *Rocky Coast Scene*

91.18.19 *Crowded Beach* CR 1380

91.18.20 *Gloucester* CR 1396

91.18.21 *Autumn in Maine* CR 1083; verso: *Sailboats*

91.18.22 *Snowscape* CR 156

91.18.23 *Deer Hunt* CR 1163

91.18.24 *Guiding the Cows* CR 1182; verso: *Sketch of Girls and Street Scene*

91.18.25 *Study St. Malo No. 9* CR 101

91.18.26 *Study St. Malo, No. 32* CR 92

91.18.27 *Study St. Malo, No. 33* CR 91

91.28.1 *St. Malo* CR 904

91.28.2 *Seaside Park with Sailboats* CR

960; verso: *Horse*

91.28.3 *Study of Tree at the Shore* CR 999

91.28.4 *St. Malo* CR 1007

91.28.5 *Road to the Village* CR 1088

91.28.6 *Venice: The Zattere* CR 1023; verso: *Flags in Piazza San Marco*

91.28.7 *Apple Tree* CR 1098; verso: *Landscape*

91.28.8 *Birches Near a Cove* CR 1104

91.28.9 *Eight Bathers in a Cove* CR 1117

91.28.10 *Exotic Nude* CR 1129

91.28.11 *Hunters* CR 1147

91.28.12 *Houses by the Harbor* CR 1207; verso: *untitled (Carrousel)*

91.28.13 *Harbor Village* CR 1263

91.28.14 *Bass Rocks, Gloucester* CR 1393

91.28.16 *Park Benches* CR 955

93.13.1 *May Day Picnic, Central Park 1902* CR 796

93.13.2 *Lady in Blue with White Boa* CR 1739

93.13.3 *The Esplanade, Boston* CR 1566

95.4.1 *Pink and Blue* CR 1172

95.4.2 *Rocky Shore with Bathers* CR 1116

95.4.3 *Pastoral Landscape* CR 1138

95.4.4 *Farmland* CR 1051

95.4.5 *Village in Summer* CR 1470

95.4.6 *Narcissus* CR 1124; verso: *Venice*

95.4.7 *Modern Nude* CR 1121

95.4.8 *Waterfront Park* CR 67

95.4.9 *Along the Shore Road* CR 241

95.4.10 *Standing Nude Model with Blue Cloth* CR 348

95.4.11 *Portrait of an Italian Girl* CR 334

95.4.12 *Three Sailboats* CR 169

95.4.13 *Egyptian Dancers* CR 1130; verso: *Modern Dancers*

95.4.14 *Lake in Maine* CR 238

95.4.15 *Portrait of a Woman in a Green Jacket* CR 346

95.4.16 *Standing Nude* CR 349

95.4.17 *Feeding the Swans* CR 1176

95.4.18 *The Birches* CR 1101

95.4.19 *Exotic Scene* CR 371

95.4.20 *Promenade on the Beach* CR 37

95.4.21 *Lighthouse at the Cove* CR 43

95.4.22 *Two Nudes* CR 1125

95.4.23 *Woman with Large Blue Hat* CR 1234

95.4.24 *The Offering* CR 1131; verso: *Tree and Frame Moldings*

95.4.25 *Fantasy with Horseback Rider* CR 1158

95.4.26 *Market Place* CR 1168

95.4.27 *Pastorale* CR 1174; verso: *Sketch of a Rider*

95.4.28 *The Riders* CR 1170

95.4.64 *Jungle Fantasy* CR 1110

95.4.65 *The Inlet Gloucester* CR 1181

95.4.66 *Bathers at Passamaquoddy Bay* CR 1115

95.4.67 *Sea Scene with Trees* CR 1381

95.4.68 *Sunset, Boston Harbor* CR 397

95.4.69 *Beach Scene* CR 1387

95.4.70 *Summer Hotel, Maine* CR 1225

95.4.71 *St. Servan* CR 393

95.4.72 *Summer Hotel, Maine* CR 1466

95.4.73 *St. Malo* CR 57

95.4.74 *St. Servan Fisherman* CR 3

95.4.75 *Lake Pavilion* CR 1369

95.4.76 *Approaching Storm* CR 35

95.4.77 *Salem* CR 42

95.4.78 *Promenade with Five Figures* CR 1213

95.4.79 *Fiesta Grand Canal, Venice* CR 725

95.4.80 *Tuileries Gardens* CR 113; verso: *New England Scene*

95.4.81 *Gloucester Harbor* CR 873

95.4.82 *Gloucester Beach* CR 1333

95.4.83 *Neponset Bay* CR 262

95.4.84 *In the Park* CR 1241

95.4.85 *Fishing Boats, Le Treport* CR 867

95.4.86 *Family Group* CR 1239

95.4.87 *Bathers and Rocks* CR 282

95.4.88 *Horse and Wagon* CR 1222

95.4.89 *St. Malo* CR 885

95.4.90 *Three Women* CR 1435

95.4.91 *Four Dancers* CR 1155

95.4.92 *The White Horse and Circus Rider* CR 593; verso: *Sketches of Roosters, Chicken, Duck*

95.4.93 *Column of St. Theodore* CR 693

95.4.94 *The Bird Cage* CR 1126

95.4.95 *Lighthouse, The Inlet, Gloucester* CR 1327

95.4.96 *Paris* CR 554

95.4.97 *Sunny Morning, Low Tide at the Beach* CR 665

95.4.98 *Rider on White Horse* CR 1179; verso: *Sketch of Venetian Bridge*

95.4.99 *Yacht Race* CR 1382

95.4.100 *Sunlight Study of a Cottage at Eu, France* CR 520

95.4.101 *The Laure Euce-Treport* CR 532

95.4.102 *Figures with Parasols Under Trees* CR 1177

95.4.103 *The Opera Cloak* CR 1696

95.4.104 *New Hampshire Village* CR 1035

95.4.105 *Maytime* CR 154

95.4.106 *Study of a Woman* CR 1472

95.4.107 *Queen, Luxembourg Gardens* CR 929

95.4.108 *Marblehead* CR 1209

95.4.109 *Three Women* CR 856

95.4.110 *Strawberry Hill* CR 1002

95.4.111 *Three Figures with Parasol* CR 1128; verso: *untitled (sketch of four nudes)*

95.4.112 *Maine Waterway* CR 407

95.4.113 *Bathing* CR 285

97.00.00 *Red Cloak with Cape* CR 1622

Museum Staff

Diane Agee, *Museum Registrar*
John R. Anderson, *Security Officer*
Ian Berry, *Curatorial Assistant*
Kenneth A. Blanchard, *Security Monitor*
Amber Chand, *Museum Shop Manager*
Melissa Cirone, *Development Associate*
Marion M. Goethals, *Associate Director*
Ann Greenwood, *Members Program Coordinator*
J. Patrick Holden, *Preparator*
Stefanie Spray Jandl, *Mellon Curatorial Associate*
Kay M. Kamiyama, *Public Relations Coordinator*
Robert T. Kove, *Security Monitor*
Silvio J. Lamarre, *Security Monitor*
Dorothy H. Lewis, *Budget Assistant*
Christine F. Maher, *Shop Assistant*
Sheila Mason, *Museum Secretary*
Nancy Mowll Mathews, *Eugénie Prendergast Curator*
Hideyo Okamura, *Chief Preparator*
Vivian L. Patterson, *Associate Curator, Collections Management*
Judith M. Raab, *Director of Membership and Events*
Barbara Robertson, *Director of Education*
Deborah M. Rothschild, *Curator of Exhibitions*
Edith V. Schwartz, *Prendergast Office Assistant*
Linda Shearer, *Director and Lecturer in Art*
Gregory J. Smith, *Art Handler*
Gary J. Sojkowski, *Preparator*
William A. Steuer, *Security Officer*
Sue Superneau, *Security Officer*
Rachel U. Tassone, *Catalogue Assistant*
Amy Tatro, *Assistant to the Director*
Theodore Wrona, *Museum Security Supervisor*

Visiting Committee

Herbert Adler
Sigmund R. Balka
Lucinda Barnes
Nancy K. Breslin
Charles M. Collins
Michael A. Dively
Margaret Stone Drewyer, *Co-Chair*
Michael S. Engl, *Vice Chair*
Romeyn Everdell, *Co-Chair*
Michael B. Keating
Thomas Krens
John R. Lane
Susan W. Paine
Randall R. Perkins
Harvey R. Plonsker
Earl A. Powell, III
Jock Reynolds
Sally W. Robinson
Dorothy D. Rudolph
Catherine C. Vare
Stuart B. Young

Members Emeriti

S. Lane Faison, Jr.
Whitney S. Stoddard

Advisory Members

Sigmund R. Balka, Chair, WCMA Fellows Program
Thomas J. Branchick, Director, Williamstown Art Conservation Center
Michael Conforti, Director, Clark Art Institute
Charles Haxthausen, Director, Graduate Program in the History of Art, Williams College
John H. Skavlem, Associate Director, Development, Williams College
Robert L. Volz, Custodian, Chapin Library of Rare Books, Williams College

Members Ex Officio

Keith C. Finan, Associate Provost, Williams College
Marion M. Goethals, Associate Director, Williams College Museum of Art
Guy Hedreen, Chair, Art Department, Williams College
Harry C. Payne, President, Williams College
Linda Shearer, Director, Williams College Museum of Art